What Is "College-Level" Writing?

What Is "College-Level" Writing?

Edited by

PATRICK SULLIVAN
Manchester Community College

HOWARD TINBERG
Bristol Community College

National Council of Teachers of English
1111 W. Kenyon Road, Urbana, Illinois 61801-1096

Staff Editor: Bonny Graham
Manuscript Editor: Lisa McAvoy
Interior Design: Jenny Jensen Greenleaf
Cover Design: Barbara Yale-Read

NCTE Stock Number: 56742

It is the policy of NCTE in its journals and other publications to provide a forum for the open discussion of ideas concerning the content and the teaching of English and the language arts. Publicity accorded to any particular point of view does not imply endorsement by the Executive Committee, the Board of Directors, or the membership at large, except in announcements of policy, where such endorsement is clearly specified.

Every effort has been made to provide current URLs and e-mail addresses, but because of the rapidly changing nature of the Web, some sites and addresses may no longer be accessible.

Library of Congress Cataloging-in-Publication Data

What is "college-level" writing? / edited by Patrick Sullivan, Howard Tinberg.
p. cm.
Includes bibliographical references and index.
ISBN-13: 978-0-8141-5674-2 (pbk)
1. English language—Rhetoric. 2. Report writing. I. Sullivan, Patrick, 1956– II. Tinberg, Howard B., 1953–
PE1408.W564 2006
808'.042—dc22

2006021700

To Susan
—Patrick

To Toni
—Howard

It is not the answer that enlightens, but the question.

Eugene Ionesco

Contents

Introduction

Patrick Sullivan
Manchester Community College

Howard Tinberg
Bristol Community College

We welcome you to a cordial, wide-ranging, substantive, and challenging discussion about one of the most important questions in our profession: What is "college-level" writing?

Just what defines college-level writing is a question that has confounded, eluded, and divided teachers of English at almost every level of our profession for many years now, and when we began this project, we set ourselves a deceptively simple task. We invited a group of professors, college students, high school teachers, and college administrators to consider the question carefully. We believed that the question at the heart of this book could only be meaningfully explored with broad representation from a variety of constituencies, and we sought to provide that representation in this book. In fact, this may be the first time such a diverse group of teachers, students, and other interested parties have been gathered together to discuss this important question.

We say "deceptively simple" because this project blossomed into something more complex, more richly nuanced, and more intriguing than we imagined possible. As it turns out (and this will probably come as no surprise), there are no simple answers to the question, "What is college-level writing?" But for those with the patience and the willingness to thoughtfully engage the complexities inherent in this question, there are certainly very satisfying, if rather complicated answers to be had. It is, after all, a question that is much more layered and multidimensional than first appears. It is a question, in fact, that ultimately requires us to consider a whole range of interrelated and interdependent skills associated with reading, writing, and thinking.

To speak very practically for a moment, we believe that this question deserves careful, patient attention because it is a question that *matters*—to us and to our students. It helps shape, in one way or another, so much of what we do: teaching reading, writing, and critical thinking at virtually every grade level; preparing students to be successful writers in middle school, high school, and college; addressing the needs of our many underprepared students on college campuses; developing composition programs at colleges and universities; engaging the important work of training a new generation of English teachers; and doing all of this within the rich context of rhetoric and composition theory. This book is designed to provide the careful attention this question deserves.

There are very different ways that teachers, scholars, and students can engage the central question this book asks, and we believe that a major strength of this collection is that it honors those differences. Of course there are certainly important commonalities here as well. In fact, as we worked on this volume together as editors, reading the essays brought a number of vitally important issues and concerns into sharp focus. It seems clear to us that strong writers develop only over a long period of time and only with considerable support from their teachers and their learning communities. As Sheridan Blau argues in his essay, this process is complicated because we find ourselves at a historical moment when the culture itself seems to have become hostile to any conception of education that is not traditionally and narrowly defined—a culture that has, it appears, become hostile to most forms of serious intellectual inquiry. We also found very real and worthwhile connections between Ronald Lunsford's discussion of attitude, Alfredo Lujan's focus on voice, Susan Schorn's comments about the need for college students to move away from the "self-centered focus of youth," Chris Kearns's argument about how meaning "*unfolds* in the shared space of acknowledgment between the reader and the writer," and Muriel Harris's discussion of reader-based writing. We thought Kim Nelson and Kathleen McCormick both had important things to say about college-level writing *assignments*, a variable that certainly needs to be considered when we talk about college-level writing. We also found great wisdom in Peter Kittle's essay, which invites our profession to move beyond "the blame game."

But there are also disagreements—splits, contradictions, fissures—that offer us much to consider as well. We think these disagreements are at least as important as the commonalities. Jeanne Gunner argues, for example, that any attempt to define (and therefore to contain and commodify) *college writing* is necessarily problematic. Ellen Knodt examines the wide disagreement among composition programs and faculty concerning the goals to be achieved in college writing programs. Cynthia Lewiecki-Wilson and Ellenmarie Wahlrab explore the structuring effects of socioeconomic differences in the academy, especially as those differences are translated into debates over standards and the kinds of writing curriculum that are designed for students. Contributors to this collection have certainly brought issues to our attention that frustrate our desire for easy answers, but they are important issues that deserve careful consideration from our profession. We think one of the strengths of this collection is that these perspectives are given clear and eloquent voice.

Taken in aggregate, we believe the essays in this book offer educators an extraordinary opportunity to engage the central question we explore in this book with renewed rigor and fresh perspective.

Our goal when we began this project was simply to begin a thoughtful, scholarly dialogue about what constitutes college-level writing—and then to see where that conversation might lead. We had no fixed end point in mind, and we were certainly not endeavoring to privilege any particular ideological or theoretical agenda. In fact, we did not know what our group of contributors might finally conclude about this most contentious question for teachers of English. But we are very pleased with the result.

We believe that our contributors have, indeed, come to some important conclusions about what college-level writing should be, and how we might move forward nationally as teachers of English to advocate for curriculum, standards, and protocol changes that will begin serving the interests of our students more effectively. We believe that this collection also offers a new degree of clarity to our profession about a variety of important and interrelated issues that help shape the daily contours of our working lives—both in the classroom and in our professional and scholarly discourse. We hope you will feel the same way.

We were lucky in this endeavor on a number of accounts. Teachers and scholars from across the nation and from a great variety of institutions responded enthusiastically to our invitation to contribute to this collection. We were fortunate as well in the quality of the contributors who agreed to participate. Many are nationally known, and all bring important teaching or research experience to this project. We also invited contributors who we knew would challenge us to think carefully and critically about this question. In addition, we also invited high school teachers, college students, and college administrators to contribute, and we think the addition of these voices and perspectives enriches our discussion immeasurably. We would like to thank all of our contributors for their eloquence, their candor, and their willingness to engage the questions we set before them in good faith.

We have a number of special features in this book, and we would like to draw your attention to them briefly:

- *Very strong variety in terms of perspective and experience*. This collection includes perspectives from college students, high school teachers, college teachers, academic scholars, adjunct faculty members, an English Department chair, a Writing Center director, a Writing Program coordinator, and a college administrator. We also have representation from a wide variety of academic institutions: high schools, community colleges, state colleges and universities, and private universities.
- *High school teachers are welcomed*. High school English teachers are among our most important professional colleagues in the grand enterprise of teaching writing at the college level—but more often than not we talk *about* them rather than *with* them. This book addresses that problem directly by inviting high school English teachers to discuss college-level writing with us. We asked our high school contributors to be as candid as possible and to "tell it like it is." As we think you will see, their essays offer us much of great value to consider.
- *A very strong focus on student perspectives*. College students in this collection are given the opportunity to speak in detail with-

out mediation in full-length essays—not just in snippets or excerpts.

- *Inclusion of the administrative perspective.* There are many administrative issues that help to shape our definition of college-level writing, and we think it is vitally important that these issues be acknowledged and explored. In this collection, they are.
- *Interactive discussion among contributors about the essays in this book.* When contributors finished writing their essays for this collection, they posted them at an online discussion Web site and then as a group we discussed this body of work. This interactive discussion is rare in scholarly collections like ours, and this is something that we believe adds a great deal to the value and usefulness of our book. We have included samples from this discussion in our final chapter. The full discussion is available online at our book's companion Web site, along with a number of additional essays and the opportunity to post comments and questions. (Information regarding the Web site is included in the appendix.)

As you will see from our table of contents, we have grouped the essays into four sections. We begin with Patrick's essay, which is a version of an essay that was originally published in *Teaching English in the Two-Year College*, and which is where the idea for this project began. Patrick's essay is followed by groups of essays from high school teachers, college teachers and scholars, college students, and college administrators. The appendix offers readers a sample of the dialogue we conducted online among contributors about the essays in this book.

One final note: A project of this scope could not have been completed without the generous support of friends, family, and colleagues. We would like to thank Kurt Austin, our editor at the National Council of Teachers of English (NCTE), and the anonymous field reviewers at NCTE, whose support and constructive criticism were invaluable. We would also like to thank our production and publicity team at NCTE, especially Bonny Graham, Lisa McAvoy, and Cari Rich. Patrick would like to thank his colleagues in the English Department at Manchester Community College for their inspiring example, their commitment to excellence, and their daily warmth, graciousness, and generosity. He would like to offer special thanks to Professors Kim Hamilton-

Bobrow and Ken Klucznik for their ongoing and enthusiastic support. He would also like to thank his wife, Susan, and his two children, Bonnie Rose and Nicholas, for their support, understanding, and love. Howard would like to thank the many colleagues who have sat around the table with him over the years to talk about what constitutes good, college-level writing—at venues such as Advanced Placement readings, department meetings, and staff meetings at the writing lab that he directs. He would like to thank his family—Toni, Miriam, and Leah—for their loving support.

We hope that you will enjoy this book and find it useful in your work. It has been an enormously gratifying project to work on.

Chapter One

An Essential Question: What Is "College-Level" Writing?

Patrick Sullivan
Manchester Community College

Introduction

I recently participated in a statewide meeting sponsored by the Connecticut Coalition of English Teachers to continue work we began on a pilot study that examined what various English teachers at community colleges around the state do when they teach composition. Our goal was to develop some common standards as well as shared expectations in terms of workload and student outcomes. We attempted, among other things, to define what "college-level" writing was. As it turns out, we found this task to be more daunting than we expected, and we found ourselves again and again returning to a variety of complex questions related to the teaching of writing. Among the questions we discussed were the following:

- What makes a piece of writing college level?
- What differentiates college-level writing from high school-level writing?
- If it is true that all politics are local, is it also true that standards related to college-level writing must be local, too?
- Shouldn't a room full of college English teachers be able to come to some kind of consensus about what college-level writing is?
- Are variations in standards from campus to campus, state to state, and teacher to teacher something we ought to pay some attention to (or worry about)? Or should we consider these varia-

tions insignificant given the complexity of what we are teaching?

- We have an increasing number of students who come to us unprepared for college-level reading, writing, and thinking. How can we best teach these students to do college-level work?
- How, if at all, do standards of college-level writing change if faculty from departments other than English weigh in on the subject?
- How do high school English teachers define college-level writing? What are the issues that most concern high school English teachers as they prepare their students for college-level work?
- And finally, how do college students define college-level writing? What experiences have students had in high school and college classrooms that might help us define college-level writing more effectively?

I subsequently found that these issues were not limited to our particular group or locale. At a meeting of the National Council of Teachers of English (NCTE)/Two-Year College English Association Northeast Conference, I conducted a session on this subject in which I encountered many of the same complexities, and many of the same differences of opinion. We discussed a variety of sample student essays at this session, for example, and the range of opinion about this work was extraordinarily varied. In one memorable case, the assessments about a particular essay ranged from A-quality, college-level work ("This is definitely college-level writing. It is very well organized, and there are no spelling, grammar, or punctuation errors. I would love to get a paper like this from one of my students.") to F-quality work ("This is definitely *not* college-level writing. Although this essay is well organized, it contains no original, sustained analysis or thought. It's empty. There is no thoughtful engagement of ideas here.").

It may very well be that these conflicts are irresolvable and that all standards related to our students' written work must ultimately be local, determined at least in part by our response to the complex realities of the communities we serve and the individual students we teach. Any discussion of shared standards may require us to ignore or discount the very powerful political and social realities that help shape students' lives on individual campuses and in particular learning communities. We must also acknowledge that much outstanding scholarly work has already been done to address this issue, especially in the area of basic writing. On the other hand, it may well be that our profession could benefit enormously from reopening a dialogue about this question. At the very least, as a matter of professional policy, it seems reasonable to revisit issues like this routinely—to open ourselves up to new ideas and insights, and to guard against rigid or prescriptive professional consensus.

At the moment, we appear to have reached an unfortunate impasse regarding our discussion of college-level writing, and this is problematic for all sorts of reasons (many of which I hope to explore in this essay). I believe that our professional discourse about this vitally important topic should be reopened. I would like to argue in this essay that as teaching professionals we should, at the very least, clearly understand the full variety of factors that help shape this debate, and carefully explore the imposing complexities that make determining a working definition of something like college-level writing problematic. I would like to argue, furthermore, that acknowledging the full range of complexities related to this issue is a necessary first step toward engaging in productive dialogue about it.

Language Is Slippery and Multivalent

Perhaps the best place to begin our exploration of these issues is with a brief discussion about the nature of language. As we know from the work of Barthes, Foucault, Derrida, and other modern literary theorists, language is no longer considered as reliable or as stable a medium for communication as it once was. In fact, modern theorists have argued that we must see language as essentially "slippery" and "multivalent," a complex term which suggests that language is "always changing, and always changing in more than one way" (Leitch 1818). Although there certainly continues to be difference of opinion about this—and about the work of writers like Barthes, Derrida, and Foucault, the theorists who have perhaps done the most to challenge us to think in new ways about language—it has nonetheless become widely accepted in academic circles that communication is complicated in many significant ways because of the nature of language. This has had significant consequences for how we now understand texts to produce meaning.

The argument that language is fundamentally unstable and slippery is only the first important premise of this new theoretical framework. A number of important modern literary theorists go on to argue from this premise that because language is slippery, the art of reading and, by extension, interpretation and evaluation must always be conducted as a conditional enterprise, with the understanding that all readings of a particular text must be, at least to some degree, "unfinished" or provisional (Culler, *Structuralist*; Culler, *On*; Derrida, *Dissemination*; Derrida, "Like"; Sullivan; see also Derrida's exchange with John Searle in "Limited Inc" and "Signature Event Context"). In Roland Barthes' "The Death of the Author," for example, Barthes challenges the traditional idea of the author who is solely responsible for putting the meaning *in* the texts we read. Once this old conception of the author is removed, Barthes argues, "the claim to decipher a text is quite futile. To give a text an Author is to impose a limit on that text, to furnish it with a final signified, to close the writing" (225). Barthes goes on to celebrate the "birth of the reader," and introduces into modern literary theory a new variable—the role that the reader plays in creating meaning with texts. Obviously, for those of us who are reading and evaluating student texts, this new theory of language helps explain how different readers can evaluate the same student texts in very different ways.

"Myths of Assessment"

Much recent scholarship related to questions regarding assessment and the teaching of writing concludes that major differences related to standards are probably inevitable and result from, at least in part, the indeterminacies of language. In perhaps the most well-known piece of scholarship on this subject, "The Myths of Assessment," Pat Belanoff argues that the strongest myth related to assessment is the one that suggests that "it's possible to have an absolute standard and apply it uniformly" (55). Belanoff goes on to conclude at the end of her essay that "we need to realize that our inability to agree on standards and their applications is not something we need to be ashamed of . . . . far from it, it is a sign of strength, of the life and vitality of words and the exchange of words" (62).

Karen Greenberg draws similar conclusions in her study, "Validity and Reliability Issues in the Direct Assessment of Writing." Greenberg finds considerable agreement about what constitutes good writing (16–17) but also considerable difference in how those standards are applied. Greenberg concludes her argument by embracing the idea that language itself is complex and that judgments about students' writing must always be provisional:

> Readers will always differ in their judgments of the quality of a piece of writing; there is no one "right" or "true" judgment of a person's writing ability. If we accept that writing is a multidimensional, situational construct that fluctuates across a wide variety of contexts, then we must also respect the complexity of teaching and testing it. (18)

Comments like this appear frequently in scholarship related to assessment. As Davida Charney notes in her review essay, "Under normal reading conditions, even experienced teachers of writing will disagree strongly over whether a given piece of writing is good or not, or which of two writing samples is better" (67; see also Huot, *(Re)Articulating*; "Toward"; Straub and Lunsford).

Professing at the "Fault Lines"

And yet, assess we must. Certainly, establishing a clear understanding of what we mean by college-level writing is crucially important for all sorts of reasons because this foundational concept affects virtually everything we do as teachers of English, from establishing placement and assessment protocols, to developing effective classroom strategies, to administering campus-wide or even system-wide writing programs. Perhaps the single most compelling reason to address this question with the careful attention it deserves, of course, is the surging number of underprepared writers coming to our colleges. As a recent report from the National Center for Education Statistics (2003) notes,

> In fall 2000, about three-fourths (76 percent) of the Title IV degree-granting 2- and 4-year institutions that enrolled freshmen offered at least one remedial reading, writing, or mathematics course. . . . In fall 2000, 28 percent of entering freshmen enrolled in one or more remedial reading, writing, or mathematics courses. (4–5)

Of special note for our purposes here is that basic writing programs were not limited to community, junior, or technical colleges. This report notes that public 4-year institutions were "also significant providers of remedial education in fall 2000" (4), as were private colleges and universities, although to a lesser degree. Obviously, it is vitally important for colleges that offer basic writing courses—and this now includes most colleges in the United States—to have a very clear sense of what we mean by college-level writing. Basic writing courses are typically defined as *precollege* or preparatory in nature. As we work to evaluate and better understand student success and retention as it relates to our underprepared students and to our basic writing initiatives nationwide, we must be able to define with some degree of precision when a particular student has passed from the basic writing stage to the college level. This is one of the most fundamental outcomes for any basic writing course or program. Obviously, if we can not clearly define for ourselves what we mean by college-level writing, how can we hope to do this for our students? Being able to distinguish and articulate clearly the differences between college-level work and precollege work has become a vitally important skill on our campuses, and I believe that this will only continue to be a more pressing need in the years to come.

This is a particularly important issue for the nation's community colleges, which now enroll approximately 41 percent of all undergraduates in the United States (see American 1; see also United States). Furthermore, our country's undergraduate population is becoming increasingly nontraditional. As the editors of *The Condition of Education 2002*, from the United States Department of Education and the National Center for Education Statistics, report,

> The "traditional" undergraduate—characterized here as one who earns a high school diploma, enrolls full time immediately after finishing high school, depends on parents for financial support, and either does not work during the school year or works part time—is the exception rather than the rule. In 1999–2000, just 27 percent of undergraduates met all of these criteria. (United States 6)

These nontraditional students bring all sorts of challenges to us, and they are enrolling at our nation's community colleges in increasing numbers. As Cynthia Lewiecki-Wilson and Jeff Sommers argued in a recent *College Composition and Communication* essay, community colleges exist on a "fault line, a site where contradictions meet" (439; see also Baker; Cohen and Brawer; Dougherty; Miller; Pickett; Pratt). Certainly, one such "fault line" is the wide range of skill levels that students bring with them to community college campuses. As we know, increasing numbers of underprepared students are enrolling at open admissions institutions, and research indicates that well over half of these students now need to do some form of college preparatory work, much of this in reading and writing. As John Roueche and Suanne Roueche note in *High Stakes, High Performance: Making Remedial Education Work* (1999),

> On average, almost 50 percent of all first-time community college students test as underprepared for the academic demands of college-level courses and programs and are advised to enroll in at least one remedial class. This percentage of underprepared students has not changed significantly across the United States in the last two decades, and there is no evidence that it will be reduced in the near future, although in individual states percentages have fluctuated. (5)

Many community college students come to us unable to produce college-level work. This situation is complicated further by English as a Second Language students, who come to community colleges with a very different set of educational needs, but who also eventually hope to work their way into the mainstream college curricula and do college-level work. Clearly, these students pose increasingly complex challenges to those who teach English at "democracy's colleges" (Griffith and Connor; Roueche and Roueche, *Between*; Roueche, Baker, and Roueche; Fox; Rose).

"Cooling Out"

This large population of underprepared students enrolling at colleges throughout the United States has affected English teachers in perhaps more profound ways that any other single group of college teachers, administrators, or staff. English teachers are first contact professionals—that is, we teach reading and writing, two of the three most essential threshold college skills (along with math) that students must master before they can move on to mainstream college courses. For this reason, English teachers spend more time—both qualitatively and quantitatively—with underprepared students than any other single group of college staff. And as any English teacher will tell you, this is some of the most challenging work we do as teachers. First of all, we are teaching reading and writing, which are difficult subjects to teach even under the best of conditions, with the most well-prepared students. Secondly, our pedagogy makes this work very demanding, particularly on the most basic interpersonal, emotional level. Because our discipline has embraced a pedagogy of draft and revision, and because our classrooms typically promote collaborative learning, and because we typically work very closely with our students as they draft and revise their essays, we often form strong bonds with our students. We become invested in our students' successes and failures in ways that are significantly different than any of our colleagues.

The kinds of professional relationships that we forge with our students have obvious and demonstrated benefits, of course, but there are also significant costs. There are heavy emotional burdens to shoulder for those of us who function in the classroom as coaches to underprepared students—especially when our students struggle or fail, as many of them do. We are the personnel on campus that most often deliver bad news to students about their ability to do college-level work. This is information, of course, that almost always has disturbing implications about students' future prospects within the college system and, beyond that, their professional lives.

This task may very well be the most difficult and heartbreaking that is required of us professionally. By any practical measure, English teachers perform much of the "cooling out" function at colleges that Burton Clark discussed in his famous 1960 essay, "The 'Cooling-Out' Function in Higher Education." Clark argued, as you may remember, that

> The wide gap found in many democratic institutions between culturally encouraged aspiration and institutionally provided means of achievement leads to the failure of many participants. Such a situation exists in American higher education. Certain social units ameliorate the consequent stress by redefining failure and providing for a "soft" denial; they perform a "cooling out" function. The junior college especially plays this role. The cooling-out process observed in one college includes features likely to be found in other settings: substitute achievement, gradual disengagement, denial, consolation, and avoidance of standards. (569; see also Bartholomae, "Tidy"; Bloom, "Freshman"; Clark, "The 'Cooling Out' Function Revisited"; Clark, *The Open Door College*; Gunner; Harris; O'Dair; Scott; Traub, "What"; Shor, "Our"; Shor, *When*)

This is painful and emotionally exhausting work—and its cumulative effect over the course of many years has yet to be adequately measured. However much we may talk about writing-across-the-curriculum programs or sharing the burden of educating our underprepared students with other disciplines or areas of the college, the fact is that English professors do much of this difficult work. One of the long-term professional effects of this is that English professors simply become worn down emotionally, and we lose the perspective that many of our colleagues share simply because they deal much less with underprepared students. All of this serves to introduce complicated emotional factors that make defining college-level work problematic. Sometimes this works in very subtle ways and is simply a matter of seeing potential rather than actual achievement, or reading a particular essay in a slightly more forgiving way. This is a type of conditioned response that I have seen exhibited routinely in our profession, and it is something that English teachers must attempt to balance every day of their professional lives with the equally important commitment to high standards. Any discussion of college-level work must take this powerful emotional reality into consideration, for it almost always becomes an important variable in any discussion of standards and definitions of college-level writing.

Political Concerns

I would also like to argue that in the political arena, where budgets are developed and approved by increasingly interventionist and activist legislatures, the need for a stronger sense of what differentiates precollege and college-level writing may be indispensable. Personally, I believe that helping underprepared students who are seeking to create better futures for themselves is an absolutely essential part of our mission, regardless of where we teach (community college, public college or university, or private college or university). But not everyone thinks this way, of course, and as we all know, the discussion related to standards and the viability of basic writing programs has blossomed into a spirited and contentious national debate (see Adler-Kassner and Harrington; Bartholomae, *Writing*; Lavin and Hyllegard; Gray-Rosendale, "Inessential"; Gray-Rosendale, *Rethinking*; McNenny; National Commission; Roueche and Baker; Sacks; Shor, "Our"; Scott; Soliday, "From"; Soliday, *Politics*). The distinction between what is and what is not college-level work has become a crucial evaluative benchmark in this discussion.

James Traub, for example, has argued in *City on a Hill: Testing the American Dream at City College* (1994) that "[t]he right to an education for which one is hopelessly underprepared is not much of a right at all" (180). This is a sentiment that is shared by many in and outside of our profession. Traub's book is, for the most part, a heartbreaking portrait of futility and desperation—about underprepared, undermotivated, and underachieving students struggling to reach the mainstream college curricula and generally not succeeding. This is a book that captures the frustration and despair regarding underprepared college students that is shared by a wide range of citizens, politicians, and teachers.

On a national level, an increasing number of taxpayers and politicians have looked with alarm at the modest success rates of underprepared students and have set out to limit the amount of money spent on remedial courses and programs, especially in state colleges. Some of these taxpayers and political leaders have argued that by funding remedial programs, we are, in effect, "rewarding incompetence." Others have argued that money spent on remedial programs is a bad investment of public resources and that we should not have to "pay twice" to educate the same student (see Roueche and Roueche, *High Stakes*; Roueche, Johnson, and Roueche; Fox). Nationwide, these ideas have found their way into legislation. In Florida, Missouri, and South Carolina, for example, all remedial courses and programs have been banned from four-year state colleges and universities (Roueche and Roueche, *High Stakes* 11). In Florida, a state statute placed explicit limits on funding for remedial curricula. Perhaps most famously, New York City set in motion a very controversial and widely reported plan to eliminate a great number of remedial courses and programs. Begun by Mayor Giuliani in 1998, the City University of New York system has removed all remedial courses from their four-year colleges in an attempt to save money and "improve standards" (see Arenson, "With"; Arenson, "CUNY"; Harden; Renfro and Armour-Garb).

Meanwhile, as some seek to challenge the validity of basic writing programs, others continue to celebrate it. Studies like Marilyn Sternglass's *Time to Know Them: A Longitudinal Study of Writing and Learning at the College Level* (1997) show how transformative such programs can be in the lives of underprepared students. Sternglass's book celebrates the triumph that can result when educational opportunities are embraced with enthusiasm and perseverance. Many of us in the profession continue to believe that offering these opportunities to our underprepared students should remain an essential component of what we do as teachers of English (see Bartholomae, "Tidy"; Bartholomae,

Writing; Beaufort; Carroll; Collins; Herrington and Curtis, *Persons*; Curtis and Herrington, "Writing"; Greenberg, "A Response"; McCourt; Roueche and Baker; Saxon and Boylan; Sheridan-Rabideau and Brossell; Tinberg).

The point I would like to make here is that however one may wish to enter this debate, the need for a better shared understanding about precollege and college-level work would appear to be essential. How can we discuss basic writing programs in a public forum in any meaningful way—regardless of what side of the issue we may be on—without a stronger shared sense of what college-level and precollege work is? Furthermore, it seems to me that having a general shared understanding related to college-level work would be vital to those of us who choose to engage this debate on the most important levels—as we talk with legislators to advocate for programs and policies we believe in. Without a more consistent, clearly articulated position on this issue, we risk failing our students in the most catastrophic ways possible. In the political arena, then, there appear to be very compelling reasons for us to develop a clear, precise, shared definition of what we mean by college-level work.

Research Related to Teacher Expectations and Student Achievement

We may also find it helpful to consider the extensive body of research that examines the effects of teacher expectations on student achievement. This research might very well be useful to us as we examine the claim made by some that we must compromise our standards in order to engage underprepared students. Although this body of research does not yield simple, universal answers (Good, "How" 29), taken in aggregate it does suggest that there is a positive correlation between teacher expectation and student performance. There appears to be, in other words, significant evidence that high expectations from teachers leads to better performance from students. In "How Teachers' Expectations Affect Results," for example, Thomas Good summarizes the research this way:

1. The teacher expects specific behavior and achievement from particular students.
2. Because of these varied expectations, the teacher behaves differently toward different students.
3. This treatment communicates to the students what behavior and achievement the teacher expects from them and affects their self-concepts, achievement motivation, and levels of aspiration.
4. If this treatment is consistent over time, and if the students do not resist or change it in some way, it will shape their achievement and behavior. High-expectation students will be led to achieve at high levels, whereas the achievement of low-expectation students will decline.
5. With time, students' achievement and behavior will conform more and more closely to the behavior originally expected of them. (26)

Good finds that "some teachers appeared to 'cause' the students to decline by providing them with fewer educational opportunities and teaching them less. These teachers were . . . overreacting to the learning deficiencies of the lows [students perceived as low-achieving] in ways that reduced both their opportunity and motivation for learning" (27; see also Billups; Brophy, "Teacher Behavior"; Brophy, "Teacher Praise"; Brophy, "Classroom"; Brookover and Lezotte; Thomas Good, "Teacher"; Rosenthal and Jacobson).

This research related to expectations has been borne out in more recent work as well. G. Alfred Hess found that higher expectations from teachers led to improved student performance, for example, in his study of the educational reform project instituted in the Chicago school system in 1988. Hess found that the reform success within this school system was the result of four important variables—and one of those variables was higher expectations (see also Wohlstetter and Odden). Festus Obiakor has explored the complex nature of teacher expectations as they relate to young minority exceptional learners, and he also finds that teacher expectations help shape student achievement. Recent work by Kuklinski and Weinstein, Jussim and Eccles, and Wentzel supports this general argument (see also Astin; Jussim,

Smith, Madon, and Palumbo; Tinto). Although there is difference of opinion about the degree to which teacher expectations affect individual student achievement, all of the literature I have reviewed suggests that teacher expectations have at least some demonstrable, quantifiable effect on student outcomes.

Although there are any number of reasons why one might argue that we must compromise standards in our classrooms, this research suggests that we probably do not serve our students well by doing so. There are many other factors that come into play, of course, in any discussion of standards, and exactly how large an effect teacher expectations may have on individual students is in doubt. It seems reasonable, however, to listen carefully to this important research as we move forward in discussing how we might establish a better understanding of what we mean by college-level writing.

The Administrative Perspective

Finally, as I discussed these issues with administrators on a variety of campuses in our state, I discovered that college deans and presidents generally have a very pragmatic perspective related to this question. One common perception among administrators that I talked to was that definitions related to college-level work are "fluid" and that English teachers respond in some very predictable and pragmatic ways to enrollment realities. One college president who I interviewed for this essay formulated it this way: Lots of demand for courses and lots of students often result in exacting standards; less demand and fewer students often result in less rigorous standards. Depending on enrollment trends, then, college-level writing might be defined differently even by the same instructor or department (see Soliday, *Politics*).

I have found this perspective confirmed informally in any number of conversations I have had with teachers over the years. All kinds of local realities at individual campuses—related to enrollment, the institution's learning culture, and the makeup of the student body—shape the way we interact with our students and influence the way we conceive of and apply standards related to our students' work. Obviously, these variables complicate the process of working toward establishing any kind of shared standards for college-level writing.

In my discussions with college administrators, I also discovered concern for the way in which different definitions of college-level work can affect articulation agreements. I had the opportunity to talk with two college presidents in our state about this, and although they both expressed their concerns diplomatically, they admitted that the twelve community colleges in our system apply different standards related to reading, writing, and thinking skills. This difference in standards related to college-level work has helped to complicate the development of a statewide articulation agreement. Both presidents noted that some of the community colleges in our system prepared students very well to be successful transfer students at their institutions. Other colleges, in their opinion, did not. They went on to note that what was college level at one institution was clearly *not* college level at others. This was an obvious cause for concern for them—but it was also an issue that they approached with great caution and wariness, keenly aware of its considerable political and professional ramifications.

Moving toward Dialogue

The poststructuralist critics like Barthes, Foucault, and Derrida, who taught us to appreciate the ambiguity of language, established this as only an important preliminary factor that must be considered whenever we communicate. They argued from this premise that because language is inherently "slippery," we must proceed with heightened sensitivity and patience as we listen, read, and write. Their argument is not that successful communication is impossible, but rather that the complicating factors related to language must be recognized and respected in order for communication to be effective.

I believe that the process of discussing what we mean by college-level writing will take the kind of patience, open-mindedness, and sympathetic engagement with others that is essential for any kind of successful communication. This kind of respectful, open-minded discourse is particularly important for this discussion because of the many variables involved, and it will be essential if we hope to avoid "going around in circles," to borrow William DeGenaro's and Edward M. White's memorable phrase, as we discuss methodological and theoretical issues. After all, every college has its own unique history, its own political and social realities, and its own learning culture. It will be a challenge, given this reality, to find common ground.

I would like to begin this vitally important dialogue by offering my own sense of what college-level writing is. First of all, I would like to suggest that we change the term *college-level writer* to *college-level reader*, *writer*, and *thinker*. I believe these three skills must be linked when we evaluate students' written work, especially as it relates to their relative level of preparedness to be successful college-level students in mainstream college courses (see Bartholomae, *Writing*; Bizzell; Bloom, Daiker, and White, *Composition*; Greene; Grego and Thompson; Horvath; Lunsford; Schreiner; Shattuck; Soles; Soliday, "From"). Good writing can only be the direct result of good reading and thinking, and this, it seems to me, is one of the foundational principles of college-level work. Furthermore, the ability to discuss and evaluate abstract ideas is, for me, the single most important variable in considering whether a student is capable of doing college-level work. Of all the components related to writing that we might consider as we evaluate student work for purposes of determining whether it is college level or not, this seems to me to be the most essential (see Berthoff, "Is"; Berthoff, *The Making*; Cooper and Odell; Corbett, Myers, and Tate; Straub and Lunsford).

I would propose, furthermore, that we consider the following list of criteria as a starting place for this discussion. This is how I would define college-level work:

1. A student should write in response to an article, essay, or reading selection that contains at least some abstract content and might be chosen based on its appropriateness for a college-level course. In fact, having a student read, consider, and respond to multiple readings grouped around a thematic question or issue would be ideal, in my judgment. The primary goal, regardless of the number of readings assigned, is to introduce students to an ongoing conversation that is

multilayered and complex. We would ask them, then, to engage the issues and ideas in that conversation thoughtfully.

Reading level or *readability* for this material might be determined by the approximate grade level it tests at according to, say, the Fry Readability Graph, McLaughlin's Readability Formula, or the Raygor Readability Estimate. Some critics argue that these various readability tests can not accurately measure complexity of content (or *concept load*) very well (see Nelson; Hittleman). My experience in using these tests for work that I assign in my own classes seems to indicate that sentence length, sophistication of vocabulary, length of sentences and paragraphs, and the overall length of each essay is a good general indicator for determining what is appropriate for a college-level reader and writer. I believe that college students should be encountering readings that require extended engagement and concentration.

2. The writer's essay, in response to this reading or group of readings, should demonstrate the following:

- A willingness to evaluate ideas and issues carefully.
- Some skill at analysis and higher-level thinking.
- The ability to shape and organize material effectively.
- The ability to integrate some of the material from the reading skillfully.
- The ability to follow the standard rules of grammar, punctuation, and spelling.

The attentive reader will no doubt wish to introduce at this point a caveat or two, perhaps formulated something like this: "That may seem reasonable, but don't you realize that phrases like *abstract content* and *evaluate ideas and issues carefully* are impossibly vague and notoriously difficult to define? And, furthermore, don't you realize that when we talk about *higher-level thinking* and *depth of thought*, we have to recognize, as Lee Odell has argued in 'Assessing Thinking: Glimpsing a Mind at Work,' that 'there are limits to what we can know or say about thinking' (7)?"

I would certainly agree. But without at least attempting to design writing tasks that will allow us to evaluate our students for these kinds of skills, how can we speak, defend, or teach within a system that makes distinctions every day between precollege work and college-level work? And how can we send our basic writing students to their other college-level courses without college-level reading, writing, and thinking skills?

Perhaps the single most important reason to conduct this discussion with full, careful engagement is political. Increasingly, we have let college-level writing be defined for us by state and national legislatures, special task forces, national testing agencies, and even some activist individuals who have strong convictions and large political constituencies. Few of the people involved in making these decisions and shaping our public policy about education are teachers, and few have more than a passing acquaintance with the college classroom. If we do not conduct this discussion ourselves, and speak with a strong voice about the issues we care about most, someone else will do it for us. If that does happen, it is very likely that the best interests of our students, and the more generally enlightened approach to the enterprise of learning that so many of us support, will be compromised. Our profession should be providing the leadership on this important matter of public policy.

As we move toward initiating a shared professional dialogue about this question, we can be guided by the work of Edward M. White and Kathleen Blake Yancey, as well as documents like the *Standards for the Assessment of Reading and Writing*, coauthored by the International Reading Association and the National Council of Teachers of English (1994); the "WPA Outcomes Statement for First-Year Composition," authored by the Steering Committee of the Outcomes Group (2001); and the recent position statements published by NCTE about teaching and assessing writing, especially "Framing Statements on Assessment" (2004) and "NCTE Beliefs about the Teaching of Writing" (2004). We can also be guided by books like Wolcott and Legg's *An Overview of Writing Assessment: Theory, Research, and Practice*, Zak and Weaver's *The Theory and Practice of Grading Writing*, Thompson's *Teaching Writing in High School and College: Conversations and Collaborations*, and Dombek and Herndon's *Critical Passages: Teaching the Transition to College Composition.*

These books provide us with a thoughtful, up-to-date overview of the issues and complexities that we must grapple with.

I would also like to suggest that we consider the following questions as we move forward with this discussion:

- What kinds of intellectual work do colleagues and students around the country associate with the concept of college-level writing?
- What are the benefits—and dangers—of standards and outcomes as proposed by documents like the Writing Program Administrators Outcomes Statement?
- What is the relationship between writing that students do as they transition to college, as they write in the first year of college, and as they write throughout their college career?
- When we look across different types of institutions, what is similar and what is different about the way college-level writing is defined?
- Should we attempt to establish some sort of shared national standard for college-level writing?

Conclusion

Just because this work is challenging does not mean that it can't be done or can't be done well. In fact, I would argue that the task of developing a clearer understanding of what we mean by college-level writing requires exactly the kind of patience, stamina, and good will that we privilege in our classrooms. We know how to do this kind of work very well, and given enough patience and good will, I think there is every reason to believe that we can accomplish it successfully.

Works Cited

Adler-Kassner, Linda, and Susanmarie Harrington. *Basic Writing as a Political Act: Public Conversations about Writing and Literacy.* Creskill, NJ: Hampton, 2002.

American Council on Education. "Choice of Institution: Changing Student Attendance Patterns in the 1990s." *ACE Issue Brief*. June 2004. 3 Sept. 2004 <http://www.acenet.edu/programs/policy>.

Arenson, Karen. "With New Admissions Policy, CUNY Steps into the Unknown." *New York Times* 28 May 1998: A1, B6.

———. "CUNY to Tighten Admissions Policy at 4-Year Schools." *New York Times* 27 May 1998: A1, A19.

Astin, Alexander. *What Matters in College? Four Critical Years Revisited*. San Francisco: Jossey-Bass, 1993.

Baker, George A. III, Judy Dudziak, and Peggy Tyler, eds. *A Handbook on the Community College in America: Its History, Mission, and Management*. Westport: Greenwood, 1994.

Barthes, Roland. (1972). "The Death of the Author." Trans. S. Heath. In Richter. 253–57.

Bartholomae, David. "The Tidy House: Basic Writing in the American Curriculum." *Journal of Basic Writing* 12 (1993): 4–21.

———. *Writing on the Margins: Essays on Composition and Teaching*. Boston: Bedford/St. Martin's, 2005.

Beaufort, Anne. *Writing in the Real World: Making the Transition from School to Work*. New York: Teachers College P, 1999.

Belanoff, Pat. "The Myths of Assessment." *Journal of Basic Writing* 10 (1991): 54–66.

Berthoff, Ann E. "Is Teaching Still Possible? Writing, Meaning, and Higher Order Reasoning." *College English* 46 (1984): 743–55.

———. *The Making of Meaning: Metaphors, Models, and Maxims for Writing Teachers*. Montclair, NJ: Boynton/Cook, 1981.

Billups, Lovely H. and Marilyn Rauth. "The New Research: How Effective Teachers Teach." *American Educator* 8 (1984): 34–39.

Bizzell, Patricia. "What Happens When Basic Writers Come to College?" *College Composition and Communication* 37 (1986): 294–301.

Bloom, Lynn Z. "Freshman Composition as a Middle-Class Enterprise." *College English* 58.6 (1996): 654–75.

Bloom, Lynn Z., Donald A. Daiker, and Edward M. White, eds. *Com-*

position in the Twenty-First Century: Crisis and Change. Carbondale: Southern Illinois UP, 1996.

Brookover, Wilbur B., and Lawrence W. Lezotte. *Changes in School Characteristics Coincident with Changes in Student Achievement*. East Lansing: Michigan State UP, 1979.

Brophy, Jere E. "Teacher Behavior and Student Learning." *Educational Leadership* 37.1 (1979): 33–38.

———. "Teacher Praise: A Functional Analysis." *Psychological Review* 88.2 (1981): 93–134.

———. "Classroom Management and Learning." *American Education* 18.2 (1982): 20–23.

Carroll, Lee Ann. *Rehearsing New Roles: How College Students Develop as Writers*. Carbondale: Southern Illinois UP, 2002.

Charney, Davida. "The Validity of Using Holistic Scoring to Evaluate Writing: A Critical Overview." *Research in the Teaching of English* 18 (February 1984): 65–81.

Clark, Burton. "The 'Cooling-Out' Function in Higher Education." *American Journal of Sociology* 1960 (65): 569–76.

———. "The 'Cooling Out' Function Revisited." *New Directions for Community Colleges: Questioning the Community College Role*. Ed. G. B. Vaughn. San Francisco: Jossey-Bass, 1980. 15–31.

———. *The Open Door College: A Case Study*. New York: McGraw-Hill, 1960.

Cohen, Arthur M., and Florence B. Brawer. *The American Community College*. San Francisco: Jossey-Bass, 1982.

Collins, Terence. "A Response to Ira Shor's 'Our Apartheid: Writing Instruction and Inequality.'" *Journal of Basic Writing* 16.2 (1997): 95–100.

Cooper, Charles R., and Lee Odell, eds. *Evaluating Writing: The Role of Teachers' Knowledge about Text, Learning, and Culture*. Urbana, IL: NCTE, 1999.

Corbett, Edward P. J., Nancy Myers, and Gary Tate. *The Writing Teacher's Sourcebook*. 4th ed. New York: Oxford UP, 1999.

Culler, Jonathan. *Structuralist Poetics: Structuralism, Linguistics, and the Study of Literature*. Ithaca: Cornell UP, 1975.

———. *On Deconstruction: Theory and Criticism after Structuralism.* Ithaca, NY: Cornell UP, 1982.

Curtis, Marcia, and Anne Herrington. "Writing Development in the College Years: By Whose Definition?" *College Composition and Communication* 55 (2003): 69–90.

DeGenaro, William, and Edward M. White. "Going around in Circles: Methodological Issues in Basic Writing Research." *Journal of Basic Writing* 19.1 (2000): 22–35.

Derrida, Jacques. *Dissemination.* Trans. Barbara Johnson. Chicago: U of Chicago P, 1981.

———. "Like the Sound of the Sea Deep Within a Shell: Paul de Man's War." Trans. P. Kamuf. *Critical Inquiry* 14 (1988): 590–652.

———. "Limited Inc." Trans. S. Weber and J. Mehlman. *Limited Inc.* Ed. G. Graff. Evanston, IL: Northwestern UP, 1988. 29–110.

———. "Signature Event Context." Trans. S. Weber and J. Mehlman. *Limited Inc.* Ed. G. Graff. Evanston, IL: Northwestern UP, 1988. 1–23.

Dombek, Kristin, and Scott Herndon. *Critical Passages: Teaching the Transition to College Composition.* New York: Teachers College Press, 2004.

Dougherty, Kevin. *The Contradictory College: The Conflicting Origins, Impacts, and Futures of the Community College.* Albany: State University of New York P, 1994.

Foucault, Michel. "What Is an Author?" Trans. Josué Harari. In Richter. 890–900.

Fox, Tom. *Defending Access: A Critique of Standards in Higher Education.* Portsmouth, NH: Boynton/Cook, 1999.

Good, Thomas L. "Teacher Expectations and Student Perceptions: A Decade of Research." *Educational Leadership* 38.5 (1981): 415–22.

———. "How Teachers' Expectations Affect Results." *American Education* 18.10 (1982): 25–32.

Gray-Rosendale, Laura. "Inessential Writings: Shaughnessy's Legacy in a Socially Constructed Landscape." *Journal of Basic Writing* 17.2 (1998): 43–75.

———. *Rethinking Basic Writing: Exploring Identity, Politics, and Community in Interaction.* Mahwah, NJ: Lawrence Erlbaum, 2000.

Greenberg, Karen. "A Response to Ira Shor's 'Our Apartheid: Writing Instruction and Inequality.'" *Journal of Basic Writing* 16.2 (1997): 90–94.

———. "Validity and Reliability: Issues in the Direct Assessment of Writing." *WPA: Writing Program Administration* 16 (1992): 7–22.

Greene, Stuart. "Making Sense of My Own Ideas: The Problems of Authorship in a Beginning Writing Classroom." *Written Communication* 12 (1995): 186–218.

Grego, Rhonda, and Nancy Thompson. "Repositioning Remediation: Renegotiating Composition's Work in the Academy." *College Composition and Communication* 47 (1996): 62–84.

Griffith, Marlene, and Ann Connor. *Democracy's Open Door: The Community College in America's Future.* Portsmouth, NH: Boynton/Cook, 1994.

Gunner, Jeanne. "Iconic Discourse: The Troubling Legacy of Mina Shaughnessy." *Journal of Basic Writing* 17.2 (1998): 25–42.

Harden, Blaine. "Reading, Writing and Ruckus: City University of New York's Tougher Standards Anger Many." *Washington Post* 2 June 1998: A3.

Harris, Joseph. "Revision as a Critical Practice." *College English* 65 (2003): 577–92.

Herrington, Anne, and Marcia Curtis. *Persons in Process: Four Stories of Writing and Personal Development in College.* Urbana, IL: NCTE, 2000.

Hess, G. Alfred. "Expectations, Opportunity, Capacity, and Will: The Four Essential Components of Chicago School Reform." *Educational Policy* 13 (1999): 494–517.

Hittleman, Daniel K. "Readability, Readability Formulas, and Cloze: Selecting Instructional Materials." *Journal of Reading* 22 (1978): 117–22.

Horvath, Brooke K. "The Components of Written Response: A Practical Synthesis of Current Views." *Rhetoric Review* 2 (1984): 136–56.

Huot, Brian. *(Re)Articulating Writing Assessment for Teaching and Learning*. Logan: Utah State UP, 2002.

———. "Toward a New Theory of Writing Assessment." *College Composition and Communication* 47 (1996): 549–66.

International Reading Association/National Council of Teachers of English Joint Task Force on Assessment. *Standards for the Assessment of Reading and Writing*. Urbana, IL: NCTE, 1994.

Jussim, Lee, and Jacquelynne S. Eccles. "Teacher Expectations II: Construction and Reflection of Student Achievement." *Journal of Personality and Social Psychology* 63 (1992): 947–61.

Jussim, Lee, Alison Smith, Stephanie Madon, and Polly Palumbo. "Teacher Expectations." *Advances in Research on Teaching. Volume 7: Expectations in the Classroom*. Ed. Jere Brophy. Greenwich, CT: JAI, 1998. 1–74.

Kuklinski, Margaret, and Rhona S. Weinstein. "Classroom and Developmental Differences in a Path Model of Teacher Expectancy Effects." *Child Development* 72 (2001): 1554–78.

Lavin, David E., and David Hyllegard. *Changing the Odds: Open Admissions and the Life Chances of the Disadvantaged*. New Haven, CT: Yale UP, 1996.

Leitch, Vincent, ed. *The Norton Anthology of Theory and Criticism*. New York: Norton, 2001.

Lewiecki-Wilson, Cynthia, and Jeff Sommers. "Professing at the Fault Lines: Composition at Open Admissions Institutions." *College Composition and Communication* 50 (1999): 438–62.

Lunsford, Andrea A. "The Content of Basic Writers' Essays." *College Composition and Communication* 31 (1980): 278–90.

McCourt, Frank. "Hope and Education." *New York Times* 21 May 1998: A33.

McNenny, Gerri, and Sallyanne Fitzgerald, eds. *Mainstreaming Basic Writers: Politics and Pedagogies of Access*. Mahwah, NJ: Erlbaum, 2001.

Miller, Richard E. "Fault Lines in the Contact Zone." *College English* 56 (1994): 389–408.

National Center for Education Statistics. "Remedial Education at Degree-Granting Postsecondary Institutions in Fall 2000." November

2003. 20 Feb. 2005 <http://nces.ed.gov/surveys/peqis/publications/2004010/index.asp>.

National Commission on Excellence in Education. *A Nation at Risk: The Imperative for Educational Reform.* Washington, DC: U.S. Department of Education, 1983.

National Council of Teachers of English. "Framing Statements on Assessment." November 2004. 21 March 2005 <http://www.ncte.org/about/over/positions/category/assess/118875.htm>.

———. "NCTE Beliefs about the Teaching of Writing." November 2004. 21 March 2005 <http://www.ncte.org/about/over/positions/category/write/118876.htm>.

Nelson, Joan. "Readability: Some Cautions for the Content Area Teacher." *Journal of Reading* 21 (1978): 620–25.

Obiakor, Festus. "Teacher Expectations of Minority Exceptional Learners: Impact on 'Accuracy' of Self-Concepts." *Exceptional Children* 66.1 (1999): 39–53.

O'Dair, Sharon. "Class Work: Site of Egalitarian Activism or Site of Embourgeoisement?" *College English* 65 (2003): 593–606.

Odell, Lee. "Assessing Thinking: Glimpsing a Mind at Work." In Cooper and Odell. 7–22.

Pickett, Nell Ann. "The Two-Year College as Democracy in Action." *College Composition and Communication* 49 (1998): 90–98.

Pratt, Mary Louise. "Arts of the Contact Zone." *Profession* 91 (1993): 33–40.

Renfro, Sally, and Allison Armour-Garb. *Open Admissions and Remedial Education at the City University of New York.* Prepared for the Mayor's Advisory Task Force on the City University of New York. June 1999.

Richter, David H., ed. *The Critical Tradition: Classic Texts and Contemporary Trends.* 2nd ed. Boston: Bedford, 1998.

Rose, Mike. "Remedial Writing Courses: A Critique and a Proposal." *College English* 45 (1983): 109–28.

Rosenthal, Robert, and Lenore Jacobson. *Pygmalion in the Classroom: Teacher Expectation and Pupils' Intellectual Development.* New York: Holt, Rinehart, and Winston, 1968.

Roueche, John E., and George A. Baker III. *Access and Excellence: The Open-Door College*. Washington, DC: Community College Press, 1987.

Roueche, John E., George A. Baker III, and Suanne D. Roueche. "Open Door or Revolving Door? Open Access and the Community College." *Community, Junior and Technical College Journal* 57 (1987): 22–26.

Roueche, John E., Laurence F. Johnson, and Suanne D. Roueche. *Embracing the Tiger: The Effectiveness Debate and the Community College*. Washington, DC: Community College Press, 1997.

Roueche, John E., and Suanne D. Roueche. *Between a Rock and a Hard Place: The At-Risk Student in the Open-Door College*. Washington, DC: Community College Press, 1993.

———. *High Stakes, High Performance: Making Remedial Education Work*. Washington, DC: Community College Press, 1999.

Sacks, Peter. *Standardized Minds: The High Price of America's Testing Culture and What We Can Do to Change It*. Cambridge, MA: Perseus, 2000.

Saxon, D. Patrick, and Hunter R. Boylan. "The Cost of Remedial Education in Higher Education." *Journal of Developmental Education* 25.2 (2001): 2–8.

Schreiner, Steven. "A Portrait of the Student as a Young Writer: Reevaluating Emig and the Process Movement." *College Composition and Communication* 48 (1997): 86–104.

Scott, Jerrie Cobb. "Literacies and Deficits Revisited." *Journal of Basic Writing* 12.1 (1993): 46–56.

Shattuck, Roger. "The Shame of the Schools." *The New York Review of Books* 7 April 2005: 66–69.

Sheridan-Rabideau, Mary, and Gordon Brossell. "Finding Basic Writing's Place." *Journal of Basic Writing* 14.1 (1995): 21–26.

Shor, Ira. "Our Apartheid: Writing Instruction and Inequality." *Journal of Basic Writing* 16.1 (1997): 91–104.

———. *When Students Have Power: Negotiating Authority in a Critical Pedagogy*. Chicago: U of Chicago P, 1996.

Soles, Derek. "Grading as a Teaching Strategy." *Teaching English in the Two-Year College* 29.2 (2001): 122–34.

Soliday, Mary. "From the Margins to the Mainstream: Reconceiving Remediation." *College Composition and Communication* 47 (1996): 85–100.

———. *The Politics of Remediation: Institutional and Student Needs in Higher Education*. Pittsburgh: U of Pittsburgh P, 2002.

Steering Committee of the Outcomes Group: Susanmarie Harrington, Rita Malencyzk, Irv Peckham, Keith Rhodes, and Kathleen Blake Yancey. "WPA Outcomes Statement for First-Year Composition." *College English* 63 (2001): 321–25.

Sternglass, Marilyn. *Time to Know Them: A Longitudinal Study of Writing and Learning at the College Level*. Mahwah, NJ: Lawrence Erlbaum, 1997.

Straub, Richard, and Ronald Lunsford. *Twelve Readers Reading: Responding to College Student Writing*. Cresskill, NJ: Hampton, 1995.

Sullivan, Patrick. "'Reception Moments,' Modern Literary Theory, and the Teaching of Literature." *Journal of Adolescent and Adult Literacy* 45 (2002): 568–77.

Thompson, Thomas C., ed. *Teaching Writing in High School and College: Conversations and Collaborations*. Urbana, IL: NCTE, 2002.

Tinberg, Howard. "Are We Good Enough? Critical Literacy and the Working Class." *College English* 63 (2001): 353–60.

Tinto, Vincent. *Leaving College: Rethinking the Causes and Cures of Student Attrition*. 2nd ed. Chicago: U of Chicago P, 1993.

Traub, James. *City on a Hill: Testing the American Dream at City College*. Reading, MA: Addison-Wesley, 1994.

———. "What No School Can Do." *The New York Times Magazine* 16 Jan. 2000: 52–57, 68+.

United States Department of Education, National Center for Education Statistics. *The Condition of Education 2002*. "Nontraditional Undergraduates." 2002. 26 July 2004 <http://nces.ed.gov/programs/coe/2002/analyses/nontraditional/index.asp>.

Wentzel, Kathryn. "Are Effective Teachers Like Good Parents? Teaching Styles and Student Adjustment in Early Adolescence." *Child Development* 73.1 (2002): 287–301.

White, Edward M. *Developing Successful College Writing Programs*. San Francisco: Jossey-Bass, 1989.

———. *Teaching and Assessing Writing: Recent Advances in Understanding, Evaluating, and Improving Student Performance*. 2nd ed. San Francisco: Jossey-Bass, 1994.

Wohlstetter, Priscilla, and Allan Odden. "Rethinking School-Based Management Policy and Research." *Educational Administration* 28 (1992): 529–49.

Wolcott, Willa, with Sue M. Legg. *An Overview of Writing Assessment: Theory, Research, and Practice*. Urbana, IL: NCTE, 1998.

Yancey, Kathleen Blake. "Looking Back as We Look Forward: Historicizing Writing Assessment." *College Composition and Communication* 50.3 (1999): 483–503.

Zak, Frances, and Christopher C. Weaver, eds. *The Theory and Practice of Grading Writing: Problems and Possibilities*. Albany: State U of New York P, 1998.

I

High School Perspectives

Chapter Two

Whistling in the Dark

Merrill J. Davies
Armuchee High School
Rome, Georgia

Thanks to you, Lacey and I are having no trouble in college composition," said Carol. "But some of the others are. Actually, we're just doing many of the same things you had us do the last two years of high school," she boasted.

We high school English teachers love to hear those kinds of comments coming from former students. Unfortunately, though, we hear other, less positive kinds of comments as well. Another student from the same class, who went to a different college, said, "Well, my first two papers were pretty bad, but my professor just expected something different, and when I learned what he wanted, I started doing better."

Having taught high school English for thirty-one years, the one thing that I have learned is that there is no guarantee that students who do well in high school composition will automatically do well in college composition. Nevertheless, the school system where I taught for twenty-seven years now claims that students who complete their rigorous Honors College Preparatory program are "guaranteed to be ready for college." This kind of claim puts the high school teacher in a position of needing to know more specifically what college professors expect in terms of writing skills.

There is an old expression about "whistling in the dark" which refers to walking along and pretending to be confident in the dark when in fact we are scared to death. That is the way I have often felt about trying to prepare students for college. I tell them what *I think* they should know and be able to do, but in reality I know that the expectations vary greatly between colleges and even among professors in the same college. Also, there is generally little communication between high school teachers and college professors. I was fortunate to have three colleges in the small town where I taught, and most of the time I knew at least one professor in each college, so I may have had a slight advantage. I also attempted to seek help through Internet searches for any information that might give me clues to college writing expectations. When I attended state and national conferences for English teachers, I took advantage of breakout sessions related to college composition. I must admit that mine were rather haphazard attempts to help students prepare for college-level writing. Nevertheless, there are four areas I have stressed with my students over the years in an attempt to prepare them for college-level writing.

First, there is the matter of *mechanics*. I have often printed out statements from colleges that tell of giving a grade no higher than a C to students who commit even one error, such as a sentence fragment, a run-on sentence, or a comma splice. It scares the pants off my students, but it gets their attention! Unfortunately, many teachers in other disciplines allow students to get by with good grades even if their writings contain gross errors in spelling, grammar, and punctuation. These students often think their English teachers are just being "picky" when they give a poor assessment to papers filled with errors.

Second, I believe that in order to be successful in college writing, students need to be able to use *analytical skills* in written responses to literary texts as well as the media. Many of my students seem to have struggled most in college composition when they have been asked to explicate a poem or analyze certain elements of a piece of literature. Early in my teaching career, I did not allow students to practice these skills early enough in high school, so they were very uncomfortable if not outright perplexed with these kinds of assignments. This resulted in very awkward-sounding comments that revealed a lack of understanding about how to talk about literary works. I would often read papers with sentences such as the following: "The author was a very good writer. He used many great literary devices in his writing and he had great themes." They could talk about what happened in the story or give the main idea in a poem, but they had little experience in discussing theme, tone, mood, or style.

Third, when students leave high school, they should also be able to *develop a specific idea in detail, supporting that idea with meaningful facts, illustrations, experiences, analogies, quotes, or whatever is needed to make the thesis or premise clear*. This skill begins to be important when students are young, but it becomes even more important when they begin to analyze literature. The more abstract the literature they read and the more abstract their own ideas become, the more important it is for students to be able to clarify their ideas with concrete details. More than once I have reminded my students that they do not convince their reader by merely repeating their main ideas over and over, but by elaborating on and discussing these ideas in meaningful detail.

Finally, not only do students need to be able to support their ideas with specific details, they need to be able to *organize* the material (in such a way that the reader can separate one idea from another) and also *provide adequate transitions* from one idea to the next so that the reader can follow easily. The often-berated five-paragraph essay is an attempt to teach students how to do this. Unfortunately, some students do not make it past this stage before they leave high school, when they should have moved beyond it in late elementary or middle school. I remember using a program called STEPS, which taught my middle school students this form. They loved it because the three points in the essay were called "Bing, Bang, and Bongo"! The program actually moved the students beyond the basic five-paragraph essay very quickly if they understood the concept of developing an idea in an organized way. Unfortunately, many teachers just kept repeating the process instead of moving the students beyond the basics.

Having given some of the areas I have stressed in teaching writing over the years, I need to add some insights that I gained during the last ten years of teaching. Basic expectations do not change much, but the emphasis does. For example, when I was in college and during my first years of teaching, the emphasis seemed to be on grammatical and mechanical *correctness* in writing. Whether it was verb usage, punctuation, documentation of sources in research, or sentence structure, the focus was on getting it right. Over the last few years, however, the emphasis seems to have shifted, and I'm hearing more about expectations of *developing a voice* and *choosing an audience* in writing. I asked some of my friends who teach at the college level what they expected and most of them mentioned *strong voice* as an important factor, along with *ability to organize ideas*, stating that the mechanics are "easier to help students fix." This is not to say that college professors no longer expect college students to write mechanically correct papers, but the focus does not seem to be entirely on correctness. There seems to be more of a balance in form and content than there used to be. I suspect that even back when I was in college and early in my teaching career, professors valued audience awareness and development of voice, but they did not evaluate those factors as much.

The real question is *how proficient* is a college student as compared to a high school student? In reality, I have had high school students who could write better than some of my colleagues who had several college degrees. But high school teachers constantly struggle with what to focus on with student writers. One teacher says that she works with students on "more formal, stylistically mature pieces such as research papers and essays" while helping them "eliminate major sentence errors like fragments, comma splices, and run-ons." She assumes that college professors will expect students who can write "grammatically correct, well-thought out pieces that present evidence of their reasoning." Still, she is not sure if what she is doing is enough. She wonders if she should be doing more literary analysis and less persuasive writing about current topics. Should high school teachers be teaching more formal papers or more informal responses to prompts?

I have always thought that high school should give students a good foundation so that they can adapt to whatever comes their way in postsecondary education, but it is difficult to identify specifically what college-level writing is and how it is (or should be) different than high school-level writing. My belief is that these lines will always be rather fuzzy, and high school teachers will have to continue to "whistle in the dark" sometimes. Given the complicated nature of writing, I am not sure we can expect college professors to come up with exact guidelines for college-level writing. Nonetheless, I would like to make two suggestions that might help us all. First, colleges need to have teacher education programs that give students specific help in the teaching of writing. Student teachers often seem much more comfortable teaching literature than they do teaching writing. Second, college English professors and secondary English teachers in the same geographic areas need to find ways to communicate on a regular basis so that high school teachers can gauge how they are doing in preparing students for college work. This dialogue could be initiated by either the college professors or the high school teachers because both would benefit.

Chapter Three

Am I a Liar? The Angst of a High School English Teacher

Jeanette Jordan, with Karena K. Nelson,
Howard Clauser, Susan E. Albert,
Karen M. Cunningham, and Amanda Scholz
Glenbrook North High School
Northbrook, Illinois

As a veteran high school English teacher, there are certain things I never want to hear. This past holiday season, Mike, a former student, stopped in my classroom to say hello. He had just graduated from college and was beginning a job search. We were having a pleasant conversation when we were interrupted by a current student hoping to clarify something about her research project. Assuming the voice of experience, Mike said, "Don't worry about it. I just graduated from college and I never *once* had to write a research paper."

I turned to him, shocked. I knew what he was saying was not true for a typical college experience. Or could it be? I thought that research-based writing was the foundation of academia. I had just dedicated six weeks of junior English to guiding (okay, maybe dragging) my students through the process by promising them that for college they needed to learn how to research, to evaluate the validity of sources, and to document their sources using MLA format. I coerced them into taking the project seriously because developing an original thesis and supporting it with evidence was critical to success in college and beyond. Now my former student returns and says he never wrote a research paper after he graduated from high school. Am I really that out of touch with what is expected of my students in their postsecondary educations? I saw my current student silently question my credibility, and I cringed.

I am convinced that my students learn to be better writers, readers, and thinkers through their high school English experiences. My colleagues and I take our jobs seriously, and we are consistently pushing ourselves to stay current with the best practices in the field. We diligently work with our students on their writing. Outside of the classroom, students work with peers and adults in the writing center to get even more feedback. Our students regularly score at the top on state assessments, and alumni overwhelmingly report that they feel well prepared for the demands of university life. Still, with 98 percent of our students going to college after they graduate from high school, it is important that I am accurate with my statements about what lies ahead for them. Again, I pondered. Was Mike's experience unique or typical for college students today? If I am mistaken about the importance of research-based writing, what other myths am I operating under? Does it matter, for example, that my students can distinguish between *who* and *whom*?

"Is Grammar DEAD—and does it really matter?" reads the cover of a recent *Chicago Tribune Magazine* (13 Feb. 2005). I plead with my students to learn the differences between phrases and clauses so that they can properly punctuate sentences. But does it really matter? I sometimes tell myself that writers need to understand the traditional rules before they can learn a sense of how and when these rules can be broken. But that theory leaves me with the feeling that I, as a high school teacher, am saddled with the burden of teaching the rules and gaining the reputation of a stickler, while professors get to sail through uncharted linguistic waters, throwing rules overboard at whim, gaining their students' approval and respect at every turn.

I wonder how strictly professors adhere to the conventional standards of grammar and format. If my students use first person in an argumentative paper, will someone assume they have been woefully underprepared for the rigors of college study? If I pound into their heads that they should avoid first person and they dutifully attempt to use third, but struggle with awkward constructions involving "one" and some mysterious "reader," will a professor somewhere shake her head at how out of touch and antiquated high school teachers are? Am I focusing on the wrong rules?

My colleagues and I work with our students to ensure that they have a good grasp of the basics of grammar and essay structure. We value nonformulaic writing and struggle to push our students beyond the very limiting five-paragraph structure that they find so comforting and familiar. Am I doing a disservice to my low-level writers, however, if I throw out this scaffold that they are still trying to master? Does putting the topic sentence as the first sentence in the body paragraph provide a security that helps them in their struggles to communicate? Is voice more important than well-structured writing? Whose definition of well-structured writing should I use as a model?

A colleague who recently returned to the classroom after a career in business wonders if writing teachers at all levels should be preparing students to write in the nonacademic world, where they will be asked to produce functional documents. He earned a small fortune consulting with businesses, enabling their employees to write clear and coherent letters, memos, and reports. He worked with college graduates—engineers, managers, business people, scientists, lawyers, even doctoral graduates—many of whom could write exquisite prose that did not mean a thing. My colleague muses that our high school-level instruction could be contributing unwittingly to the output of soulless techno-jargon that plagues business and government writing today. Should we focus our students on writing functionally in plain simple English rather than on developing elaborate theses supported by passages from the text, documented on a works cited page, and stylized by an occasional periodic sentence? I wonder how all the potential audiences for my students define good writing.

I see in my own department a diversity of views on what a good paper looks like. Beginning writing students looking for a single template that they can apply to all writing situations are frustrated and confused by these myriad opinions. They don't understand that different writing tasks require different writing forms. Instead, they blame their teachers. I remember working as a writing tutor in graduate school and listening to students struggle to integrate these sometimes mixed messages. "But my high school teachers always told me my thesis had to be one sentence!" or "Everyone else wants me to use research, but he says it should be entirely original!" they would complain. I sympathized, but I also found that the more I got to know a professor and his or her assignments, the more they made sense, even if the students were convinced an assignment was the most ridiculous thing they had ever been asked to do. So how do I impart to my high school students that different writing tasks and audiences expect different outcomes? How do I prepare them for what may seem like moving targets and conflicting goals without turning them into complete relativists?

Although I taught a variety of college writing courses when I was a teaching assistant working my way through graduate school, that was fifteen years ago. My perception of what is expected may be dated. What I do know is that my colleagues and I do our best to prepare our students for the challenges that will face them after they leave us. I would like a clearer idea of what those challenges are at the college level today.

I wonder what frustrates college writing instructors the most about the level of writing preparation students have before entering college. I am sometimes disappointed that in four years of high school, we often repeat very basic lessons over and over again ("show, don't tell," "specific is terrific!"). I believe that students learn in spurts and slips and false starts, and that seeds that I have planted may not blossom for years, especially when the growth is in the most difficult areas. But I wonder, at times, if there are basic competencies my students are missing. What are those basic competencies? To know how to use a semicolon? To understand the idea of intellectual property and how to use textual support without plagiarizing? To value their own voice and feel that they have something to say?

My visions of college English are updated mainly by alumni who visit and share their experiences with me. I eagerly listen to what they have to say as I question them: "What kind of writing do you do?" "What have you written about?" "What are you reading?" "What was the most difficult part about writing at the college level?" "Did you feel prepared for it?" "What advice do you have for us as high school English teachers?" Cate, a student of mine who graduated ten years ago, prompted the revamping of our research paper project when she shared the scathing remarks a college professor made on her first college research project. His many negative comments evidenced his anger and frustration with her writing. "Your paper is entirely meaningless" was just one of the criticisms of the piece. Cate was an honors student and National Council of Teachers of English Achievement Award nominee! If she experienced this difficulty with research-based writing, we knew we needed to revise our project to better prepare our students for what awaited them. That was nine years ago; however, a lot has changed since then. My doubts return, and I consider that my skills may not be current anymore. Is Mike's experience a more accurate reflection of contemporary university expectations? Are we now spending too much time on a project that is irrelevant to postsecondary success? I know that my students' experiences vary by college and class, but I think that there must be some consistencies. These consistencies are what I need to hear about so that I can confidently tell my students, "Yes, you will need to do this when you write in college."

The Salem Witch Trials: Voice(s)

Alfredo Celedon Lujan
Monte del Sol Charter School
Santa Fe, New Mexico

B*oring*: College-level writing must have a strong thesis statement. College-level writing is tightly woven and unified—buttressed by topic, transitional, and parallel sentences that flow seamlessly and thematically from paragraph to paragraph. College-level writing must have an introduction, body, and conclusion. It is demonstrated in essays, papers, stories, journals, research projects, lab reports, reader responses, articles, etc. It conforms to state and national standards and adheres to the conventions of correctness. *Boring.*

"Rewind, *ese*" (from the movie, *Selena*, 1997). In 1965, I was a sophomore in high school, and I was bound to go somewhere. Most likely, I was headed for the army and Vietnam, like my classmate Robert Steven Trujillo—Bobby, who is gone but not forgotten (high school graduate, May, 1967; missing in action, January 7, 1968).

In Pojoaque, our remote northern New Mexico town, the term *college bound* was somewhat foreign. Girls were on the clerical track (Typing I, II, III, and Bookkeeping), and they all took Home Economics. Boys took Drafting, Vocational Agriculture, and Shop (woodworking, leather crafting, or auto mechanics). We also took required courses, of course. And there were exceptions—the brains who took Advanced Algebra, Geometry, Trigonometry, Calculus, and were also straight-A students in English I through IV. They were the few who would definitely go to college. Many of us, however, had been counseled to join the military, to serve our country, to become men. John F. Kennedy's motto had been coined and ingrained in our collective consciousness: "Ask not what your country can do for you, ask what you can do for your country." The poster on the wall of the counselor's office pointed at *me* and said, "Uncle Sam wants *you*." *Chale, bro*—no way, *Jose*.

Generally, our main objective was to attend school every day, 180 days a year; get a certificate for perfect attendance; stay on task; get the diploma; go into the service and/or work for the rest of our lives. So what did the Salem Witch Trials mean to me? Nothing. *Nada. El zilcho.*

Our English teacher said we should learn to do research in case we went to college. English classes back then were largely grammar-based with plenty of sentence diagramming. We started on page one of Warriner's, or *English 2600* (Blumenthal). Our goal was to finish the book by the end of the year while learning, reviewing, relearning (not Re: Learning), and reiterating the parts of speech, the subject, the predicate, the four types of sentences; auxiliary verbs; the six comma rules, capitalization rules, and prepositional phrases among other things: cursive penmanship, independent clauses, dependent clauses, subordinate and coordinate clauses, the use and over-use of semicolons and colons, the conjugation of verbs . . . *perfecto* tense.

Sophomore year, when I did my first research paper in case I went to college, I was stumped. Our teacher gave us a handout that illustrated the essential parts of the paper, including a bibliography. When she wrote our research options on the blackboard, the only one that jumped out was the Salem Witch Trials.

I swear the first image that came to my mind was the Salem cigarette pack and TV commercial with green meadows, a babbling creek, a misty waterfall, *menthol*. The second word that grabbed my attention was *Witch*. *Brujas* were real in our part of the country, so I was curious to know more. I don't even remember the other topics we might have chosen. I had two weeks to do my research paper. It was hard homework, homework that I had never done before. Good thing my parents had bought a set of encyclopedias from a traveling salesman when I was in junior high.

A week later I realized my research paper was due Friday, and it had to be typed! I asked my mom if she would type it at work because we didn't have a typewriter at home. She told me she'd type it during her lunch hour Thursday, but I'd have to write it by Wednesday. I initially had trouble finding the Salem Witch Trials under T for *the*, but eventually I found my topic under S in the encyclopedia. The print was small, and the story was long, so I skipped a lot of it because it was time to write the paper.

I took out my pencil and paper, and I started copying from the sections of the encyclopedia that I had skimmed. I put what I read into my own words; I changed "and's" to "but's" and "or's" to "nor's," so to speak. My paper became ten pages of encyclopedia text that I had rearranged and copied almost directly from the book. How else does a high school sophomore write ten pages? It was okay because I honestly (if naively) thought it was the kind of research and writing I'd have to do if I decided to go to college. My mom typed it for me, as promised. I turned it in when it was due. When I got it back, a B- was at the top of the page with no other marks on the paper. In retrospect, I should have gotten an A+ for plagiarism, and the teacher should have received a C- for effort.

Preparing for college writing today is no longer just encyclopedia "research." There are heaps and layers of printed and electronic texts accessible to students now. How do we help them plow through the material and cultivate college-level writing without copying or clipping and pasting? What is acceptable and genuine student writing today?

I'd say good writing rings true with *voice* authenticity (Ken Macrorie, Peter Elbow, Nancy Martin [may she rest in peace], Donald Graves, Peter Stillman). As far as I know, the nebulous term *voice* has been kicked around for the last quarter of a century, *mas o menos*.

What is voice in writing? To simplify, it is, perhaps, when the writer recognizes in her or his prose or poetry a style, tone, personality, and rhythm that work. And the writer must have an ear for detail (Macrorie); this helps establish the writer's voice. In "A Letter to Gabriela, A Young Writer," author Pat Mora encourages young writers to listen with all of their senses. "Listen to the wrinkles on your *tia's* face," she advises.

"Voice is the imprint of ourselves on our writing," says Donald Graves in *Writing: Teachers and Children at Work*. "Divorcing voice from process is like omitting salt from stew, love from sex, or sun from gardening. Teachers who attend to voice listen to the person in the piece and observe how that person uses process components" (227). Students should feel free to express themselves, to choose their diction, to take risks in their writing. Writing without voice is breathing without rhythm—is speaking without body language, accent, dialect, or inflection. When a student writes, she or he is talking on paper.

Inevitably, the writer engenders a rhetorical stamp—a linguistic habit that consists of "spelling, diction, grammatical accidence, syntax, internal biographical evidence, psycholinguistic material" (Foster). One's personal writing technique produces unique, thoughtful prose or poetry that includes literal and figurative language—seriousness, analysis, and humor on paper. It's akin to Buzz Lightyear's "falling with style" (*Toy Story*), but this is *writing with style.*

One of my first classes at the Bread Loaf School of English was Nonfiction Prose, taught by Ken Macrorie (*The I-Search Paper*; *Writing to Be Read*). We thought on paper—what a concept! We wrote, and we rewrote. Many of our first drafts were timed, stream-of-conscious freewrites. The topics varied; the philosophy was simple. Writers learn to write by writing; writers write to be read, and writers revise. Papers that were returned by Ken had no grade at the top, but they had plenty of feedback: "This is good . . . flesh this out . . . include dialogue . . . great image . . . good ear . . . your conclusion needs work . . . don't explain . . . your paper starts here," etc. Those comments reminded me of the first time I felt like a teacher had truly read my paper. I was a freshman at New Mexico State University in the fall of 1967. The professor's name was John Hadsell. (We always remember the names of teachers who respond to our writing.)

We were reading *Writing Prose: Techniques and Purposes*, a literature anthology with segments on mechanics and usage, grammar, and writing. We used the writers in the anthology as models. We wrote essays. The grading system was plus (+) for exemplary, check (√) for good, and minus (-) for needs work. That was it: a plus, check, or minus at the top of the paper, but the paper always had Mr. Hadsell's comments on the margin. One assignment was to write an argumentative paper. We had read "Boxing with the Naked Eye," an essay from *The Sweet Science* in which A. J. Liebling asserts that watching boxing live is far better than watching it on television. We were asked if we agreed or disagreed with Liebling. Our objective was to convince the reader that watching sports on television was better than watching them live or vice versa. I argued in favor of watching baseball on television because the replay option was not available at the stadium. I wrote something like, "[I]n the stadium, a loudmouth with a hotdog or a bag of popcorn in his hands could jump up right in front of you and block the view of a pin-striped Yankee sliding chest first into third base." Mr. Hadsell checked the passage and on the margin wrote something like, "good concrete image, tone, and choice of words." This meant more to me than any A, B-, plus, check, minus, whatever. It wasn't even good writing perhaps, but finally someone had recognized *my words*, even if they mimicked the author's. I had stumbled upon my voice.

As a teacher of English I try to replicate Hadsell's and Macrorie's pedagogy. I comment on passages that seem unique to my students' voices, and I hope the comments guide them through revisions and future papers. I also mark spelling, mechanics, and usage, of course, but the emphasis is placed on passages that stimulate the reader's senses. Below are some final draft excerpts of student writing that I consider college level.

Bianca and Colin wrote the following identity poems after reading Pat Mora's *My Own True Name*.

I Am . . .

I am from Cuautemac, Chihuahua.
I am from the desert mountains.
I am from the smell of "*bizcochitos,*"
still fresh, just out of the oven.
I am from the taste of "*pan dulce,*" sweet as candy.
I am a small star in the dark cloudy sky,
just starting to shine.
I am like the sound of "*cumbias,*"
tun, tun, tun, tun, tun, tun.
I am from Mexico.
I am me.

Glossary

bizcochitos:	Mexican sugar cookies
pan dulce:	bread with candy (like donuts)
cumbias:	a Mexican kind of dance

Bianca Madrid, 7th grade
Monte del Sol Charter School, Santa Fe, New Mexico

The Solver of the Real Homework

I am the forgetful one, the one who probably forgot his homework today. In fact, I am the one who forgot his homework today, and I am the one who forgot it yesterday, and I am the one who will probably forget his homework tomorrow too.

"Why?" you might ask.

"Because," I would answer, "I am busy trying to find the answers to my homework."

I would not, however, tell you that I do not mean my math homework or my French homework but the unassigned homework—the real homework—the homework that we will all have to "cash in" on someday; the homework that is unwanted because it is hard and because people are scared of it. It's unwanted because humans created something that none can control. Too many things are masked to such a point by the textbooks that were rewritten by the media. Few can see the truth or their real identity, and some have lost sight completely, only thinking of war and their own good being. But there is a way we can see the truth—"the light"—and our real identities again, and that is what I am working on instead of doing my homework. This way is hard and long but worth it. This way is to do the real homework. It is your homework, my homework, everybody's homework. This homework includes solving the hard problems like world hunger and homelessness.

This is the world that I have come from, and this is the world that has masked my identity from me to such a point that I could say hi to my identity on the street and not recognize him. But for some reason I feel that part of my identity is the forgetful one and also a big part of my identity is the solver of these big problems like world hunger that I like to call The Real Homework.

Colin Strauch, 7th grade
Monte del Sol Charter School, Santa Fe, New Mexico

The following pieces were written by Ben and Briana after they were asked to write about an interest/passion that they have.

My Batting Routine

When I'm in the on deck circle, waiting for my turn at the plate, I like to put pine tar on the handle of my bat. The pine tar is sticky so it helps me get my grip. As the batter in front of me gets on base or is out, it is my turn at the plate. I walk up to the box. While I am getting my signs from the coach at third base, I flex my fingers on and off of the stickiness of the tar. I step into the box, and dig in with my cleats (so I have good footing) . . .

Ben Balkcom, 7th grade
Monte del Sol Charter School, Santa Fe

My Own Stage

In the wings,
dark and quiet,
pulse quickening

Concentrate. Settle down. Breathe.
Your turn.
You are out on stage,
lights bright,
shining on your dazzling costume.
You say your line,
and as the play goes on,
the character thrives in you,
and you become the character.

You take a bow.
The lights dim.
The play is over.

Briana Thomas, 7th grade
Monte del Sol Charter School, Santa Fe, New Mexico

The following poem was written by Sinay in response to "My Father's Hands," a poem from Nora Naranjo-Morse's *Mud Woman.*

AMÁ

Las manos de mi amá
son muy importantes
Desde que nací
sus manos han hecho todo
para tenerme vivo
trabajaban para el dinero
cocinaban para comer
me bañaban para tenerme limpio
me tocaban y me cariciaban para sentirme amado
Y ahora que ya están en la mitad
de su vida, todavía me dan de
comer, trabajan, y con sus manos me
sigue amando

Sinay Alvarez, 10th grade
Monte del Sol Charter School, Santa Fe, New Mexico

Below is Nolan Ellsworth's entry, which was written on a train ride across the United States. His teacher is Amy Bebell at the Brooklin School in Maine. I recently read his reading journal. I loved this entry and its communicative format (a letter to his teacher), so I'm including it even though he is not a student of mine.

Reading Journal, 9-30-04

Dear Mrs. Bebell,

I found another book to read called *The Ghostmobile.* It's about a boy named Ryan who moves to Wisconsin from Evanston with his family, his brother Josh, his sister Carrie, and his other sister Brook. They're all miserable camping in the middle of a cornfield until a giant glowing bus lands in the middle of their driveway!

But wait, on my way to Wyoming I stayed in a hotel in Boston and went to a giant bookstore. I got the 5th *Spiderwick* book, which is about these three kids named Jared, Simon, and Mallory who discover their great, great uncle's field guide to fairies, and start seeing strange creatures everywhere . . . it's a great book!

From,
Nolie

P.S. I'm not writing in cursive because the train ride was too bumpy.

Nolan Ellsworth, 3rd grade
Brooklin School, Brooklin, Maine

The two following excerpts are reader responses by Jamaica and Guy after they read sections of Walt Whitman's "Song of Myself."

Song of Self

I am a 14 year old girl, who likes many things.
I was born on September 12, 1990. I am a Virgo.
I was born of Aileen Lopez and Ruben Gonzales,
  my supporting parents.
I am the oldest of 4 children.
I am a Catholic/Christian, who believes in God and all His
  mysterious ways.
I am of Hispanic, White, Mexican, French, German,
  and other heritages.

I am from Carlos Gilbert Elementary School
  and Monte del Sol Charter School.
I like math, English, history, and choir.
I have been in a lot of sports in my life:
  basketball, soccer, tennis, cheerleading, and track.
And I have been in a lot of dance programs:
  ballet, Spanish, drill team, NDI, and hip-hop.

I like to imagine, and I love to read.
I am smart, and I am dumb.
I am good, and I am bad (I make good and bad choices).
I am a friend and an enemy.
I am placed in this world to make a difference
  (everyone can make a difference).
I am who I think I am; I am Jamaica Ashley Gonzales.

Jamaica Gonzales, 8th grade
Monte del Sol Charter School, Santa Fe, New Mexico

I Stand

I am from my mother and my father,
I am from the weak, and I am from the strong,
I am from the power of those who came before me . . .

I am from late night phone conversations, sleeping in late, and
procrastinating until everything seems hopeless.
I am from effort, and I am from laze.
I am from a vocabulary that rivals that of many adults.
I am from my mother's unrelenting love and my father's some-
times hard to identify but equally powerful affection.

I am from my name, Guy, its meaning is unimportant; my name
is who I am no matter what. People have made fun of my
name; they've even made fun of my parents for naming me so.
I don't care what other people think about my name, it's MY
identity and only mine . . .

I am from feeling the rhythms as I tap dance, no choreography,
all improvised.
I am from the searing pains in my legs that I know are good for
me during ballet class—all form, all choreography.
I am from the style of my Jazz classes . . .

I stand for the democratic process;
I stand for people working together to achieve what they want;
I stand for "Anyone but BUSH 2004," one of my favorite
bumper stickers.
I am from the Presidential debates that seem to be the only
important thing.
I stand for believing in John Kerry's and John Edwards' beliefs; I
also stand for respecting the beliefs of George Bush and Dick
Cheney as much as I may believe they are wrong.
I stand for uniting our country rather than separating it with
political tools like religion and sexual orientation and political
stances . . .
I stand for this country.

I do not stand for a country divided.
I am an American, not a Democrat nor a Republican
I am not independent.
I am an American.

I also stand for the world, the economy, the United Nations. I
stand for peace treaties and global trade.
I stand for the affairs of the whole world as well as my country.
I stand for the Islamists, Hindus, Christians, Catholics, Bud-
dhists, Pagans, Muslims, Unitarians, and all the religions of
the world. I believe in a nondiscriminatory world, one without
sexism, racism, or the struggle for oil underneath the soil of
other countries.

I stand for a world not terrified by the chances of global destruction from nuclear warfare, or even interplanetary warfare.
I stand for the farmer who can barely afford to feed his cows and harvest his crops.
I stand for the scuba diver, the coal miner, the vegan, and even the millionaire.
In order to be a world free of terrorists and dictators, we must be a united world, one without conflicts and warring countries.

I not only stand for nations and the world, I stand for myself and my immediate community.
I stand for my school, my family, myself.
I stand for nurturing myself and others.
I stand for the power of the individual, for the people who can stand alone for what they believe in.

People who have the power to stand alone will gain followers; people respect people who have the courage to stand up and say, "This is what I stand for," people like Gandhi, Martin Luther King Jr., Abraham Lincoln, Susan B. Anthony and even the people who didn't make a national or global difference, the people who changed one village, one city, one state. These are the individuals that I believe in.

I also stand for youth. I stand for the children and teens of this country that will rise in the next generation to lead the world. If the world is to change into a better place, we need to nurture and develop our youth. The people who understand this best are teachers. They understand that by teaching they are building the power of the youth. A world of uneducated leaders in the next generation cannot possibly fare well. So I stand for the youth of this world and of my country. Though we may seem disrespectful and noisy, even ignorant, we usually catch the important things, and we almost always internalize these things to use later in our lives . . .

I am me. I am me. I am me . . .
I stand.
I stand for me.
I stand for my community.
I stand for my country.
I stand for my world . . .
. . . I don't plan to leave this world without making a mark . . .
I do stand.

Guy Mannick, 8th grade
Monte del Sol Charter School, Santa Fe, New Mexico

The following double entry journals were written after close readings of several texts.

Double Entry Journal, 11-8-2004

"What are your blooms, your thorns, your roots?"

Pat Mora
"Dear Fellow Writer"
My Own True Name
p. 1–3

I really, really liked this quote because Pat Mora brings us into the book. She's like inviting us into the book so that we can tell her what we think or what's the answer to her question. She is asking the readers what were their good times, their bad times, and also when they learned a lesson. In my opinion, I'm going to enjoy this book.

Double Entry Journal, 11-7-04

"My pen is like music."

Pat Mora
"A Letter to Gabriela, a Young Writer"
English Journal, September, 1990
pp. 40–42

In my opinion this was the best sentence. I really liked this sentence because when she said that her pen is like music. It, well, told me that the pen or pencil that we are writing with just says on the paper what we think. Because sometimes when I'm thinking . . . I just write it on paper, and I feel more relaxed because . . . I shared my thoughts with someone . . .

Bianca Madrid, 7th grade
Monte del Sol Charter School, Santa Fe, New Mexico

Double Entry Journal, 11-7-04

"Listen to the wrinkles on your *tia's* face."

Pat Mora
"A Letter to Gabriela, a Young Writer"

The Salem Witch Trials: Voice(s)

English Journal, September, 1990
p. 41

I liked the phrase because if you imagine it, it's funny . . . if she's talking to you, and you're looking at her wrinkles, you're not even paying attention to her.

Vanessa Quintana, 7th grade
Monte del Sol Charter School, Santa Fe, New Mexico

Double Entry Journal, March 7, 05

"The Kiowa came one by one into the world through a hollow log."

N. Scott Momaday
"I"
The Way to Rainy Mountain
p. 16

They say a woman "swollen with her baby" got stuck in the log and no one else could get through, and that is why the Kiowa is such a small tribe. This story of creation interests me. I have never heard anything like it. I really like it because I can imagine it in my mind, and it really gives a good explanation instead of just saying people appeared one day. A lot of religions have a story like this—that pueblo people came from a hole in a kiva or that God made Adam from sand. They all have an explanation, but this one I really like. It makes me wonder what's on the other side of this log.

Gabby Seredowych, 7th grade
Monte del Sol Charter School, Santa Fe, New Mexico

Double Entry Journal, March 11, 2005

"They formed a great circle, enclosing a large area of the plain, and began to converge upon the center."

N. Scott Momaday
"II"
The Way to Rainy Mountain
pp. 18–19

I think that this is interesting because the circle is very important to the Kiowa. It represents equality and unison, and in this text it tells how they came together in a circle to hunt. This is important to me because the meat from the hunt will help everybody, and doing this will make up for the greediness of the ancient chief.

Double Entry Journal, March 11, 2005

"At first there is no discrimination in the eye, nothing but the land itself, whole and impenetrable. But then the smallest things began to stand out of the depths."

N. Scott Momaday
"I"
The Way to Rainy Mountain
pp. 18–19

I think that this is very important in life because when you first look at things you just see a whole of something. If looked at closer, you can see everything big is made up of something smaller.

Tova Lecuyer, 7th grade
Monte del Sol Charter School, Santa Fe, New Mexico

The following poem was written by Alicia when she was a seventh grader. She wrote it after a prompt that asked students to observe their families doing something specific to their cultures.

Chile

Four people are seated in front of a wooden square table,
my mom, my aunt, me, and my grandma,
In front of us are two big plastic bags of mild green *chile*,
3 tin platters, 2 yellow bowls, and that week's newspapers.

The only sound is the steady whirring of the ceiling fan.
My eyes are burning, and my face is itching.
I glance out of the corner of my eye, and I see my grandma.
She can't see what she is doing, but she has peeled *chile* so many times, she can do it by memory.

Her wrinkled hands are not very agile anymore, so she goes slowly.
"What are you doing?" I ask.

"Estoy pelando chile. Qué quieres?"
I get up to wash my hands to leave, but I see my grandma still peeling, so I sit back down. After-all, I need her help.
My grandma, she can't see.

Alicia Armijo, 7th grade
Monte del Sol Charter School, Santa Fe, New Mexico

[The following poem was written by Daisy after an "I am" prompt when she was in the seventh grade. She made it clear that she is *not* the Little Girl in the poem. "Little Girls" are seventh graders struggling with their middle school identities.]

Little Girls

The little girl can't breathe.
Tight clothes squeeze the air from her
Every time she bends.
Her boyfriend sucks it,
Straight from her lungs,
Each time their lips meet.
She used to breathe in wild flowers
In airy sun dresses.
But now it's stretch hip-huggers.
Tight T-shirts.
And she's suffocating alone,
At a dinner table full of parents, brothers, sisters.
Suffocating alone in a room
Full of people.
Suffocating alone at a desk in a classroom.
A classroom full of little girls.
12, 13, 14.
Little girls suffocating,
Suffocating, too.

Daisy Bond, 7th grade
Monte del Sol Charter School, Santa Fe, New Mexico

So what is good college-level writing today? I'd say *a good choice of words* at any level. Good writing is a student thinking on paper, using words unique to her or him—voice, a rhetorical stamp, citing the text, attributing quotes, answering the question thoughtfully, creating intelligent prose, poetry, or poetic prose. And when there is doubt about the assignment, I would say that college writing is being able to "manipulate the task," as one of my teachers, Nancy Martin, used to say (and by this, she meant "Be resourceful and make the assignment your own!").

When does good college writing begin? Yesterday. Students in elementary, middle, and high school have to write and write often in multigenres: stories, personal essays, critical essays, parodies, poems, freewrites, letters to teachers, journals, jingles, reader responses, lists—and teachers have to read most of it (some writing should be for just the fun of it—not for assessment). One genuine little check mark and a comment like "Yeah!" or "Great!" or a suggestion like "good, now flesh the details out," on a passage ringing true with a student's authentic voice, may be the moment at which the writer recognizes that he or she has something valuable to say, and when it complies with the "conventions of correctness," it is college-level writing.

Works Cited

Blumenthal, Joseph C. *English 2600*. New York: Harcourt, Brace, 1962.

Elbow, Peter. *Writing without Teachers*. London: Oxford UP, 1973.

Foster, Donald. "Email to Jameson." 17 Nov. 2003. 7 June 2006 <http://www.jameson245.com/foster_page.htm>.

Graves, Donald. *Writing: Teachers and Children at Work*. Exeter, NH: Heinemann Educational Books, 1983.

Liebling, A. J. "Boxing with the Naked Eye." *The Sweet Science*. New York: North Point, 2004. 17–29.

Macrorie, Ken. *The I-Search Paper*. Rev. Ed. Upper Montclair, NJ: Boynton/Cook, 1988.

———. *Writing to Be Read*. Upper Montclair, NJ: Boynton/Cook, 1984.

Martin, Nancy, ed. *Writing across the Curriculum Pamphlets: A Selection from the Schools Council and London University Institute of Education Joint Project: Writing across the Curriculum*. Upper Montclair, NJ: Boynton/Cook, 1984.

Mora, Pat. "A Letter to Gabriela, a Young Writer." *English Journal* 79.5 (1990): 40–42.

———. *My Own True Name: New and Selected Poems for Young Adults, 1984–1999*. Houston: Piñata Books, 2000.

Naranjo-Morse, Nora. "My Father's Hands." *Mud Woman: Poems from the Clay*. Tucson: U of Arizona P, 1992.

Selena. Dir. Gregory Nava. Warner Bros. 1997.

Stillman, Peter. *Writing Your Way*. Upper Montclair, NJ: Boynton/Cook, 1984.

Toy Story. Dir. John Lasseter. Walt Disney Pictures. 1995.

Warriner, John E. *English Composition and Grammar*. New York: Harcourt, 1988.

Whitman, Walt. "Song of Myself." *Leaves of Grass*. New York: Penguin, 2005.

Chapter Five

The Truth about High School English

Milka Mustenikova Mosley
Sequoyah High School
Canton, Georgia

When I was contacted about writing an essay concerning college-level writing, I was excited. I love to write, but rarely do I make time for professional reflection. I am usually too busy planning and reading my students' papers. Since I am familiar with both worlds, high school and college, I saw this essay as an opportunity to express my observations about student writing. I have been teaching high school English for fifteen years and college composition since 1998 (part time). I do believe I have an idea of what is going on in both worlds, and I would like to share my experiences regarding student writing at both the high school and college level.

In general, I would call high school writing *formulaic*. We have too many students and too little time for grading, so we often allow students to follow a formula to produce a product. This strategy helps both students and teachers: students learn how to get to the point quickly and organize their ideas logically, and teachers are able to grade a large number of papers more efficiently. Otherwise, if we just assign a topic without any type of guidance to our inexperienced writers, we will receive poorly written papers that will be time-consuming to grade. For example, whenever I assign an essay, my students and I write one together *orally* first. I explain the assignment and with their help write a working outline on the board. I then discuss with them the specifics necessary for the completion of this essay. This strategy helps me provide more writing opportunities to my beginning writers and helps them acquire and use their skills to write papers not only for my class but for their other classes also.

In contrast, I believe college-level writing should focus more on the student's ideas and exhibit his or her individuality. College-level writing differs from a piece of high school writing because of its greater level of sophistication, as well as a certain degree of eloquence and the use of rich vocabulary. I know this is not evident and rarely accomplished in lower-level college classes, but I believe that students in upper-level classes should be *expected* to write intelligent papers because of their exposure to diverse and rich academic materials, their age (especially the aspect of independence my high school students dream of), and their rich cultural environment. All of these will contribute to the originality and the uniqueness of a piece of college-level writing.

High school–level writing is usually very predictable. High school students typically write mainly to conform. They want to know exactly how many words they need to write, when the assignment is due, and whether or not they are allowed to say "I" in their piece. Occasionally, they will look up some synonyms and try to incorporate new vocabulary into their essays, but oftentimes these words do not work well within the context of their essays. This is due to their lack of reading and writing experience, to their youthfulness and age, and to already established routines. All they have done since kindergarten has been conforming to the requirements set before them by their educators. It sounds harsh, but, for their age, the application of certain rules and regulations protect and guide young students as they begin to develop into writers and thinkers.

However, in order to prepare students for careers in today's competitive world, college students are required to produce very specialized writing tasks in their classes such as "lab reports, case studies, research papers, proposals, literature reviews, memos, arguments, interpretations, historical narratives, impact statements, and essay questions based on different sources of information and specific professional models" (Gottschalk and Hjortshoj 4). Many college professors and especially English instructors seem frustrated by the poor quality of work students produce in their classes, and they often wonder whether high school English teachers are aware of their students' incompetence in writing and, if they are, what they are doing to prepare young adults for college.

My response to this concern is yes, high school English teachers are somewhat familiar with college-level writing expectations. After all, teachers are college graduates, and we have taken all kinds of courses in different subject areas during our college careers. However, once a teacher becomes a member of the real high school world of teaching, everything changes. All the theories and practical applications that college English instructors swear by often go out of the window because college theory and high school practice differ greatly. I am reminded of this discrepancy whenever I work with a student teacher. From my experience as a classroom supervisor, I find that most of the time student teachers are highly enthusiastic and, on the basis of what they studied in college, they are oftentimes convinced that what we do in high school is outdated and inefficient. However, once they start working within the prescribed curriculum that our school systems have established, they realize that there is more to teaching high school English than just fun drama improvisations and writing creative poetry.

Just like the students, high school English teachers have to conform to and cover the curriculum approved by our school boards because everything we do is closely monitored by standardized testing. If our school receives poor reports on standardized tests, we are labeled as a nonstandard school and put on probation, which would greatly complicate the running of our normal school activities because time would need to be allotted for many additional administrative procedures and meetings, along with lots of paperwork, to rectify the situation. We often have to suspend our curriculum instruction to prepare our students for all types of schoolwide standardized testing such as the End of Course Test, Georgia High School Graduation Test, Preliminary Scholastic Assessment Test (PSAT), Scholastic Assessment Test (SAT), and the Prewriting and Writing Assessment Tests. All of these disruptions take away from class time, which we could otherwise use for teaching writing. Besides testing, we also have to deal with daily interruptions such as assemblies and pep rallies and sometimes even discipline problems. Also, since every student has an English class, students are taken out of our English classes for any schoolwide activity such as picture day for the school yearbook.

Nevertheless, as a group we English teachers usually take everything in stride. We adjust our lesson plans and go about our work. Preparing our students for standardized tests does not mean that we strictly teach to the tests. On the contrary, we provide our students with various learning activities to prepare them for college. However, it is important for college educators to understand that our English classes are not composition classes, but are *surveys of literature classes*, mainly surveys of different genres of literature, but also surveys of World Literature, American Literature, and British Literature. We also cover study skills, grammar, and vocabulary. Through the study of literature, high school English classes provide students with a window to the world, so they can understand and appreciate the universal aspects of the human experience. The various readings acquaint students with different cultures from ancient civilizations through modern times and enrich student awareness of the world so they can build on the life experience, wisdom, and knowledge of others. This is especially important in today's multicultural, Internet-dependent, and CNN-connected world.

This does not mean that all we do in high school is read and discuss literary work. In my case, for example, we also follow the county's *Language Arts Curriculum Guide*, but we have some freedom in deciding how to teach the items listed in our program of study. Much depends on what is available at our particular school: textbooks, supplementary materials, videos, audiotapes, and computer labs. When it comes to writing, we do provide students with many writing assignments as well as various creative projects so they can learn to express their knowledge to their peers. For example, I am fortunate to teach Honors English 2. I have small classes, intelligent students, and parents with great expectations. I do my best to provide my students with practice for the PSAT and the Practice Writing Assessment test because these scores basically predict how well students will do on their SAT and Georgia High School Graduation Test. Plus, from the Practice Writing Assessment scores, the Advanced Placement (AP) World History teacher gets a sense of what our students need to work on in order to do well on the AP World History exam. Usually, the same students who take Honors English 2 also take AP World History.

Besides these classroom activities, I work closely to cover the material listed in our program of study. For example, last semester I covered two chapters of grammar, provided my students with a few vocabulary practices, and exposed them to eight classic pieces of literature: *Wuthering Heights*, *Jane Eyre*, *Julius Caesar*, *Oedipus Rex*, and excerpts from *Gilgamesh*, *The Once and Future King*, Hamilton's *Mythology*, and the *Iliad*. The county *Language Arts Curriculum Guide* listed more titles than these, but this was what I was able to cover with my students. Along with the readings, the students completed many different types of projects such as PowerPoint presentations, video enactments, live newscasts, and writing activities such as narratives, creative writings, journals, essay/essay questions, and research/summaries. They also took several quizzes and tests and completed two impromptu argumentative essays. Teachers of different subject matter in the AP department work closely because we teach the same students, and these reading, writing, speaking, and listening activities will prepare our students for their AP language and AP literature classes taught in their junior and senior years. They also provide writing skills for other subject matter AP exams such as biology and history. Our honors and AP students usually perform very well on the AP exams, and many of them earn college credits, which allows them to skip basic-level college English classes: this means that lower-level college instructors do not have the chance to work with good students who are good writers.

Most of the students who take freshmen college composition classes are our college preparatory students whose program of study differs greatly from our honors and AP curriculum. The reason for this is because the college preparatory classes are large (usually over thirty students per classroom) and the learning ability level varies to accommodate all learners. Since the college preparation-level curriculum is not as dynamic, students are not exposed to as wide a variety of readings, writings, and creative project assignments. When it comes to the students in the college preparation program, I have noticed a trend: a lack of confidence in their writing abilities. Many are the times when the college preparatory students in my Advanced Composition class (an academic elective) come to me and say, “I am good at storytelling, but I am not good in grammar.” I hear similar statements in my English 1101 class at the university. This is because most of the students’ formal papers, which carry the most weight toward their final grade, are evaluated with the *infamous* grading scale (points are taken off for every little mistake), and the low grades cause them to doubt their writing abilities. I believe giving students failing grades on formal papers without a chance for revision is an ineffective practice. Just like anyone else, failure negatively influences the fragile psyche of the high school student and the first-year college student. I often wonder if the grading scale is a real gauge of students’ competence in writing! Maybe we need to rethink and modify the point system to match the quality of writing and the sophistication of ideas.

When it comes to the college preparatory writing assignments, it is important to take into account the large class size. Oftentimes, teachers avoid assigning much writing because they have very little time to grade it. Depending on the number of students, the load can often reach around 150 papers per writing assignment. We all know that the class size will not decrease, but the writing has to increase because of the new SAT writing requirements. Maybe Laura Vanderkam’s solution deserves some attention: “Pay to make grading fly. Students learn grammar, mechanics, and grace when teachers demand—and correct—three or more drafts of each paper. NCLB [No Child Left Behind] can cool teachers’ ‘grading hell’ by giving grants to outsource grading—not to India, but to freelance writers or grad students looking for cash” (2). I do not think this will ever happen, but for some reason college preparatory teachers do not realize the fact that everything does not have to be graded with the grading scale. Some of the pieces can be shared orally (for some reason, teachers forget the *speaking* aspect of teaching English) or graded for completion or graded for certain skills because it is better for students to have many writing opportunities that will help them find their voice and gain confidence in their writing abilities. Plus, the extra grades will help students’ overall grades. Nevertheless, without a chance for revision and improvement of formal papers, extra writing opportunities will not help our young writers. For example, Amy Horacek, a student of mine, stated:

> "I remember a D on a junior research paper. . . . I went to college. . . . I ran into the same high school approach. Write the paper. Hand in the paper. Receive the grade and the feedback with no instruction in writing. I withdrew with the first attempt because I made a D on the paper. I see the teaching approach changing. For the class I took three years ago . . . The professor gave feedback on each section and conferenced with each student. In the current class, I see the same workshop approach with more conferencing than I've ever witnessed in any English class."

My student feedback confirms my belief that writing and revising is what will help students become competent writers. After all, using the grading scale on all student writing and doing all that math is time consuming, especially for us, English teachers, who are *allergic* to math.

From my personal experience, I have realized that when I provide my students with extra help before I collect the final drafts, I have more enjoyable papers to read. I usually hand out an essay checklist so they can personally eliminate from their papers all that I mark with the dreaded *red or green* pen. I provide them with peer editing sessions, consultations, and, of course, opportunities for revision. I believe that only through revision can students learn from their mistakes and avoid repeating them again. We just have to make sure that we talk about writing to students with *fervor* and model and share our own pieces so they can become excited and connect with us as fellow writers. I also believe that we must, if necessary, extend the due date or take a late paper because *a missed writing assignment is a wasted opportunity*. Once students see the teacher as a fellow learner, they care more about their work and try harder.

On the other hand, it is important to notice that most high school English departments have their own departmental procedures, which protect and justify their actions when it comes to explaining graded papers to students' parents, and often are not up to date with the latest in teaching writing because many of them lack the exposure to English graduate classes and university-held workshops. I personally believe that each teacher should attend some of the workshops held by the National Writing Project because this is the place where regular teachers, assisted by university experts, teach regular teachers. I believe my involvement with the Kennesaw Mountain Writing Project for three separate institutions has not only given me confidence in what I am doing professionally but has enriched my teaching repertoire by allowing me to share lesson plans and experiences with my colleagues. It also provided me with writing opportunities that helped me gain confidence in my own writing. This is the reason why I believe that teachers need to incorporate some of their graduate-level English work or experiences into their classes. It is true, many of my colleagues do have graduate degrees, but many are not in English. Their graduate degrees are in health, administration, or counseling. Teachers often try to complete graduate programs that are convenient and inexpensive (and fit into their busy schedules) in order to receive a pay raise. For example, I was fortunate to receive my masters in rhetoric and composition and was able to experience and then apply *the true essence of reading, writing, speaking, and listening in the classroom*. The most convenient and affordable option for my specialist degree, however, was the administrative program. For this reason, we need workshops conducted by college English instructors in order to learn what we are required to do to prepare our students for college. Most high school teachers think that a grammatically correct piece is what is needed for college. I believe they have to be reminded to consider the sophistication of ideas as well.

Fortunately, besides teaching high school English, I am a part-time college instructor at the local university, and I have been able to make a few observations about the attitudes of both groups towards writing and schoolwork in general. I have noticed that the first couple of papers by freshmen college students lack originality and are poorly written. However, first-year college writers show great interest in writing and excel at a much faster pace than high school writers do. All of a sudden upon entering college, students become serious and responsible and try hard to keep the scholarships they have obtained, justify the school expenses to their parents with good grades, or hold two jobs to pay for their college classes personally. I often hear statements such as "I have to keep HOPE" (a scholarship provided by the Georgia lottery) or "My parents are paying for my education" or "I am working two jobs to pay for my college tuition." I believe that maturity is an important aspect when it comes to students and their attitude towards schoolwork. This is an issue that is not present at the high school level, and that is why high school students need more writing opportunities to improve their writing skills.

One of the most exciting aspects of teaching a first-year college composition class in comparison with high school English is the diversity that I encounter in the college classroom. It is enjoyable to hear not only different gender perspectives on an issue, but also different age and even cultural perspectives. When it comes to writing, even though I provide instruction and all types of handouts to help students eliminate their grammatical errors, my first-year college students do poorly on the first couple of formal papers. The reason for this is, of course, not having enough writing practice at the high school level and not being familiar with the grammatical jargon. I see this during individual consultations and during peer editing workshops, which my students and I find very productive. For example, in her reflection about one of the college writing classes I taught, Francis Garcia said, "I like the fact that you explain everything in detail, how to write an essay and what to do in order to achieve the best score . . . I also like the fact when you return our essays you talk to us individually telling us what we need to do next and give us an opportunity to make a better grade on it by rewriting it." I have noticed that after the second paper and two consultations, students' papers dramatically improve because they are mature enough and care about learning. I am always pleased when they make comments in their reflections such as, "The interest that I have developed in writing is almost a surprise . . . This class has encouraged me to pursue many dreams that once I thought would be impossible" (Olson). It is wonderful teaching and discussing writing with a *willing* audience! When it comes to high school, this process is much slower. I guess that is why we have year-long courses.

One concern that I have about the college first-year English classroom is the English as a Second Language (ESL) writers. Their learning process takes much longer. Besides the problems they encounter with language and grammar, oftentimes they are not familiar with the requirements of formal essay writing and, most of all, they have hardly any knowledge of the worst offense in writing: plagiarism. It was just last semester when, during our consultation on her argumentative essay, one of my ESL students told me that she does have a thesis statement and that it is in the conclusion because it makes a better emphasis there! Another serious problem is the poor use of the Modern Language Association style of documentation and wide application of patchwriting. ESL students often simply cut and paste words and phrases from the text and occasionally change tense or include a synonym. This is a cultural issue, and educators have to be patient and understanding. That is why I often allow my ESL students to revise their papers two or three times, and still I do not think they are ready for the next class. Even though I am a nonnative English speaker (I was born and raised in Macedonia) and am aware of their personal situation, still I cannot help them in one semester. I do believe they should take more remedial courses before they sign up for a regular first-year class.

In order to understand our separate worlds, high school and college, I propose that we establish a line of communication between high school English teachers and first-year college composition instructors. College instructors have to become aware of our reality and take into consideration all the responsibilities we high school teachers have in our daily English classes and provide us with advice and practical workshops so we can help our students become better prepared for college-level classes. Some may say the professional magazines offer everything teachers need. However, even though we receive the *English Journal* and other journals, unless we are working on a graduate class, we rarely have the time to read about the latest in theory and practice when it comes to teaching writing. However, if we had practical workshops where both sides could share student writing samples and teaching experiences during our staff development days, we would gain much more than listening to a motivational speaker or a sales person discussing teaching strategies, just to sell his or her textbook. I believe we need *teamwork* where we can visit each other's territory and immerse ourselves into specific teaching/learning situations in order to help both high school and college-level writers.

Works Cited

Garcia, Francis. Reflection on English 1101/36. 12 December 2004.

Gottschalk, Katherine, and Keith Hjortshoj. *The Elements of Teaching Writing: A Resource for Instructors in All Disciplines*. Boston: Bedford/St. Martin's, 2004.

Horacek, Amy. Reflection on English 1101/36. 11 December 2004.

Olson, Michael. Reflection on English 1101/36. 10 December 2004.

Vanderkam, Laura. "Writing a Wrong." *USA Today*. 1 Dec. 2004. 12 Dec. 2004 <http://www.keepmedia.com/pubs/USATODAY/2004/12/01/664742>.

II

College Perspectives

Chapter Six

Good Enough Writing: What Is Good Enough Writing, Anyway?

Lynn Z. Bloom
University of Connecticut

Good enough student writing isn't bad, it isn't great. And although it ultimately isn't good enough, it's what many of us will settle for much of the time. Although many American colleges and universities claim to strive for excellence, they will be reasonably contented with Bs. For most have adopted a de facto standard for college-level writing: whatever is good enough to warrant (note that I do not say merit) a B in whatever course it is written for at that particular school is good enough writing. Yes, this definition is pragmatic, rather than utopian. Its contours are determined locally, rather than nationally, by individual teachers in individual classes—though more exacting teachers or "hard graders" may continue to measure against the ideal.[1]

Yet we can discuss the concept of good enough writing in general because B is the standard grade in American undergraduate education in general, and in composition courses as well.[2] It is widely based on the following characteristics. B-level writing is college-level writing that exemplifies the following characteristics judged according to local standards. B-level writing is good enough to satisfy first-year writing standards and to meet norms of acceptable writing in more advanced classes. It is thus good enough to serve as the lingua franca for writing throughout the writer's home institution, and presumably, to meet the standard for writing beyond that college—the larger community, and the student's future professional world. If this writing is also good enough to satisfy the student writer's own expectations, so much the better, but that's an unexpected bonus, not a given. Although the following definition is embedded in a discussion of first-year composition, the features of good enough writing are equally discernable in academic writing required in any other college course up, down, or across the curriculum except for creative writing, which is beyond the scope of this discussion.

As I will explain in this essay, good enough writing is characterized by a clutch of Academic Virtues. These include: *Rationality*; *Conformity*, *Conventionality*—which is attained by using Standard English, following the rules, and otherwise maintaining proper academic decorum; *Self-Reliance, Responsibility, Honesty*; *Order*; *Modesty* in form and style; *Efficiency*, and *Economy*. When accompanied by *Punctuality*, turning the papers in on time, according to the demands of the academic schedule, a great deal of student writing that meets these criteria—perhaps most of it—should be good enough to receive a good enough grade, a B, in most institutions.[3] (Nevertheless, any teacher—and we have all met them—can override the norm using individual or idiosyncratic criteria, such as "Any paper with more than three spelling errors gets an F.")

Many teachers would also insist on evidence of "the ability to discuss and evaluate abstract ideas" as crucial to college-level writing (Sullivan 384). Critical thinking is more variable than the tidier Academic Virtues, more dependent on the individual teacher's expectations and frames of reference, and often difficult to measure. It will be addressed in the last two sections of this essay. Otherwise, my analysis assumes that although we say we value and expect critical thinking, when awarding the final grade we cave on this quality. If throughout the semester we have received a preponderance of technically and politically correct papers that reflect all the other Virtues, we will deem that writing good enough for a B.

Although composition studies handbooks and rhetorics hold out the Platonic ideals of excellence, particularly when their illustrations are from professional writers, classroom teachers perforce read these through the realistic lenses of "good enough." The label, "good enough writing," is an analogue of British psychoanalyst D. W. Winnicott's concept of the "good enough mother," neither negligent nor a smother-mother, but good enough to provide adequate physical and psychological nurture that will ensure the development of a distinctive individual, a healthy child (17–19). Most of us tend to teach to the class average (or slightly above, but still within B range), yet oddly enough, given the tacit acceptance throughout the country of this pervasive concept, it has never been given a label that stuck.[4] Like Molière's Bourgeois Gentleman, who was delighted to finally have a label to acknowledge that he had been speaking prose all his life, the label "good enough writing" tells us what we've been teaching our students to do all along. Now we know what to call the resulting work; if good enough writing is not the best outcome, it is certainly the normative practice that we tolerate.

The Characteristics of Good Enough Writing

Rationality

The academy purports to be nothing if not rational—a virtue as old as Aristotle. The academic writer, from student on up to faculty researcher, is constrained to write rationally, to produce nonfiction prose usually construed as expository or argumentative writing, critical or otherwise. This must be organized according to a logical plan or purpose and proceed by a series of logical steps from its initial premise to a logical conclusion. In pursuing this goal—the logical consequence of the five-paragraph theme construed as a heuristic rather than a template—the writer is expected and advised in all the Handbooks[5] to be reasonable, balanced, fair-minded, and "respectful of the feelings of [the] audience," to "avoid rhetorical fallacies" and "learn from others' arguments." Thus the writer should be able to "distinguish fact from opinion," "take a position" and "make claims" derived from "supporting evidence" based on "verifiable and reliable facts." He or she should "respond to diverse views," considering "at least two sides of the issue under discussion" (Glenn, Miller, and Webb 502–27).

Although ethical and emotional appeals receive a nod (a paragraph apiece in this 876-page book), the emphasis throughout the *Handbook*, as in the course it sustains, is on the rational.

Emotion and *passion*—which might signal the operation of a host of nonrational elements—are not indexed; *play* refers only to the literary genre. The dead seriousness that dominates academic discourse, allegedly the epitome of rationality, must prevail. William H. Gass contends that the article (or essay) as a genre—and by extrapolation, most academic writing—is far less rational than it purports to be, that it is in fact a "veritable Michelin of misdirection; for the article pretends that everything is clear, that its argument is unassailable, that there are no soggy patches, no illicit inferences, no illegitimate connections; it furnishes seals of approval and underwriters' guarantees" (25). In point of fact, as all researchers and writing teachers know, every piece of academic writing has a point of view and presents an argument, explicit or implicit, and evidence to reinforce the author's bias. Just because a piece of writing sounds objective (including, say, the essay you are reading right now) doesn't mean that it is; though one can—and should, in a rational universe—be fair, one can never be objective.

Conformity, Conventionality

Conformity, conventionality, and their consequent predictability are the necessary hallmarks of respectable academic writing. Academic readers expect academic writing to exhibit decorum and propriety appropriate in style and thought to the academic universe in general and to their discipline in particular. Teachers expect students to use Standard English, and follow the rules (see, for instance, Sullivan 385); and maintain decorum of thought as well as expression. Thus, as will be clear from the following discussion, the authors of good enough papers must color—and think—within the party lines, however loosely or tightly they are drawn at any given institution. However clearly or vaguely these are spelled out at any given school, most students are acculturated to understand them. When they don't—if, for instance, they are from another culture or their first language is not English and even if they know the words they don't understand the music—their failure to conform may land them in big trouble, as the following discussion reveals.

Adherence to Standard English and Rules

No matter how informal or slangy one's speech may be outside of class, teachers and textbooks and college standards concur on the importance of Standard English as the lingua franca for writing in the academy (again, creative writing excepted), reinforced by conventional grammar, mechanics, and spelling. Failure to follow the rules will result in papers that are not good enough, no matter what other virtues they exhibit. Although the National Council of Teachers of English (NCTE) manifesto on "Students' Right to Their Own Language"—a defense of nonstandard English, among other things—was promulgated in 1974 and is still on the books, teachers detest error and devote much effort to stamping it out, as Connors and Lunsford's research in "Frequency of Formal Errors" reveals. Likewise, Mina Shaughnessy's sensitive analysis of the "stunningly unskilled," error-laden writing of thousands of open admissions students in *Errors and Expectations* leads ultimately to the expectation that sensitive, insightful teachers will assume that their students are "capable of learning" what they themselves have learned, and what they now teach—Standard English (292). Three semesters of basic writing will, if done right, give students Standard English facility with syntax, punctuation, grammar, spelling, vocabulary, "order and development," and "academic forms" (285–86). Though Mike Rose's equally sympathetic work, *Lives on the Boundary*, identifies many pitfalls that must be overcome on the road to successful academic writing, he shares Shaughnessy's vision of the ultimate goal. And, as David Bartholomae argues in "Inventing the University," when entering students have learned to talk the talk, they can walk the walk.

So taken for granted is this normative view of language that it is manifested from kindergarten through college in workbooks, grammar and usage tests, and spelling lists. Standard usage and grammar are addressed today in college and admissions (and exit) testing and placement. But these are the end of the line that now—as a consequence of the highly problematic, very politicized No Child Left Behind legislation—begins with mandatory testing in the primary grades and continues as long as the child remains in school. Despite objections from individual teachers and professional educational organizations, the law of the land reinforces adherence to the rules.

Decorum

Student writing must stay within the decorous boundaries of expression, and—for many teachers—suitable (however they define it) parameters of thought and ideas, even at the risk of hypocrisy. Sarah Freedman's classic research reveals that students whose writing is seen as insubordinate—too friendly, familiar, casual, presumptive of equal status with the teacher—may be penalized with lower grades (340–42). Making academic and professional norms explicit, *Harbrace* emphasizes that "respectful writers do not use homophobic" or racist or sexist language, and are "sensitive to ability, age, class, religion, and occupation" (287–89). Although the advice is couched in terms of language—"avoid the stereotyping that careless use of language can create" (289)—its implications are clear: if the writer's true sentiments are subversive or transgressive, they should be suppressed in the writing.

Students socialized in American high schools arrive in college with an understanding of the deep as well as surface meaning of many types of writing assignments. Most of them steer clear of the cultural undertow in which they might drown, even when to do so means evading the underlying moral issues—a potential breach of ethics far more serious than surface impropriety. The heated discussion of "Queers, Bums, and Magic," a gay-bashing paper in which the Kuwait-born student author also confesses to urinating on and beating up a homeless person in "San Fagcisco," makes it clear that students who violate the prevailing moral imperatives, whether by intention or in innocence, run the risk of incurring the teacher's wrath or even legal sanctions that could get them thrown out of school, into jail, or both (Miller; see my discussion in "The Good, the Bad, and the Ugly").

Self-Reliance, Responsibility, Honesty

Composition teachers, ever Emersonian in spirit, stress the importance of self-reliance, despite the constraints on independent thought and language imposed in the interests of decorum. "Your work must be your *own* work," we say, even in collaborative classrooms. "*Yours* is the most important voice in a paper that has your name on it," echoes the *Harbrace* (264). Yet, paradoxically, teachers distrust the personal voice (except in narratives), which signals ownership of the subject. And teachers emphatically discount the unsubstantiated opinion. Indeed, the most elaborate discussion of a single topic in the *Harbrace*, 16.6 percent of the total, is devoted to finding, using, and citing sources responsibly (548–693); the most responsible writing, students might well infer, is that which is most heavily and accurately cited. The emphasis on citations is also intended to nip irresponsibility in the bud. From sea to shining sea, as proscribed by decrees and honor codes throughout American colleges and universities, plagiarism and piracy, now complicated and confounded by the easy accessibility of materials on the Web, are the writer's cardinal sins. The *Harbrace* epitomizes and updates conventional wisdom, beginning with a harsh opening sally: "Taking someone's words or ideas and presenting them as your own leaves you open to criminal charges" (597). This is followed by, "In the film, video, music, and software businesses, this sort of theft is called *piracy*. In publishing and education, it is called *plagiarism* or *cheating*. Whatever it is called, it is illegal" (597). The ensuing discussion again typifies the paradox of requiring students to be self-reliant in finding and using sources while simultaneously distrusting them to do this accurately or, more particularly, honestly: "Although it is fairly easy to copy material from a Web site or even purchase a paper on the Web, it is just as easy for a teacher or employer to locate that same material on the Web and determine that it has been plagiarized" (598–99). Gotcha!

Order

Most arenas of the academy, except those encouraging artistic creativity, depend on order—in calendars and schedules, procedures, and written documents. The academic world runs better when the participants can know, respect, and follow a predictable, conspicuous pattern. Thus good enough writing is reasonably well organized. Writing that looks disorganized is as disreputable as disorderly conduct, for disorder implies mental laxity, if not downright confusion, and shows disrespect for one's readers. We even like to see the organizational scaffolding; witness the popularity of PowerPoint presentations that threaten to become caricatures of order, arrangement made explicit in a series of short sentences or sentence fragments. Five paragraph themes likewise serve as their own caricature.

Nevertheless, the late Richard Marius's views on order in *A Writer's Companion* represent the academic norm. He asserts that "A Good Essay Gets to the Point Quickly" and "Stays with Its Subject" (47–53). It is well integrated and does not drift without clear purpose from item to item. Thus, says Marius, "A good essay will march step by step to its destination. Each step will be clearly marked; it will depend on what has gone before, and it will lead gracefully to what comes afterward" (53). Marius's advice, the antithesis of postmodernism, is proffered more categorically than, for instance, that of Strunk and White, who say, "Choose a suitable design and hold to it" (#12) (15). Their realistic analysis accommodates both the necessity of good design and the vagaries of the procedures by which it may be attained: "A basic structural design underlies every kind of writing. Writers will in part follow this design, in part deviate from it, according to their skills, their needs, and *the unexpected events that accompany the act of composition*" [italics mine]. Writing, they say, "to be effective, must follow closely the thoughts of the writer, but not necessarily the order in which those thoughts occur. This calls for a scheme of procedure." However, they add, "In some cases, the best design is no design, as with a love letter, which is simply an outpouring" (15). Nevertheless, academic necessity puts most teachers in Marius's camp; students write no love letters on our watch.

Modesty in Form and Style

Good enough writers are advised to keep out of sight, even while taking responsibility for their own ideas. For good enough writing is moderate and temperate, its qualities of style, form, and tone quiet, steady, and inconspicuous. This is a pragmatic response to the ethos of the academy, for academics expect papers to be written in the form, language, and style appropriate to their respective discipline. When they are reading for substance, they cannot afford to be distracted by departures from conventions of form, or language that calls attention to itself, what my agriculture colleagues object to as "flowery writing."

To violate the normative literary conventions of the discipline in which one is writing is to mark the writer as either highly naive or very unprofessional. Or so the academy believes.[6] Thus *Harbrace* identifies the particular conventions and illustrates them with sample papers: "Writing about literature follows certain special conventions" ("Use the full name of the author of a work in your first reference and only the last name in all subsequent references"); "Reports in the social sciences follow prescribed formats to present evidence"—along the lines of introduction, definitions, methods and materials, results, discussion and critique; and "Writing in the natural sciences is impartial and follows a prescribed format" to ensure that the experiments can be replicated (694–703).

The sense of style conveyed in Polonius's advice to Laertes ("rich, not gaudy"; "familiar, but by no means vulgar") is reiterated today in the rules of Strunk and White, who together constitute the American Polonius: "*Place yourself in the background*" (#1) (70); "*Do not inject opinion*" (#17) (79–80). It would be as hard for anyone educated in American schools in the past thirty-five years to escape the influence of advice embodied in *The Elements of Style* (itself a direct descendant of conventional eighteenth-century advice) or its analogues as it would for any post–World War II American baby to escape the influence of Benjamin Spock's *Baby and Child Care.* "The approach to style," say these books, "is by way of plainness, simplicity, orderliness, sincerity" (Strunk and White 69). This precept governs much of the normative stylistic advice to students: "*Be clear*" (#16); "*Prefer the standard to the offbeat*" (#21); "*Avoid fancy words*" (#14); "*Use figures of speech sparingly*" (#18). And be patriotic: "*Avoid foreign languages*" (#20) (70–81).

The author's individual, human voice is generally not welcome, particularly in papers written by teams of authors, as in the hard sciences, where convention dictates anonymity. Yet when the first person is permitted, Gass observes that such writing must appear voiceless, faceless, "complete and straightforward and footnoted and useful and certain" even when it is not, its polish "like that of the scrubbed step" (25). This suppression of the self, that might otherwise be manifested in the individual writer's voice and distinctive features of syntax and vocabulary, has the effect of making a given piece of academic writing sound like every other piece in the same field. For a single writer's voice to speak out would be to speak out of turn, and thus be regarded as immodest—calling attention to the speaker rather than where it properly belongs, on the subject.[7] The emergence of the authorial self, a necessary attribute of personal writing, may be one reason curmudgeonly diehard academic critics dislike and distrust this genre.

Efficiency, Economy

Good enough academic writers squander neither time nor words. Concepts such as George Orwell's "Never use a long word where a short one will do" and "If it is possible to cut a word out, always cut it out" (176) and Strunk and White's "Omit needless words"—"a sentence should contain no unnecessary words, a paragraph no unnecessary sentences" (23)—govern American textbooks and much of our red-penciling. In *A Writer's Companion*, Richard Marius reiterates, "Write Efficiently. Here is one of the fundamentals of modern English style: Use as few words as possible to say what you want to say" (10). Efficient prose, direct, honest, and to the point, enables readers to be efficient, as well, "without having to back up time and again to read it again to see what it means" (11). Although this advice could be interpreted as designed to produce a svelte body of Word Watchers in, say, advertising or the sciences, it seems just as likely to meet good enough writers where they live—writing to fulfill the letter of the required assignment (forget about its spirit) and get on with the more engaging aspects of their lives beyond the paper at hand.

By this criterion, the writer's ideal composing process would be equally efficient. I question how often the ideal is actually met, for it is antithetical to the unruly, wasteful, disorderly means by which creation usually occurs, even in good enough writing. Thus, although Lunsford and Connors in the second edition of *The St. Martin's Handbook*, for example, accurately explain that the writing process is "repetitive, erratic," recursive, "and often messy," rather than proceeding "in nice, neat steps," they hold out the hope that "writing can be a little like riding a bicycle: with practice the process becomes more and more automatic" (3–4). To the extent that process follows format, this may be true. It may be possible to write on automatic pilot if writers are working with predetermined forms of academic and professional writing, such as research reports, business memos, literature reviews, lab reports, and writing against deadlines where time is truly money. Nevertheless, by the fifth edition, Lunsford has abandoned this concept: "It is inaccurate to envision a single writing process. There are, in fact, as many different writing processes as there are writers—more if you consider that individual writers vary their writing processes each time they sit down to write!" (32).

Whereas economy and efficiency are subordinated, if not suppressed, in Lunsford's commentary, these concepts drive *Harbrace*'s discussion of writing against real-world deadlines. In what is likely a reflection of the writing process of many good enough students, *Harbrace* considers the fact that "[i]t may sometimes be necessary to abbreviate the writing process," and therefore to cut corners by narrowing "the topic to a manageable scope" and drawing on one's store of academic or experiential knowledge—"but stay away, if possible, from a topic that requires much research" (482). Check the topic and approach with your instructor; do the best you can in the time allotted, emphasizing the main points and a strong conclusion; proofread. And "[s]ubmit your work on time" (483).

Punctuality

The academic and business worlds must run like clockwork in order to function well. Only selected creative writers and major thinkers—Proust and James Joyce come to mind—are expected to meet Matthew Arnold's criterion of "the best that has been known and thought in the world," and allowed by the workaday world (to which they are sublimely indifferent) to take their sweet time about attaining this standard of excellence. But for the good enough student writer this is irrelevant; a balance must be struck between procrastination and production. If the writing produced against deadlines is simply good enough to do the job but no better, that's all right for most people, most institutions, most of the time. When the Muse must report for duty on time, at least the work gets written.

The Upshot

If student papers meet all these criteria, are they guaranteed a B? Probably yes, for teachers oriented to the universe of good enough papers. But, as I indicated at the outset, not necessarily. Teachers for whom some criteria or types of error weigh more heavily than others, or who employ other local or institutional norms, may mark down or fail students who don't measure up. (As in the use of sentence fragments. Which I've now done twice in the same paragraph. So flunk me!) Teachers who value critical thinking, originality, discovery, experimentation, and other attributes of creativity—striking metaphors, dazzling language, a powerful individual voice—may also downgrade papers that are unoriginal, vacuous, faceless, voiceless, or otherwise bland. Let us examine why, for these teachers, good enough writing is simply not good enough.

The Consequences of Being Good Enough: What's Missing and What's Possible

We get what we ask for, a plethora of procedural virtues. Thus we get student writing that is rational, well-organized, decorous, modest, and efficient; that plays by the rules of Standard English and academic discourse; that follows the disciplinary conventions of form and style, and is turned in on time. Handbooks, rhetorics, dictionaries, usage directives, study guides and checklists, tests reaffirm these academic values and virtues. Student writing that meets the letter of these expectations should, in many venues, be good enough to earn the B that all involved in the transaction—students, teachers, their institutions—will settle for. By and large, these are the qualities we can teach and reinforce. If, as a consequence, student papers—at least, on the introductory level—also seem predictable, pedestrian, perhaps boring, well, maybe we're implicitly asking for this as well.

Beginning students can learn the conventions before they gain the knowledge and authority that will enable them to make genuine intellectual contributions to the ongoing dialogue in their field. Whether this writing could ever become better than good enough —supply the adjective—amazing, engaging, groundbreaking, earthshaking, or exciting in a myriad of other wonderful ways may be beyond our capacity to teach. But maybe not. Students may just have to cross the great divide between As and Bs on their own—but we would be remiss as teachers if we didn't try to help them on the ascent.

Beyond this great divide are, of course, the characteristics missing from the list of those that constitute good enough writing. These include: evidence of the writer's critical thinking; grappling with multiple, perhaps contradictory, sources and ideas; questioning both authority and one's own convictions; experimentation with genre, language, and other attributes of form, style, persona, and voice. Any and all of these have the potential to transform a good enough paper into a great one. In the process, student writers must transform, transcend, violate, or ignore a number of the attributes of good enough writing. In this section I address some of the possibilities for writing that could change the meaning of "good enough" from the merely acceptable to the genuinely good.

Because these attributes of genuinely good writing are much more variable, they are more difficult to categorize and to define, although we—and our students—know them when we see them. Whether these can be taught to first-year student writers is debatable, but students can certainly be exposed to the concepts. Success depends in part on how automatically the students can deal with the essentials of good enough writing so they can concentrate on the more challenging and creative aspects of the assignment at hand. Success depends also on the teacher's own appreciation of, understanding of, and ability to write with creative, confrontational, or otherwise original thinking and expression, for it's hard if not impossible to teach what one cannot do. All my life I have advocated writing in the genres we teach, for ourselves and our students (see "Why Don't We Write What We Teach?"). After writing a dissertation that was a critical analysis of the methodology of literary biography ("How Literary Biographers Use Their Subjects' Works"), I wrote the biography of America's best-known living author, Benjamin Spock, to learn firsthand what I could about writing biography (see "Growing Up"). It turns out that I learned a lot. Long experience as a teacher and author of textbooks convinces me that students write best about literature when they write as insiders, creators of texts in the genre, mode, and even the sensibility of the work they are studying.

Indeed, today many Readers, which are textbook collections of articles and essays, complement the readings with demanding assignments intended to "draw on students' creative imaginations and analytical skills to turn them from passive consumers into active producers of critical and creative texts" (Scholes, Comley, and Ulmer v)—an application of Scholes's theory articulated in *Textual Power*. Among the more thoroughgoing are Scholes, Comley, and Ulmer's *Text Book: Writing through Literature*, now in its third edition (2002), Bartholomae and Petrosky's *Ways of Reading*, the seventh edition also published in 2004, and my own books, including current editions of *The Essay Connection*, *The Arlington Reader*, and *Inquiry*, although it would be possible for imaginative teachers to create such transformative writing assignments from nearly any contemporary textbook.

Whereas outsiders read and write as aliens trying to second-guess the teacher's understanding of unapproachable iconic texts, insiders are reading and writing "through literature," as Scholes et al. explain, to produce original texts of their own. Space does not permit here a comprehensive analysis of the scope, variety, depth, and level of difficulty of assignments intended to transform student writers from outsiders to insiders. There is room, however, to briefly illustrate this pedagogical philosophy with some of my own assignments from "Coming of Age in American Autobiography," a course I have taught recently to honors first-year students and (in a separate course) to upperclass undergraduates. The central readings in each course are six canonical American autobiographies: Benjamin Franklin's *Autobiography*, Frederick Douglass's *Narrative*, Thoreau's *Walden*, Annie Dillard's *American Childhood*, Richard Wright's *Black Boy*, and Maxine Hong Kingston's *Woman Warrior*. To enable the students "to identify some of the issues and problems of the autobiographers's art—as readers, critics, and writers" (one of the course aims), I ask them in discussion and in writing to "examine the ways autobiographers see themselves (and others) and shape their vision and self-presentation—as children in an idyllic or problematic era; as members of a particular gender, social class or ethnic, regional, or racial group; as people fulfilling particular destinies or roles; as individuals in family, occupational, or other group contexts." They do this, however, not as ventriloquists of high culture criticism, which would put them in the conventional roles of outsiders trying to unlock iconic texts and characters, but insiders trying to recreate these figures through interpreting the subjects' self-interpretations, central ideas, milieus; psychological, intellectual, and social growth and development.

Thus one assignment requires students to work in pairs to "[w]rite a dialogue between Franklin and Douglass in which they discuss, debate, and ultimately define the meaning(s) of one of the following concepts as it pertains to either coming of age as an individual or as a nation (or both): independence, self-reliance, defiance of authority, citizenship, maturity, contributions to/engagement in the larger society." Another assignment asks pairs of students to "[d]esign a 21st century house for Thoreau, in an appropriate setting. One of you (as Annie Dillard) is the decorator. The other is the environmental engineer and landscaper. Remembering Frank Lloyd Wright's dictum, 'form follows function,' this dwelling and its environment should reflect, be symbolic of the predominant values of the people involved. You may include a drawing, floor plan, sketches, photos, whatever, ad lib." Of course, to fully experience autobiography as a genre, it is essential for the students to write one on the theme of the course: "Tell a true story with yourself as the central character—of some experience; event; relationship with a person or group; recognition of a belief or value system; or other phenomenon that was pivotal in your coming of age and/or understanding of the world."

Other briefer writings involve keeping a Thoreauvian journal, telling a joke Dillard's family would appreciate, making a list in the style of Richard Wright, and constructing a Kingstonesque cautionary tale.

The students lit up when they read these papers—every single one—aloud to their primary audience, the class; their discussions were energetic, enthusiastic, and engaged. So it was not surprising that when I asked the students to evaluate each assignment individually, they loved "trying new modes of writing and getting into the heads of the authors we were reading." With the exception of one paper, we all loved the results: varied, imaginative, on target, and—a bonus for me—virtually unplagiarizable because they are so specifically geared to the texts and context of the course. (Surprisingly, none of the twenty-four chapters in Buranen and Roy's otherwise comprehensive *Perspectives on Plagiarism* addresses writing assignments.) As one student commented, "I was pleasantly surprised with the assignments. I liked them a great deal more than the simple, mechanical, and stereotypical critical papers I was used to." The autobiography, assigned two-thirds of the way through the class (I shared my own "Living to Tell the Tale"), was voted "the best paper of the year," and further validation of insider writing: "It gave everyone a hands-on experience with the genre. While I found writing about myself exceedingly difficult, this assignment gave me a great appreciation of the subject matter of this course."

There are other types of real-world writing assignments so thoroughly embedded in innovative course material that they require extensive original investigation and very careful writing and revising—much of it conducted in groups. Linda Flower in *The Construction of Negotiated Meaning* and Thomas Deans in *Writing Partnerships: Service-Learning in Composition* explore a variety of writing courses and projects that ask students and teachers to situate their work and their writing in disciplinary as well as wider nonacademic communities with which the classes form partnerships (Deans 9). The writings thus become reports, bulletins, brochures, operating manuals, position statements, case studies, and a host of other materials described in the four programs Deans examines in detail, as well as in the appendix of courses offered in sixty-one other schools (219–44; see also

Deans's textbook, *Writing and Community Action*). The students are described as highly invested in their work, which is perforce original and usually takes a great deal of time, because the students have to learn to understand the subject to which it pertains and the contexts in which it will be read. Much of it, intended for business, professional, or community audiences, has to be technically proficient. Whether it is intellectually innovative as well, or essentially only good enough is beside the point of Flower's and Deans's research, though the students have considerable incentive, encouragement, and models to make their writing clear, accurate, and to the point.

Truly Good Enough Writing

It should be apparent by now that in the final analysis good enough writing may not really be good enough at all, even if, as realists, we're willing to settle for it. If we're good enough teachers, are we only good enough to help students navigate the upward (and sometimes slippery) slope, but not good enough to get them to the summit? Should we, dare we, ask more of ourselves—as teachers? As innovative writers who understand from the inside out how to break the mold? If not, can we ask more of our students? If so, if we do fulfill our escalating demands on ourselves, perhaps our students still won't want to scale the peak. But, with creative assignments and latitudinarian pedagogy, we can set that vision before them, point them in the right direction, coach them for the climb, and expect the best. When we get it, that writing will truly be good enough.

Notes

1. For instance, in "What Is 'College-Level' Writing?" Patrick Sullivan reports that his informal survey of community college faculty and administrators reveals their common understanding that what is "'college-level' at one institution [is] clearly not college-level at others" (383).

2. *Evaluation and the Academy*, Rosovsky and Hartley's thoroughgoing survey of the research literature from the 1960s through the mid-

1990s provides comprehensive evidence to demonstrate that large-scale surveys show that "the number of A's increased nearly four fold" during this time, from "7 percent in 1969 to 26 percent in 1993, and that the number of C's declined 66 percent (from 25 percent in 1969 to 9 percent in 1993)"; that "across all institutional types GPA's rose approximately 15–20 percent from the mid-1960s through the mid-1990s," by which time "the average grade (formerly a C) resided in the B- to B range. More recent research [1995] across all types of schools shows that only between 10 percent and 20 percent of students receive grades lower than a B-A" (p. 5 includes the authors' extensive citations).

3. Some portions of the discussion below are adapted from my analysis of "Freshman Composition as a Middle-Class Enterprise," though here the orientation is different.

4. A literature search reveals only a single, fleeting use of the concept, likewise derived from Winnicott, by Peter Elbow: "By 'good enough writing,' I do not mean mediocre writing with which we cannot be satisfied. But I do not mean excellent writing, either. . . . In my view, the concept is particularly appropriate for required writing courses where many students are there under duress and are more interested in satisfying the requirement acceptably than in achieving excellence. (Can we hold that against them?) Yet in elective writing courses, 'good enough writing' is also appropriate because students there are more ready to develop their own autonomous standards" (87).

5. I am using as the source of normative advice *The Writer's Harbrace Handbook* (Glenn, Miller, and Webb), the 2004 descendant of the ubiquitous ur-Harbrace, with thirty-nine editions 1941–98, a status warranted by its longevity and ascendancy in the market for years.

6. For example, to claim in a paper of literary criticism on Shakespeare that "Shakespeare was a great writer," though true, is considered a mark of critical naiveté, for everyone (however that is determined) knows this. Nevertheless, if a noted critic were to make that claim, the cognoscenti would attribute this apparent banality to extreme sophistication—since the critic couldn't possibly be that naive—and try to puzzle out what arcane meaning she or he intended by making such an obvious statement.

7. *Harbrace*, surprisingly, says that "The first person is typically used" in literary analyses (718), though a brief survey of the industry standard, *PMLA*, reveals that of eight substantive articles in the January 2003 issue, only three (by John Carlos Rowe, Lori Ween, and Michael Bérubé) used the first person, Rowe and Ween very sparingly and impersonally: "I admit there is a tendency" (Rowe 78); "I will mention

only" (Rowe 83); "I extend to the marketing of novels James Twichell's observation" (Ween 92). This seemingly idiosyncratic advice is not borne out by other widely used handbooks, Lunsford's *St. Martin's Handbook*, fifth edition (2003); Kirszner and Mandell's *Brief Handbook*, fourth edition (2004); or Hacker's *Writer's Reference*, fifth edition (2003).

Works Cited

Arnold, Matthew. "The Function of Criticism at the Present Time." 1865. *The Norton Anthology of English Literature*. Ed. Stephen Greenblatt. 8th ed. Vol. 2. New York: Norton, 2006.

Bartholomae, David. "Inventing the University." *Writing on the Margins: Essays on Composition and Teaching*. Boston: Bedford/St. Martin's, 2005. 60–85.

Bartholomae, David, and Tony Petrosky. *Ways of Reading: An Anthology for Writers*. 7th ed. Boston: Bedford/St. Martin's, 2004.

Bérubé, Michael. "American Studies without Exceptions." *PMLA* 118.1 (Jan. 2003): 103–13.

Bloom, Lynn Z., ed. *The Essay Connection: Readings for Writers*. 8th ed. Boston: Houghton Mifflin, 2007.

———. "Freshman Composition as a Middle-Class Enterprise." *College English* 58.6 (1996): 654–75.

———. "The Good, the Bad, and the Ugly: Ethical Principles for (Re)Presenting Students and Student Writing in Teachers' Publications." *Writing on the Edge* 13.2 (2003): 67–82.

———. "Growing Up with Doctor Spock: An Auto/Biography." *a/b: Auto/Biography Studies* 8.2 (1993): 271–85.

———. "Living to Tell the Tale: The Complicated Ethics of Creative Nonfiction." *College English* 65.3 (2003): 278–89.

———. "Why Don't We Write What We Teach? And Publish It?" 1990. *Composition Theory for the Postmodern Classroom*. Ed. Gary A. Olson and Sidney I. Dobrin. Albany: SUNY P, 1994. 143–55.

Bloom, Lynn Z., and Louise Z. Smith, eds. *The Arlington Reader: Canons and Contexts*. Boston: Bedford, 2003.

Bloom, Lynn Z., Edward M. White, and Shane Borrowman, eds. *Inquiry: Questioning, Reading, Writing*. 2nd ed. New York: Prentice-Hall, 2003.

Buranen, Lise, and Alice M. Roy, eds. *Perspectives on Plagiarism and Intellectual Property in a Postmodern World*. Albany: SUNY P, 1999.

Connors, Robert, and Andrea Lunsford. "Frequency of Formal Errors in Current College Writing, or Ma and Pa Kettle Do Research." *College Composition and Communication* 39 (1988): 395–409.

Deans, Thomas. *Writing and Community Action: A Service-Learning Rhetoric and Reader*. New York: Longman, 2003.

———. *Writing Partnerships: Service-Learning in Composition*. Urbana, IL: NCTE, 2000.

Elbow, Peter. "Writing Assessment in the 21st Century: A Utopian View." *Composition in the Twenty-First Century: Crisis and Change*. Ed. Lynn Z. Bloom, Donald A. Daiker, and Edward M. White. Carbondale: Southern Illinois UP, 1996. 47–62.

Flower, Linda. *The Construction of Negotiated Meaning: A Social Cognitive Theory of Writing*. Carbondale: Southern Illinois UP, 1994.

Freedman, Sarah Warshauer. "The Registers of Student and Professional Expository Writing: Influences on Teachers' Responses." *New Directions in Composition Research*. Ed. Richard Beach and L. S. Bridwell. New York: Guilford, 1984. 334–47.

Gass, William H. "Emerson and the Essay." *Habitations of the Word: Essays*. New York: Simon & Schuster, 1985. 9–49.

Glenn, Cheryl, Robert Keith Miller, and Suzanne Strobeck Webb. *Hodges' Harbrace Handbook*. 15th ed. Boston: Thomson/Wadsworth, 2004.

Hacker, Diana. *Writer's Reference*, 5th ed. Boston: Bedford, 2003.

Kirszner, Laurie G., and Stephen R. Mandell. *The Brief Handbook*. 4th ed. Boston: Thomson/Heinle, 2004.

Lunsford, Andrea. *The St. Martin's Handbook*. 5th ed. New York: St. Martin's, 2003.

Lunsford, Andrea, and Robert Connors. *The St. Martin's Handbook*. 2nd ed. New York: St. Martin's, 1992.

Marius, Richard. *A Writer's Companion*. 4th ed. Boston: McGraw-Hill, 1999.

Miller, Richard. "Fault Lines in the Contact Zone." *College English* 56 (1994): 389–408.

Molière, Jean-Baptiste. *The Bourgeois Gentleman*. Trans. J. Miller and H. Baker. Mineola, NY: Dover, 2001.

National Council of Teachers of English. NCTE Position Statement: "On the Students' Right to Their Own Language." 1974. 6 June 2006 <http://www.ncte.org/about/over/positions/category/lang/107502.htm>.

Orwell, George. "Politics and the English Language." 1946. *A Collection of Essays by George Orwell*. Garden City, NY: Doubleday, 1954. 162–77.

Rose, Mike. *Lives on the Boundary: The Struggles and Achievements of America's Underprepared*. New York: Free Press, 1989.

Rosovsky, Henry, and Matthew Hartley. *Evaluation and the Academy: Are We Doing the Right Thing?* Cambridge, MA: American Academy of Arts and Sciences, 2002.

Rowe, John Carlos. "Nineteenth-Century Literary Culture and Transnationality." *PMLA* 118.1 (Jan. 2003): 78–89.

Scholes, Robert. *Textual Power: Literary Theory and the Teaching of English*. New Haven: Yale UP, 1985.

Scholes, Robert, Nancy R. Comley, and Gregory L. Ulmer. *Text Book: Writing through Literature*. 3rd ed. Boston: Bedford/St. Martin's, 2002.

Shaughnessy, Mina P. *Errors and Expectations: A Guide for the Teacher of Basic Writing*. New York: Oxford UP, 1977.

Strunk, William, and E. B. White. *The Elements of Style*. 1979. 4th ed. Boston: Allyn and Bacon, 2000.

Sullivan, Patrick. "What Is 'College-Level' Writing?" *Teaching English in the Two-Year College*. 30.4 (2003): 374–90.

Ween, Lori. "This Is Your Book: Marketing America to Itself." *PMLA* 118.1 (Jan. 2003): 90–102.

Winnicott, D. W. "The Relationship of a Mother to Her Baby at the Beginning." *The Family and Individual Development*. New York: Basic Books, 1965. 15–20.

Chapter Seven

Whose Paper Is This, Anyway? Why Most Students Don't Embrace the Writing They Do for Their Writing Classes

Michael Dubson
Editor, *Ghosts in the Classroom: Stories of Adjunct Faculty Members—And the Price We All Pay*

When student essays are turned in to me, often my name is written larger on the cover page than the student's. Sometimes my name is placed in such a way that it looks like I myself wrote the paper. When I request that students provide a self-addressed, stamped envelope for the return of assignments submitted at or near the end of a semester, very few students actually provide them—although I always get a slew of follow-up e-mails about grades. When I have left graded assignments in boxes visibly marked with my name and course in an easily accessible space—the mailbox room, the faculty secretary's office—most assignments remain unclaimed, growing dust mites long into the next term. Whatever is in the box, however hard the students worked, few want it back.

Also, assignments regularly show up in my mailbox long after the original due date has passed, when any feedback I can provide will probably be of little use to the student. At other times, usually between the end of classes and the final examination period, a late assignment (or many late assignments from an excessively absent or negligent student) appears in my mailbox. Does the student believe that *writing* the assignment was the only thing he or she needed to do? What about evaluation? Reflection? Feedback? After all the work of the semester, why do these suddenly become irrelevant?

And the winner for the most disheartening experience is returning a set of papers that I have corrected and seeing one (or two or three) glibly tossed into the garbage when I leave the classroom at the end of the period. I might have spent ten, fifteen, twenty minutes reading that essay, asking questions of the writer, marking sentence errors, offering suggestions on additional development, and this is what happens. Perhaps the student scanned the paper quickly, saw the grade, liked or disliked it, and discarded the paper accordingly. Perhaps he or she read over the comments and committed them to memory. Or perhaps, all they wanted to do more than anything was to get that paper out of their life.

How many other papers meet the same fate? How many ride unread in tattered folders until they are hurled into end-of-the-semester dumpsters? Do the students not realize that this might be a project they will want to do more work on later? Do they think there is nothing in this paper they can't learn from?

When college writing assignments, perhaps struggled over for hours or days, can simply be tossed into the trash, what did this writing ever mean to the student, in their class, in their mind, in their life?

Who are these students writing this paper for? Why are they writing these assignments? Where do they, as writers, fit into the writing?

My answer is that, as a group, the students who fill my college writing classes don't care enough or don't care enough in the right way about the work they are doing. Obviously, this is the opposite of what is supposed to be happening in a college writing course, and it is very different than my own personal perspective and very different as well from my attitude in college about the writing I did for my classes.

Who Am I?

I went to college because I was a writer. I started writing what my family called "little stories" when I was eight. A writing teacher

I once had called me a born storyteller. I spent a good amount of time in high school writing novels full of adolescent angst that were supposed to be serious but in retrospect were hilarious. I spent my post-high school years writing and marketing short stories of every stripe.

When I enrolled in college after being out of high school for several years, I went to Parkland College, a community college in Champaign, Illinois, initially with journalism dreams dancing in my head. The first thing I did after registering for courses was to stop by the student newspaper office. Within weeks, my byline was all over the newspaper, and I was read weekly by friend and foe. I grew as a person and as a writer when teachers and fellow students would speak to me about an article I had written, and I grew with pride and a sense of accomplishment as I filled one bulging scrapbook after another with clips. After moving to Boston to complete my undergraduate degree, I spent my junior and senior years writing for a new student paper, and continued to do so briefly as a graduate student.

Since completing college, I have worked for "real" newspapers, had fiction and nonfiction published, published two books, and edited two literary magazines. I have tinkered with song and film writing, and I wrote a play that was produced in Boston. And there is more, much more writing that I wish and intend to do, sandwiched in between my day job. So I am speaking here as a writer.

Between writing articles for the newspaper, I had many writing assignments to do in my classes. I always poured myself into them, often exceeding expectations (and length requirements). While writing, in my mind, I would picture my professors reading my work, imagining their surprise, their shock, their delight at my observations, my analyses, my language. In the end, however, I dug into my writing with energy and gusto because I loved writing, and I loved the work that I produced. I took pride in the work, and I earned the good grades I received.

During the second semester of my first year, after having fallen in love with college and the classroom, I decided to pursue a career teaching college writing instead of journalism. My story isn't unusual. Those of us who love reading and writing go into teaching writing to share our love and joy of writing, and to share our knowledge of a valuable skill.

The other half of my story, sadly, isn't unusual either. After six years of college teacher preparation, I found myself readily and immediately hired at multiple campuses as an adjunct, and I have stayed there. I wanted to teach college writing, and boy have I been able to do that. I wanted a career as a teacher, and I guess I've had one.

As a career adjunct, I have been praised by my supervisors, had outstanding course evaluations and glowing classroom observations, and I have worked steadily every semester, usually being offered more work than I can accept. During searches for full-time faculty positions, I, like other adjuncts, have been called in for token interviews. Ultimately, most of us are passed over for the sparkling stranger from Shangri-la, Antarctica, Transylvania. Afterwards, I am handed my adjunct assignments, patted on the head, and sent off to work.

I have finally realized that it doesn't, and will probably never, matter what I do, how well, or for how long. I will never be awarded the lofty full-time, tenure track job. I will never be allowed to cross the great divide. Personally, I am much happier since I accepted this. But still the resentment grinds when I listen to administrators in their satin robes tell graduating students that hard work will always pay off. That's when I remember the self-deluded promises and/or deliberate dishonesties of my own faculty mentors in graduate school on how good teachers get jobs.

This is the perspective I am writing from. My observations are based on my experiences as an adjunct teacher in a multitude of different school situations. For the most part, I have worked in the Massachusetts community college system, and working at a community college was what I wanted to do because of my own initial college experience. Each community college is a universe unto itself, with different student demographics and different student skills. I have also worked at several universities, both public and private, and a couple of places that were so hideous, they don't even deserve to be called colleges.

The Student Paper Trail

After fifteen years of teaching developmental writing and first-year composition, I have come to believe that most students don't especially care about the work they do for their college writing courses. This makes a mockery of the idealism teachers bring with them into college classrooms, as well as making a farce of what a college writing course is supposed to be.

College writing courses are supposed to give students experience in writing. In doing so, they should become familiar with the various stages one has to go through to write, the generalized process that we all experience, as well as learning and understanding more about their own working habits and the working mechanisms of their own minds. In the process, we teach them how to write different kinds of projects—the descriptive, the expository, the narrative, the argument-persuasive, the analysis, the dreaded research paper. All of this to strengthen their sentence skills, their composition skills, their thinking skills—which will help them in their other coursework and in the real world.

Of course, some skill level may improve if students simply do what is asked of them, over and over, semester after semester, year after year. But how much more improvement would there be if as many students as possible could be more involved in their own process as much as possible, if there was a real investment in the work for as many students as possible, true claim of and true pride in the product produced? Like the person cramming for an exam, the necessary material may be in the person's head when going into the exam. But when the bluebook is closed and the exam is finished, what happens? All that was crammed for furiously flies away, forgotten. A student writing a paper with minimal interest or ownership may experience the composition equivalent of an exam cram.

I think there are many factors that come together to alienate students from the work they do in all their college classes, especially the undergraduate core curriculum courses. That alienation is present in the college writing class, but because of the kind of skill and experience writing is, that alienation is more problematic. Some of the causes of this distance come from the students themselves, some from the teachers, some from the institutions, and some from our larger real-world society.

Student Attitudes about Writing and Writers

Students come into writing classes with some pretty deeply ingrained attitudes about writers and writing. Students who are least likely to embrace the work they do, and who are consequently getting less out of the writing class experience, are students who are likely going to dislike writing, fear it, or not understand it. These students may have had minimal writing experiences in their own lives and have had unpleasant, often error-oriented writing instruction through elementary and secondary school.

Writing is personal, emotional, visceral. To dig into one's own mind and pull up memories, values, experiences, and ideas and put them out there is a very brave and sometimes frightening act, even for experienced writers. Inexperienced and unconfident writers may be more sensitive to this than experienced or exhibitionistic writers because their sense of vulnerability, of embarrassment, of fear of failure or rejection may be much higher. No student comes in with a failing grade from another course and says, "I got an F on *my* math," or "I got an F on *my* history." The distance between those fields of study and the work done is obvious. But they do say, "I got an F on *my* paper, on *my* writing." The relationship between this work and the worker is much more intertwined. It is, therefore, natural that they will put some emotional distance between themselves and the work they do, doing work they may emotionally disown.

Students with negative attitudes or ideas about their own writing are probably going to be much more obsessed with the cultural stereotypes of the writer as a *nerd* or a *dweeb*. Only the writer of the trashiest romance novels is ever deemed *hot* by the popular culture. Students in late or early postadolescence may resent or fear such labels being attached to them by their peers, particularly if they do not enjoy writing enough to risk it. Those of us who love writing and reading realize, sooner or later, that we are complex individuals with a variety of interests and are not especially bothered by stigmatizing and minimizing labels such as *nerd*.

Another phenomenon that affects student attitudes about and ability in writing is the image-heavy/text-light world most of our students have come of age in. Many have read less and written less than generations before them, and therefore have lower entry-level skills at every stage in their education. Many have been weaned on the revolting five-paragraph essay in high school.

When they get to college and are asked to write sustained discourse on a variety of issues, many of their models of serious discourse have been the shallow snippets on the evening network news passed off as "in-depth information you need to know" and the sensationalistic dysfunction of talk and reality shows—noise without analysis. Writing is a difficult process, as generation and revision pirouette around the tension between writer agenda and audience awareness. And if there are any grammar problems, known or unknown, forget it. Consequently, when students come into college writing courses, all of these beliefs and experiences may come between them and the writing that we ask them to do.

Finally, for students who dislike or fear writing, there may be a grudging respect for the successful writer, whether hot or nerd, a fellow student or a successful professional, because they believe that such a person has *talent*. If someone comes into writing class thinking writing is a talent they do not have, a cloud hangs above everything we ask them to do. They think their work is of little value because they aren't talented, or they may think that being asked to write is a waste of time. Our job, of course, is to show them that writing is a skill, a craft that can be acquired, developed, and perfected by anyone. We can do that by acknowledging that some people will develop the craft faster than others, and some will have a greater interest and aptitude in it than others. But nevertheless, the idea that writing is a skill that everyone can develop and improve upon may take more time to sink in than the relatively few weeks students spend in first-year composition courses, in the same way that long-standing writing problems take more than a few semesters to be permanently eradicated.

Student Baggage

And if this wasn't enough . . .

Other forces put upon students, more directly related to their college experience, lead to a greater distance between them and the work they do for their college writing courses. One of them is our cultural attitude about going to college.

Today's economic market is flooded with those special savings programs for parents who want to be sure their three-year-old will be able to attend college in fifteen years. The pressure on parents to send their children to college has probably never been greater, ironically at a time when tuition has never been higher and government support and financial aid have become much tighter. Before the social movements of the 1960s opened the doors to many previously disenfranchised students, most people who went to college were the well-to-do and/or those with high grade point averages. And back in the day, as my students say, reasonable employment could be obtained without a college degree. Economic and social shifts have changed the face of colleges, making college education an economic necessity. Declining population trends have made many of the schools, which were founded to accommodate the baby boomers, desperate for their survival (though that trend is reversing somewhat as the baby boom echo hits college age).

Most of today's high school graduates are simply expected to go to college. Others who might wish to take some time off or do something else are pressured or forced to go by parents legitimately concerned about their children's future or, grotesquely, about how this looks to friends and neighbors. Other people proudly become the first generation to attend college, seeing the entire experience as the ticket to the good life, an unrealistic expectation fostered by ignorance about the kinds of jobs and careers the basic college degree can initially lead to. The marketing techniques colleges use—promises of bright futures and successful lives, all of which will occur *after* graduation—are not only misleading, they negate the value of the college experience as it occurs.

In addition, there are often personal or cultural judgments made about the intellectual capacity of the person who does not go to college. Getting into college is seen as a marker of intelligence, of potential, of not being a dummy.

Great Cultural Irony #1

Students don't want to be identified as nerds, dweebs, or bookworms, but at the same time, they don't want to be seen as dumb. Being a successful college student suggests the former; not going to college at all suggests the latter. So those who go to college want to be in the middle of these two points, which means they go to college, they want to be considered smart, but they are careful not to put too much effort into their work so they won't be labeled nerds.

Consequently, college becomes a necessary evil, something students have to get through in order to get to the other side where all the glory is. The work that students do then becomes a means to an end, something not of intrinsic value unto itself but for what it leads to. Students take classes in order to get a good grade, to get a degree, to get a job or a career. In classes with subjective measurements of achievement, as the grading of student writing often is, the significance of the work becomes even more unclear because it cannot be quantified in an easy to understand formula, as a math test can be.

Attitudes about going to college and the work done in college often mirror our cultural attitudes about work in general. Students go to school to pursue careers, but the conventional cultural message is, sadly, that work is something undesirable to do. It is something we have to do to survive, or to afford things, but something so disagreeable and unpleasant, we yawn our way through or escape from it every chance we get. Those messages are embodied in much of the advertising that students have been saturated with since they first opened their eyes, whether it's advertising for beer, travel agencies, or what's new on Cinemax.

The parallels are frightening. Class work, unpleasant but necessary, equals grade, equals degree, equals job. In the best of all possible student fantasy worlds, that means the best grade, the best degree, and the best job for the least amount of work. Then, job equals work (albeit often undesirable), equals paycheck, equals paying the electric bill and buying the new car and the $150 concert tickets. The best situation to be in is to do the least amount of work for the most amount of money.

In both cases, it seems that the experience gained or the service performed is not seen as valuable per se, but only for what the return is. When we ask students who already have issues with writing to write, we ask them to jump through hoops to get grades in the grade book, which leads to the *final grade* at the end of the term. The writing they do is something that they are not going to necessarily embrace with open arms. They will do it because they have to, not because they want to. This attitude puts a distance between the writer and his or her work. Merely doing what they are told to do without any innate or internal interest in the work is going to prohibit or seriously compromise the kind of learning and growth that we want to encourage.

Cultural Irony #2

Students go through college with hostile attitudes about their college work because it is a means to an end in terms of getting a good job. After they get the job because of their college degree, their attitude about their work often continues to be negative.

Faculty Attitudes and Agendas

This is what I believe we see when our students file into our college writing classes on that happy first day. And what most of us do builds on the disenfranchisement of the students and their writing. It's not completely our fault, but I think we need to be aware of what's going on.

When students come into our classes with preexisting attitudes about writing and a mindset about the work they will do in college, they sit in writing classes with a fair amount of hostility toward the whole process, and often, initially, the teacher. In theory, a bunch of strangers, who may remain for the most part strangers, are going to be led to literary achievement by another stranger. And how do we do that?

With contrived writing assignments that represent *our* interests and *our* values. Textbooks are marketed to us. We pick the texts we want, we choose the readings we like, but all that may mean very little or nothing to the students. Even worse, many composition teachers communicate, with or without words, what is and what is not the appropriate response the student should deliver. One English teacher I knew, for example, said she would not read papers that disagreed with her position on certain political issues, particularly abortion. In an environment like this, how can we expect our students to own the writing they do for our college writing classes?

"What do you want?" is a question I'm often asked. My answer is that I want them to take my assignment and make it their own and care about what they have to say. For some students, who have been trained to give teachers what they want, that may be very difficult, if not impossible.

Of course, our assignments are designed to make students *think* about an issue, and our goals may be lofty and valuable. Nevertheless, if students are put off by an assignment, or uninterested in it, many do all the deadly things that inhibit successful thinking, writing, and learning: procrastinate, bullshit, or both. Ultimately, they will not take pride in or ownership of the work produced, and if they take a hit in the grade book, it will put further distance between themselves and their writing.

If a student has written five pages of empty air on a serious topic, it may be because the student did not put the time or energy in. But it may also be that they just could not find a way into the assignment in order to claim it as their own. We might say they should have, in the same way a boss might say an employee should care about doing his or her work. Or we might remind them that they will have to do things they aren't especially interested in or thrilled about in the working world. But what do we want our college writing classes to be? Places where the sheep bend mindlessly to the will of the shepherd, or places where students embrace writing in general, and their own in particular? If what we return to the student is something they never cared about before, during, or after its creation, then what does it matter?

The alternative may be open-ended, write-what-you-want assignments. Those have a great deal of appeal to the self-motivated student, but those who already have issues with writing may find these assignments problematic. Such students, forced to think of and, by necessity, claim a topic, may procrastinate or blow the assignment off all together. Others may fill up pages with baloney passing off as discourse. Still others may resort to less scrupulous ways around it: inadvertent or deliberate plagiarism, or outright dishonesty—a bought paper. This is easier for our Internet-savvy students to do than ever before. We can issue moral platitudes against the student who plagiarizes until dehydration sets in, along with threats of course failure and college expulsion, threats that most likely ring hollow in a world where scoundrels, liars, and hypocrites of all stripes continue to rise to positions of prominence and hold on to them even after public scandal. But behind all the judgmental epithets of *cheater*, *liar*, *incompetent* is a student who clearly does not embrace the writing assignment, does not feel engaged in the work of writing, does not care about his or her own writing, does not feel capable of doing it.

And then there's us, the red pen people. Unfortunately, the teacher-student relationship is fundamentally adversarial in many ways. We have the right, the responsibility to judge, censor, criticize, and evaluate student writing in order to, theoretically, help them improve. The perspectives of teacher and student are very different. From our perspective, we are helping students improve. From their perspective, we appear to be judging and criticizing their work, often covering it with comments and observations and marking errors. When they get their homework back, it can look violated, a violation that can sting even more if the final grade is a big fat red F or D. Students, expecting a marked-up paper, may distance themselves before the assignment is returned—just because they aren't emotionally or intellectually prepared to deal with and understand this evaluation.

Teacher comments may be cryptic or obtuse, sometimes illegible, and are often read at a point in time too far removed from the writing of the paper to be fully effective. A margin comment or question about a passage in the paper will not mean anything if the student can't remember what the passage was about. What percentage of first-year composition students are going to reread the entire paper to get a holistic sense of the essay in order to fully understand the comments?

The attitude students often take is that teachers *correct* their papers—an idea that implies both an already flawed product and one that only the teacher can fix. A flawed product, particularly something someone doesn't have a clue about how to fix, is not something they are going to embrace, and a marked up essay is going to be even more alienating.

Our own attitudes about students and student skills are not going to help this process, and if we have negative attitudes about them, we will communicate this to them one way or another, whether in our grading comments, our classroom attitude, or our pre- or postessay discussions. But we've all heard these comments, and we may have said them ourselves: laments at faculty meetings about the distressing levels of error in student writing, the bellyaching about student work in adjunct faculty ghettos. If we feel hostile about their work in any way, students are going to pick up on this one way or another.

I've seen the reverse of this as well, in assessment exam readings, where student writing is fussed over and picked at, and the gap between a developmental writing course and college-level course appears to grow wider than the gap between kindergarten and graduate school. The graders seem to forget that First-Year Composition is not a senior honors English course. This attitude is not going to help the students embrace their writing, or the writing they do in our classes if it comes back to them with our baggage.

The negative attitudes many in academia have about First-Year Composition are clearly reflected in who ends up teaching it. In the four-year colleges and universities, what I've seen is that full-time tenured faculty prefer and usually get specialized courses that they particularly like, and if required by their institution to teach First-Year Composition, teach as few sections as possible, one a semester or one a year. In the community colleges, the full-time faculty may teach more sections of the first-year writing courses, but they also have their pet courses they turn to, as well as the ever-popular course release for committee work (or whatever) to keep the workload down. By and large, teaching first-year writing is seen as a dreary, undesirable task that many established faculty avoid.

Consequently, first-year writing is farmed out to the least powerful, the most disenfranchised, the most exploited members of the academic community—adjuncts, teaching assistants, graduate students. Adjuncts may be teaching for fun, or on the side of a regular job or career, or they may be *career adjuncts*—colleagues making a living at teaching and hoping for that great big *full-time job* break.

I have been a member of this group, and I have known many teachers who work at multiple campuses teaching courses in numbers that would send the average, complacent, full-time faculty member reeling right into a retirement home, choking on their own sense of entitlement. Because of workload issues, it is often just not possible to give each student the individual attention they deserve, no matter how much we might want to.

Full-time faculty do not necessarily have the time to do it either. Although they, ironically, may teach fewer classes and have an office, there are always other time-consuming duties to attend to, and institutional policies and regulations continue to interfere with how much faculty can do for each student. Complacency, arrogance, and laziness also become factors with some tenured faculty.

Graduate students and teaching assistants may have more optimism and energy that more seasoned faculty lack, but they also lack the experience, and in between designing assignments and reading essays, they have their own work to do. In the end, the students lose out, and in the end, the distance between themselves and the writing they do for school grows.

Cultural Irony #3

First-Year Composition is considered a fundamental course needed by all students to lay some kind of foundation that will help them in all the other classes they will take, and in their working and personal lives as well. And yet, teaching this course is seen as undesirable, and the conditions under which it is taught are such that they create more harm than good. In addition, academic institutions as a rule treat very poorly the majority of the people who perform this most profound, fundamental work.

Institutional Inconsistencies

Many things colleges are doing now are part of the reason students find themselves distanced from their writing. Assessments that are used to determine placement in an appropriate class end up putting a menagerie of students in one single class that they choose to take based on schedule convenience. Little or no attention is paid to attitudes about writing, fear or dislike of writing, or writing history and experience when making placement decisions.

Consequently, many students who would rather go white water rafting backwards in the dark than write find themselves in classes with people who love to write. The poorly skilled may find themselves in the same classes with the highly skilled. This can be useful because there is something to be learned in this situation, but it can also be intimidating. But what about those times when students who don't like writing or fear writing or are poorly skilled at writing all end up in classes together?

Either way, the results are problematic. The teacher can either teach to the lowest or the highest denominator. And what happens to those students who don't fit into the group?

One of the biggest issues in writing classes is class size. The number of students increases a teacher's workload. The more students, the more impersonal and factory-like the faculty member's response must be. The less time and attention per student, the greater the chance that the student will remain disengaged from the writing they do for their class.

At the schools I have worked at, maximum class size ranges from place to place. In some schools, it's twenty-two. At others, it's twenty-five. Some schools have a double standard in terms of maximum enrollment for full-time faculty versus adjunct. For example, at one school, full-time faculty, who have the time, office space, and institutional engagement, have a class size maximum of twenty-two. For adjuncts, it's thirty. Most of the schools, bless their hearts, tend to give adjunct courses the same enrollment maximum that full-time faculty receive.

I used to work at one little diploma mill that offered affordable tuition because it had no academic standards. They did not believe in enrollment limits. I have to give credit where credit is due and admit that this greasy spoon gave me my first postgraduate "professional" job. I was hired over the telephone after I sent a cover letter and resume. Being too naive to know any better, I was thrilled with the opportunity.

How clearly I can still remember those first few days of my brand new English 101 semester as new students rolled in every day until add/drop was over. Thirty, thirty-five, forty students—in a writing class! At one point, I had to send the students out to look for other chairs, which they had to force into the room. Even in my naiveté, I knew better than to send those students back to the registration desk. That would have ended my first job before it had even started.

How was I supposed to respond intelligently and personally to the work of all these students? Even though I was still idealistic from graduate school, I knew this wasn't going to work. But that didn't stop the school from collecting all those nice, juicy tuition dollars. And I didn't have to worry about grading all those assignments. By midterm, half the students had dropped.

Was it because I was a lousy teacher? Was it because they were immature and irresponsible? Or was it because, lost in a sea of strangers where one teacher could not possibly give them the personalized attention they deserved, all the factors added up and made dropping out (and having to enroll in and pay for the class) again the lesser of two evils? All those delicious tuition dollars—but at whose expense?

The problem with colleges is the robber baron mindset they have adopted, perhaps in response to political and economic changes and declining support for higher education by corporate society. Too often the goal is to get the students in, get their tuition dollars, and then let academic Darwinism take over. Whether they sink or swim, it's their fault, or it's the teacher's fault—especially if the teacher is an adjunct. In the end, in the college writing class, the potential growth that could occur in the writing assignments of the maximum number of students doesn't happen.

Cultural Irony #4

Though everyone must go to college to receive an education, the institutions that mandate this, including corporations and governments, are often less than willing to support those institutions, and then blame colleges when students graduate without appropriate writing skills.

Solutions?

My suggestions for improving the situation aren't especially realistic in the political and economic climate of today's real world, but so what? What is life without an impossible dream?

Obviously, the best way to deal with student writing is to help *each and every student* find and develop their own ideas, ideas we know are their own, and to work closely and individually with each student to develop a piece of writing through its various stages, pointing out error without marking up a paper, offering suggestions for development and revision without there being midnight comments scrawled illegibly in the margins. This means more than lectures on how to write a paper, forced class discussions or small group work on textbook selections, and more than a five-minute paper conference. And it means more than fifteen minutes reading, or five minutes scanning, student papers and scrawling comments. Yet most likely, this vision wouldn't get anything more than a chuckle from the standard academic dean. Aren't we supposed to be able to do it all now?

If close, semester-long individual attention could be the experience of all students in college writing classes, more students would emerge with stronger skills and a sense of pride and ownership of their work. But, unfortunately, this will cost money. More significantly, it calls for a revision in the paradigm of how most of us envision college. In today's political climate, where the cost of college is higher than ever and government support for it lower then ever, when unions, administrators, and entrenched full-time faculty are frequently resistant to change, the college world will go on as it is. Teachers will make assignments, students will hop through the ring of fire to do them, the papers will be graded and returned a week or two later, and maybe some writing skill or personal growth will occur for some students.

Failing any major changes in the system, what can we do? As a teacher, I intend to talk about the value of thinking, the importance of being curious, the type of work that can be done for its own sake as well as for external and ultimate gain, and for good writing being of value above and beyond a grade.

But I also know there's always the garbage dumpster at the end of the semester, eagerly awaiting all those essays students didn't care enough about to save.

Chapter Eight

The Boxing Effect (An Anti-Essay)

Jeanne Gunner
Chapman University

You may remember a Monty Python sketch in which a man (Michael Palin) enters an office and announces to a man behind a desk (John Cleese), "I want to have an argument." The Cleese character responds, "No, you don't." What ensues is a maddening series of contradictions, with the Palin character asserting that contradiction does not constitute real argument, the Cleese figure responding that it can, and the sketch continuing in the usual brilliant Monty Python way, the Palin character ultimately paying five pounds for the privilege of being contradicted, insulted, and frustrated. Yet, despite his experience, he remains poignantly hopeful of engaging his tormentor in meaningful exchange, forking over another five pounds when his time is up.

If you are in the field of composition, this absurdist routine can't help but be familiar to you, simply because as compositionists, we are all caught up in the usually thankless argument about what constitutes college-level writing, a public wrangling characterized by a maddening series of contradictions that we strive to synthesize into a legitimate intellectual discourse, only to be refuted, dismissed, and mistreated. And, given working conditions in the field, it's fair to say that we, like the hapless Palin character, pay for the privilege of suffering such ill-considered abuse, having in some way been coerced into believing that it ultimately can make sense. But when decades of methodologically diverse research and historical study, of classroom experience across institutional types, of epistemological paradigm shifts of immense order cannot disrupt knee-jerk contradictions of our field's claim that writing is not a monolithic skill open to simplistic psychometric measurement and behaviorist training techniques, then perhaps it's time to stop asking the question that sets off this absurd response. To speak of *college writing* is to invoke a formulation that encourages the commodification of writing, writing students, writing curricula, and writing instructors, a formulation that reifies a system of nonporous institutional boundaries. If college writing is an object that has to be defined in order to be produced efficiently, then we become mere delivery people uninvolved in packaging the contents of the boxes we hand out.

This *boxing* effect entails the following interlocking processes, beginning with the commodification of writing but extending throughout a system of containing devices that work against real writers' writing and rhetoric as social action.

Writing Is Commodifed, the Result of Capitalist Culture

The boxing effect is implicit in the contexts of our work. Institutions of higher education can't be disentangled from the (often pseudo) public-interest accountability trend and the larger capitalist culture. As compositionists, we teach in a corporate administrative context as part of a service industry. The business program in my own institution (ostensibly a liberal arts college) articulates this blunt relation of writing and capitalism: "Our curricula point toward preparing students for the processes of creating wealth and adding value for enterprises" ("Draft" 8). The purpose of the liberal arts core is understood as itself serving this end:

> Our graduates will be equipped with solid academic preparation for the challenges of leading firms in a turbulent market environment as well as the professional skills necessary to succeed in the marketplace, such as oral and written communications skills, teamwork skills, leadership skills, and analytical skills.

In this discourse, writing is one among several commodifiable skills, and our job becomes the cultivation of this valuable—that is, wealth-creating—commodity. Once writing is commodified, every point of educational *interface* reinforces this construct of a disembodied skill, as David Russell argues:

> The genres of core researchers in a discipline (e.g., research articles) are translated into other genres for practitioners (e.g., research reviews, instructions, teachers' manuals, etc.) and for consumers of various kinds, such as customers (trade book popularizations, warning labels, advertising), clients (intake forms, brochures), and beginning students (teaching materials, Cliff's Notes, and—most predominately—textbooks). (85)

When I volunteered in my daughter's elementary school classroom one year, my job was to dispense prefabricated teaching materials, a curriculum that literally came in a box. At a Writing Program Administrators meeting with publishers' representatives, I listened to enthusiastic pitches about how a new text came "bundled" with pedagogical add-ons. No wonder, then, that my students now are to be "equipped with solid academic preparations." They are "product."

Efficiency of production, then, is really the one way to add instructional value, and so we're institutionally encouraged to find ever-better ways—that is, more time-efficient ways—of producing writing skill. College-level writing is thus abstracted from any individual purpose and comes to function as every other commodity, as a thing to be owned, a thing which we're contracted to provide as standard equipment.

As a Commodity, College Writing Becomes Disembodied and Asocial, with Writing Separated from a Writing Subject

These systemic cultural forces work to coerce us into answering the question "What is college writing?" with an isolable, prescriptive, testable set of bundled standards, located outside of a writing subject—a real student. The question of what college writing is disembodies writing from the social agents who not only produce it, but who might otherwise (were they ever to be allowed to write outside the box) have the potential to determine its purposes and values. Writing as a disembodied skill thus comes to be a credential that can be impersonally produced. Students in turn can be labeled *haves* and *have nots* according to this commodified notion of writing, their worth determined by their use value: do they have good writing skills?

The central aim of the extensive longitudinal research on writing conducted by the late Marilyn Sternglass is to dismantle this writing reification process:

> Early instruction in composition is critical to fostering critical reading and writing skills, but the expectation that students have become "finished writers" by the time they complete a freshman sequence or even an advanced composition course must be abandoned. (296)

Yet writing continues to function even at her home institution as a possession, "equipment" that determines access to the university, and students become modular compendia of useful skills. College writing is one element in an assembly process.

This system of usefulness, of worth defined as "adding value to [business] enterprises," redefines not only students but teachers of writing as well ("Draft" 8). Teaching becomes a matter of boxing, bundling, and otherwise delivering learning packages through a writing process that standardizes all products. Unable to resist the cultural imperative to reify writing, we find ourselves participating in the boxing effect. Kurt Spellmeyer argues that

> [m]any textbooks still uphold the dictum that a sentence "should contain," as William Strunk long ago insisted, "no unnecessary words," and "a paragraph no unnecessary sentences, for the same reason that a drawing should have no unnecessary lines and a machine no unnecessary parts." Just as widely endorsed is the advice of Henry Seidel Canby, offered in 1909 but repeated, with a few up-to-date modifications, by authors of the latest handbooks and rhetorics. "When a man prepares to write a theme [. . .] he should have a definite idea in his own mind as to just what points he is going to make [. . .] he should write a theme as an engineer builds a bridge, planning it first and then building from his plan." Legacies of a specific time and place, these injunctions now possess a timeless self-evidence, a cultural purchase inversely proportional to their diminishing visibility [. . . .]

> [T]oday these claims are neither true nor false; they are common sense, ideas a teacher might endorse even after his experience has failed to support them. . . . (3)

Instead of leading to a Kuhnian crisis and revolution in the commodity paradigm, the teacher's experience with real human subjects writing in real social locations reinforces the disembodiment of college writing. Divorced from actual writers and their social contexts, writing operates in/as Platonic form, and the pale, inferior imitation that an individual student produces becomes evidence of college writing as a good that he or she does not possess.

Epistemological *Container* Theories Support the Commodification Process

Despite the resurgence in rhetorical instruction, then, much of our work as writing teachers remains under the coercive influence of reductive cognitive models of linguistic competence, a situation exacerbated by an often equally reductive assessment culture. As a writing teacher, I come under intense pressure to be instrumentalist in approach, behaviorist in pedagogy, consumerist in curriculum, all forces leading to the reification of reading and writing. Almost twenty years ago, educational theorist Patrick Shannon analyzed this commodification process:

> [W]hen they reify reading instruction, teachers and administrators lose sight of the fact that reading instruction is a human process. . . . [T]heir reification of the scientific study of the reading process as the commercial materials means that their knowledge of reading and instruction is frozen in a single technological form. . . . [S]chool personnel's reification of science requires that they define their work in terms of efficiency of delivery and students' gains in test scores. (190)

Consider the larger cultural nostalgia for mechanistic models of reading, given new strength by continued strides in mandatory, state-sponsored testing. In a pre-social-construction model, college (or any educational level) reading *skill* can be easily assessed, since the model separates readers from interpretation; in such a model, the text *contains* its own meaning. The student reader's task is to read the text and extract that meaning. Success can be measured through various forms of comprehension testing, for correct answers have a close to absolute relationship with the text—an idea or point either is or is not in the text, and a student either has or has not understood it. It's a container model of knowledge; open the text's lid and scoop out the meaning from the text box. It powered much of the pedagogy of English classes through at least the 1980s. Its appeal is clear: if knowledge exists in bits or chunks, then it is easily measured, in a text or a student's performance, according to a scale of simple to advanced. In turn we get a theory of teaching and learning that is incremental, that posits basic skills as necessarily prior to other, higher-order cognitive skills. The boxes, in other words, can be neatly labeled.

Curricula built on this model assume that texts hold knowledge, that we mine knowledge from texts, and so that if we read the right texts, we will get the best knowledge and become the best people. This is a commodity model of reading infused with a ruling class ideology—he (sic) who reads the most of the best naturally rises to the top, but only he who is naturally superior will understand these hard books. The notion of inherent textual meaning is compelling because it idealizes out of existence some otherwise troubling phenomena, like the unequal performance of white students and students of color on standardized tests. If the boxes are identical, then any difference in their unpacking can be directly attributable to the individual student. Min-Zhan Lu locates this neutrality as a scientistic element of composition textbooks, which

> empty writing of the social and historical, operating to authorize a notion of "good" writing structured on the binary of 'human' universality vs. social, historical differences. . . . [T]hese texts . . . offer 'new,' 'scientific' justifications for maintaining the neutrality of "good" writing. (70)

The writing curriculum is the production end of this meaning collection. Students learn to mine a text box's ideas and then recast them in a box he or she has decorated, as this current online guide to writing puts it:

> An essay can have many purposes, but the basic structure is the same no matter what. You may be writing an essay to argue for a particular point of view or to explain the steps necessary to complete a task.
>
> Either way, your essay will have the same basic format.
>
> If you follow a few simple steps, you will find that the essay almost writes itself. You will be responsible only for supplying ideas, which are the important part of the essay anyway. ("Guide")

Such a model of writing supplants the concept of the rhetorical, the recognition of language as a social practice, of communication as an exchange with a purpose, as a context-dependent process of negotiated meanings. The container model posits reading and writing as a linear process of incremental skill that moves hierarchically from the simple to the complex. What is prior is simpler, and what is later is more challenging. Applied to students, this model rewards students from certain cultural backgrounds and justifies itself in the face of poor performance by others. Applied to the institutional level, this container model produces the differing degrees of cultural capital that can be named community college, four-year school, research university.

Commodification Is Replicated in Institutional Structures

Where curricular control is removed from the teachers who teach the curricula, instruction is always already corrupted. External curricular control means not only debased curricula and limited access for students, but it also debases the field and faculty. Commodified college writing is therefore also a formula for maintaining the distinctions between institutional levels.

In "Our Apartheid," Ira Shor describes the stratification of educational institutions and employs the metaphors of "tracking" and "apartheid," both of them forms of social and institutional containers. He argues that the community college system is a means for the social tracking of students, but his argument also clearly suggests that the control placed on the community college system correlates with a cultural impulse to discipline the bodies of certain faculty—of those who lack cultural capital, who are reified via the tightly structured bureaucracy of state control of curriculum.

Within a university context, *community college* is a monolithic term, a kind of icon for a set of assumptions, a primary one being that there is no need for differentiation, that community colleges are relatively identical boxes. The differentiations that are commonly made among four-year institutions—Research I and II, comprehensive universities, state schools, regional schools, private liberal arts schools—are usually not used by faculty and administrators at these schools when it comes to thinking about relations with two-year schools. This attitude is reinforced by the perception of the two-year school as a place of reduced autonomy. In "Pleasure and Pain: Faculty and Administrators in a Shared Governance Environment," Sally Fitzgerald (then a community college dean) discusses the problems administrators face in working collaboratively with faculty. She explains some of the constraints on hiring and course assignments, constraints imposed not by her administrative superiors at the college but mandated by state legislators. The degree of external control, the restrictions on autonomy, that pervades the state's institutions at the community college level is striking in its ability to box in faculty status as well. Just as students in the writing classroom traditionally have been constructed more by assumptions about their institutional affiliation than by their critical awareness, so, too, have faculty.

The institutional relations have been formed by a linear notion of relationship: two-year school education precedes university education, a temporal frame that discourages serious attention to what happens in the two-year school, just as has been the pattern of relations between secondary schools and college. The relations of two-year school, four-year school, and research university faculty are thus limited by a class-based ideology, one that overrides the material connections that exist between them. Materially, colleagues at two-year, four-year, and research institutions have common means of contact. We often work together, especially those of us in the rhetoric-composition field, since the number of part-time instructors is so high in both types of institutions, and this part-time population is likely to teach at both. We share students, since a primary mission of many two-year schools is to send a significant number of graduates to four-year institutions. We have course articulation agreements that acknowledge the parallel work of our curricula. We belong to many of the same professional organizations, such as the National Council of Teachers of English, attend many of the same conferences, such as the Conference on College Composition and Communication (CCCC), and read many of the same journals, such as *College Composition and Communication*, *College English*, and *Journal of Basic Writing*, sharing a common theoretical knowledge. We were graduate students together. Clearly, a powerful ideological system operates to justify the divide that is apparent despite these material connections.

Each institutional faculty is boxed into its own institutional container, and these are dialogically nonporous. A deeply ingrained notion of hierarchy in education, a social construct of linear relations, produces a static relationship in which one group must always speak *up* to the next group even as it works *down* against a response from this group. The seemingly democratic nature of shared work in the national professional organizations constructs its equality via a base of dues-paying members even as it enables status distinctions through the cultural capital of its status-graduated conferences and journals. The egalitarian unity of a CCCC, for instance, is one of the "utopias—nowheres, metacommunities" that Joseph Harris cites in his critique of the idea of community (100); it is unrelated to the material conditions of our daily lives in our stacked institutional boxes.

Writing out of the Box

When we reify writing, we tacitly endorse a set of beliefs that assume generic shape as common sense: writing, after all, is concrete, a thing you can produce, use, sell. Richard Ohmann critiqued the ideological agenda behind the Strunk and White dictum to students to "use definite, specific, concrete language" as having the effect of "encourag[ing] them to accept the empirical fragmentation of consciousness that passes for common sense in our society, and hence to accept the society itself as just what it most superficially seems to be" (250). Writing in college has a material reality that cannot be contained in a set of disembodied descriptors or idealized prescriptives.

Writing in college, as elsewhere, happens among people, in real places, over time, for a vast range of purposes. When people writing in college environments write, we see embodied instances of college writing. To attempt to define college writing outside this human social context is to invite its commodification, to erase the subject himself or herself, to justify mechanistic curricula, and to support institutional atomism. All the contemporary professional calls for a rhetorical curriculum speak against such commodification, and all the emerging works of alternative discourses embody the subversion of it. We've paid enough for our arguments over what college writing is.

Works Cited

"Draft Strategic Plan." Memo to the Provost, Chapman University, Orange, CA, 2 Aug. 2004.

Fitzgerald, Sallyanne. "Pleasure and Pain: Faculty and Administrators in a Shared Governance Environment." *WPA: Writing Program Administration* 21.2/3 (1998): 101–05.

"Guide to Writing a Basic Essay." 30 Aug. 2004 <http://members.tripod.com/~lklivingston/essay/>.

Harris, Joseph. *A Teaching Subject: Composition Since 1966*. Upper Saddle River, NJ: Prentice Hall, 1997.

Lu, Min-Zhan. "Importing 'Science': Neutralizing Basic Writing." *Representing the "Other": Basic Writers and the Teaching of Basic Writing*. Eds. Bruce Horner and Min-Zhan Lu. Urbana, IL: NCTE, 1999. 56–104.

"Monty Python's Flying Circus." Created by Graham Chapman et al. British Broadcasting Corporation. 1969.

Ohmann, Richard. "Use Definite, Specific, Concrete Language." *Politics of Letters*. Middletown, CT: Wesleyan UP, 1987. 241–51.

Russell, David. "Activity Theory and Process Approaches: Writing (Power) in School and Society." *Post-Process Theory: Beyond the Writing-Process Paradigm*. Ed. Thomas Kent. Carbondale: Southern Illinois UP, 1999. 80–95.

Shannon, Patrick. "Commercial Reading Materials, a Technological Ideology, and the Deskilling of Teachers." *Becoming Political: Readings and Writings in the Politics of Literacy Education*. Ed. Patrick Shannon. Portsmouth, NH: Heinemann, 1992. 182–207.

Shor, Ira. "Our Apartheid: Writing Instruction and Inequality." *Journal of Basic Writing* 16.1 (1997): 91–104.

Spellmeyer, Kurt. *Common Ground: Dialogue, Understanding, and the Teaching of Composition*. Englewood Cliffs, NJ: Prentice Hall, 1993.

Sternglass, Marilyn. *Time to Know Them: A Longitudinal Study of Writing and Learning at the College Level*. Mahwah, NJ: Lawrence Erlbaum, 1997.

Chapter Nine

What Does *the Instructor Want?* *The View from the Writing Center*

Muriel Harris
Purdue University

When I first confronted the question posed by the editors of this volume, "What is college-level writing?" my initial response was a desperate desire to evade answering. Then a feeling of utter helplessness set in when pondering a question much like one of those all-encompassing questions we used to debate over endless mugs of coffee in college coffee houses. Everyone in those discussions had different answers on different days to the same question. Sometimes we argued whether the question of the day could even be asked. But then, I'm supposed to be more experienced now, having directed and tutored in a writing center for almost thirty years. I'm tempted to offer an answer similar to U.S. Supreme Court Justice Potter Stewart's often-quoted reply when asked how to recognize pornography. As he said, "you know when you see it" (Jacobellis). Can't I, I wondered, recognize college-level writing when I see it?

Yet, as a tutor, I have to admit I am not always sure which college-level writing I am supposed to recognize. For example, one rainy fall afternoon a student dragged himself into the writing lab where I tutored, flung himself into a chair next to me, and with a truly dejected look produced a paper he had written. His first comment was that he was an A student in the first-year Advanced Composition course. And then he admitted that the paper lying limply in front of us was considered a disaster zone by the faculty member who taught his engineering course. As I read his paper, I admired the elegant sentences, the careful use of transitions, the introduction that led readers smoothly into the subject, the clear thesis statement, and so on. This would be an A paper in any composition course, but for his engineering instructor it was inappropriate and, therefore, poorly written. The student was mystified as to what the engineering instructor wanted, despite the notation across the top of the title page: "GET TO THE POINT." From the student's perspective, there was indeed a clear thesis sentence. What did the professor want?

That was merely one example of what others in this book and elsewhere have pointed out—the variety of programs and goals as well as the fundamental problem of lack of universally similar responses from readers. As Patrick Sullivan notes, when he raised the problem of defining college-level writing because of the lack of stability both in language and in readers:

> A number of important modern literary theorists . . . argue . . . that because language is so slippery, the art of reading and, by extension, interpretation and evaluation, must be conducted as a provisional enterprise. . . . (376)

Ellen Andrews Knodt confirms the disparity among standards that exists and notes that it stems from the "wide disagreement among composition programs and faculty about the goals to be achieved in college writing programs" (146). Exploring the causes of this divergence in goals, she sees one of the problems with uniformity as arising from "many college writing programs [that] have come to serve many purposes" (146). Other contributors to this book confirm the problems of lack of similar goals, standards, readers, programs, and institutional structures and populations. The official Outcomes Statement of the Council of Writing Program Administrators prefers instead to define *outcomes* or *types of results* and declines to specify *standards* for first-year composition because, as the Outcomes Statement explains: "The setting of standards should be left to specific institutions or specific groups of institutions" (Council).

If we are not likely to reach agreement through the prism of standards, and if the Council of Writing Program Administrators chooses to present outcomes instead of standards, how do we recognize when the outcomes have indeed been reached? For example, one outcome in the Writing Program Administrators Outcomes Statement is that by the end of a first-year composition program the student should be able to focus on a purpose; another outcome is that first-year students should be able to control surface features such as syntax, grammar, and punctuation. But how are we to determine what constitutes *control* of such features? The Writing Program Administrators Outcomes Statement is a noble attempt to recognize and cope with diversity among institutions and still determine what students should be learning in their first composition courses. It is a description of goals and does not attempt to answer the question of how to recognize when the outcomes are met.

So, once again, we cycle back to the question of what college-level writing is, looking for a place to become specific enough to be useful across broad differences among institutions, programs, and instructors. One thing we can do is to return to the basic question of underlying characteristics of writing that define experienced writers, concepts that lie at the intersections of that welter of programs, goals, and varied reader interpretations. Ronald Lunsford concludes that college-level writers should be able to respond to texts that contain abstract content, should be able to "deal with complex issues that challenge students to read against their biases" (196). The list of aptitudes that define characteristics of college writing is, of course, still plagued by the very basic divergence of reader responses, but we can continue to try to work on the list of abilities such as Lunsford has done. My contribution to that list is that college-level writing should demonstrate the writer's ability to write effectively to his or her particular audience. Moreover, I hope to expand on the problems caused by lack of audience awareness.

Audiences vary, of course, but when a student's writing does not succeed with its intended reader, as with that engineering instructor who condemned the student's paper because the point was not immediately obvious to that reader, the student has not attended appropriately to the audience. This does not mean that the problem automatically lies with the writer because it may be that the student was not appropriately made aware of various genre and instructor guidelines or that his first-year composition course had not made him aware of differences among audiences. But nevertheless, that paper for that teacher in that class was not a piece of successful writing. I also do not mean that every genre has tight, uniform standards or that all engineering faculty want concise documents that boil down the prose to its essence. However, I have met with students writing papers for many fields whose instructors had impressed upon them the need to be concise. But I have also worked with students whose writing met the standard of conciseness but were writing for faculty who found some students' writing too elliptical, too tightly packed. One such instructor wanted his students to be able to write for the business world where, from his experience with outside consulting, a different, more relaxed tone prevails, despite the added verbiage this might cause. (As I found out in a conversation with this faculty member who encouraged informality, "thou shalt not use passive voice" should be the eleventh commandment. He had clearly drunk from the fountain of Strunk and White.) In the responses Susan Schorn received from colleagues at her institution, she notes that an instructor in the School of Business at her university shares this emphasis on audience: "If I had to pick one thing that separates adult-level writing from adolescent-level writing, it is the ability to reflect the needs of the audience in your writing. To be able to empathize with the reader and present the material in a way they can best receive and comprehend it" (336). Further on in her response, the Business School instructor notes that this includes "[leaving] behind the self-centered focus of youth" (Schorn 336).

The literature of composition is filled with references to the need for writers to move beyond writing for themselves, and composition texts explain and explain the need for audience awareness. And the Writing Program Administrators Outcomes Statement includes the ability to respond to the needs of different audiences (Council). But for some students, this simply does not register or is not meaningful in any useful way, does not seem as urgent as getting the commas in the right place or avoiding fragments or getting the thesis statement in the first paragraph. If so, the student is not yet able to produce college-level writing. The variety of audiences out there is not only real in academia (as the literature of writing-across-the-curriculum documents), it is also critically important when writers address the basic prewriting/planning questions such as "who am I writing to?" "why?" and "what do they need to know?" The answers to these questions will determine whether that writer "leaves behind the self-centered focus of youth" that the Business School instructor in Schorn's institution sees as a defining criterion of adult-level writing. This move from the self-centered focus of youth, however, may not be just confined to youth. When Linda Flower introduced the powerful concept of writer-based and reader-based prose, she invited us to look deep into our own composing processes, as well as our students', to see what writer-based prose is, how it appears on paper, and what we can do to move the writer to reader-based prose.

Flower begins with a question: "[W]hy do papers that do express what the writer meant (to his or her own satisfaction) often fail to communicate the same meaning to a reader?" (19). She continues: "[E]ffective writers do not simply *express* thought but *transform* it in certain complex but describable ways for the needs of the reader" (19). We see here the movement that Flower describes. Writer-based prose is not merely inadequate prose but prose, possibly in its early states, that has not yet been transformed. Farther into her discussion of writer-based and reader-based prose, Flower reminds us that this earlier form of writing, writer-based prose, is common to us all, prose that she notes is "a major and familiar mode of expression which we all use from time to time," characterized by "features of structure, function, and style. Furthermore, it shares many of these features with the modes of inner and egocentric speech described by Vygotsky and Piaget" (20). Inner speech may be that shorthand we use mentally, and it often shows up in student papers that are incompletely informative, often as a first draft being passed off as a finished paper. Lisa Ede calls such writing egocentric, but not writing that implies selfishness; rather, moving beyond one's self as the audience is a skill children must learn as they acquire the ability to decenter and begin to envision viewpoints of others (145). As a tutor, my task as a reader might be to ask the writer to clarify or expand on what is being discussed because I seem to be missing content that will explain an argument, a line of thought, or a connection between two ideas. We recognize some writer-based prose, then, when it is confusing, not completely developed, or lacking certain parts of an analysis or even a description that we, as intended readers, need in order to understand and move forward. When I turn to a writer and ask what was meant at the point of my confusion, that writer may stop and verbally fill in the blanks needed for me to proceed. Then, we need only look back at the paper to see that the missing information may have been in the writer's mind but not on the paper. In short, the writer was writing to himself or herself until a reader stopped him or her to indicate what is missing. If the writer fills in the blanks with the awareness of what the reader needs, he or she is on the way to transforming the paper into *reader-based* prose. Sayanti Ganguly, a writing center tutor experiencing the incompleteness that writer-based prose causes, describes her pedagogy in action as she works with students:

> When I come across sentences and paragraphs that are unclear because of word choice, word order, or simply because they are too brief, I ask students to tell me what they mean. In explaining, the student usually talks about the idea he/she is trying to convey in much greater detail. They use three sentences to explain what they have said cryptically in one. (11)

Flower's concept of writer-based and reader-based prose was widely acknowledged after her 1979 article in *College English,* but it has tended to fall off our agendas or awareness of how to fold it into our thinking about college-level writing, despite Flower's description of writer-based prose as "the source of some of the most common and pervasive problems in academic and professional writing" (19). How then can we unpack this complex notion of writer-based prose caused by lack of awareness of audience needs? What are the characteristics of this use of language that Vygotsky calls "inner speech"? When we can recognize it, we are on our way to being able to distinguish it from reader-based prose, which is a major characteristic of college-level writing. One feature of writer-based prose, in Flower's taxonomy, is that it is highly elliptical, condensed, because we may not need to spell out who or what the subject is or perhaps even the context of the thought. "Not now" might be a bit of inner speech that, when expanded for someone else who does not share the thought or situation, might mean "I won't have time to make that phone call because I need to leave the house now." An instructor's response to a similar writer-based sentence or paragraph might well be "expand on this" or "tell me more" or "what does this mean?" or "please explain" or simply "confusing." From a tutor's perspective, when I met with a student whose writer-based prose contained such instructor responses, I found that some students needed help in realizing that a reader would need such explanation. Good writers are more likely to come to the writing center to ask a tutor to read a draft and to answer the writer's question: "Does this make sense?" or "Do you get what I'm trying to say?" In that case, the writer already recognizes the need to transform the prose but is not sure if sufficient transformation has taken place. Elliptical writing, however, is not the only cause of lack of development in a paper. Some students do not know what else to add to a paper that is supposed to be 500 words but is only 425. That is more likely not writer-based or elliptical writing; instead, the writer may need invention strategies, though Theodore Clevinger views audience analysis as inherently a heuristic procedure (qtd. in Ede 142). Certainly I have used audience analysis that way in tutorials when I ask not "What else can you say here?" but instead assume the role of the intended reader and ask "Why are you telling me this?" or some other reader question to turn the writer's attention to my need to know why I should be reading some sentence or paragraph or paper.

A second characteristic of writer-based prose, as Flower teases out its elements, is that it uses words "saturated with sense"(21), words that do not necessarily carry their public meanings. Again, we are back to private or idiosyncratic language, language laden with connotations in the writer's mind that are not publicly shared. For example, a student with whom I worked in a tutorial began an *issue paper* (that is, not a research paper but a statement of the writer's opinion on some issue) with the following:

> Dodgers really tick me off. It seems that these people in society today are the ones that get all of the benefits. This is a huge problem, not only because they are not productive for America but they are making the productive people in society less productive.

It seems that *dodgers* in that writer's mind are the people who live on welfare and dodge working. Or maybe they are the people who slip through various cracks and don't pay taxes or get free health care. Or maybe *dodgers* encompasses more in that student's mind. I never was able to understand fully what that word meant to that writer. Nor was the writer sympathetic to my need to understand the private use of this word. Other examples are those words that call up memories, smells, contexts in one person's mind that are not universally shared. *Grandmother* for some recalls a lovely lady who always had a home-baked pie in the kitchen; for others, it's a sick, frail person whom it was difficult to talk to. (I cite this example because of a tutorial with a student who was writing about divorce and its repercussions. One of the effects of a divorce discussed in the paper was that some children must then live with grandparents. For that writer, this was not a positive outcome, but that was not evident in the writing. As a reader, I could not tell whether that result was intended as a problem caused by divorce or some compensation for the upheaval in a child's life.) And here, we are back to the slipperiness of language. And sometimes the this-is-what-I-mean word choice can lead to lack of specificity. Endless science lab reports were carried into our writing lab with vague phrases such as the "hot liquid" listed as the cause of a synthetic coating to crack. The instructor notation in such a case is "how hot? Be precise."

The third characteristic of writer-based prose, as described by Flower, is the absence of logical and causal relations, the lack of transitions:

> In experiments with children's use of logical-causal connectives such as *because*, *therefore*, and *although*, Piaget found that children have difficulty managing such relationships and in spontaneous speech will substitute a non-logical, non-causal connective such as *then*. Piaget described this strategy for relating things as *juxtaposition*: "the cognitive tendency simply to link (juxtapose) one thought element to another, rather than to tie them together by some causal or logical relation." (21)

We are all familiar with the disconnect or lack of logical flow of ideas caused by lack of transitions in a piece of writing. And sometimes, writers who have not explored in their own minds how or why sentence B follows after sentence A will disguise the lack of logical connection with sentences strung together with *and* or, as Piaget noted, with *then*.

Such are some characteristics of writer-based prose, writing that has not been transformed into prose that indicates awareness of audience. The problems that can result from this elliptical, private writing are familiar to us all. One such difficulty is a lack of organization in a writer's paper because, as Flower explains, "it is the record and the working of his own verbal thought . . . the associative, narrative path of the writer's own confrontation with her subject" (19–20). Some of us might call this kind of narrative a *mind dump*, that is, putting into words all that spills from the writer's mind as he or she thinks about it. Research papers, lab reports, proposals that have not been transformed into *reader-based* prose often have this sort of narrative, tracing the path of what the writer did, what problems she encountered, how she overcame them, and so on. These are narratives of progress, usually reported in the chronological order of what happened or how the writer got to the result, thesis, or information. These "home movies of the writer's mind" (Flower 25) often contain endless uses of "I found" or "I realized" or "so then I tried to" or "then I found." There is, of course, the writer's desire to share with readers all that he or she went through to get to the discovery or result (particularly prevalent in papers that required some research). But again, that's a lack of reader consciousness, a lack of awareness that the reader may not really care about the path to the point, only what the point, outcome, or result is. As a tutor, I have tried as gently as I could to ask writers whose papers are just these narratives of their process or path why they are telling me all that. Some writers acknowledge the desire to show how hard they worked, but other writers do not easily see why the narrative should not dominate the paper.

There are also grammatical problems that result from lack of awareness of what information readers need. Ambiguous pronoun references are usually not ambiguous for the writer when writing for himself or herself; fragments might result when a thought trails off in the writer's mind or is merely the detached phrase or dependent clause that follows the previous sentence. Textbooks invoke the need to gain distance from a piece of writing so that the writer can see what revisions may be needed for the reader, but that assumes an easy transition to a reader stance, an understanding or ability to recognize what readers will need. Sentences drained of any internal punctuation can reflect the writer's ability to decode for himself or herself what he or she has written, without realizing how to chunk the information for the reader.

Lest we get carried away with condemning writer-based prose as mere problem-ridden discourse, Flower happily notes that writer-based prose "is not a composite of errors or a mistake that should be scrapped. Instead, it is a half-way place for many writers" (37) before the needed transformation into reader-based prose has taken place. However, we are still left with the question of who the reader is. The literature of composition has recognized to various degrees the fiction behind the notion of a knowable audience. Beginning with Walter Ong's seminal essay demonstrating that the audience a writer constructs is a fiction, scholars have explored the implications and nature of this fictional audience. As Fred Pfister and Joanne Petrick point out, fictionalizing an audience is an act of constructing in the imagination a replica of the readers who actually exist out there in the world (213–14). Lisa Ede and Andrea Lunsford, in an effort to move away from any simplified conception of audience, distinguish two different audiences a writer might envision: the audience addressed, which emphasizes a real audience out there who can be observed and analyzed (the audience that Ede and Lunsford see as privileged by Pfister and Petrick), and the audience invoked, the audience writers construct because they cannot know the reality of who is out there. This audience that is invoked is a created fiction in which writers indicate the role they want readers to adopt in responding to text. Readers, then, cannot simply invoke some idiosyncratic need and deem prose less than college level if, for some personal reason or bias, the writing is unclear or inappropriate. By noting that college-level writing is writing that is appropriate for its intended audience, we have to expand the concept of audience or reader to include the fictionalized aspect as well.

But, just to muddy up the waters even further, there is yet one more aspect of audience as a factor in determining if writing meets college-level standards, and that is to recognize the growing complexity of audiences in academia and beyond. Today, the transformation that Flower notes as needed for text to become public is far more complex, given the ever-growing numbers of students with diverse cultural backgrounds and/or students whose first language is not English. Whereas a more homogeneous audience might once have been a construct to work with, the diversity of cultures, primary languages of readers, even the diverse and constantly changing world of business and commerce, would ask a reasonably competent writer to rise to the sophisticated level of being able to write for discourse communities that college writers have little knowledge of. But if we do not ask that writers be able to recognize all the various facets of diversity that exist, student writers should still exhibit some awareness of diverse audiences other than those who share the writer's beliefs and background. As students progress through their college education, they can be expected to grow in awareness so that what is expected of a first-year college writer is less than what is expected of a graduating senior. For example, a first-year composition student who strongly defends the need to halt immigration to the United States should show some recognition of the benefits of immigration, some awareness that there are opposing views that should be accounted for. Thus, students writing argumentation papers should be learning how to seek common ground but should be excused from not envisioning all the complexities of various groups who are concerned with immigration. Later in the student's college career, that recognition (we hope) will grow and deepen. So, college-level writing needs to show maturation from year to year as students progress through their academic career, a fact that the Outcomes Statement of the Council of Writing Program Administrators also emphasizes when it notes that as students move beyond first-year composition courses, their "abilities not only diversify along disciplinary and professional lines but also move into whole new levels where expected outcomes expand, multiply, and diverge" (Council).

If audience awareness should be a major topic in composition pedagogy, we will have to confront the question of how to teach it. Lisa Ede is not sure how teachers can develop audience awareness (147), while Linda Flower and John Hayes suggest creating real assignments with real audiences with real needs (qtd. in Ede 147). Barry Kroll offers three views of audience and examines the theoretical and pedagogical implications (172). But even with strong pedagogy to help writers make that necessary transformation from writer-based to reader-based prose, we should recognize that audience awareness for some students will not quickly develop beyond writing for the teacher. But instructors at all levels of academia who assign writing in their classes can assist in this by providing students with clear descriptions of who the intended audience is and what they need in order to find the writing effective and appropriate.

And, finally, we return to a question that must still nag at us. If we can't specify standards that allow for divergence of programs, goals, and so on, and writing program administrators talk in terms of outcomes, how do we recognize college-level writing? If I have made a sufficient argument for the importance of audience and how it affects so much of the quality of a written document, then one criterion might be any permutation of a set of questions to ask a reader how he or she is positioned to be the reader of that document. Such a reader can ask, "Am I the appropriate reader of this paper? If so, does the writing make sense? Is it clear? Do I need more information? Do I find it free of distracting surface errors?" When the reader is the appropriate reader, given the complexity of that term, and finds the writing satisfactory in such terms, then perhaps we might have some confidence in considering that we have begun to identify college-level writing.

Works Cited

Council of Writing Program Administrators. "WPA Outcomes Statement for First-Year Composition." Nov. 2003. 15 Oct. 2004 <http://wpacouncil.org/positions/outcomes.html>.

Ede, Lisa. "Audience: An Introduction to Research." *College Composition and Communication* 35.2 (1984): 140–54.

Ede, Lisa, and Andrea Lunsford. "Audience Addressed/Audience Invoked: The Role of Audience in Composition." *College Composition and Communication* 35.2 (1984): 155–71.

Ganguly, Sayanti. "Learning through Trial and Error: Working with ESL Students at the Writing Center." *Writing Lab Newsletter* 29.2 (2004): 10–12.

Flower, Linda. "Writer-Based Prose: A Cognitive Basis for Problems in Writing." *College English* 41.1 (1979): 19–37.

Jacobellis v. Ohio. No. 378 U.S. 184. Supreme Court of the United States 22 June 1984.

Knodt, Ellen Andrews. "What Is College Writing For?" *What Is "College-Level" Writing?* Ed. Patrick Sullivan and Howard Tinberg. Urbana, IL: NCTE, 2006. 146–57.

Kroll, Barry. "Writing for Readers: Three Perspectives on Audience." *College Composition and Communication* 35.2 (1984): 172–85.

Lunsford, Ronald F. "From Attitude to Aptitude: Assuming the Stance of a College Writer." *What Is "College-Level" Writing?* Ed. Patrick Sullivan and Howard Tinberg. Urbana, IL: NCTE, 2006. 178–98.

Ong, Walter J., SJ. "The Writer's Audience Is Always a Fiction." *Proceedings of the Modern Language Association* 90 (1975): 9–21.

Pfister, Fred R., and Joanne F. Petrick. "A Heuristic Model for Creating a Writer's Audience." *College Composition and Communication* 31.2 (1980): 213–20.

Schorn, Susan E. "A Lot Like Us, but More So: Listening to Writing Faculty Across the Curriculum." *What Is "College-Level" Writing?* Ed. Patrick Sullivan and Howard Tinberg. Urbana, IL: NCTE, 2006. 330–40.

Sullivan, Patrick. "What Is 'College-Level' Writing? *Teaching English in the Two-Year College* 30.4 (2003): 374–90.

Vygotsky, Lev. "The Genetic Roots of Thought and Speech." *Thought and Language*. Ed. and trans. Alex Kozulin. Cambridge, MA: MIT P, 1986. 94.

Chapter Ten

It's Not the High School Teachers' Fault: An Alternative to the Blame Game

Peter Kittle
California State University, Chico

The question posed by this volume's title, taken from Patrick Sullivan's thoughtful essay included in this book, is one that is manifestly at issue within the profession of teaching writing. I often encounter colleagues, at my own university and beyond, who lament the poor writing of incoming college students. Almost inevitably, an attempt to assign responsibility for this apparent deficit ensues. College faculty assume high school teachers aren't doing their jobs; high school teachers complain that middle schools don't prepare students adequately; middle schools wish elementary schools did a better job; elementary schools decry the family situations that provide too many students with a literacy-poor start to life. My own career history as a high school English teacher (1987–1992), graduate student composition instructor (1993–1998), assistant (now associate) professor of English (1998–present), and writing project teacher-consultant (2000–present) has given me ample opportunity to see this blame game played out at all educational levels. But it is a game I choose not to play. Rather than be defensive and accusatory, I would like to be descriptive of my continually evolving perceptions and representations of what constitutes college-level writing, and in the process examine the pedagogical implications of that evolution. How did my sense of what it means to write at the college level develop? What light does that evolution shed on issues surrounding the teaching of college preparatory writing at the high school level? What kinds of practical steps can be taken to facilitate more shared assumptions about the composition pedagogy among writing teachers at high schools, colleges, and universities? It is my hope that answering these questions will be more productive than trying to lay blame at anyone's door.

When I began to teach English at Kelso High School, the centerpiece of a small lumber-mill city in southwest Washington, I found the prospect of teaching writing daunting. I was a successful writer myself, if the grades in my college English courses were any indication, but I discovered that the ability to write did not translate into the ability to teach writing. The curriculum in my school specified separate courses in literature and composition at each grade level, with the composition courses devoted to teaching in the *modes* paradigm: informational, comparison/contrast, definition, persuasive, and research essays. I duly followed the curricular materials provided, but never felt that my students were particularly engaged in the writing tasks they were given. On those occasions when students did seem engaged, it was usually due to having the opportunity to argue about extremely polarized issues like abortion or gun control—topics that aren't particularly amenable to reasoned discourse due to a lack of shared underlying assumptions.

It wasn't as though my undergraduate major had neglected to anticipate that I would one day need to teach writing; in fact, I had taken a class specifically devoted to the teaching of writing. Taught by Suzanne Clark at Oregon State University in the mid-1980s, the course provided smart, provocative readings in the theories that inform writing instruction (*Teaching Writing: Essays from the Bay Area Writing Project* and Erika Lindemann's *A Rhetoric for Writing Teachers* both remain prominent in my memory). While the intent of the class was to help me understand effective practices in composition pedagogy, its actual impact on me was more personal than pragmatic: I learned about my own writing processes, which was revelatory enough in its own right. It wasn't until I was in my own classroom, facing those small-town high schoolers, that I began to wish that I had been better able to contextualize the rest of that writing course's content.

While laboring under the constraints of the high school classroom—with its large class sizes, limited time, and exhausting workload—I found few opportunities to revisit the ideas from Professor Clark's course. Instead, I fell back on the resources at hand: the textbooks adopted by the school, the quick advice of colleagues, and my own memories of what writing assignments in high school were like. Still, I mostly floundered at teaching writing, especially when it was isolated from literature. This was an idea shared by my colleagues; by the time I left Kelso High, we had transformed English coursework into year-long courses that covered both literature and composition. At the time, we made the argument—and it's a compelling one—that it's more sensible to teach the complementary literacy skills of reading and writing together. And I'm sure that we believed it. But I think that, for me, part of what made the change in curriculum attractive was that the teaching of writing in isolation, which daunted me, would disappear, and the already-overflowing literature curriculum would easily spread to fit the larger timeline. And because most English teachers love literature (myself included), the pushing aside of non-literature-based writing assignments was more than palatable.

In practicality, then, this change of curriculum allowed me to continue to offer students somewhat watered-down versions of the kinds of writing I was asked to produce in college English courses. Character analyses, explications of themes, authorial stylistic techniques—these were the subjects I asked students to address in their writing. To maintain some connection to the old modes, I asked students to compare and contrast John Knowles's novel *A Separate Peace* and the then-recent film *Dead Poets Society*. But my assignments, as a whole, followed what Margot Soven (borrowing from Rexford Brown) has called the "contract of vagueness," wherein English teachers provide fuzzy directions for writing, and students accept the situation because they implicitly understand that unclear assignment parameters are part of the culture of English classes (135–36). But even if I was less than confident about my specific writing pedagogy, I nonetheless believed that I was duly preparing students for college writing. In reality, I was propounding some well-worn and firmly entrenched myths about college-level writing.

One of the most common of these myths involved correctness: "College professors," I would intone to my students, "will give you an F if you make more than three errors in a paper." This particular belief was widespread in my school; every English teacher used it as something of a cudgel to motivate students to proofread carefully. Somehow, the fact that neither I, nor anyone in my acquaintance, had ever received an F for reasons of correctness escaped our recollection. While always able to produce clean written work in compliance with the rules of standard English, I'm sure that typos, misreadings, and sloppy editing must have added up to at least three errors in a few of my college papers. But no Fs (and yes, I do know that that's a fragment).

Still, I faithfully followed this myth, all too often applying the archetypal red pen with liberal abandon. If I'm honest about it, I focused on error due to the fact that—as Patricia Dunn and Kenneth Lindblom compellingly assert—beyond observing that my students had committed surface errors in their writing, I didn't "know what else to tell them" (45). In fact, I'm certain that on more than one occasion, I overvalued papers with marginal insights simply because they were relatively error free. Some students even revised their work to make it less complex—filled with simple vocabulary and safe sentence structures—to assure that it had fewer errors. While this in itself was bad enough, what is worse is the mistaken impression that I'm certain many of my students gained from my instruction: clean presentation trumps smart, complex argument.

The second myth I freely propagated concerned form. I taught the five-paragraph essay to my students. I even had a variety of bright, colorful bulletin board themes devoted to this odd genre, perhaps most notably a large, laminated picture of a hamburger, with the buns representing the introduction and conclusion, and meat, cheese, and lettuce standing in for the three body paragraphs found in each five-paragraph essay. While I readily enough taught this form of writing, I honestly cannot say I looked forward to reading the student work with any relish. But I told my students, as well as myself, that this writing form would serve them well in college. I was a (willing) victim of what Mark Wiley has called the "pedagogical blindness" that goes hand-in-hand with formulaic writing instruction (61). The insistent focus on form made other, very important aspects of writing become, in practical terms, invisible to me.

I do not mean to downplay the role of either correctness or form here, both of which are indisputably important to clear writing. However, correctness and form attain meaning only through the purposeful communicating of important, relevant ideas. Why, then, did I teach writing in these ways, focusing on correctness and form to the detriment of more substantive issues? The answer lies in expedience. I taught the five-paragraph essay because it was easy to teach, not because I thought it was the best way to teach writing. I marked papers for grammatical errors because it was easy to see and circle those mistakes, not because they were the most important aspect of my students' writing. I admit this not with pride, but at least with honesty; expedience and efficiency matter tremendously when facing five classes a day, with over thirty students per class. If I had had better strategies for responding to student writing more productively, or (better still) for creating writing assignments that would lead to rigorous, interesting, and insightful student work, I hope that I would have employed them. But the fact was that I had only vague ideas about what was expected of students when they had to perform at college level, and even less-firm ideas of how to teach students to reach that level.

Despite my shortcomings in the field of teaching writing, I became an effective classroom practitioner during the five years I taught at Kelso High. I developed a professional teaching persona, able to maintain discipline, communicate efficiently, and establish meaningful rapport with students. In short, I had become confident in my abilities as a teacher. When I entered the PhD program at the University of Oregon in 1992, therefore, I actually felt affronted that I—with over 4,000 hours of classroom teaching under my belt—would have to be *trained* in teaching, including classroom apprentice work, before I could be assigned to teach first-year composition. In fact, I went so far as to appeal for a waiver from these requirements. As it turns out, the decision by Jim Crosswhite, then the director of composition, to deny my appeal was one of the best things that came from my graduate program. He did not question my ability to teach—the *how* of teaching—but wanted to ensure that the *what* of my teaching would be in keeping with the university composition program's philosophy.

That philosophy, based on the central tenets of John Gage's *The Shape of Reason*—namely, situating enthymeme-based inquiry within active, engaged classroom discourse communities—radically reshaped my own understanding of what constituted college-level writing. I suppose that the primary revelation involved my own renegotiation of the role of the teacher in a *discourse community* classroom. This model places primacy on the idea that "[s]tudents write at their best when they have something to say and someone to say it to" ("Program Philosophy"). The "someone" to whom the writing is addressed is not, importantly, the teacher alone; rather, it is the classroom community, whose values and assumptions have been shared and made explicit. In such a context, the teacher's role is decentered. Students address an audience of classmates who are well informed regarding the questions at issue within the essay. Course participants' ideas are written in response to what others have said—be they fellow students, the instructor, or a published writer. The writing produced by students was not expected to merely demonstrate compliance with mandates regarding form and correctness, but to represent focused inquiry into issues that the class had agreed can be answered in different ways by reasonable people.

The teacher in this college-level writing class was akin to a mentor, facilitating specific avenues of inquiry, guiding discussions and classroom activities in productive directions. For such a class to operate effectively, the students must be able and willing to take responsibility for engaging with the course materials and discussions. This, for me, was the primary difference in assumptions about writing education between college and high school. As a high school teacher, I found the institutional context to privilege a pedagogy of compliance, wherein students were expected (and accustomed) to simply follow directions and do their best to meet the teacher's expectations. There was, in other words, a tacit understanding on the part of students (in the form of consent) that the teachers were in exclusive possession of academic power. The college writing classroom, on the other hand, resisted such a stance actively, often using as anchor readings texts that call into question traditional educational practices (e.g., excerpts from Freire's *Pedagogy of the Oppressed* or selected writings by John Dewey on democracy and education).

One of the interesting outcomes of my new position teaching college composition was the ability to see how the myths I had formerly spread affected students entering college. Often, students would produce, in response to a course assignment, a rather bland five-paragraph essay with few surface errors; they would then be particularly nonplussed to find less-than-complimentary feedback given to work that would likely have been praised by their high school teachers. Of course, this also gave me pause, since such students were only behaving in ways that I would have encouraged when I had been teaching high school. While I readily admit that my practices as a high school teacher were underinformed, I always felt confident that my teaching at that time was in keeping with something of an educational Hippocratic tenet: First, do no harm. Upon seeing the cognitive dissonance evident in students trying to seamlessly use the five-paragraph form in the college classroom, though, I had to rethink that confidence.

I want to pause here and clarify a couple of things I've said so far. First, I am not trying to write an academic version of evangelical transformation. A testimonial of conversion—"I was a blind, sinful high school teacher until I saw the light and became a born-again writing instructor"—is not my object. Such a perspective (aside from being simply unseemly to me) implies a highly judgmental attitude toward high school teachers, for whom I have deep respect. Second, I am not attempting to make a case that all high school teachers believe, behave, or teach the way I did, but I have spoken to enough teachers to know that my story is not unique, either. What I hope to be outlining instead is that two factors strongly affect the transition of writers from high school to college. First is that the circumstances and contexts of high school and college writing classes are very different, and those circumstances and contexts strongly impact pedagogy. Second, the avenues of communication between high school and college teachers of writing are not nearly as open as they should be. The effect of these two factors is widely differing sets of expectations among students, high school faculty, and college writing teachers.

While the pragmatist in me suspects that there is little to be done to minimize the difference in contexts of high school and college classrooms, my involvement in a number of collaborative programs helps me hold out hope for improving the sharing of knowledge among writing teachers at all levels. I have collaborated with local high school teachers through work with the Northern California Writing Project, as well as through California State University programs like the Collaborative Academic Preparation Initiative and the Early Assessment/Academic Preparation Programs (EAP/APP). In each of these experiences, I have learned much about the curriculum and practices of secondary teachers in my area, and the insights shared by those teachers have productively informed my own practices as a university teacher. Creating learning partnerships between college and high school, with genuine give and take on each side, is in my view imperative to minimizing the propagation of myths about college-level writing.

I have been fortunate enough to have forged just such a partnership with Rochelle Ramay, a colleague from the Northern California Writing Project who chairs the English Department at Corning High School. Ramay and I have team-taught professional development institutes ranging from 25 to 120 hours throughout northern California. Focusing on academic reading and writing in high school, these institutes have allowed Ramay and me to read professional books together, synthesize various perspectives into some coherent theoretical tenets, and implement the same ideas—albeit with some variance to account for different populations and abilities—within our respective classes. There is no hierarchy or posturing in our partnership; we are simply two reflective, inquisitive teachers who collaborate on issues in teaching writing, and share our findings with others (through inservices, institutes, conference presentations, and articles). We are, through our work together, both better able to understand the expectations and constraints put upon writers at the high school and college levels.

While a one-to-one partnership such as mine with Ramay is ideal, it is far from being easily replicated en masse. But other, more widespread programs are making the attempt to bridge the gaps between high school and college. The EAP/APP initiative, sponsored by the Chancellor's Office of the California State University (CSU), seeks out potential CSU students and assesses their readiness for college writing. Using an augmented set of questions on a standardized test administered during the junior year of high school, the early assessment portion identifies specific students who would benefit from reading and writing instruction tailored especially to smooth the transition from high school to college.

The creation of the curriculum for that transition period came out of the CSU Task Force on 12th Grade Expository Reading and Writing, of which I was a member. Comprised of CSU faculty from seven of the university's campuses (representing composition, reading, and English education), as well as high school teachers and administrators, the task force began by drawing connections among three key documents: the *Reading/Language Arts Framework for California Public Schools*, which outlines content standards and pedagogies for English; Harrington's *Focus on English*, which describes the English Placement Test taken by incoming CSU freshmen; and *Academic Literacy: A Statement of Competencies Expected of Students Entering California's Public Colleges and Universities*, a text created by a joint committee of faculty from community college, CSU, and University of California campuses. The former two emphasize discrete skills that are to be mastered and measured, while the latter focuses instead upon "habits of mind" shared by students who succeed in higher education.

As we discussed ways of articulating these documents' shared characteristics, a basic template emerged for creating assignment sequences that began with reading and ended with writing. What we tried to do was ensure that the skills in reading and writing outlined by the standards (both for public school and for college admission) were wedded, with explicit scaffolding, to the academic dispositions described in the *Academic Literacy* document. For instance, the habit of mind described as "read[ing] with awareness of self and others" may be rightly expected of students, but is unlikely to be directly taught. The task force template ensures that such metacognitive aspects of reading and writing, which are usually invisible to the outside observer but are integral to academic habits of mind, become specific targets of pedagogy. With strategies such as using different highlighter colors to identify passages that would be important to a variety of readers, the idea of reading with "awareness of self and others" becomes an intellectual practice, not just an ideal abstraction.

While the task force has created a curriculum that, we believe, will help California's students make it through the transitional period from high school to college, it will be for naught if it is not implemented. And this, really, is the sticking point. The CSU Chancellor's Office has committed to providing professional training in the new curriculum to all twelfth-grade English teachers in the state, in the form of three days of training conducted by teams of CSU and high school faculty. At the time of this writing, these trainings have only just begun. But while I hold out hope for their success, I am cautious about showing real optimism. This is because, as I outlined above, I firmly believe in the need for genuine, long-term partnerships between public school and college teachers. As a high school teacher, I experienced many afternoon workshops, day-long inservices, and other one-shot professional development scenarios that I found interesting and provocative, but that in the end did not particularly impact my actual teaching practices. Real change takes time—sometimes very significant quantities of time, carefully structured to allow for experiencing and discussing new ideas, experimenting, and reflecting on how those new ideas can be meaningfully incorporated into already-existing curricular frameworks. I fear that, without being able to establish the kinds of professional relationships that are predicated on mutual respect for teaching abilities, subject matter knowledge, and academic values, any ideas being propounded by college writing teachers will be seen as just another mandate from above.

What needs to be kept in the forefront of discussions surrounding contentious ideas—including what constitutes college-level writing—are the concerns shared by the interested parties at all levels. Writing teachers need to avoid assigning blame for the level of student work, and instead collaboratively describe what we do, why we do it, what our struggles are, and how we might serve our students better. As a university instructor, of course I care about having well-prepared students enter my institution.

But when I think about literacy education in a more global manner, I care more that all students—college bound or not—are prepared to read and write critically and competently enough to be active, informed citizens. I suspect that most teachers of writing, at whatever educational level, feel the same way. The challenge that faces us in easing the transition from high school to college, then, involves finding, establishing, and maintaining the goals for writing shared by faculty at secondary and postsecondary institutions. Such collaboration would require genuine change, not just on the part of individual high school and college faculty but also on the institutional structures that limit collaboration. My overwhelmingly positive work with the Writing Project, where long-term partnerships are the norm rather than the exception, reinforces my belief that the potential for lasting, far-reaching rewards make such reformative efforts worthwhile.

Works Cited

Academic Literacy: A Statement of Competencies Expected of Students Entering California's Public Colleges and Universities. Sacramento: Intersegmental Committee of the Academic Senates, 2002.

Dead Poets Society. Dir. Peter Weir. Silver Screen Partners IV. 1989.

Dewey, John. "Between Traditional and Progressive Education." *Reading Our Histories, Understanding Our Cultures: A Sequenced Approach to Thinking, Reading, and Writing*. Ed. Kathleen McCormick. Boston: Longman, 1999. 298–304.

Dunn, Patricia, and Kenneth Lindblom. "Why Revitalize Grammar?" *English Journal* 92.3 (2003): 43–50.

Freire, Paulo. *Pedagogy of the Oppressed*. Trans. Myra Bergman Ramos. New York: Continuum, 1992.

Gage, John. *The Shape of Reason: Argumentative Writing in College*. 4th ed. New York: Pearson/Longman, 2006.

Harrington, Mary Kay. *Focus on English*. Long Beach: The California State University Office of the Chancellor, 2002.

Knowles, John. *A Separate Peace*. New York: Bantam Books, 1988.

Lindemann, Erika. *A Rhetoric for Writing Teachers*. New York: Oxford UP, 1982.

"Program Philosophy: The Composition Program at the University of Oregon." University of Oregon. 17 July 2004 <http://darkwing.uoregon.edu/~uocomp/philosophy.htm>.

Reading/Language Arts Framework for California Public Schools, Kindergarten through Grade Twelve. Sacramento: California Department of Education, 1999.

Soven, Margot. *Teaching Writing in Middle and Secondary Schools: Theory, Research, and Practice*. Boston: Allyn and Bacon, 1998.

Sullivan, Patrick. "An Essential Question: What Is 'College-Level' Writing?" *What Is "College-Level" Writing?* Ed. Patrick Sullivan and Howard Tinberg. Urbana, IL: NCTE, 2006. 1–28.

Teaching Writing: Essays from the Bay Area Writing Project. Ed. Gerald Camp. Portsmouth, NH: Boynton/Cook, 1982.

Wiley, Mark. "The Popularity of Formulaic Writing (and Why We Need to Resist)." *English Journal* 90.1 (2000): 61–67.

Chapter Eleven

What Is College Writing For?

Ellen Andrews Knodt
Penn State Abington

Patrick Sullivan, one of the editors of this volume, notes that there is often broad disagreement among English faculty evaluating student papers and asks an excellent question: "What is college-level writing?" As he participated in a workshop attended by a number of English faculty from different institutions, he explains,

> We discussed a variety of sample student essays at this session, for example, and the range of opinion about this work was extraordinarily varied. In one memorable case, the assessments about a particular essay ranged from A-quality, college-level work ("This is definitely college-level writing. It is very well organized, and there are no spelling, grammar, or punctuation errors. I would love to get a paper like this from one of my students") to F ("This is definitely *not* college-level writing. Although this essay is well organized, it contains no original, sustained analysis or thought. It's empty. There is no thoughtful engagement of ideas here"). (375)

To arrive at an answer to Sullivan's question, we first need to ask: What is college writing *for*? I suggest that the wide disparity in evaluation that Sullivan experienced stems in part from a wide disagreement among composition programs and faculty about the goals to be achieved in college writing programs. In recent years, many college writing programs have come to serve many purposes. Some orient first-year students to campuses, serving as foci for ethics training including discussions of diversity on campus, plagiarism and cheating, binge drinking, and proscribed sexual behavior such as stalking, date rape, and intolerance of gays. Other programs seek to shake students out of their complacency by introducing them to political and social movements with which they are not familiar or with which they might disagree. Some programs continue to emphasize current traditional rhetoric. And even within programs, individual faculty educated at different times and in different universities may have goals different from their fellow faculty. George Hillocks, Jr., vividly makes that case in his 1999 study *Ways of Thinking, Ways of Teaching.*

Acknowledging the difficulty of determining writing curricula, Edward White says:

> There is no professional consensus on the curriculum of writing courses, at any level. There is also no shortage of advice from researchers and practitioners; whatever approach to instruction an individual instructor might elect or inherit seems to have its prominent exemplars and promoters, and the profusion of textbooks is legendary. How can we arrange a sensible and useful syllabus in the face of so many theories, texts, research findings, pedagogical truisms, content suggestions, and methodologies? (419)

This is not to say that this variety of goals for writing programs is necessarily wrong, though some have argued that composition programs have been led away from their main mission of teaching writing to indulge the desire of college instructors to teach something else (see Hairston; Wallace and Wallace, "Readerless"). However, such variety may cause problems in assessment of outcomes across programs at colleges and universities and may pose complications for universities that accept many transfer students who may have completed their composition courses at institutions with far different writing programs. This essay will attempt to analyze the major types of college composition programs currently in use and to illustrate how the goals of such programs may affect assessment of outcomes for their students. While the types of programs discussed below are not the only curricular variations, they are the most common types of programs.

The Traditional Five-Paragraph Essay Program

Though one may not find compositionists to support this type of program, it is alive and well in American colleges and universities. A Google search produced dozens of college Web sites devoted to the five-paragraph essay or to its revised versions. Most instructors using this organizing principle acknowledge it as a formula but find it useful for beginning writers who have little sense of organization. They also point out that it is a quick way to organize an essay exam answer in history or psychology or other such courses. Programs using this approach often take their university service role very seriously, feeling that their main function is to prepare students to present information they have learned in an organized, coherent essay.

Such programs require students to do different types of work from, for example, a program at New York University described by Dombek and Herndon that defines college-level writing as being about creating something new, something original, a "hybrid kind of academic writing" that asks "writers to pose rigorous questions and speculate about multiple possible answers, analyze several texts at once, sustain complicated trains of thought, wrestle with contradiction and paradox, and develop new ideas" (4). As seen in Sullivan's example above, there is a fundamental disagreement over composition as conveying information in an organized way and composition as a creative process that produces new knowledge or insights. In one schema, a student's essay may be successful, but the same essay being evaluated under a different schema may not be deemed successful.

Students successfully completing one program may produce quite different texts from students completing another program, and assessment of such different texts may be problematic.

The Classical Rhetoric Program

Such programs are based on analysis of classical sources of rhetoric such as Plato and Aristotle, usually as a basis for analysis of contemporary essays. In their written work, students are expected to read, summarize, and apply classical rhetorical concepts to the contemporary essays they read. For an example of this approach, see Marvin Diogenes' "An Honors Course in First-Year Composition: Classical Rhetoric and Contemporary Writing." Students in such a program will be expected to learn and apply terms like *pathos*, *logos*, and *ethos*, among other concepts, which students in other programs may not be exposed to, at least in the same words. Admittedly, Diogenes' course is for honor students, but classical rhetoric curricula may be found in several texts and is taught at many traditional liberal arts institutions.

The Sociopolitical Program

Another variant program goal is making students more politically and socially aware. James Berlin has declared that the mission of a composition course is to "bring about more democratic and personally humane economic, social, and political arrangements" (116). One clear description of such a program comes from Karen Fitts and Alan France in "Advocacy and Resistance in the Writing Class: Working toward Stasis":

> Our politics are materialist-feminist, and they are central to our pedagogical and professional ethos. It is important to us, for example, that our teaching practices actively challenge the white, middle-class consensus that Americans can afford to ignore the poverty-strangling inner-city life, the general erosion of women's reproductive rights, and the growing ecological threat of Western technologies. . . . At the same time, as professors of rhetoric, we are also committed to open democratic forums, free expression of conflicting arguments, and an empathetic classroom environment for our students' apprenticeship in the public discourse of self-governance. (13–14)

In their discussion of class assignments, the authors explain that among other topics they ask students to investigate gender practices of other societies and to examine advertisements or other media representations of gender. Their analysis in the article of their students' papers from the course concentrates on students' "rhetorical strategies to avoid confronting" (17) certain issues, not on whether their students were more or less successful in explaining their views.

Again, one can see that a student successfully passing this course would have an entirely different background in terminology and technique from a student who had taken the classical rhetoric course described above. Would a transfer student from one institution understand what is expected of him or her in subsequent writing courses at the new institutions? Would the respective instructors be able to evaluate papers from each other's classes?

The Writing Across the Curriculum Program

Beginning in the 1970s, Writing Across the Curriculum (WAC) programs are sometimes housed in English departments and sometimes are campus-wide programs administered separately from English departments. Shared assumptions are that students need to learn to write in many college disciplines and that many (or all) members of the faculty need to be involved in creating writing opportunities for students. Students in such programs write reports, observations of experiments, summaries of readings, in addition to essays. Readings are often in many disciplines. Responsibility for teaching and grading a WAC course is often shared between an English faculty member and faculty from another discipline or is the sole responsibility of the English faculty but with curriculum decided on by multiple disciplines. WAC programs share a service emphasis with other service-oriented programs mentioned here.

Following the Boyer Commission recommendation in 1998 to link writing to coursework (V,1), Kerri Morris suggests that composition reform should remove the first-year writing course from the English department and place writing instruction in the hands of all faculty (120). Such a move has many implications, of course, but for composition students, this change might further fragment the goals of the course because now faculty from many disciplines with presumably even more varied notions of what college-level writing entails would be teaching the subject.

Students participating in a WAC program would have quite different writing backgrounds from students participating in several of the other programs discussed here. Their assignments would depend on the kinds of writing that faculty both inside and outside the English department feel is important to success at that institution.

The First-Year Orientation Program

This program sees first-year composition as an opportunity to reach all or most first-year students in order to introduce them to academic life. At the University of Wisconsin Oshkosh, Odyssey, a summer reading program, becomes the common subject matter of composition which places "the composition program directly in the service of the administration, so that its retention goals become the primary object for the first weeks of the class" (Helmers 91). Odyssey chooses one book as the focus of discussion for the first-year students in their writing course. Issues for such programs are the creation of a unified intellectual experience for entering students and focuses on the shared reading assignment as a way to engage students in academic discourse. Such programs are often unique to the particular institution both in the readings chosen and in the activities engaged.

The Professional Writing Program

Some institutions envision their composition programs as preparing students for the writing they will do *after* college. Donald Samson advocates teaching students to write "proposals, reports, letters, memos, resumes, briefing materials, speeches," etc. because "our function as writing instructors should be in part to prepare them to succeed in the writing they will have to do" (124–25). Samson's program emphasizes writing to provide information for different audiences rather than what he sees as writing for personal development or writing to prove what the students have learned (writing as testing). While some schools have business or technical writing courses that address Samson's goals, he feels that this professional approach to first-year composition would engage students more fully than what is currently offered on most campuses.

An Overview and a Practical Suggestion

While all of these programs have legitimate rationale for their approaches, especially within the context of their colleges and universities, they offer very different experiences. Students completing one such composition course (at one institution or even from one instructor) might approach a writing assignment at another institution or even a later course at the same institution in quite different ways. And a statewide assessment of college writing skills with students from multiple institutions would be even more problematic, leading to just the experience Patrick Sullivan describes in his opening essay.

So what are we to do? Do we want just one universal approach to composition? And if we did, what one might that be? It seems to me that a single approach is both unrealistic and undesirable. However, we might do a better job of talking to each other in our English or writing departments about what we are doing and why. We might also begin dialogues with institutions that our students transfer to or with institutions from whom we receive transfer students to discuss what we both think are the important writing experiences that our students should have. To aid in these dialogues both within and without our institutions, perhaps the Council of Writing Program Administrators (WPA) Outcomes Statement for First-Year Composition could serve as a template or touchstone for discussion. The Outcomes Statement does not dictate content of readings, types of assignments, or political approaches, but focuses on the kinds of writing experiences and skills that a broad spectrum of experts think are desirable:

> The Council of Writing Program Administrators adopted the following Outcomes Statement for First-Year Composition in April 2000. [I have included here the statements for composition classes only, not the advice to faculties in other programs and departments on how to extend this knowledge.]

Introduction

This statement describes the common knowledge, skills, and attitudes sought by first-year composition programs in American postsecondary education. To some extent, we seek to regularize what can be expected to be taught in first-year composition; to this end the document is not merely a compilation or summary of what currently takes place. Rather, the following statement articulates what composition teachers nationwide have learned from practice, research, and theory. This document intentionally defines only "outcomes," or types of results, and not "standards," or precise levels of achievement. The setting of standards should be left to specific institutions or specific groups of institutions. . . .

These statements describe only what we expect to find at the end of first-year composition, at most schools a required general education course or sequence of courses. As writers move beyond first-year composition, their writing abilities do not merely improve. Rather, students' abilities not only diversify along disciplinary and professional lines but also move into whole new levels where expected outcomes expand, multiply, and diverge. For this reason, each statement of outcomes for first-year composition is followed by suggestions for further work that builds on these outcomes.

Rhetorical Knowledge

By the end of first year composition, students should

- Focus on a purpose
- Respond to the needs of different audiences
- Respond appropriately to different kinds of rhetorical situations
- Use conventions of format and structure appropriate to the rhetorical situation
- Adopt appropriate voice, tone, and level of formality
- Understand how genres shape reading and writing
- Write in several genres

Critical Thinking, Reading, and Writing

By the end of first year composition, students should

- Use writing and reading for inquiry, learning, thinking, and communicating

- Understand a writing assignment as a series of tasks, including finding, evaluating, analyzing, and synthesizing appropriate primary and secondary sources
- Integrate their own ideas with those of others
- Understand the relationships among language, knowledge, and power

Processes

By the end of first year composition, students should

- Be aware that it usually takes multiple drafts to create and complete a successful text
- Develop flexible strategies for generating, revising, editing, and proof-reading
- Understand writing as an open process that permits writers to use later invention and re-thinking to revise their work
- Understand the collaborative and social aspects of writing processes
- Learn to critique their own and others' works
- Learn to balance the advantages of relying on others with the responsibility of doing their part
- Use a variety of technologies to address a range of audiences

Knowledge of Conventions

By the end of first year composition, students should

- Learn common formats for different kinds of texts
- Develop knowledge of genre conventions ranging from structure and paragraphing to tone and mechanics
- Practice appropriate means of documenting their work
- Control such surface features as syntax, grammar, punctuation, and spelling

These outcomes may seem unreachable in their entirety for many students in many programs, but I suggest that as departments and institutions discuss their approaches to composition as compared to this list of outcomes, they may clarify their priorities and may reach some consensus as a department on their goals for their students. (Council)

Conclusion

As I see it, departments could use the WPA Outcomes Statement for First-Year Composition as a checklist to ascertain whether their departmental program is meeting the needs of their students, regardless of the overall approach the department had decided to follow. For example, a department following a professional writing approach could ensure that the proposals, reports, and speeches that students write are sufficiently complex to challenge students' rhetorical knowledge by requiring them to write for different audiences, vary the formality and tone of their content depending on audience and situation, and understand the different purposes of their communication. Similarly, students using a professional writing approach should have experiences leading to the outcomes of critical thinking, reading, and writing, understanding writing processes and common conventions of writing. Such a course can succeed through peer group discussions, drafting and revising written work, integrating information into texts, and other classwork. Activities and assignments can be structured to accomplish most, if not all, of the WPA goals within each department's approach.

There still remains the difficulty a student may have transferring from one college's writing program to another that may use quite different readings and writing assignments. For example, let us imagine a student moving from a program in which a student writes a report analyzing moving a factory to a country outside the United States and the resultant implications for a business and a community to a program in which a student is expected to analyze the different realities of the two sisters in Alice Walker's story "Everyday Use." If, however, the instructors in each program are making students conscious of the WPA outcomes and are explaining students' writing tasks in similar terms, students will have a much easier time adapting their writing to meet these new writing situations. Perhaps our biggest failure in helping students and colleagues to understand what is college-level writing is our failure to be explicit in what we seek.

Works Cited

Berlin, James A. *Rhetorics, Poetics, and Cultures: Refiguring College English Studies*. Urbana, IL: NCTE, 1996.

The Boyer Commission on Educating Undergraduates in the Research University. *Reinventing Undergraduate Education: A Blueprint for America's Research Universities*. 24 April 1998 <http://naples.cc.sunysb.edu/Pres/boyer.nsf/>.

Council of Writing Program Administrators (WPA). *WPA Outcomes Statement for First-Year Composition*. April 2000. 19 July 2006 <http://wpacouncil.org/positions/html>.

Diogenes, Marvin. "An Honors Course in First-Year Composition: Classical Rhetoric and Contemporary Writing." *Strategies for Teaching First-Year Composition*. Ed. Duane Roen et al. Urbana, IL: NCTE, 2002.114–32.

Dombek, Kristen, and Scott Herndon. *Critical Passages: Teaching the Transition to College Composition*. New York: Teachers College P, 2004.

Fitts, Karen, and Alan France. "Advocacy and Resistance in the Writing Class: Working toward Stasis." *Pedagogy in the Age of Politics: Writing and Reading (in) the Academy*. Ed. Patricia Sullivan and Donna Qualley. Urbana, IL: NCTE, 1994. 13–24.

Hairston, Maxine. "Diversity, Ideology, and Teaching Writing." *College Composition and Communication* 43 (1992): 179–93.

Helmers, Marguerite. "Constructing Bridges between High School and College Writing." *Strategies for Teaching First-Year Composition*. Ed. Duane Roen, et al. Urbana, IL: NCTE, 2002. 89–96.

Hillocks, George, Jr. *Ways of Thinking, Ways of Teaching*. New York: Teachers College P, 1999.

Morris, Kerri. "The Service Myth: Why Freshman Composition Doesn't Serve 'Us' or 'Them.'" *Reforming College Composition: Writing the Wrongs*. Ed. Ray Wallace, Alan Jackson, and Susan Lewis Wallace. Westport, CT: Greenwood, 2000. 113–22.

Samson, Donald. "Preparing Composition Students for Writing in Their Careers." *Reforming College Composition: Writing the Wrongs*. Ed. Ray Wallace, Alan Jackson, and Susan Lewis Wallace. Westport, CT: Greenwood, 2000. 123–36.

Sullivan, Patrick. "What Is 'College-Level' Writing?" *Teaching English in the Two-Year College*. 30.4 (2003): 374–90.

Walker, Alice. "Everyday Use." *In Love and Trouble: Stories of Black Women*. New York: Harcourt Brace Jovanovich, 1973. 47–59.

Wallace, Ray, and Susan Lewis Wallace. "Readerless Writers: College Composition's Misreading and Misteaching of Entering Students." *Reforming College Composition: Writing the Wrongs*. Ed. Ray Wallace, Alan Jackson, and Susan Lewis Wallace. Westport, CT: Greenwood, 2000. 79–98.

Wallace, Ray, Alan Jackson, and Susan Lewis Wallace, eds. *Reforming College Composition: Writing the Wrongs*. Westport, CT: Greenwood, 2000.

White, Edward M. "Philosophical Statement." *Twelve Readers Reading: Responding to College Student Writing*. Ed. Richard Straub and Ronald Lunsford. Cresskill, NJ: Hampton, 1995: 419–21.

Chapter Twelve

Scripting Writing Across Campuses: Writing Standards and Student Representations

Cynthia Lewiecki-Wilson
Miami University

Ellenmarie Cronin Wahlrab
Miami University Middletown

In this chapter we respond to the question, "What makes a piece of writing college level?" by investigating the institutional history of Miami University of Ohio. Why Miami? We believe it is a productive site of inquiry into changing definitions of college-level writing because the evolution of its composition program parallels in many instances the development of the field of composition and rhetoric.[1] What makes Miami even more useful for a case study is that its selective and two-year open-admissions campuses allow us to look through dual lenses. This comparative vision lets us examine two different kinds of institutional sites and consider how the tiering of institutions alters expectations for writing.

Taking up Mary Soliday's call for more local material histories and Gail Stygall's challenge that rhetoric and composition scholars "take seriously those public documents that educational institutions . . . produce" (7), we first examine documents in Miami's English department to study changes in its definitions of college-level writing. In the second part of our essay, we turn to one of Miami's open-access branch campuses (Miami Middletown) and its scripting of students for work-based competencies. We describe a composition class designed to develop rhetorical skill not only for work, but also for academic and community life. We aim to historicize and make visible the multiple, often competing desires of teachers, students, institutions, and communities that intersect in a writing classroom. We believe this institutional history and comparison sheds light on the structuring effects of socioeconomic differences in the academy, especially as those differences become translated into debates over standards and the kinds of writing curriculum students need. The history we compose from our archives shows how a two-year open-admissions college became identified with the *remedial* student, who then becomes scripted as needing a technical education and simple communication skills.

In *The Politics of Remediation*, Mary Soliday traces the history of remediation and the changing material conditions of the City College of New York (CCNY), arguing that the politics of access are at least as important as curricular reform in shaping the direction of writing programs. Our local research led to a somewhat different twist in the story of the politics of access and standards. Similar to Soliday's findings, we argue that our institution has used *access* and *standards* for its own purposes—to craft an ever more selective marketing profile for itself—by creating open-access campuses and then over time more sharply differentiating their missions and students from those of the "main" campus. However, in addition to the politics of access and standards, we posit the importance of the politics of assessment. We identified assessment as a crucial third element in the story of access and standards. The history we recount shows that assessment has always been embedded—but often remains invisible—in curricular decisions and often is driven by institutional needs, rather than to benefit students or improve curricula. We end by arguing that educators need to develop richer ways of assessing the complexity of rhetorical knowledge and skill of students, so that assessment serves students, improving their learning, as well as leading to improved curricula and teaching.

Tiering Campuses, Tiering Student Writing

Miami University, a state-assisted university founded in 1809, is located in a rural area of southwest Ohio. The university remained small and focused on undergraduate education before World War II: In 1941 it had about 3,500 students, mostly undergraduate, and no doctorate programs (Shriver and Pratt 197). By 2004 the university had about 15,000 undergraduate and 1,700 graduate students and offered 50 areas of study for the master's degree and 11 for the doctoral degree ("About Miami"). In the period of postwar expansion, Miami developed graduate programs and off-campus instructional sites that in the 1960s evolved into two open-access regional campuses. The main campus in Oxford, Ohio, today bills itself as a selective liberal arts "public ivy." When Miami Middletown, located twenty-five miles away in a steel town, was founded, locals hoped it would evolve into a four-year college, while the university's goals for the campus were more limited (Shriver, Letter). Today, with about 2,500 students, Miami Middletown emphasizes a two-year curriculum, although its mission continues to undergo changes.

As early as 1960—at a time when the momentum to create the regional campuses was coalescing—an exchange of memos between an English department faculty member and the president of the university makes clear that the institution was planning for increased selectivity among both future students *and* faculty members. The exchange began with a long letter to the university president from an English department faculty member, proposing a new kind of first-year writing course with lectures, increased class size, and a reduced number of papers. In his reply, the president acknowledged the burden of teaching many sections of composition and expressed the hope of recruiting new faculty with PhDs and reducing the number of composition classes that new hires would have to teach (Houtchens 2; Millett).

This and other documentation from the late 1950s and early 1960s indicate that the English department and university were promoting a growing selectivity in admissions and faculty recruitment. The language of these memos suggests the acceptance of a culture of hierarchical tiering, a culture also evident in the practice of assessing students for placement into regular or advanced tracks. Standardized assessment before and during a writing course served the purposes of sorting students, primarily according to their knowledge of mechanical writing conventions. The presumed "standard of excellence" was maintained by segregation based on "ability," purportedly measured by national standardized test scores, or demonstrated by a student's knowledge of mechanical conventions as measured by the department's qualifying test.

Yet, amid this traditional test-based curriculum, a thread of a more complex story of writing pedagogy also appears in the small details. We'll turn below to a discussion of pedagogy, but it is important to note that the actual practices of writing instruction contained a mix of approaches and philosophies that the official syllabi and tests sometimes belie. Based on our research, the story we compose of Miami's composition curriculum can be neither a triumphal tale of constantly progressing pedagogy nor an ironic institutional critique, delivered from a present-day position of enlightened hindsight.

Other department documents suggest that the changing idea of the first-year writing course occurred over a long period of time within the context of wider institutional changes and desires. The 1960 exchange of memos cited above, for example, employs rhetorical arguments about the university's goals of attracting doctoral-level research faculty by freeing them from the perceived drudgery of teaching writing through the marking of weekly papers. The memo writer argued that his proposal would make the course more intellectually challenging and more college level, apparently referring to the lecture method of delivery. Such a scheme would have restructured the writing course along the familiar lines of other college lecture courses such as history and shifted focus away from grammar and mechanics, but not toward any specific writing instruction.

In 1969–1970, shortly after the English department developed a PhD program in English, it did change first-year writing, moving to themes—for example, *alienation*, *pollution*, *the black experience*—as a way to respond to a university report that was critical of the curriculum ("Proposal"). However contemporary the themes approach may appear, memos about the new curriculum did not specifically address writing instruction either, focusing mostly on what students were to read (primarily fiction, poetry, and drama). This curricular reform marks a further shift away from a composition and rhetoric focus to one on literary study, and writing continues to be defined by models extrinsic to writing instruction. This is not just our critique but was also pointedly raised as a question by the University Requirement Committee. A committee member from the Communication department objected that the first-year English courses taught literary criticism rather than persuasive writing and attention to specific audiences, while the committee's representative from English argued that students should learn to write logically for a universal audience (Minutes January 31; Minutes February 7). There was soon a widespread backlash against the theme model. The lack of a common curriculum became fodder for those wishing to change the core requirements and snatch the universal first-year courses from English. But the debate sketched above seems more than a mere power grab, as it touches on key conceptual differences that still fuel debates about a single standard of logical writing versus a rhetorical view of writing.

The English department responded to the threat of losing the course by claiming its expertise and commitment to composition: First, it set a new policy, requiring all English faculty to teach composition; later in the 1970s it added composition and rhetoric graduate courses and moved toward the creation of the composition and rhetoric PhD. These measures solidified the English department's control over the first-year composition requirement. Ironically, a nearly complete reversal had occurred in the approximately fifteen years since the president's 1960 memo in which he expressed his wish that in the future English faculty "would not be required to take more than two sections of freshman English" and "could have at least one advanced section of English" (Millett).

Miami's history thus confirms a number of Soliday's claims. As elsewhere, it was also true for Miami: "midlevel institutions struggled to upgrade their status by shedding a pure teaching mission, offering more professional and graduate education, and requiring some research as conditions for faculty hiring or advancement" (Soliday 13). And, just as at CCNY, Miami's main campus has always had a "remedial" population of students, before *and after* the creation of its open-access campuses and the growing emphasis on selectivity on the main campus. Soon after the opening of the Middletown Campus in 1966, the chair of the English department and his counterpart at Middletown proposed creating a basic writing class for the Middletown campus only. Students would be placed into it based on the American College Test (ACT) scores. Yet, despite the fact that 20 percent of the main campus students' scores fell below the cutoff, the chair and his counterpart did not suggest that the Review of English Fundamentals course proposed for Middletown should also be offered at the main campus in Oxford (Peterson).

By locating basic writing only on the regional campuses, Miami's tradition of sorting students into different tracks took on a main campus/regional campuses distinction, with different rules and expectations for the different student bodies. From the 1950s to the present, writing curricula on the Oxford campus evolved from a grammar and skills focus (defined in internal memos as "remedial") through many different iterations of what a college-level course should be—from the study of rhetorical modes, to the reading and interpreting of literary texts, to a focus on the improvement of student texts using sentence combining, to expressivist and process approaches, and in the 1990s to socially oriented critical inquiry and currently a new rhetorical emphasis.[2]

With the inception of the PhD in Composition and Rhetoric in 1980, student writing became the centerpiece of composition courses in Oxford, national scholars came to lead workshops on the teaching of writing, and Miami hosted national writing conferences. The department ended its testing of basic grammar conventions and later a timed essay proficiency exam. Today each campus handles placement of students in its own way.[3] No advanced first-year composition classes are available on the open-admissions campuses, and no basic writing course is available on the Oxford campus, although there are students on all three campuses who could benefit from both of these options. We conclude that composition curricula generally flowed from the center to the periphery (from Oxford to the regional campuses). When discordances became visible, Oxford allowed the regional campuses to develop their own solutions, as long as those solutions operated solely on the regional campuses so as not to disfigure the portrait of the selective main campus.

The development of the Miami Middletown campus echoed the national trend that Ira Shor argues was one of the strongest forces for the institution of two-year colleges. According to Shor, universities themselves saw it as desirable to split off the first two years of general education from the university so that the university could devote itself to the research and training of professionals, which was becoming its desired mission (51). While initially all of Ohio's universities practiced open-door policies, today most have moved to selective admissions for the main campus and relegated open-admissions students to branch campuses and community colleges. Burgeoning enrollments from the 1960s on and "the responsibility of developing more extended graduate programs for able college graduates" ("Education Beyond the High School" 7) were claims used to argue for this tiering of access, but economic and political aims may have been operating as well. Shor contends that universities may have wanted to slow "the upward rise of the non-traditional student" (51).

Our archival research suggests to us that the mission of the Middletown campus has been and continues to be in flux, waxing and waning according to how the major players in its existence construct its market(s)—and therefore its functions—from servicing returning vets to deferring admission of "less able" students to the main campus ("Education Beyond the High School" 7), from fanning a small city's hope for the campus's intellectual and cultural drawing power to relegating technical education to the less-visible branch campuses. Competing views about the campus's mission remain unresolved to this day. Nonetheless, how the mission of a two-year college is defined may have enormous material consequences for its students and for the continuing inequality of wealth and power in our country.[4]

We turn in the next section to bring the two stories together—composition curricular change and campus histories—by suggesting that the way students are scripted by institutions for intellectual or technical futures can be used as a point of inquiry in a writing classroom. On the two-year campus, for example, where composition classes are expected to prepare students for work-based communication competencies, these expectations can themselves become the subject of rhetorical inquiry. We argue that composition curricula should not script student writers as needing *only* academic *or* workplace writing skills, depending on their social and economic location, but should serve to develop rhetorical skill needed for any writing situation by foregrounding and investigating the demands and desires of self and others for the writing that they produce. In the next section, we show how the demand for work training on a two-year campus can be turned on its head and used as the fulcrum for developing rhetorical skill and intellectual inquiry, preparing students for work *and* academic *and* community life.

Teaching Rhetorical Skill and Illuminating the Material Conditions That Organize Learning

In every writing class, teacher and students discover themselves in always specific and complex rhetorical situations with a multitude of rhetorical forces pressing upon them. Teachers bring a curriculum that has been shaped by particular and general forces —by their own interests and accumulated practices, departmental programs, and extradepartmental pressures for academic writing or workplace communication skills. Other forces that press upon the writing classroom might include the institution's position in a community: What does a community expect from this institution of higher education? Is it expected to produce a trained local workforce, business leaders, professionals, informed citizens? To what segment of a population does the institution market itself and what kind of educational profile does it construct of its students and graduates? Intellectuals? Artists? Technical workers? Job seekers? And what about students' own rhetorical expectations or assumptions about writing in college and the realities of their lives outside the classroom? Whether or not a space is made for students' desires to surface, they are surely a force in the writing classroom.

This complex rhetorical knot makes the notion of standards in "the plural singular sense of the word" (Fox 6) counterproductive because a single standard erases the many rhetorical demands writers face. As students learn to juggle these demands and make choices that meet their own purposes *and* those of the many other interested parties to their writing, they are developing rhetorical skill.

A pedagogy that foregrounds the knotted conditions of writing offers students opportunities to unravel and identify the strands of exigencies, and reweave them for their own rhetorical purposes. The following example of such foregrounding grew out of the actual material conditions of a specific two-year campus and student body and should not be taken as a model of an ideal pedagogy, but as an example of how a composition class might be focused.

A large National Science Foundation (NSF) grant designated for the development of learner-centered education on the Middletown campus provided the framework and funding for Ellenmarie to develop this first-semester composition curriculum. The knotted conditions of this writing classroom included many strands. The class's students were diverse, ranging in age from seventeen to fifty years and older; they were black, white, biracial, Appalachian; urban, small-town, farm, and suburban; first-generation college (and even high school) students; public high school graduates as well as General Education Development Test holders; workers—in one or more jobs in factories, construction, medical support, restaurants, banks, delivery services; women and men, with more than half of the class being parents. Their diversity is typical of two-year campuses nationally.

Their purposes for being in the class were, more often than not, driven by the desire for a "better" job, which for some meant more money while others "just wanted something more" out of their work and their lives. Several were aiming for a two-year degree—in nursing, for example, or business technology, with sometimes the hope of eventually completing a four-year degree. Others did not have a plan but were responding to the twentieth-century version of the American dream: a college education equals upward mobility.

The Miami Middletown faculty's perceptions of college-level writing were also an ever-present strand, whether surfacing through students talking about the evaluation of their writing in other classes or through complaints overheard in the faculty lounge bemoaning the dismal state of student writing. Ellenmarie brought her own frustration into the classroom: The campus, in fact the university, construed the branch campus students as cut from a different cloth than those at Oxford, and this construction lent itself to the replication of class structure.

The NSF grant was especially targeted for, but not limited to, educational innovation in the teaching of science, mathematics, engineering, and technology (SMET). The SMET proposal stated that its primary goal was "to create an active, learner-centered educational community," but a close reading of it revealed the impetus behind the initiative as well as the opportunity to turn that impetus on its head (Governanti and Lloyd 4).

Of the seven desired learner outcomes, four explicitly targeted work readiness competencies or technological skills called for by the corporate world. The others promoted the development of critical thinking, decision-making, and problem-solving learning strategies, as well as increased opportunities for cooperative and collaborative work. The proposal claimed that two-year colleges are "uniquely qualified to carry out learner-centered curriculum reform"; should maintain "strong ties to the needs of area business and industry"; and should "provid[e] services of both an academic and technical nature, [offering] curricular choices that blur distinctions between the pursuit of 'academic' and 'technical' learning" (Governanti and Lloyd 4–5).

This "blur" hid several disturbing assumptions about the curriculum of the two-year college: that technical learning is an end in itself, linked to the goals of business and industry; and that the strategies learned could be used in any context, thereby construing learning as decontextualized from any larger concerns (e.g., ethical or political). The "blur" covered over the glaring absence of one of the key aims of Miami's liberal education goals—understanding contexts—goals stressed on the main campus that supposedly apply to the branch campuses as well. This emphasis on decontextualized skills embedded, at a fundamental level, hierarchical class differences in expectations about the human potential, career opportunities, and civic responsibilities of the main and branch campus students.

The opposing realities identified here are not new; in fact, this struggle between vocationalism and professionalism existed within the two-year college movement from its inception to the present. In a larger sense, this struggle over the purposes of education in a democracy reflects the underlying dynamic of how equality has variously been construed in the service of the economy and social order. Two-year college faculty are urged to shape their curricula and evaluation practices to ensure work-ready students, whereas the work of the university lies down another path, creating critical thinkers who will carry on the higher order thinking of the academy and the critical work of the culture at large.

The opportunity presented by the NSF grant for curriculum development allowed Ellenmarie to juxtapose several persistent questions facing the Middletown English faculty: Must this institution's composition instructors consider their students only as future (or advancing) workers? Could the critical thinking that is central to the university's work be taught hand-in-hand with work-based competencies? To answer these questions, she designed a first-level composition course that would attempt to address these two goals: a course based on a dual approach to the theme of work. This critical inquiry-based course would investigate work itself while integrating workplace activities into the classroom.

If work was the dazzling vision that drove student ambition, curriculum design, and corporate and foundation support, the curriculum developed with the support of the NSF grant would not try to divert the collective gaze but would instead put work right into the center of inquiry in the course: How do we construct the work we do? How has it been constructed for us? What are its satisfactions, injustices, aesthetic pleasures, ethics, politics, and purposes? The class would study the actual work situations of students' lives through reflection, critical inquiry, problem posing and problem solving, decision making, talking, and sharing workplace, personal, and academic writing—including the writing produced by the academy necessary for it to do *its* work. Through interweaving academic, campus workplace contexts for writing, and students' own life and work locations, the notion of workplace competencies would be complicated by examining how they are embedded in real social and historical locations. Another benefit was that students' workplace knowledge would be validated as learning and accomplishment and also would be open to revision and improvement. Students would draft workplace writing—meeting minutes, memos, and proposals—all in the context of a problem-based scenario; write personal narratives and self-reflections; and read and critique campus and academic documents, as well as drafts of Ellenmarie's research on the history, functions, and mixed results of the two-year college movement in which they were now knowingly participating.

A writing curriculum that supports the development of rhetorical skill situates instruction in actual classroom conversations. For example, Ellenmarie drew on the class's surprised and thoughtful responses to two essays on Black English to set up the situation calling for minutes. In an excerpt from "Linguistic Chauvinism," Peter Farb traces the history of Black English, arguing that Black English is a language in its own right, with a complexity of structure and rules comparable to those of Standard American English, and expressive of a rich, if painful, cultural heritage. Conversely, Rachel Jones argues in "What's Wrong with Black English?" that she doesn't speak "white" but "right," and that those who do not become articulate in Standard American English hurt their own chances for success in a white-dominated culture. Most of the class initially found the Farb essay daunting to read, with its interweaving of linguistic explanation, history of the development of Black English, and argument for the legitimacy and value of Black English as a language. The class met in small groups to analyze the main points of each author's argument. Then spokespersons from each group led the class in an evolving understanding of the language issues at stake. What came up again and again was Farb's illustrative example of a young African American girl's ability to read fluently a story written in Black English that she could not read in Standard American English. His point was that this student would have to learn a new language while learning how to read in order to succeed in the school system she was in, and that this need would not be recognized as the demanding additional learning situation it entailed but rather as a deficit.

To move the discussion into their everyday lives, Ellenmarie asked students to form work groups hypothetically composed of parents, teachers, and administrators from an elementary, middle, or high school. Their task would be to develop a policy and related program for addressing the concerns raised by both authors. How would their school recognize and value the home languages of all of their students and also address their students' needs to become fluent in the dominant culture's language? Their added task would be to write minutes of their meetings, which came to be numerous and complex. Their working groups became so involved in their discussions and research that Ellenmarie organized time at almost half of the weekly class meetings for the issue groups to continue to meet. Some researched what their own school districts were doing concerning language issues and brought back what they found to their groups.

Near the end of the semester when the groups critiqued each other's proposal rough drafts, however, they were dismayed to realize that they had reduced the complexity of language issues explored in their group discussions and research to one of deficit. All of the plans were based on remedial instruction with just a token nod, if any, to the value of students' home languages. Their group minutes, however, traced the circularity of some of the discussions, the research done, and the struggle to design a policy and program that addressed the concerns raised by the readings. The minutes thus had a substantive writing function; the groups could go back to them and use them to revise their proposals to more fully reflect their group conversations. These students experienced collaborative problem solving as a complicated, rich, frustrating, and ongoing rhetorical situation, as in out-of-class life, not artificially tied up into a neat solution, as the traditional academic form of the argumentative research paper imposes.

Facing and discussing the widespread tendency to reduce differences to deficits also provided an opportunity for reflection: In what ways did their own positions at an open-admission campus create the perception of deficit? In what ways did the material conditions of their lives—families, work, school systems, money, etc.—lead them to the campus? What did *access* mean literally and figuratively in their lives? How could they sort out what and who defined them?

Students at first resisted this move to study their own positions. Many have internalized derogatory attitudes toward two-year college students that are common on both the main and branch campuses. Yet the course focus on critical inquiry into work led students to a deeper contextual understanding of how they were positioned. For some students this eventually became empowering, leading them to more confident self-reflection and voicing of their own views and interests. One student wrote that the critical inquiry into work had helped him understand more clearly what he valued—"personal contact with people, high ethical standards, job security, the ability to work outside, competence in my job, and respect from those I work with" (Slusser 4). He included this personally meaningful story in his final reflective essay:

> Recently at work, my co-worker and I had a meeting with a prospective client. I had worked with this gentleman [previously] . . . so I had already established a relationship with him. During the meeting I actually felt a stronger confidence in myself and in my ability to provide this customer what [he] desired. . . . I know this increased measure of confidence is largely due to what I have learned during this class. I have been asked several times why I am going to college at forty-five years old. My normal response was . . . for a higher position at work and also for personal fulfillment. My perception of work has changed so drastically; now I cannot imagine success at work that doesn't include a large measure of personal satisfaction. I no longer just think of my "paid job" when I think of work. Webster has at least fourteen definitions of the word "work" and only a few of them are concerned with employment. An athlete *works* to develop his or her body; an artist displays a body of *work* whether it be a play, a movie, a painting, or a song; a cabinet maker *works* to turn a cherry tree into a beautiful hutch; teachers prepare their students for *work*; and parents *work* every day to prepare their children for their own life's *work*.—Work consumes a tremendous portion of our lives and we cannot afford to let it be all about money. (Slusser 6)

Other students did not feel empowered but worried. They were still grappling with the nets and snares they had uncovered in their research. For example, the two-year college's push for work-readiness training tangled with the dreams of some of the students who hoped to pursue bachelor's degrees on the Oxford campus after completing an associate's degree on the Middletown campus. One assignment asked students to map their educational goals and university pathways to those goals. In doing their research, they uncovered the fact that a number of courses counting toward an associate's degree in business would be useless for meeting the requirements of a bachelor's degree in business, should a student plan to go on.

This example of discouraging four-year degree expectations is, unfortunately, not an anomaly. Though most who begin their higher education at a two-year college may say they expect to earn a four-year degree and the advantages it accrues, their ambitions are "cooled out," as Burton Clark noted nearly forty years ago. He claimed that failure to achieve their aspirations may be "inevitable and [actually] structured" into the higher education system itself (qtd. in Brint and Karabel 10).[5]

After reading some of Ellenmarie's research on two-year colleges, one student wrote poignantly of the pull to give up:

> As I look back I see myself at the beginning of the longest road you can imagine, but I have only [gone] a short ways down it and now I am thinking I should have taken the short cut through the woods instead of taking the long route around the woods (school). It has been really rough working long hours, then going to school [in] the evenings . . . . I still love work and learning new stuff at school, but nobody's body should ache like you're 70 when you're only 20. I got this feeling that I might be one of those junior college dropouts. I just have to get my priorities on track before I derail myself and really mess up my future. (Swank 1)

Revising the Script, Assessing Writing for Learning

The "cooling out" effect Clark described results not only from the structure of the two-year college but from the university's refusal to address the material conditions of students' lives (so eloquently voiced by the student above). Composition curricula and methods of assessment that limit rhetorical knowledge to a narrow set of easily measurable grammatical skills and a narrow range of writing further compound this cooling out effect.

Assessment is both conceptual, like curricula, and material, like institutional practices such as access, and it may work for the institution's benefit and purposes rather than for the benefit of students or improved curricula. When we assess and fail students based mostly on correctness of a decontextualized writing sample, we are—in effect—closing the doors even further, dropping or *stopping students out*[6] of higher education before they have had the opportunity to develop and apply rhetorical knowledge and skill.[7]

It is not that correctness and workplace communication skills are unimportant or unreachable goals, but that these goals are too limited. Students need opportunities to voice their own passions and interests and to struggle with the complex rhetorical demands of writing for work and life, as well as for the academy.

It is possible to assess what students can *do* and what rhetorical skills they are able to apply to different writing situations but not by basing assessment on a single text taken out of its rhetorical context.[8] In response to the question of what makes writing college level, we pose other questions: What kinds of rhetorical knowledge and practices are expected of students in future writing situations inside and outside many kinds of classrooms? Can more complex and accurate ways of assessing students' rhetorical skills be designed so as to encourage more effective ways of teaching those skills? Pursuing answers to these questions will lead to different kinds of assessment practices requiring more than reading and scoring discrete texts against a concept of a universal standard.

Notes

1. A Miami composition director was active in the formation of the Conference on College Composition and Communcation and served as its chair in 1966; its English department developed a PhD in composition/rhetoric in the late 1970s and since the 1980s has been home to the Writing Program Administrators and a site of the Ohio Writing Project.

2. The current first-year curriculum contains elements of Miami's expressivist and socially oriented past syllabi, while emphasizing the interanimating tensions among writer, audience, purpose, context, language, and genres. Students write in a number of different genres, and study, practice, and reflect on how to make rhetorical choices that can serve their own (and often other) purposes in a writing situation.

3. The Middletown campus has developed its own placement process; for a description of it, see Lewiecki-Wilson, Sommers, and Tassoni. The

Hamilton campus uses ACT's COMPASS test. On the Oxford campus, students may be placed into Advanced College Composition or exempted from both sequences of the first-year composition requirement through scores on advanced placement (AP) exams or the Miami Writing Portfolio Program. Students on the branch campuses may also earn AP or Writing Portfolio credit, but have no options for taking Advanced College Composition.

4. The American Association of Community Colleges reported that the median earnings for a person eighteen years or older in 1999 with an associate's degree was $29,457 as compared to earnings of $36,525 for those with a bachelor's degree ("Median Earnings"). The disparity in economic value between a two-year and four-year degree persists over a lifetime, according to Kathleen Porter in "The Value of a College Degree." She cites Day and Newburger's 2002 statistics that "associate's degree holders earn about $1.6 million; and bachelor's degree holders earn about $2.1 million."

5. Ira Shor is blunter: "Working-class and minority students are being cooled-out en masse in the lesser institutions and lesser tracks set up just for them" (qtd. in Tinberg 56). See also Brint and Karabel: The two-year college offers the masses the promise of upward mobility while also managing their ambition by serving as a gatekeeper for further education and diverting, with greater or lesser success, many of its students to terminal programs which lock in their positions in the class system (9–11).

6. *Stopping out* is a term used to describe the process of students leaving college before completing a program or earning a degree but who intend to return. Many students at our two-year campus at Middletown stop out and reenroll—sometimes more than once—usually due to financial circumstances and their multiple family and work responsibilities in addition to the demands of their academic work.

7. Longitudinal studies such as those by Marilyn Sternglass and Anne Herrington and Marcia Curtis show that students develop writing fluency, confidence, and skill over the course of several years, not in a single course.

8. William Condon and Diane Kelley-Riley, reporting on large-scale assessment at Washington State University, found that student writing often showed an inverse relation between correctness and critical thinking; that is, correct papers tended to be superficial, and papers rated higher on their critical thinking rubric were not as error free (66). They note that teaching writing must occur all across a campus and involve faculty from all disciplines since writing and critical thinking are rhe-

torically situated; excellent writing is different for different contexts and purposes. They conclude that “multiple measures within robust assessment systems yield a more complicated portrait of what faculty teach and what students learn” (69).

Works Cited

“About Miami.” Miami University Web page. 6 June 2006 <www.miami.muohio.edu/about miami/>.

Brint, Steven, and Jerome Karabel. *The Diverted Dream: Community Colleges and the Promise of Educational Opportunity in America, 1900–1985*. New York: Oxford UP, 1989.

Clark, Burton. “The ‘Cooling-Out’ Function in Higher Education.” *American Journal of Sociology* 65 (1960): 569–76.

Condon, William, and Diane Kelley-Riley. “Assessing and Teaching What We Value: The Relationship between College-Level Writing and Critical Thinking Abilities.” *Assessing Writing* 9 (2004): 56–75.

“Education Beyond the High School with Emphasis on Finance and Organization.” Preliminary Report. Cleveland: League of Women Voters of Ohio, April 1962.

Farb, Peter. “Linguistic Chauvinism.” *Word Play: What Happens When People Talk*. New York: Knopf, 1981.

Fox, Tom. *Defending Access: A Critique of Standards in Higher Education*. Portsmouth, NH: Boynton/Cook, 1999.

Governanti, Michael, and Baird W. Lloyd. “Furthering Advances toward Learner-Centered Education.” Grant Proposal to the National Science Foundation. 30 July 1998.

Herrington, Anne, and Marcia Curtis. *Persons in Process: Four Stories of Writing and Personal Development in College*. Urbana, IL: NCTE, 2000.

Houtchens, Larry. Memo to President John D. Millett. 18 Jan 1960. 1–3. Miami University English Department.

Jones, Rachel. “What’s Wrong with Black English?” *American Voices: Multicultural Literacy and Critical Thinking*. Ed. Delores La Guardia and Hans P. Guth. Mountain View, CA: Mayfield, 1993. 506–9.

Lewiecki-Wilson, Cynthia, Jeff Sommers, and John Paul Tassoni. "Rhetoric and the Writer's Profile: Problematizing Directed Self-Placement." *Assessing Writing* 7 (2000): 165–83.

"Median Earnings for Persons 18 or Older by Educational Attainment." American Association for Community Colleges. 6 June 2006 <http://www.aacc.nche.edu/Template.cfm?Section=Statistical_Guide&template=/ContentManagement/ContentDisplay.cfm&ContentID=4778&InterestCategoryID=244&Name=Statistics&ComingFrom=InterestDisplay>.

Millett, John D. Memo to Gordon Wilson. 20 Jan. 1960. Miami University English Department.

Minutes of the University Requirement Committee, February 7, 1973: 1–5. Miami University English Department.

Minutes of the University Requirement Committee, January 31, 1973: 1–3. Miami University English Department.

Peterson, Spiro. Memo to Karl E. Limper, Dean, College of Arts and Sciences. "A Proposal for a New Course at the Middletown Campus, English 04 Review of English Fundamentals." 2 June 1967. Miami University English Department.

Porter, Kathleen. "The Value of a College Degree. ERIC Digest." 31 July 2004 <http://www.ericdigests.org/2003-3/value.htm>.

"Proposal for a Thematic Organization of Freshman English, 1970." 1–5. Miami University English Department.

Shriver, Phillip R. Letter to Honorable James A. Rhodes. 26 Aug. 1966. 1–2. Miami Middletown Archive. Gardner-Harvey Library.

Shriver, Phillip R., and William Pratt. *Miami University: A Personal History*. Oxford, OH: Miami UP, 1998.

Shor, Ira. *Culture Wars: School and Society in the Conservative Restoration 1969–1984*. Chicago: U of Chicago P, 1992.

Slusser, Richard. "It's Not All about Money." Final essay. English 111, Spring 2000. Miami University Middletown.

Soliday, Mary. *The Politics of Remediation: Institutional and Student Needs in Higher Education*. Pittsburgh: U of Pittsburgh P, 2002.

Sternglass, Marilyn. *Time to Know Them: A Longitudinal Study of Writing and Learning at the College Level*. Mahwah, NJ: Lawrence Erlbaum, 1997.

Stygall, Gail. "Unraveling at Both Ends: Anti-Undergraduate Education, Anti-Affirmative Action, and Basic Writing at Research Schools." *Journal of Basic Writing* 18.2 (1999): 4–22.

Swank, John. "Essay 5." Final essay. English 111, Spring 2000. Miami University Middletown.

Tinberg, Howard. "An Interview with Ira Shor—Part I." *Teaching English in the Two-Year College* 27 (1999): 51–60.

CHAPTER THIRTEEN

From Attitude to Aptitude: Assuming the Stance of a College Writer

RONALD F. LUNSFORD
University of North Carolina at Charlotte

As I think about the task of defining college writing, I remember two important mentors in my academic life: William E. Coles, Jr., and Kellogg Hunt. Bill Coles often uses the phrase "get your money up" to insist that if one is going to talk about writing, one had better bring along samples of student writing that illustrate concepts being explained and support claims being made. Kellogg Hunt was not one to prescribe what others should do, but the care he took with his own research has often stood me in good stead. Hunt avoided, at all costs, making claims that he could not support; as a case in point, consider his analysis of complexity in syntax, entitled *Syntactic Maturity in Schoolchildren and Adults*. Knowing that it would be virtually impossible to define *good* writing, he based his study on two important assumptions: namely, that as writers grow older, their writing gets better; and that those who have been published in two quality magazines, *Harper's* and *The Atlantic Monthly*, can be assumed to be good writers. With those assumptions in place, he undertook a study that described the changes in students' writing over time—from the early grades to high school—and he contrasted the writing style of the best student writers with writing chosen from the pages of those two literary journals.

So what, you may be asking, do these reminiscences about my two mentors have to do with the task at hand? Just this. Mindful of my mentor, Bill Coles, I will endeavor to "get my money up." That is, I will illustrate and support the claims I am making about college writing with samples written by college students. And, like my other mentor, Kellogg Hunt, I will begin with an important assumption, viz., that any writing we receive from students attending college is, ipso facto, college writing. With this assumption firmly in place, I will proceed to describe the qualities I see in the writing of three college writers.

Before you despair, thinking that I have completely misunderstood the task we have been set, i.e., to analyze the qualities of college writing, let me explain a bit further. There is a sense in which this task is an impossible one. What exactly could one mean in asking what differentiates college writing from that which is not college writing? Do we mean to suggest that college writers come to us as college writers? If so, what exactly are we supposed to be doing to (or for) them in the one or two college writing courses they are required to take? Surely, we have things to teach them. Are we, then, supposed to be moving them from the status of *college writers* (which status we assume they have attained in order to matriculate at our institutions) to that of *advanced college writers* and eventually *postcollege writers?*

As an alternate reading, by college-level writing we may refer not to products they are capable of producing when they come to us, but rather to the skills, knowledge, and attitudes they bring to college, assets that will allow them to develop their abilities to produce the types of writing we value in our institutions. I prefer this reading. It allows me to say that when they come to us, students only have to produce a piece of writing in response to the first writing assignment we give them in order to become college writers. However, some of them come with certain assets that make it likely that they will be able to learn how to produce the kinds of products we value. Others, lacking these assets, are not likely in the brief span of time we have them to learn how to produce these products. What are these assets I speak of?

This would seem to be the time for me to "get my money up." Let's look at a text written by a student who has what it takes to develop the kind of writing we're looking for. This text, written by a first-year college student, was in response to an assignment given in a Philosophy of Biology course:

A Critique of "The Propensity Interpretation of Fitness"

In an Advance Biology class, Darwinian fitness was introduced to me as the reproductive success of an organism. At the time, I considered that concept simple and logical. I could see how it followed, what I then perceived as, the theory of evolution. I even noted that this definition insinuated that those organisms who may seems quite fit (in a physical sense or such) are not fit in the scheme of natural selection if they do not indeed reproduce. All of this seemed easy enough prior to our class "Philosophy of Biology" and such essays as Susan K. Mills and John H. Beatty's, "The Propensity Interpretation of Fitness." I was previously content with fitness for the same reason that R. Levins accentuates when he says, "Fitness enters population biology as a vague heuristic notion, rich in metaphor but poor in precision." It has been often noted that there are circular problems in defining fitness for natural selection and the theory of evolution. The purpose of the paper by Mills is to propose one approach that provides a non-circular and logical definition of fitness. I understood why the authors felt the need for this new interpretation. I also pointed out what I felt were the points of confusion, points of weakness, weak extrapolations, ideas that were well thought out, and finally the overall usefulness of this new interpretation.

It is very easy to be pleased by my old Advance Biology definition of fitness [Darwinian]. But when the questions, what is the definition of fitness and what is the measure of fitness, are asked simultaneously an obvious flaw is exposed; intuitively the answers are the same. The authors of this essay were so bothered by this flaw that they opted to present the propensity interpretation. In this case, the definition of fitness does not include the phrase "those that survive," thus interrupting the previous circularity of other arguments.

There were many minor points of confusion in the essay, but that very well could be the fault of the reader more so than that of the authors. However, I did feel that there was one rather important part that was confusing. After presenting the bulk of their argument, the authors attempted to expand their idea in to a mathematical sense (refer to pages 15, 16 in Sober). I can see the appeal of conveying the idea in another manner such as this, however I felt the practicality of it was low. When I approached this portion of the paper I felt the tone of the issue switch to that of a very intricate calculus word problem. And I was not prepared for nor did I benefit from that transfer. Obviously, I am noting this as a point of confusion and therefore I am not saying that it is fallible in any sense, or that I wouldn't validate it completely with more explanation.

I did not outright disagree with much of what Mills and Beatty presented in their paper; and the paper was relatively sound except one analogy the authors made. This analogy was placed on page 9 in Sober, and it deals with "the propensity of salt to dissolve in [pure] water." It seems to me that fitness is far too different from chemistry for a proper analogy to be drawn. For example, I believe it is much less controversial to say, "the guarantee of salt to dissolve in [pure]," because from my understanding that is just what it is. There are two other smaller weak points that are more specifically weak extrapolations. The first deals with the authors' statement that they have improved the definition of natural selection by introducing this propensity interpretation. They take a good effort to qualify this statement, however the claim is of gargantuan proportion and is based largely on "common sense." The claim seems to merit (and quite possibly require) a whole other paper. The sentiment is that the authors received a "two for one" deal here, however the reward of this claim is of too much importance to be awarded so easily. The second extrapolation is criticized pretty much for its brevity. The statement is contained in the very last sentence of the paper, where the authors express that they see no reason why "a similar reconstruction could not be given for the case of macroevoluntionary change." There is absolutely nothing in this paper to validate that claim and therefore I couldn't stand to let that extrapolation pass uncommented.

So far I have been very critical of this paper, however I believe it was warranted. Regardless there were some very clear points that really stood out in the paper. I felt the separation of propensity fitness into "fitness1" and "fitness2" was really helpful. For one reason, there was a need to differentiate between the fitness of an organism and of a genome (with alternate alleles). Kudos is given to Mills and Beatty there. Also I enjoyed and grasped a hold of the concept of propensity as a graduated spectrum (refer to page 11 in Sober). I felt it did the job in explaining the specific idea of propensity that the authors had in their mind. I do believe the authors succeeded in presenting a notion that can explain when the fittest do not survive to reproduce, however I am still troubled by the reality of the statement. Tom Bethell taps into my reservation with his statement, "If only there were some way of identifying the fittest before-hand, without always having to wait and see which ones survive." And since my intuition says we can never know this vital information of "who is fittest" before the fact, I'm almost moved to say, "Why bother?"; conversely I also understand that new discoveries in science can only come about through (philosophical) questioning even in a skeptical situation.

> The conclusion of Mills and Beatty maintains that their interpretation of fitness "allows us to reconstruct explanations of microevoluntionary phenomena in such a way that these explanations appear to be entirely respectable and noncircular." However, much like the rest of the paper this conclusion is open to skepticism. The phrase "appear to be respectable" alone causes me to be reticent about supporting the conclusion. How can you rely on appearance? One of the most commonplace sayings I can think of is, every thing isn't as it appears. And what does it mean for the explanation to be respectable? A good informed guess can certainly be respectable, but yet it can also be wrong.

Now that I've put my money on the table, let me be clear what assertions my "money" is supporting. I am not saying this is the type of writing we want college students to be doing; in many ways, it's not what we want from them when they come to college—and it certainly isn't the kind of writing we want from them when they complete a college-level writing course. It isn't necessary to detail all the ways it fails to meet those standards. Suffice it to say, they include editing problems, such as subject-verb agreement errors, failure to understand the meaning of individual words, awkward phrasings, and equivocation. There is enough here to keep a teacher's red pen busy for some time.

Even so, my claim is that this essay, written during the student's—let's call him Adam—first month of college, demonstrates those assets that he will need to succeed as a college writer. How so? Let's start with the basics. We have said that this writing contains problems in basic editing. True enough. But, those cases seem to be the exception rather than the rule. Most of Adam's verbs agree with his subjects; most pronouns are properly connected with antecedents; most words are spelled correctly. At the level of the sentence, we also find basic competence. The writer seems to have an intuitive sense of what makes a sentence different from a nonsentence.

At a somewhat higher level, we find some sophistication in sentence structure. To see that sophistication, we need look no further than the first four sentences of the first paragraph:

> In an Advance Biology class, Darwinian fitness was introduced to me as the reproductive success of an organism. At the time, I considered that concept simple and logical. I could see how it

> followed, what I then perceived as, the theory of evolution. I even noted that this definition insinuated that those organisms who may seems quite fit (in a physical sense or such) are not fit in the scheme of natural selection if they do not indeed reproduce.

The paper begins with a passive sentence. While Adam certainly overuses the passive, here he uses it quite effectively, to highlight the subject of his investigation. The second short sentence is made emphatic by the rather complicated sentences that follow it. The third sentence offers an embedded clause (*how it followed*) as the object of the verb *see*; and within that embedded object, the writer uses an embedded clause (*what I then perceived as*) to modify the object of *followed*. The fourth sentence is equally complicated with two right-branching *that* clauses modifying each other. If this grammatical terminology isn't to your liking, simply read the sentences and note the skillful use of complex clause structures.

Now that we have established that the writer can handle the basics of usage and sentence structure, let's move up a level to coherence. Adam provides a basic plan for the paper in the last sentence of the first paragraph: he will critique the article entitled "The Propensity Interpretation of Fitness," by Susan K. Mills and John H. Beatty. The rest of the paper attempts to offer support for the claims that the article is confusing at points, that it has weaknesses, but that, overall, it presents a useful interpretation. As support, Adam offers:

1. the confusion caused by the attempt to translate their idea into a mathematical formula;
2. their reliance on an analogy that does not work;
3. their attempt to pair two different claims, offering support for the first, and assuming the reader will not notice that support has not been offered for the second;
4. their introduction of a final claim that has no support whatsoever.

Of course to know how good this writing is, we would have to examine the text Adam is writing about to see whether these criticisms are warranted. However, we don't have to consult that other text to determine that this writer knows a great deal about writing and thinking. It is clear that he knows that analogies provide a good place to attack any argument. Even more importantly, Adam knows that a writer is responsible for offering support for all the claims that are made. He seems almost indignant in the last sentence of paragraph five, where he says: "There is absolutely nothing in this paper to validate that claim and therefore I couldn't stand to let that extrapolation pass uncommented." A writer able to work up this kind of steam over an unsupported claim comes to a college writing class with one essential building skill for the work ahead.

But the writer has additional important skills. In paragraph six, he turns to strengths he finds in this article. In doing so, he shows his ability to analyze (sorting the various issues found in the article) and to evaluate—"I do believe the authors succeeded in presenting a notion that can explain when the fittest do not survive to reproduce. . . ." In this same paragraph, Adam illustrates his ability to bring other voices into the conversation he is having with the reader: "Tom Bethell taps into my reservation with his statement, 'If only there were some way of identifying the fittest before-hand, without always having to wait and see which ones survive.'"

In addition to these basic writing skills, this writer also demonstrates a good deal of knowledge about language and logic. First, let's look at language. In paragraph one, Adam tells us that he has noted "that this definition insinuated that those organisms who may seems quite fit (in a physical sense or such) are not fit in the scheme of natural selection if they do not indeed reproduce." From this sentence, we can deduce that this writer knows something about the role of implication in language. Even though *insinuated* may not be the best word for what he means, the writer seems to be moving toward an understanding that a word's meanings are not limited to neatly packaged assertions. And in this same sentence, he shows his understanding of polysemy: an organism may be *fit* physically and yet not be deemed *fit* in the context of an evolutionary process.

Next, let's look at what Adam knows about logic. Paragraph two begins as follows:

> It is very easy to be pleased by my old Advance Biology definition of fitness [Darwinian]. But when the questions, what is the definition of fitness and what is the measure of fitness, are asked simultaneously an obvious flaw is exposed; intuitively the answers are the same. The authors of this essay were so bothered by this flaw that they opted to present the propensity interpretation. In this case, the definition of fitness does those include the phrase "those that survive," thus interrupting the previous circularity of other arguments.

Although he has not stated his case clearly, Adam seems to be attempting to point out the circularity in the reasoning of those who have been attempting to define fitness. He praises the writers of this article for attempting a definition of fitness that does not "include the phrase 'those that survive,'" revealing his understanding that a definition can be circular even when a concept presented in the subject of a sentence is paraphrased in the complement, i.e., to be satisfactory, a definition must add new information in the complement.

Another logical insight can be seen in the following passage taken from paragraph four:

> There are two other smaller weak points that are more specifically weak extrapolations. The first deals with the authors' statement that they have improved the definition of natural selection by introducing this propensity interpretation. They take a good effort to qualify this statement, however the claim is of gargantuan proportion and is based largely on "common sense." The claim seems to merit (and quite possibly require) a whole other paper.

Like most students who are stretching their vocabularies, Adam sometimes seems to push his prose to the breaking point, e.g., using *accentuates* for *emphasizes* (paragraph one) or using *transfer* for *change* (paragraph three). However, his use of *extrapolations* in the passage above seems to drive home an important point he is making about this article. To extrapolate one proposition from another is to make an inference or a conjecture. Unlike a corollary principle, which is proved incidentally by proving a related principle, an extrapolation must be proved separately from the principle from which it was extrapolated.

Clearly this writer comes to college with important skills and knowledge. But even more importantly, he comes with the right attitude. To see what I mean in saying this, let's think of the various related meanings of the word *attitude*. It can be used to express emotion, as would be the case if we talked about a child with a belligerent attitude. Certainly such a child is evincing an emotion, but at the same time he is evincing an orientation; there is a clear relationship between this use of attitude and its use in describing an airplane. Just as an airplane takes a certain orientation toward the earth and the sky, a writer takes certain attitudes toward his or her writing, subject, and readers.

What are these attitudes? Another way of asking this question is, how does the writer orient himself or herself in this writing situation? I would argue that at the core of a writer's attitude are that writer's beliefs. If a writer believes a reader is lazy and/or uninformed, then, ipso facto, the writer takes a certain attitude toward that reader. If the writer believes a particular subject is serious and important, the writer then brings a certain attitude toward that project. If the writer believes certain fringe groups to be kooks whose point of view or arguments should not warrant serious thought, then his or her writing about these people and their arguments will reflect that attitude. So, what kinds of attitudes does this writer bring to his writing in this essay?

We don't have to look very far to see important evidences of these attitude-forming beliefs:

> In an Advance Biology class, Darwinian fitness was introduced to me as the reproductive success of an organism. At the time, I considered that concept simple and logical. I could see how it followed, what I then perceived as, the theory of evolution.

We mentioned above the complicated syntactic structure of the last sentence in this passage. That complication reflects the complicated beliefs that this writer assumes, viz., that his perceptions about the world do not reflect the reality of that world and that what he believes at one point may well be changed at another point in his life. It is hard to overestimate the importance of this attitude. With it, the writer opens himself up to learning of all kinds—most immediately, he opens himself to learning about a subject during the process of his own writing. We see this openness again in paragraph three when the writer tells us: "There were many minor points of confusion in the essay, but that very well could be the fault of the reader more so than that of the authors." The writer believes that he is in part responsible for making the meaning he takes from a text, and he brings a careful attitude toward that process—realizing that misunderstandings often reflect a failure of writer and reader to connect.

I mentioned above that the kind of open attitude this writing reflects permits him to learn from his own writing. We see that kind of learning most powerfully in a conversation that the writer has, in a sense, with himself (paragraph five):

> Tom Bethell taps into my reservation with his statement, "If only there were some way of identifying the fittest before-hand, without always having to wait and see which ones survive." And since my intuition says we can never know this vital information of "who is fittest" before the fact, I'm almost moved to say, "Why bother?"; conversely I also understand that new discoveries in science can only come about through (philosophical) questioning even in a skeptical situation.

Here the writer is pushing the limits of his thinking—in fact, of thinking itself. Just as the quantum physicists had to push their thinking past the boundaries of what seemed intuitively possible in order to move past Einstein, our everyday thinking requires us to bring a skeptical attitude to the most intuitively established truths when those truths seem to represent a roadblock to continued thinking.

Of course when a writer brings this attitude to his or her own thinking and writing, it is a relatively logical step to bring that attitude to the writing and thinking of others. From the beginning, we see that this writer brings a questioning attitude to the authorities whose article he is to critique. When they offer claims without support, he becomes animated in discussing this weakness. But at the same time, he analyzes and evaluates positively those points in their article that seem valid to him.

To this point, it may seem that I am protesting too much about the assets this writer brings to the college writing situation. In part, I am doing so because the paper is so lacking in some of the niceties of college writing that we would want to see in those texts that we hold up to our paying public. I want to look beyond the surface form to the underlying abilities this student brings to a college writing class. We may see these abilities more clearly by contrasting this student's writing with writing that lacks these qualities.

"The Right to Pray"

It is nine o'clock a.m. seven years ago in a small classroom. A bell rings to signify the beginning of school. "Would everyone please stand for the flag salute and a moment of silence," blares over the intercom. Twenty-seven sixth graders noisily shift chairs and stand to their feet. After they salute the flag, the teacher asks, "Who would like to lead us in prayer today?" Every child raises a hand and shouts, "Me, me, me!"

These days have been long lost. Prayer in schools has been abolished because it has been argued that it interferes with some of the children's religious preferences. But what about the other kids? They are being deprived of a religious freedom. To give both the religious preference and freedom the constitution grants, prayer should be present, but optional, in schools.

We believe the reason this country is in such a bad shape is because it has turned away from God. One example is taking prayer out of schools. With all of the trouble and evil in the world, we want our children to learn to ask for God's protection. Now more than ever protection in school is essential. Schools are now corrupt with drugs, fights and murders, and they are getting worse as times passes. God is the only one able to protect kids while they attend school.

The people who oppose prayer in school say school is not the place for prayer. Schools are for learning. Anywhere can be the place for prayer. The prayer does not have to be long and extensive. It can be a short simple prayer, like thanking God for waking me up this morning and giving me strength to attend school, that will not interfere with time used for getting an education. The prayer does not even have to be aloud. God sees the heart. Silent prayers are just as effective. One prayer that I used to use in class went like this: Dear God, I want to thank you for my life, health, and strength. I ask that you protect me through the day. Amen."

Atheist are among the people who wanted prayer out of school. These people do not believe there is a God. Naturally, they pass it on to their children. They do not want their children

> exposed to religion in school. Some say the prayer was forced on the students. If prayer was optional in schools, the students would be given a choice.
>
> Opposite of the atheist's beliefs, some parents believe in God and want Him in every aspect of their child's life. These are the people that suffer from the decision to take prayer out of school. They can not practice their religious beliefs and therefore they have no religious freedom. One of my friends told me, "I was really shocked when they [Congress] passed the law taking prayer out of schools. How could they do that? Religious freedom is given to us by the constitution. I felt so deprived!" How would the opposition feel if one of their inalienable rights, such as liberty, taken away from them? They would be very upset. Well, this is how we feel. This is a grave injustice to some of the Americans.
>
> In the 1700's and 1800's, thousands of people set out for this country. Many had suffered beatings and imprisonment in their home country because of their religious preferences. News had gotten to them that they would be able to practice their choice of religion in the New World. It was known to some as a religious haven. During this journey, which sometimes lasted for three months, many contracted diseases and some lost their lives. Now, some of their descendents are being deprived of that selfsame freedom. No compromises were made when the decision was finalized to remove prayer from schools. These people have a right to practice their religious beliefs. Just as students are given the choice of saluting the flag, they should be given the choice to pray.

As I indicated above, I don't believe this student will likely succeed in a college writing course. I will pass over the obvious problems with writing skills to deal with what I see as the more important limitations of this writer—the attitudes she brings to this writing assignment. Here is the assignment as her teacher presented it to her:

> Reflect on your experience and choose a controversial issue that is particularly interesting to you. Write a paper in which you attempt to convince your readers to accept your views on the topic. Be sure to target your essay for readers who are in need of some convincing on this matter.

This is not an assignment that I would give; it may well contribute to the student's failure to write successfully by asking her to attempt to convince people who see the world differently than she does to accept her world view. I would much prefer an assignment that asks her to explain her reasoning (her position) rather than to persuade others to change theirs. Even so, there are things this student, let's call her Donna, could have done to show she is ready to matriculate in a college writing course.

As I noted above, this assignment asks Donna to talk to people who see the world differently from the way she sees it. It assumes that there are issues on which reasonable people disagree. And we as writing teachers assume that a good bit of that disagreement comes about because of the different ways in which people use language to describe, define, and evaluate the worlds in which they live. This assignment invites the writer to enter into and, indeed, struggle with the complexities of this world.

She declines. She is writing a rote speech that will stand for the set of beliefs she brings to this assignment. There is no awareness of an audience that will question assertions made. We see this attitude in the very first paragraph when we are told that when the teacher asks for a volunteer to lead in prayer, "Every child raises a hand and shouts, 'Me, me, me!'" What would happen if we were to question this student: "Somewhere out there don't you suppose there was a shy child, or a sick child, or a mean little child—someone who would not have shouted his or her desire to lead in prayer?" I suspect that if she answered honestly, she would say something like, "You know what I mean. Quit asking silly questions."

Of course we cannot quit asking these "silly" questions. We have to ask what she means by saying (in paragraph two) that "prayer should be present, but optional in schools." And we must understand what she means in saying (in paragraph four) that "prayer does not even have to be aloud." Who would (or could) deny students the right to pray silently while they sit in their seats, walk to and from classes, or take a test?

It is tempting to say that this student just can't think well. Or to say she doesn't understand the rhetorical situation, i.e., she can't put herself in the place of her readers and speak to them in a way that they can understand her. But I'm not satisfied with that answer; I don't think it gets to crux of the matter. This student approaches this writing situation with an attitude that prevents the kind of thought and rhetorical awareness we would encourage.

In order to explain what I mean, I need to review her essay attempting to read the text in the way she meant for it to be read. Speaking for people who believe the way she believes, she argues that to take prayer out of school is just as much of an infringement of the rights of her group as leaving prayer in is for those who oppose prayer—or more so, since her group is in the majority. She recognizes that those who oppose prayer say it takes time away from learning. So she is willing to stipulate that the prayer they use should be very short and simple—and not take very much time away from education. But she knows that this will not satisfy. She knows that some extremists on the other side are going to say that the words of a prayer will offend nonbelievers. So, in a situation in which there is a nonbeliever present, she might be willing to go so far as to say there could be a few moments of silent prayer—and of course the nonbeliever would not (could not) be forced to pray. What could be more fair?

Those of us who have come to write (and think) in the way we do are appalled at this simplistic thinking. And it is tempting to label her as one unable to think in the ways we do. I don't believe that is true—at least not of many students who write this way. Rather, they are like the Hopi Indians who had only two words for hot and cold colors. The extreme Whorfian hypothesis would have us believe that, limited by their language, the Hopi could see no shades of color, that blue looked no different from green. Most linguists today would argue against that view. When (and if) they see a need for these differences, and are given the language to do so, the Hopi are perfectly capable of seeing these shades of meaning.

So what exactly does this have to do with Donna? Well, Donna has not yet come to understand the importance of using language in the subtle ways we would want her to use it. Donna is like a person who buys a toothbrush, takes it home and opens it up, but then decides that she doesn't like it. She takes it back and asks for her money, only to be told by the clerk that once opened, a toothbrush is not returnable. But Donna insists she hasn't used the toothbrush, hasn't even touched the head of the brush. The clerk does not disagree, but asserts that, in principle, once a toothbrush has been opened, it is contaminated by definition. Donna goes away shaking her head at this ridiculous rule that ignores what she knows to be the truth.

Donna would feel the same way about those who would try to complicate the prayer in schools argument with such hypotheticals. They would argue that atheists would not be the only ones to object to the Christian prayers she would like said in her schools. Muslims, Jews, and even some sects of Christians would be left out of the prayers she (and other members of her "we") would espouse. Donna would look around her at the twenty-five children all shouting "Me, me, me" and say, "Where are these dissenters? They don't come to this school. When they do, we'll deal with them; for now, why complicate and impoverish our religious lives with these distant, hypothetical worries?"

So What Is College-Level Writing?

Since I'm taking this question from the title of an article published by one of the editors of this collection, Patrick Sullivan, let's begin with his list of standards for defining college-level work. After saying that a student should write "in response to an article, essay, or reading selection that contains at last some abstract content" (385), Sullivan offers the following criteria for college-level writing:

- A willingness to evaluate ideas and issues carefully
- Some skill at analysis and higher-level thinking
- Some ability to shape and organize material effectively
- The ability to integrate some of the material from the reading skillfully
- The ability to follow the standard rules of grammar, punctuation, and spelling.

I am not sure whether Sullivan means for us to use these criteria to determine whether a student should be admitted to a college-level writing course or whether the student should receive a passing grade for a college course. Depending upon how these criteria are defined and interpreted in specific situations, they could be used to exclude a large percentage of the students currently in college writing courses.

Let's examine how the two pieces of writing we have looked at so far might fare when judged by these criteria.

Our first writer certainly shows a willingness to evaluate ideas and issues carefully. Even though it is difficult to define analytical and higher-level thinking, I think most college instructors would give this student high marks in this area. I would anticipate some debate as to whether and how this student shapes and organizes his material. Although he does not use a great deal of source material, he does seem to know how to integrate sources into his own writing. And in general he can follow the rules of grammar, punctuation, and spelling. So if this standard is in place to determine whether he should be admitted, there is rather substantial evidence that he should be admitted; if this is an exit standard, he might be judged deficient by some.

The other writer would clearly fail two of the criteria—willingness to evaluate ideas and higher-level thinking. Even though these are difficult criteria to define, I am confident that most of us can look at her writing and say it is lacking in these areas. However, many would find her writing acceptable in terms of two other criteria: organization and standards of usage.

So where are we then? If Sullivan's criteria are to be used as exit criteria, then he is right to suggest, as he does, that there is considerable work to be done in defining and operationalizing these criteria. How could we weigh certain criteria to make sure that the second writer is not given credit for a college writing class? But even more difficult is the question of whether the first writer should be given credit, since his work embodies so many of the most important (in my opinion) criteria, while falling short in other areas. I believe we can do this work, and I am heartened by the realization that the essay we have from the first writer is his first submission in a college course. This writer can easily learn to master the criteria in Sullivan's list.

With that pronouncement made, I move to the question I find more interesting at this junction, viz., what criteria should we use in determining which students should enter a college writing course? Somewhat facetiously above, I made the point that students are college writers when they write in college. But a more serious response to this question would be to say that not all students who graduate from high school are ready for a college writing course. If that is the case, and if we have the opportunity to screen students entering a first-year college writing course, how do we decide which ones are ready for that course and which are not? I believe that when such screening is done, it often fails to look at the most important quality a student brings to his or her writing: attitude.

To explain what I mean, let me offer one final piece of student writing:

"What If Drugs Were Legal?"

What if drugs were legal? Could you imagine what it would do to our society? Well according to John E. LeMoult, a lawyer with twenty years of experience on the subject, feels we should at least consider it. I would like to comment on his article "Legalize Drugs" in the June 15, 1984, issue of the *New York Times*. I disagree with LeMoult's idea of legalizing drugs to cut the cost of crime.

LeMoult's article was short and sweet. He gives the background of the legalization of drugs. For example, the first antidrug laws of the United States were passed in 1914. The laws were put in effect because of the threat of the Chinese imagrants. In addition, he explains how women were the first to use laudanum, an over the counter drug, as a substitute for drinking; it was unacceptable for women to drink. By explaining this he made the reader feel that society was the cause of women using the substitute, laudanum, for drinking. LeMoult proceeded from there to explain how the money to buy drugs comes from us as society. Since drug addicts turn to crime to get money we become a corrupt society. Due to this we spend unnecessary money protecting innocent citizens by means of law enforcement, jails, and etc. LeMoult says that if we legalize drugs that "Overnight the cost of law enforcement, courts, judges, jails, and convict rehabilitation would be cut in half. The savings in tax would be more than $50 billion a year."

LeMoult might be correct by saying that our cost of living in society would be cut in half if drugs were legalized, however, he is justifying a wrong to save money. In my opinion legalizing

> drugs is the easy man's way out. Just because crime is high due to the fact that the cost of drugs is unbelievable it doesn't make legalizing them right. We all know drugs are dangerous to the body and society without any explanation, therefore, you shouldn't legalize something that is dangerous.
>
> My only and most important argument to LeMoult is the physical harm it would bring by legalizing drugs. People abuse their right to use alcoholic beverages because they are legal. For example, LeMoult himself says the amount of drug addicts is small compared to alcoholics. Why?—of course it is because of the legalization of alcohol. When you make something legal it can and will be done with little hassle. Why allow something to be done with ease when it is wrong? LeMoult's points are good and true but I believe he is approaching the subject in the wrong manner. Drugs are wrong, therefore, should not be legal!

While this essay has many flaws, it has qualities that make it more appealing than Donna's school prayer essay. The writer, let's call her Mary, seems to try to listen to the argument of the LeMoult text and rather than offering pronouncements of the beliefs of a certain group, she qualifies certain statements with such phrases as "in my opinion."

However, when we look closely at this text, there is little to recommend it over Donna's. It is written in response to another text, so it gives us a chance to examine the writer's ability to interact with the thinking of another writer—you'll remember that Sullivan recommends that judgments about college-level writing be made on texts that are written in response to other texts. If you were able to compare Mary's essay with the LeMoult text, you would see some very real problems with her ability to interpret this text. Chief among them is her failure to identify the thesis of LeMoult's article, as stated in the last sentence of his essay: "I do not suggest that we legalize drugs immediately. I ask only that we give it some thought." It is clear from his article that LeMoult is leaning toward a position of legalizing drugs, but he asks only that his readers consider how our current drug laws are working and give some thought to other ways of dealing with drugs.

This is something that Mary will not do. She knows that drugs are wrong, and she knows that we should not legalize things that are wrong just because it might cause a reduction in crime to do so. In her defense, it seems that she would have made alcohol illegal given the chance, since the use of alcohol is clearly wrong.

I Don't Like Your Attitude

I don't think either Mary or Donna is ready for a first-year college writing course. Having been both a director of composition and a department chair, I am aware I will have to come up with something more than "I don't like your attitude." But in a real sense, that's the truth. And I don't want to stand behind some smoke screen, e.g., pointing to problems in grammar and mechanics or even sentence structures. Those problems can be found in Adam's paper also.

No, I mean it when I say I don't like certain students' attitudes, because it is their attitudes that are going to keep them from the growth in writing, reading, and thinking that we want to see in a college-level writing course. Our attitudes position us for learning in the same way that an airplane's attitude positions it for landing. In fact, our attitude determines our aptitude, and interestingly enough, both words come from the same Latin word, *aptitudo*.

What then can we tell our students like Mary and Donna, and what do we do to help them prepare themselves for college-level writing? I think Patrick Sullivan offers us some crucial tools here. I think he is absolutely right that what the writing students do to illustrate college-level competence should be in response to texts that contain abstract content. I might push a little further here to say those texts should deal with complex issues that challenge students to read against their biases. The writing they do in response to these prompts should require them to show their ability to think about difficult topics abstractly and with some openness. We need not analyze that writing in the detail that I have analyzed Adam's text, but that analysis should show some of the ways in which we can find college-level abilities in writing that is far from perfect.

Then what? What can we do for those students whose writing does not demonstrate such abilities? What we don't do is relegate them to classes in which we torture them with drills on correctness and elegant sentence structures. Those things come in time as writers become more and more engaged with their writing.

Another thing that we don't do is respond to their texts with the litany of questions that a cross-examining attorney barrages a hostile witness with. When a writer says, "We all know drugs are dangerous to the body and society without any explanation, therefore, you shouldn't legalize something that is wrong," it will avail us (and the student) little to write in the margin such responses as:

- Do we all know anything?
- Are all drugs dangerous to the body? What about aspirin?
- What do you mean "without any explanation"? Don't we have to explain ourselves?
- Do we make all wrong actions illegal?
- Do you think it's wrong to insult someone? Should it be illegal?

I base this claim on the assumption that the writer who writes this way is like the person taking a toothbrush back that has been opened. This person knows he or she did not use the toothbrush and so sees no point in engaging in theoretical discussions about the fact that an opened toothbrush indicates that one could have used it. This person might understand the need for that discussion more if the clerk simply accepts the toothbrush and then gives back a replacement—one that has been opened and repackaged in a makeshift cellophane container.

As for our student writers, it may be much more helpful to give them complex texts to read, write, and talk about. Rather than asking them to imagine hypotheticals, we should encourage them to interact in situations where people think and define the world differently. It is one thing to talk abstractly about the problems with prayer in school. It is quite another to have a conversation with people whose beliefs (or nonbeliefs) differ from yours. Such conversations may provide students ways into texts that they might not otherwise have. Most importantly, they may encourage students to want to deal with the complexities that they would otherwise avoid.

Works Cited

Coles, William E. Jr. *The Plural I: The Teaching of Writing*. New York: Holt, Rinehart and Winston, 1978.

Hunt, Kellogg. *Syntactic Maturity in Schoolchildren and Adults*. Chicago: U Chicago P for the Society for Research in Child Development, 1970.

Mills, Susan K., and John H. Beatty. "The Propensity Interpretation of Fitness." *Philosophy of Science* 46 (1979): 263–86.

Sullivan, Patrick. "What Is 'College Level' Writing?" *Teaching English in the Two-Year College* 30.4 (2003): 374–90.

Chapter Fourteen

Do You Believe in Magic? Collaboration and the Demystification of Research

Kathleen McCormick
Purchase College, State University of New York

Coming out of a workshop I'd just run for high school teachers in which we discussed George Hillocks's *The Testing Trap*, taking a coffee break from a summer staff meeting for first-year writing faculty at my college, or leafing through the *Boston Globe* while on vacation, I lately find myself confronted with the question: What exactly is college-level writing? While clear definitions are hard to come by, what the media bombard us with is that whatever it is, students are not doing it: they can't analyze in depth; they can't synthesize disparate (or even similar) texts; they don't know how to follow an argument in a scholarly source, or maybe even in the *New York Times*, and they certainly don't know how to cite the source according to Modern Language Association (MLA) format in a research paper. The list of complaints goes on and on. We've all heard them, and no doubt in moments of weakness made them ourselves.

While there is obviously no one answer to the question of what college-level writing is, this essay articulates a set of skills with which I think few would disagree as being required for college-level research paper writing. I focus on research because while college-level writing takes many forms, research is often the most challenging for students, and I believe that it is the most undertaught type of writing by teachers. Plagued by plagiarism—or the fear of it—the carefully researched essay, which should be central to college-level writing, is often seen by students and faculty alike as something to fear and, if possible, avoid.

Using both the concept of epistemic rhetoric put forth by James Berlin and lately analyzed in depth by George Hillocks, and the notion of *flow*, first developed by psychologist Mihaly Csikszentmihalyi and put into a carefully scrutinized practice by Michael Smith and Jeffrey Wilhelm, this essay describes a pedagogy that can enable first-year students to learn college-level writing skills when writing researched essays and suggests to teachers strategies for teaching these skills. In the classroom setting I discuss, students work collaboratively on the process of research; they discuss and debate perspectives in a carefully structured, student-centered setting; and they genuinely revise their writing. All of these skills are essential for college-level writing, but they are often not explicitly taught stage by stage to students when they are engaged in writing research papers. If students are expected to possess skills that they are often not taught, they regard themselves as incompetent, as unable to write correctly, as already failures at college-level writing. If, however, these skills are enacted in the classroom, students can learn and understand them so that they can move with a fair degree of competency away from the formulaic you've-got-to-pass-the-state-test writing for which they were so frequently rewarded in high school to writing in which they take up positions of their own that actively engage experts in a field. This, in my view, is writing that is appropriate to the college level.

In *The Testing Trap*, George Hillocks reports on his studies that analyze the theories of knowledge employed in teaching writing on the high school level. Not surprisingly, "current traditional" rhetoric, in which teachers report that they tell students that "truth is directly apprehensible," is the most common intellectual approach to writing instruction. The characteristic pedagogical practice Hillocks discovered that accompanies such an approach is to lecture on the forms of writing. There is little need to talk about content since correct answers are "in the book" or "in the lecture" (25).

A small percentage of teachers in Hillocks's investigations teach from an "expressivist" standpoint in which personal insight is valued and students are expected to develop their ideas both through the writing process itself and through discussion with others (25). While Hillocks sees expressivism as "constructivist" and values the emphasis placed on the writing process and on individual thought, he sees the student-centered "workshop mode" of instruction that typifies an expressivist approach as insufficiently coordinated by the teacher to enable students to move beyond merely exchanging ideas and instead develop genuine arguments that interact with texts and ideas beyond the their own experiences (27–28). So while most students come to college having learned standard writing forms—particularly the five-paragraph essay—and while even fewer come having learned to express their own ideas, neither of these two groups of students arrive at college with a complex conception of how knowledge is developed or with an understanding of its socially constructed nature—assumptions that often seem so *natural* to teachers in college that they are not even discussed.

The intellectual approach valued by Hillocks is one that stems from James Berlin's concept of "epistemic rhetoric," which Hillocks notes "remain[s] very unusual in American schools" (27). From an epistemic approach, students learn that rhetoric is "a means of arriving at the truth" (Berlin 774), that truth is arrived at dialectically through a collaborative process in which the personal subjectivity that is allowed to thrive in an expressivist environment is "ameliorate[d by] . . . allowing others to scrutinize and criticize our ideas" (Hillocks 24). Because the epistemic classroom is so unusual, Hillocks describes its characteristics in detail—and it is these characteristics that I suggest are essential in a college classroom to teach college-level writing. In an epistemic classroom, Hillocks argues:

- Student discussion is maximized.
- Discussion focuses on structured problems that are complex and not subject to simple solutions.
- Discussions often serve as preparation for writing but may also serve to help students learn strategies for critical thinking that they will later use in writing, although not necessarily about a given topic of discussion.
- Discussion takes the form of deliberative thinking about alternatives.

- Ideas and their development are central, with form emerging from them. (27)

A crucial distinction between the epistemic and expressivist classrooms is that while there is a focus on students in each, the epistemic environment is much more highly structured. Teachers do not allow students simply to pursue topics of interest willy-nilly, but rather establish problems for students to work on collaboratively before they work independently (Hillocks 28). Hillocks further notes that in epistemic classes, students learn "sets of fairly specific strategies" and that "learning tasks are scaffolded so that students have support as they encounter new tasks" (28). Thus collaborative work takes precedence over lecturing; it is a prerequisite for independent work because it helps to establish methods of study, critique, and evaluation of student work. Each aspect of the epistemic learning environment is crucial, I believe, for teaching students how to read, think, and write at the college level. Thus, throughout the process I describe below for the teaching of research, I employ an epistemic approach.

Michael Smith and Jeffrey Wilhelm adapt the concept of *flow* described, first by Mihaly Csikszentmihalyi, to create a pedagogy that, they argue, is essential for student engagement in the classroom. Flow, according to Csikszentmihalyi, is what we experience as "joy, creativity, the process of total involvement with life" (Smith and Wilhelm xi). Translating this psychological concept into the classroom, Smith and Wilhelm isolate four characteristics that they argue are central to the creation of such a spirit in the classroom: "a sense of control and competence; a challenge that requires an appropriate level of skill; clear goals and feedback; a focus on the immediate experience" (28, 30). They discovered in their study of middle and high school boys—and argue that it can be easily generalized to girls as well—that many students will resist trying something new for fear that they will not be competent at it (31). This happens particularly in school settings in which students tend to feel that all of the control resides in the teacher (33). The classrooms in which students feel the least control and therefore will take the fewest risks and likely learn the least are those that are "monologic," focused around teachers' lecturing (129). Smith and Wilhelm, in an argument that is similar to Hillocks's, suggest that frontloading information (83–84), giving students genuine choices in collaborative projects, and creating workshop settings (111–13) increase students' feelings of competence and likelihood of learning.

When students are asked, say, at the end of a term in a lecture class, to write a research paper, they often feel overwhelmed. Such assignments, I frequently argue in workshops for high school and college teachers, are invitations to plagiarize because students do not feel that the assignment matches the environment of the class. If they have been required to sit passively in class, to regurgitate information from their textbooks or from lectures on exams, being suddenly asked to take on one of the most potentially active kinds of writing—a researched essay—seems inappropriate. Smith and Wilhelm point out that if students feel "overmatched" in school, many will just "give up" (37). They argue for the importance of carefully sequencing assignments so that students move gradually from one level of difficulty to another in a setting in which skills build upon each other.

Students also reported disliking "the ambiguity of tasks in English" (Smith and Wilhelm 115), which makes it difficult for them to know if they have the skills or even the right sense of a particular assignment to succeed. Clear goals and feedback, the third classroom characteristic required for success, is frequently something that teachers at all levels can see as potentially constraining to students. I have spoken to so many high school and college teachers who feel that assignments like "Analyze Aristotle" are liberating to students because they allow students the freedom to focus on both the task and its content themselves. But from the perspective of the students Smith and Wilhelm worked with, such assignments are frightening and discourage the very creativity teachers expect them to spawn in students.

The fourth characteristic advocated by Smith and Wilhelm is a "focus on immediate experience." They argue, following Csikszentmihalyi, that "healthy work" is immediate and "largely unconscious" (67), and they contrast it with "instrumental" work, which is done for a future gain, such as getting into a good college, but which is not presented by teachers or experienced by students as having any immediate reward. Smith and Wilhelm make clear that in advocating such a goal, they are not talking about pandering to students, but rather about presenting schoolwork in such ways that students will find themselves engaged. Quite surprisingly, students argued that in-depth work seemed more immediately purposeful to them, and they provided powerful critiques of superficial work (104).

All four of the aspects of flow, interwoven with epistemic rhetoric, form the basis of the classroom environment I describe below: it is the one in which I have seen students learn to read, think, and write best at the college level. And it is one in which they have taken the most pride in their work and experienced the greatest degree of competency.

Part I: The Unsilencing of Teaching: Teaching as a Scholarly Activity

Much contemporary pedagogical analysis attempts to bridge the gap between theory and practice. This involves neither simply teaching theory in the canonical and uncritical way in which literary texts have been and still are often taught, nor simply reporting on "what I did in my classroom" yesterday. Rather, it requires making our pedagogies visible—to ourselves so that as faculty we can all discover ways to create enriched and more productive learning environments, and to our students so that they can learn how to *enact* the theories that underlie our teaching practices—whether they are theories of reading literature, theories of writing, or various disciplinary perspectives. When given the opportunity to develop theoretical knowledge by enacting it, students become more than good students, simply able to mouth the latest ideas of the profession (or the professor); rather, they become capable of actively engaging in the current practices of the discipline. This can happen most successfully in a collaborative, epistemic environment in which students are challenged at an appropriate level of difficulty. In such a context, they feel competent and thus take on increasingly complex tasks over which they feel ownership. For it is only in enacting that one can develop, critique, and grow, and eventually generalize one's reading, writing, and interpreting abilities beyond literature and beyond the classroom.

As undergraduates, many of us were taught in ways that deeply conflict with the pedagogies I am advocating. We were taught by a *silent model* in which teaching and learning occurred behind closed doors and were not really thought about or talked about. New Criticism, which suggested that focused staring at a text would somehow bring insight to students, suited this silent method quite well. One did not theorize or enact how one read, taught, or wrote. It all supposedly "just happened," rather in the spirit of Allan Bloom's notion that one should "just read the text" (344). Except, of course, that it didn't just happen for many students.

While I functioned pretty effectively under this method as an undergraduate, I also discovered that teachers not thinking consciously about the theories underlying their teaching could force students into a variety of unproductive roles. The classroom—one of my favorite places then as now—could all too easily become a scene of deception. Students did not just magically develop deep insights by carefully looking at a poem. Their insights were frequently based on extratextual knowledge that the student had picked up somewhere along the way and seemed to just know (and therefore felt like a privileged insider, "to the classroom born") or that was consciously sought out by reading such guides as *Twentieth Century Interpretations*. These books, however, were not discussed in class by students or teachers because acknowledging that one read them took away the magic, the illusion of spontaneity and genius. Students lacking strategies for gaining what was supposed to be *innate* knowledge became painfully aware of their status as incompetent outsiders. And because of the lack of clearly articulated goals, group discussions, or collaborative projects, these students were usually not helped by the teacher or their fellow classmates. Students' feelings of control and competence in the classroom were not thought to be, as Smith and Wilhelm argue, something that teachers could be a part of by "shar[ing their] . . . secrets with students" (132); rather, these feelings were something students had to create on their own.

Increasingly over the last twenty-five years, a variety of factors have come into play that have called into question the silent model of teaching. Some of these are very material details of professional and institutional life. For instance, with budget shortages, faculty are required to teach more courses outside their specialty, even while, paradoxically, specialties in graduate schools are narrowing. The requirement of teaching a wider variety of courses for which one is not prepared by graduate study has created a need for learning about teaching. English faculty have also had to teach an increased number of composition courses—which are difficult to teach effectively (let alone enjoyably) without some degree of theorizing about pedagogy. Some of this thinking necessarily spills over into the teaching of literature. Greater connections have developed between college faculty in English and high school teachers, leading college faculty to think more explicitly about how they teach.

There has also been some response to repeated calls from the MLA for teacher training to be included in graduate curricula. Increasingly, as a profession, we have had to acknowledge that most jobs are in non-PhD-granting, primarily teaching-oriented undergraduate colleges. The rise of cultural studies has given significant credibility to the study of specifically educational practices and institutions. Further, over the last half century, more students have been going to college. This increase in the college student population necessarily means that a number of students may well be less prepared for college-level work. Teaching underprepared students is more difficult, and it highlights what should have always been acknowledged about college-level teaching: that teachers not only impart a body of content knowledge, but also a set of practices and pedagogies that enable or disenable learning as much as the content itself. While all of these changes can be seen and have been represented at times as negative, together they functioned positively to legitimate the analysis of teaching as a scholarly activity and to help break the silences surrounding teaching and make pedagogy visible.[1]

When teachers show how theories can be enacted and how even apparently commonsensical practices are rooted in complex theories of knowledge, they and their students cannot easily sustain the idea that deep thoughts or good papers just happen. If teachers theorize the very material ways in which genuine learning occurs for different types of students in different contexts—and if they give students the opportunity to enact these theories in a collaborative, epistemic classroom—they can enable many more students to become actively engaged and productive learners.

Some may ask whether demystifying assignments for students in ways I am about to suggest doesn't in some way do the work for them or "dumb down" a course. Such a question results from a confusion between *telling* students *what to say* in a paper and *instructing* students explicitly in the processes of *how* to engage in an assignment, a practice that helps to level the playing field for students who may come to college less versed in academic conventions. While it may seem paradoxical, as Smith and Wilhelm demonstrated (115), students do not work as hard when their assignments are mystified because romantic notions then take over—they wait for inspiration that doesn't come, or they feel defeated from the start. When teachers make the practical and theoretical underpinnings of their pedagogies visible to students, they give students concrete opportunities and specific strategies for working productively, and they can more easily set rigorous standards that students can achieve. As a practical example, I will focus on a teaching process that many of my colleagues and I use by which research can be theorized and demystified (and more effectively learned) in an undergraduate classroom.

A great deal of guidance exists in textbooks telling students how to engage productively in college-level research, and no doubt on occasion, this guidance is helpful for students who are already sufficiently trained in research techniques to be able to follow it. Students are told repeatedly, for example, to be sure that their research question is broad enough so that they can find material, but narrow enough to make the project doable and to enable them to develop a focused thesis statement (Rosa and Eschholz 302–3; Lynn 207–10; Fulwiler and Biddle 916–18; Trimbur 528–29; Behrens and Rosen 178–79; Ballenger 77–79, 81–82). They are encouraged to find "patterns" among source texts (Rosa and Eschholz 309), to "make one source speak to another" (Rosenwasser and Stephen 229), thinking of them as a "collaborative *chain* of thinking" (Rosenwasser and Stephen 221), and to realize that research is a "recursive process" where "backtracking and looping [are] essential" (Behrens and Rosen 177).

This is all good advice and describes processes that most would probably agree should occur in college-level writing; however, many students do not seem to end up learning from it. I believe that students are unable to translate such practical, but fundamentally abstract, lessons about research to their own work for two reasons. First, in all of the textbooks and in most conventional classes, students do their research alone. At most, they work with a librarian and their teacher. Despite all of our advances in peer review and collaborative work in the writing process, when it comes to writing a research paper, where students usually need the most help in all of the areas listed above—narrowing a topic, finding patterns among source texts, rereading, developing thesis statements, redrafting, thinking recursively—students are left alone. This student isolation in writing a research paper is a key factor in keeping research writing at a fairly static level, in lowering students' enthusiasm for doing research, and in encouraging plagiarism.

Second, despite the detailed practical advice given by these books, there is a point at which each of them mystifies part of the research process. Crucial strategies on how one moves from one stage to another are silenced in a romantic leap of faith—a moment of magic—suggesting that if one waits and works hard enough, a coherent, well-argued paper will eventually emerge. At some point, most authors actually do begin to hint that the whole process of engaging in research at the college level is not quite so straightforward as it sounds. They acknowledge that students may feel "overwhelmed and lost" (Lynn 205), "pretty frustrated" (Fulwiler and Biddle 916), or find themselves "facing an impossible deadline at the last moment" (Rosa and Eschholz 301). Students are told to anticipate problems and are given various pieces of advice. Repeatedly, they are told to be "flexible" (Lynn 205; Behrens and Rosen 103; Trimbur 544), "patient" (Lynn 205), and to be willing to "modify" their "thinking" (Rosa and Eschholz 309; Trimbur 544–45).

It is at this stage in many of the textbooks that what I term *magic*—or at least a romantic ideology of the individual writer's mind—appears to take over. Things are supposed to happen that are not really explained, so that we see the mystifying of the research process and of writing on the college level begin again.

Students are told to wait, and that somehow their papers will all fall into place. What they should actually do at these stages is not quite clear. Fulwiler and Biddle discuss a student, Jessica, at the early stages of her research. Just when she is getting frustrated at the library because she is finding too much information that is not quite relevant, a librarian shows up to ask if he can help (916). A bit later, after she had "been in the history library for an hour" and "wasn't feeling very encouraged" (917), Bill the librarian shows up again and helps her find more relevant material. So within just an hour or so of frustrated waiting, Jessica is well on her way to finding good sources.

Rosa and Eschholz similarly assure students who cannot seem to make their sources fit together that "by looking at evidence on both sides, you will refine your topic and begin to see possible organizational plans" (309). Behrens and Rosen advise students to "be comforted that through back tracking and reformulating you will eventually produce a coherent, well-crafted essay" (103). Lynn is perhaps the most explicitly magical: even though he has told students that they don't have to rely on "luck" (206), he recognizes that there will be a point at which students will be "waiting for the facts to fit together" (204) and advises them to "start writing anywhere" (222), assuring them that if they have done enough research, they will find that they, like the student Anna in his book, will be "ready to put it all together" (234).

While all of this advice is salutary, it does not address the reality that many students do not achieve success as easily as happens in the textbooks. Sources can be harder to find than they were for Jessica. Librarians don't always turn up. When students have collected a number of sources, they do not necessarily fall onto two sides. A number of students do spend time reviewing their sources on their own and still never find coherence among them and do not write well-crafted essays. Finally, the idea of starting to write anywhere is frightening to many students who do not feel as ready as Anna to "put it all together."

This remystification of the research process will not affect students who know what to do while waiting. But for everyone else, these stories can be defeating, suggesting that if students wait and nothing happens, they have somehow personally failed to be able to write on the college level. Further, success stories like Jessica's and Anna's may suggest to some students that research is actually much simpler than the textbooks have been letting on and that a quick throwing of something together, after one has done sufficient research and a lot of staring and waiting, isn't so bad after all.

As in my own undergraduate experience and as a teacher—and like most faculty—I find that there are always a few "good students" who do whatever is assigned to them quite well and apparently naturally, and who would easily be able to follow the advice of textbooks like these. But there are many more students who cannot. I think that we have to face the fact that large numbers of students come to college not having been taught how to do the intellectual work of research effectively, and as a consequence, the processes of research need to become public, not private, and actively enacted in the classroom in multiple sites of a student's college career. Research, like reading in the days of New Criticism, cannot be regarded as simply a private experience. Clearly, teachers and the textbooks I have cited do not mystify stages of research for reasons of perversity, but rather because the processes in which they want students to engage seem so commonsensical to them that they have often remained untheorized, even in the face of weak student research papers.

In her important work on task representation in *Reading-to-Write: Exploring a Cognitive and Social Process*, Linda Flower argues that one of the reasons students frequently perform poorly on written assignments is that their task definition does not match the teacher's (37–43). Students, for example, do a summary rather than a synthesis; they write a "gist and list" paper rather than develop an argument (44–53). In the very act of theorizing the kinds of writing students have engaged in, Flower helps teachers and students to understand the vast array of writing choices students have when they begin an assignment, the contexts in which one choice may be more appropriate than another, and the series of complex tasks that are nested in each of our writing assignments. These tasks are underpinned by theoretical assumptions about the nature of writing and thinking of which teachers are frequently not fully cognizant and often do not articulate to their students. This silence decreases students' possibilities of understanding the assignments themselves, let alone completing them successfully. While Flower's work on task definition does not address research writing per se, it has obvious implications because of the myriad tasks that are imbedded and never articulated in a research assignment.

The suggestions that I offer in this chapter for breaking the silence that surrounds the research process are not meant to be definitive articulations; rather, they provide some ways of making the theoretical assumptions behind particular pedagogies visible. They are, further, meant to encourage readers to think about how their assumptions about research may differ from as well as overlap with mine, and to then explore how they make their particular assumptions explicit to their students.

Part II: Demystifying Research Processes in the Classroom

Many students come to college with negative views of research, at least in part because they have been asked to write research reports, which are basically summaries, rather than researched essays—that is, carefully integrated arguments in which student writers enter into genuine conversation with a group of experts (Ballenger 6–7). While this *report* task definition of research usually leads to a disengaged process for students, it is relatively easy to accomplish. So, although students frequently complain about it, they often hold tenaciously to it because it has worked in the past, because it is not all that demanding, and because, for many, it is the only way they know how to write a research paper. A number of students, therefore, come to college needing faculty to help make visible to them the excitement of research, not because they are lazy or cognitively deficient, but because they literally do not have a conception of research as something engaging, exciting, and potentially empowering, a conception of research that is the essence of college-level work. Many textbooks cited above acknowledge this (Ballenger xix–xxii, 4; Lynn 205; Rosa and Eschholz 302; Fulwiler and Biddle 919).

Theorizing the ideological underpinnings of most college students' attitudes toward research can lead to productive changes in how we teach. If Hillocks is right that over 80 percent of high school students are taught from a right/wrong current traditional rhetoric perspective, we can assume that little of such theorizing has occurred in high school. Thus, we need to acknowledge that, for particular social and historical reasons, students come to us not only with a fear of or disdain for research, but also with a genuine lack of understanding of how to engage in effective research processes and of why they are important. Rather than giving them—and ourselves—yet further experiences of failed opportunities, we can create contexts in which we dramatically reposition research so that students can learn to enjoy it, despite all that militates against such an attitude.

I am proposing that, especially at the beginning of students' college education, we abandon notions of research as primarily an individual endeavor and create a research environment in which students work collaboratively to learn what the textbooks say are the major goals of research—to do research in stages; to narrow one's research questions; to analyze sources critically; to develop multiple options for thesis statements; to use sources effectively, putting them in conversation with one another; to organize and synthesize; to build effective arguments; and to read and write recursively. After they have learned all of these skills collaboratively, students can still, in the end, write individual research papers. Collaborative work in class can make visible the processes by which one does research, processes that tend for many students to seem abstract and difficult until they actually witness them come alive in the classroom. Because research capacities are so vital to academic work, it is well worth the time to have students themselves actively develop and then display these skills in class.

I have found that research becomes most engaging and productive for students when they are required to find and analyze sources as members of a research team rather than individually. This makes the process of doing research more "immediate" and gives them a sense of "control and competence," two crucial aspects for flow and engagement (Smith and Wilhelm). Subsequently, students use these collaboratively developed sources in their individual research papers. So, from an epistemic approach, students' collaborative work is highly structured by the teacher and it is meant to provide scaffolding prior to independent work (Hillocks 28). During the research process in this type of assignment, the class functions together, in the words of one of my students, "as one great mind," and the insights they develop can be startling both to the students and to the teacher.

The collaborative research process I am proposing can be best explained in seven stages, which I will elaborate and justify below.

- Teachers develop a collaborative research paper assignment that is similar in kind to other work students have done in the course.
- The collaborative research paper assignment has a number of facets that are defined by the teacher; students choose which facet they will focus on in collaborative research teams.
- The teacher specifies the types of sources that best suit the needs of each research team, including both preliminary and more focused research.
- Students work collaboratively to select appropriate sources; each team makes four or five sources available to the class to read in advance of their team presentation.
- Each research team formally analyzes its source texts with the class, suggesting research questions, thesis statements, and points of dialogue among the texts of the team.
- Between team presentations, the class engages in *synthesis days* in which students develop short written statements that develop relationships among source texts from *different* teams. On these days, students analyze and evaluate source texts recursively to develop new and more complex ideas, to debate alternative perspectives, and finally to determine potential thesis statements for their research papers.
- Students draft and redraft papers, peer review, and analyze the papers in and out of class; synthesizing sources across teams, students begin to think in new and original ways about the research topic.

The whole process takes about five weeks. It is a structure that is adaptable to all disciplinary content. By creating contexts for radically redefining students' conventional notions of research and for encouraging genuine engagement and productive writing, it has the potential to break the silence surrounding the research process. In what follows, I spell out in some detail what is likely to happen at each of these stages, not because I expect any of my readers to be unfamiliar with the skills addressed in each stage, but because I expect that they may not be used to explicitly providing a space in which students can *enact* them.

1. Teachers develop a collaborative research paper assignment that is similar in kind to other work students have done in the course.

Teachers often feel that students will engage in research more actively if they are free to choose their own topic, but the possible pleasure of researching something in which one is individually interested—particularly for students just entering college—is often quickly erased by the sense of isolation and confusion experienced in the research process. We need to recall Smith and Wilhelm's powerful evidence that in the absence of clear goals, students lose motivation, that the idea of "giving students freedom" is often perceived by the students as a failure to provide them guidance (50). While research assignments generally ask students to read their sources critically, often such evaluation is made impossible when faculty encourage—or at least allow—students to do research on topics about which they know virtually nothing. If, in contrast, students are asked to collaboratively research a topic with which they and their classmates feel somewhat familiar, they are likely to choose sources more critically because they will have a knowledge base from which to evaluate these sources and opportunities to negotiate their choices publicly. Students, as Smith and Wilhelm have demonstrated, feel a greater sense of control and competence when they are actively working collaboratively. And they feel greater motivation if they believe that they are being challenged at an appropriate level.

A teacher, for example, might assign a research paper on particular aspects of the production and reception of Arthur Miller's *The Crucible* in a course in which the class has read other American plays, read critical texts provided by the teacher about those plays, and already written at least a short paper or two. The research paper, therefore, is similar in its task definition to other papers students have written, but probably larger in scope, and requires students to provide most, if not all, of the critical material. It will be easier for students to approach their research if the fundamental task of the paper is one with which they are familiar. Students already understand the fundamentals of the assignment: it has clear goals and they have already received clear feedback if they have written similar papers earlier in the term.

If students, in contrast, have not been asked to read any critical texts before a research paper is assigned, too many variables can change in the research assignment. In such an instance, students are likely to be overwhelmed, not only because research is difficult but also because they may not understand how to integrate criticism into a paper or even how to read it. The task definition has changed too much and students may feel *overmatched* and possibly defeated before they begin. This kind of confusion about the task that often results in frustration for students and teachers alike can be avoided if the only new task students are asked to perform in a research paper is the research itself. Further, if the research assignment is seen by the class as extending an inquiry already begun in the course, its significance and validity becomes clearer and more immediately understood to students.

As they become more knowledgeable in a particular subject area, usually their major, in their junior and senior years, students can begin to extrapolate from course material and do projects that move further afield. I would still argue, however, that in most courses in the major, students need far more support for their research—from teachers and peers—than they usually receive in conventional assignments and conventional classrooms where they are often expected to be carrying out their research on their own while other material is required to be read for class lectures and discussions. The need for an inquiry-based epistemic approach to teaching research does not end in the first year if students are to learn to read, think, and write from the critical perspectives expected in college.

2. The collaborative research paper assignment has a number of facets that are defined by the teacher; students choose which facet they will focus on in collaborative research teams.

A team approach to research works particularly well with a group of approximately twenty to twenty-five students and with four or five research areas so that there can be approximately five to six students in each team. The system of organization teachers choose for dividing the research teams will work best if it makes sense to students in terms of the overall theory and method of the class, again increasing students' sense that they are competent to perform the assignment. In this way, students can see their research as an integral part of the course, not something added on that is fundamentally disconnected. They will also see that earlier work is helping to scaffold later work. So for example, if a teacher's approach has been historical, she or he might divide students chronologically (group one: 1900–1925; group two: 1926–1950; group three: 1951–1975; group four: 1976–present), and each group would research the same set of issues in different time periods.

Thus, in one class that focused on banned books, each group chose as the focus of their research a banned book from their assigned time period that the class had not studied. They felt a clear sense of control, not only because they chose the focus of their research themselves, but also because they already had experience working in groups and reading published responses to banned books earlier in the term. Or teachers might have groups organized by competing issues in a single time period. Students might look at issues in the contemporary family: one group would focus on single-parent versus two-parent families, another on religion and the family, another on socioeconomic status and the family, etc. Whatever the topics, teachers oversee them to be certain that students will be working in areas sufficiently different to make the topic complex, but that can also be integrated enough so that students will be able to think deliberatively and critically about alternative perspectives.

3. The teacher specifies the types of sources that best suit the needs of each research team.

Many teachers—and textbooks—are concerned that students will use *unreliable* sources when doing research. Such problems can be solved, however, if students are given clear guidelines on the types of sources they should use, and if they work collaboratively to help each other find and analyze sources. Rather than hoping that a librarian will happen upon a lost student who doesn't know where to turn first in the library, teachers can build guidelines into a team's research requirements that help them do their research systematically and relatively successfully. For example, teachers can specify that students doing historical research are required to find a certain number of academic and popular articles, and they can specify the time periods from which those texts must come, and they can explain to students the rationale for finding such types of sources. Teachers can also give students criteria for evaluating sources that resemble those in the textbooks, and they will find that students heed these criteria to a much greater extent when they are working collaboratively than when they are working alone. The clear goals of the assignment enable students to feel that they are competent to complete the task. The structure of the assignment will help students set up problems that are bound to have multiple perspectives. The collaborative nature of the work—both that students are trying to find good sources together and that they will eventually share their best sources with the entire class—lends an immediacy to the assignment that motivates students. Finally, the clarity of the assignment begins to take the magic away from the process of beginning to do research. Students will see, through the various stages of their work, that research is comprised of a set of skills that can actually be specified by the teacher and enacted by the student. The playing field is being leveled because research secrets are being revealed.

4. Students work collaboratively to select appropriate sources; each team makes four or five sources available to the class to read in advance of their team presentation.

While, as teachers, we tell our students about the importance of carefully selecting source texts, because we usually give them no practical way of moving these choices from the individual to the collective, we do not publicly validate a practice we supposedly endorse. Consequently, we send students mixed messages: choosing your source texts is important, but it's not important enough for the teacher or the class to actually get involved. When given such a message, most students will opt for the easier course of action and simply choose the first books or articles they find. If students work in research teams to find texts to share with the entire class, however, the dynamic of selecting sources can change dramatically. The research process is not so daunting when students work collaboratively. They feel freer to ask questions of the teacher and of librarians when these questions are shared by the whole team; moreover, students are much more likely to critique the books and articles they are considering for their research if they can talk about them with other students, both inside and outside the classroom.

Students develop a more critical attitude toward their source texts in such a context primarily because of the collaborative nature of both the source selection and dissemination process. When members of a team read each other's texts, their sense of the immediacy of the task is so strong that they begin to do audience analysis. They can no longer simply decide to use the first texts they find. Rather, because every team knows that the rest of the class will use some of their texts in the final research paper, students tend to reject a number of sources after they have read them if they do not meet fairly stringent criteria. Most groups try to select articles that are readable, interesting, and informative, criteria that students largely maintained for themselves as a result of the productive peer pressure and sense of flow that comes from collaboration. Students want positive responses to their texts from the rest of the class. They want other students to be able to find patterns and connections among them. They want their texts to suggest answers to certain research questions. I have found that when students do not have to share their source texts with anyone in the class, they are much less discerning: they are less concerned about interest level, points of connection, and even about whether they meet particular criteria I have established.

The number of sources that each research team is responsible for finding can vary with the level of the class and with whether the class is a general education class or a course in the major. My own preference in a first-year or general education class is to keep the number of total articles for a team approximately equal to the number of students on the team. For example, if there are five students on the team, they could be responsible for providing the class with five good source texts, though their bibliography can be more extensive. In upper-level classes, I might require a team to find more sources, but I will still ask them to give only a subset of these to the entire class. Since much of the research process at the undergraduate level is about teaching students the practice of reading, analyzing, and synthesizing texts, it is important that the number of texts that the entire class shares not become too high. If this happens, students will simply be too overwhelmed to do the work.

5. Each research team formally analyzes its source texts with the class, suggesting research questions, thesis statements, and points of dialogue among the texts of the team.

Once all of the teams have decided on what their source texts will be, the next stage is to make visible more of the skills that are at the heart of good research—analyzing source texts, developing and choosing among research questions, determining thesis statements, and putting texts in dialogue with each other. These skills are often mystified because they are usually required to be performed by students alone. They can be demystified by having each research team, on different days, share their sources with the entire class and formally analyze them in a presentation and discussion. This process works most effectively when teams give their source texts to the class in advance of their presentation and when class members are required to read and write about the texts before discussing them with the research team. I ask students to read other teams' research actively, looking for points of connection or areas of tension among the viewpoints presented in the texts, and to write a page or two about what they imagine the research question and thesis of the research team will be. Students complete these assignments before they hear each presentation, using specific quotations, paraphrases, and summaries to support their speculation. This scaffolding enables students' presentations of their research to result in genuine epistemic work.

Knowing that their sources will be scrutinized in an ongoing way encourages each team to become increasingly responsible not only about the particular sources they select, but also about the ways in which they present their material to the class. Similarly, because all class members realize that they must use the texts provided by other teams in their final research paper, they become significantly more attentive to each others' work, come to value each group's contributions, and want to engage actively in discussing each team's research. When students build hypotheses about the relationships among a team's source texts before coming to class, they are prepared for informed and animated discussions. In these discussions, students engage in and make visible the kinds of epistemic thinking that underlies good research, in which researchers try to develop research questions and discussions of complex problems, link disparate sources, speculate—often many times—on how they might form a chain of thinking, try out and scrap a lot of ideas, think consciously about alternative perspectives, and debate the relative merits of particular positions.

These are all the kinds of processes advocated by the textbooks discussed above and that most faculty expect, on some level, that their students will do on their own. Most students, however, would not engage in this recursive and ongoing analysis of sources on their own both because this process is usually not part of research as they knew it in high school, and because—and we might as well face facts—it is too hard to do, at least initially by oneself. However, these tasks are easily made visible and become quite doable when students work together in class, in a low-stakes environment, well before they begin to write their papers. Class discussions help prepare students for writing, but, as Hillocks notes of the epistemic class, they also help students practice critical thinking skills that they will use later, in other contexts.

6. Between team presentations, the class engages in synthesis days in which students develop short written statements that develop relationships among source texts from **different** *teams. On these days, students analyze and evaluate source texts recursively to develop new and more complex ideas, to debate alternative perspectives, and finally to determine potential thesis statements for their research papers.*

Hillocks argues that "writing is thinking" (198), and in this stage of the research process, students come to see this for themselves. In the previous stage, students discover that developing multiple and complex relationships among different texts of a single research team is a key part of research. Although new, this task is likely to be manageable for most students because the research team will have worked to create a selection of texts that speak to each other.[2] Thus, while the previous stage of synthesizing texts from one team is an excellent starting point and helps to make even weaker students feel a sense of control over the material, it must be regarded as scaffolding for the more difficult task that occurs in this stage, which more realistically reflects the challenges of actual research—finding connections among the texts of *different* research teams.

And here is one instance in which the student-centered nature of epistemic methods of instruction is also highly structured. Without adequate intervention by teachers at this stage, many students can become overwhelmed, and the careful sense of flow established thus far can easily evaporate. To help keep the challenge of integrating an increasing number of disparate texts at an appropriate level, teachers can alternate classes in which research teams present their work with classes that focus on developing relationships among texts across teams.

If a course has four research teams, for example, a teacher could schedule a number of "synthesis days" to help the class stay in control of new material and to keep the experience immediate and flowing. These synthesis days can occur after group two's work, in which students would be asked to find patterns among the sources of groups one and two; after group three's work to find relationships among groups one, two, and three; and after group four's work to find patterns among groups one, two, three, and four. To prepare for these synthesis days, each student might be asked to write one page for homework that would consist of three parts: (a) write a one-sentence statement that connects one group's research with another group's research; (b) list quotations from various sources that support this connection (some students will be surprised that this will require rereading source texts with a particular idea in mind—a vital stage of research); (c) write one paragraph expanding the initial statements, with the quotations from the source texts in mind.

The advantages of such synthesis assignments that explore relationships among the texts of different research teams are many. Students are told by textbooks that rereading their sources will eventually help them develop a thesis about these sources. But, as Smith and Wilhelm have argued and as Dewey pointed out nearly ninety years ago, when any aspect of education is presented as preparation or instrumental rather than immediate, students suffer a "loss of impetus" (Dewey 90, as qtd. in Smith and Wilhelm 66). Synthesis assignments keep students engaged and in the immediate: when students write to connect two or more team presentations and when these connections are discussed in class, students actually see the logic of engaging in the kinds of recursive work discussed in the textbooks "where backtracking and looping [are] essential" (Behrens and Rosen 177).

Being asked, in a clear and concrete assignment, to create patterns from the research of different groups—patterns that have not been planned because research teams work independently—helps students to reread, reevaluate, and synthesize previously read work. It requires that they develop more complex and comprehensive ideas about the subject, well before having to start writing the paper. When done gradually and systematically, students find themselves developing unanticipated relationships among source texts from different research teams. They begin to see recursive work as a vital stage of research because they are actively enacting it together rather than simply being told to do it on their own. The process most students usually follow in conventional research paper writing of finding one's sources, reading them, and then trying to write a paper about them—often in one or two sittings—is not a successful strategy. But students cannot be told this abstractly by teachers or textbooks; they will learn it, however, if given the chance and support to experience it collaboratively in recursive assignments.

7. Students draft and redraft papers, peer review, and analyze papers in and out of class; synthesizing sources across teams, students begin to think in new and original ways about the research topic.

Before students are required to start drafting their research papers, they have been engaging in complex discussions that they have taken seriously because they were not overmatched. Because they had a chance to develop ideas about relationships among source texts out of class, every student has come to class with something to say. Because rereading was not optional, students have become increasingly expert in the subject matter and have had increasingly nuanced discussions. While these discussions were a preparation for writing the research paper, they also had an immediacy and integrity about them. The teacher has worked to keep the students on track, but because they are, for the most part, comfortable with the task definition at each stage, because the teacher provides clear goals and feedback, because there has been significant scaffolding, students usually need remarkably little guidance once the synthesis class discussions begin to occur. In these discussions and before they have seriously started to write their research paper *per se*, students have already analyzed their source texts, debated various research questions, explored alternative perspectives, and suggested possible thesis statements in class. They have also tried out a variety of ideas in short pieces of writing, critiqued those together, and developed multiple patterns of connection among their sources.

Engaging in all of this work publicly, with texts provided by one's classmates, makes research come alive for students and aids enormously in the drafting process. Because the work is done incrementally, students do not find themselves facing a blank screen when they have to begin writing their research papers. By the time they have to write a first draft, they feel competent and in control. Although not all students are fluent writers, they all have some ideas and they are familiar enough with the issues and the texts to be able to write a first draft of their papers.

As students share paper drafts, the class as a whole can observe itself using the same materials, but usually coming to very different conclusions. Because they know that the development of their own ideas in dialogue with each other and with their source texts is central to the course, because they know that truth must be argued through a dialectical process, and because they have experienced their own viewpoints being modified by other students' critiquing of their ideas in class discussions (see Hillocks 26), at this stage, students work to support each other's alternative perspectives. While they may not fully agree with the argument a fellow student is developing, they will nonetheless help that student better support it, so long as they feel it is viable.

Rather than simply coming out of their own individual research (or off the Internet), students' final researched essays synthesize a subset of the research from all groups in the class. The essays they produce actually meet the requirements that textbooks and most faculty set for students, but that students rarely achieve on their own: students intellectually negotiate a variety of texts and they work recursively to articulate and then answer a particular research question. They do this with a clear and usually well-developed position, which they actually believe in. They write with strong ideas supported by a well-organized pattern of sources. They take into account alternative viewpoints. Because the processes of research were a part of an epistemic classroom rather than something students were simply expected to do on their own, all stages of the processes of research were demystified, and thus the personal engagement and personal investment in as well as the intellectual level of student papers dramatically increases.

One colleague, who was initially skeptical of this collaborative research process, asked me whether, in a process such as this, all students wouldn't end up writing basically the same paper. He assumed that with all of our discussions, we would come to a class consensus, which students' papers would then merely echo.

This seems to be a reasonable question particularly because the research paper in an academic setting is so invested with a sense of privacy, even though collaboration is actually the more common mode of professional research done outside, and increasingly inside, the humanities. A number of my colleagues and I have used this process many times and have never found a class or even a subset of the class using the same thesis statement in their final paper.

Although it may initially seem paradoxical, this collaborative model supports individual thinking. When students are doing their own research and sharing it with the class, they have a high degree of ownership that prevents them from reaching a class consensus. Students have worked individually as much as they have worked collaboratively. While they have collaborated to find articles, to present team groupings of research, they have each worked on their own to read, write about, reread, and reconceptualize research questions, theses, alternative perspectives, and patterns of connections among source texts. Perhaps ironically, students have done much more individual processing of their source texts than they would normally do if they were working on their own, because they were responsible to the whole class every day for their individual work. Thus, most students have already determined at least a working thesis before they begin writing their research paper, and they are often highly invested in its difference from other students' theses.

Peer reviewing conventional research papers, in which students have all written on different topics and have no texts in common, is often frustrating for students and teachers alike. The most that peers can do if they have little or no knowledge of the content is to line edit, checking grammar, punctuation, and citation style. While this can be useful, it is intellectually thin. Peer editing of papers written from a collaborative process, in contrast, is exciting and deeply informative. Students enjoy critiquing each others' papers from the point of view of a relative expert. That is, they not only can explain to other students that they should develop or refute or at least take account of a particular point in more detail, but they can also suggest sources by which to do this.

The drafting and redrafting process, therefore, is dynamic, exciting, and rigorous in ways that I have never seen either with conventional research assignments or with assignments in which I have provided all of the readings. Students, as well as teachers, feel the difference, and many students and faculty have reported that they can hardly believe that students are this excited about a research paper. Significant numbers of students—for the first time—have realized that it is actually possible for them to create new knowledge. They see that this originality is not based simply on personal opinion and feeling. Rather, it is the result of understanding a spectrum of expert contemporary and historical ideas on a subject and configuring those ideas to build an argument that exists in dialogue with the research on which they are drawing. This definition of originality (as opposed to the *personal opinion* definition) requires careful scrutiny and an honest use of sources. Students, rather than the teacher, can usually monitor each other on this because they are so close to their source texts.

And the final test of this pedagogy? The papers are better. Much better.

Part III: Conclusion

What strikes me most about breaking down the research process into various stages is that at each stage, students discover many helpful skills. They thereby inadvertently show me the gaps in their strategies, the places where, if left on their own, they would have probably failed or felt frustrated because they would not have known what to do, and I would not have been aware of what they did not know. Yet it is impossible for a teacher ever to predict what all of these gaps will be. They will differ from student to student and class to class. Enacting the research process collaboratively and in stages, however, breaks the silence, as students show the teacher and each other their areas of strength and weakness and learn from each other. Students are particularly receptive to learning from their peers in this setting because their work is so collaborative; nonetheless, they know that they will be writing their own short recursive assignments and their own final paper. Thus, they need to learn as much as they can from each other as well as from the teacher because the supportive environment of our functioning as one great mind will eventually end.

In trying to develop effective strategies for teaching research, my colleagues and I are making our pedagogies more visible not only to our students, but also to ourselves. We are beginning to recognize that assigning research carries with it significant responsibility for the teacher, as well as for the students. We are spending the time to explore with students the complex hidden strategies within processes of research and to give them multiple opportunities to enact these strategies, not just to be told about them. In so doing, we believe that we are helping to level the playing field for students so that they can actually learn what college-level research writing is. Further, we are giving them the opportunity to understand and develop the skills necessary to eventually conduct productive research on their own. We are facing the fact that application is harder than theory, that there is no magic, that good research won't just happen, and that the silent model of teaching doesn't work any more, if it ever did.

So, we have been forced to confront our own assumptions about our assignments, our subject matter, and our students in general. In such a context of demystification, everyone benefits. And when our pedagogies are clearly articulated and out on the table, revising them is also easier—as teachers, we can figure out what we might want to change about an assignment that did not quite work, and we can more fully think through the underlying theoretical or practical reasons for such changes.

Finally, when teachers theorize their teaching practices, they have the potential to engage others to become conscious of the assumptions underlying their own teaching. This occurs because teaching has been changed from a private space that happens behind closed doors to a public, theorized, discursive practice that has consequence, that can be analyzed, and that, like the research our own students are doing, can be altered by the arguments and practices of others.

Notes

1. One of the most recent examples of the rise in the status of teaching as a scholarly activity is in the development of the journal *Pedagogy* in 2001. Studies throughout the country, such as the Boyer Commission's report *Reinventing Undergraduate Education* (1998) and MLA's report *Professional Employment* (Gilbert 1997), increasingly are addressing the need for radical change in the teaching of undergraduates and in the training of university educators.

For scholarly work on teaching over the last twenty-five years and for some discussions of reasons underlying it, see the journals *College English*, *College Composition and Communication*, *College Literature*, and *Reader*. See also books in the MLA *Approaches to Teaching* series, which began in 1980 and reflects the discipline's increasing concern with pedagogy. See also such edited volumes as Kecht, *Pedagogy Is Politics* (1992); Clifford and Schilb, *Critical Theory and Writing Theory* (1994); Sadoff and Cain, *Teaching Contemporary Theory to Undergraduates* (1994); Slevin and Young, *Critical Theory and the Teaching of Literature* (1996); Kent, *Post-Process Theory* (1999); Shamoon et al., *Coming of Age* (2000); Helmers, *Intertexts: Reading Pedagogy in College Writing Classrooms* (2003).

Of the many single-authored volumes on the subject, one can perhaps best look to those books that have won MLA's Mina Shaughnessy Prize, and to the development of this award itself in 1980, which focuses on the teaching of language and literature. Recent books focusing on the history of the discipline also now give teaching practices a much more foregrounded place than they would have had twenty-five years ago. See, for example, Scholes's *The Rise and Fall of English* (1998) and Crowley's *Composition in the University* (1998).

2. By watching the class analyze their texts, members of the research team can also discover that there are multiple ways to read even quite tightly organized texts—for invariably, the class will find points of connection and tension, and will ask research questions that the research team did not anticipate.

Works Cited

Ballenger, Bruce. *The Curious Researcher: A Guide to Writing Research Papers*. 2nd ed. Boston: Allyn and Bacon, 1998.

Behrens, Laurence, and Leonard Rosen. *Writing and Reading Across the Curriculum*. 7th ed. New York: Longman, 2000.

Berlin, James. "Contemporary Composition: The Major Pedagogical Theories." *College English* 44.8 (1982): 765–77.

Bloom, Alan. *The Closing of the American Mind*. New York: Simon & Schuster, 1987.

Boyer Commission on Educating Undergraduates in the Research University. *Reinventing Undergraduate Education: A Blueprint for America's Research Universities*. New York: Carnegie Foundation for the Advancement of Teaching, 1998.

Clifford, John, and John Schilb, eds. *Writing Theory and Critical Theory*. New York: MLA, 1994.

Crowley, Sharon. *Composition in the University: Historical and Polemical Essays*. Pittsburgh: U of Pittsburgh P, 1998.

Dewey, John. *Democracy and Education: An Introduction to the Philosophy of Education*. New York: Free Press, 1916.

Flower, Linda. *Reading-to-Write: Exploring a Cognitive and Social Process*. New York: Oxford UP, 1990.

Fulwiler, Toby, and Arthur Biddle. *A Community of Voices: Reading and Writing in the Disciplines*. New York: Macmillan, 1992.

Gilbert, Sandra. *MLA Committee on Professional Employment: Final Report*. New York: MLA, 1997.

Helmers, Marguerite, ed. *Intertexts: Reading Pedagogy in College Writing Classrooms*. Mahwah, NJ: Lawrence Earlbaum, 2003.

Hillocks, George. *The Testing Trap: How State Writing Assessments Control Learning*. New York: Teachers College P, 2002.

Kecht, Maria-Regina, ed. *Pedagogy Is Politics: Literary Theory and Critical Teaching*. Urbana: U of Illinois P, 1992.

Kent, Thomas, ed. *Post-Process Theory: Beyond the Writing-Process Paradigm*. Carbondale: Southern Illinois UP, 1999.

Lynn, Steven. *Texts and Contexts: Writing about Literature with Critical Theory*. 2nd ed. New York: Longman, 1998.

Rosa, Alfred, and Paul Eschholz. *The Writer's Brief Handbook*. 3rd ed. Boston: Allyn and Bacon, 1999.

Rosenwasser, David, and Jill Stephen. *Writing Analytically*. 2nd ed. Ft. Worth: Harcourt, 2000.

Sadoff, Dianne, and William Cain. *Teaching Contemporary Theory to Undergraduates*. New York: MLA, 1994.

Scholes, Robert. *The Rise and Fall of English: Reconstructing English as a Discipline*. New Haven: Yale UP, 1998.

Shamoon, Linda, Rebecca Howard, Sandra Jamieson, and Robert Schwegler. *Coming of Age: The Advanced Writing Curriculum*. Portsmouth, NH: Boynton/Cook, 2000.

Slevin, James, and Art Young, eds. *Critical Theory and the Teaching of Literature: Politics, Curriculum, Pedagogy*. Urbana, IL: NCTE, 1996.

Smith, Michael W., and Jeffrey D. Wilhelm. *Reading Don't Fix No Chevys: Literacy in the Lives of Young Men*. Portsmouth, NH: Heinemann, 2002.

Trimbur, John. *The Call to Write*. New York: Longman, 1999.

CHAPTER FIFTEEN

A Community College Professor Reflects on First-Year Composition

JOHN PEKINS
Tallahassee Community College

Appropriately enough, I am freewriting this opening with one of my first-year composition classes, as that is the best—and often only—way I get any writing done, once the semester lifts off. Four first-year composition sections (three of which are English Composition [ENC] 1101), thirty writing students per section, but I'm not complaining. After all, I have a job teaching a subject I love. Anyway, as I write I am remembering the just-returned sets of diagnostic grammar test results for my three ENC 1101 sections. An English department requirement, the test is a forty-question, minimum-competency instrument written at the ninth-grade level, and class averages for the three sections are 56 percent, 60 percent, and 61 percent, respectively. Five-paragraph, minimum-competency diagnostic essay results are often equally disappointing, with many essays demonstrating what I call *flat-line* reasoning, as well as equally *flat* control of sentences and paragraphs. These essays often read as if even this minimum exercise is a disturbingly unfamiliar experience for these students now embarking on a long journey through college-level, scholarly discourse.

At the start of each semester, my reaction to these results is always the same: heartfelt concern for these people sitting before me—men and women, some younger, some older—all of whom have arrived at my classroom with admirable goals related to acquiring satisfying careers for themselves and secure futures for their families. They have registered at this community college to help bring their dreams to reality. This course, ENC 1101 College Composition, is the anchor course for their dreams, as its purpose is to expose them to the practices of what many call *academic discourse*. Whatever the major, all students participating in the college enterprise traditionally engage in this mode of discourse, involving thesis, organization, development of support, etc. In spite of this long-standing tradition, though, I believe that those who participate in first-year composition these days—teachers and students alike—face severe problems accomplishing the course's purposes. Perhaps I should rephrase that point: teachers and students, in my view, face severe problems even agreeing on what the course's purposes should be, as the definition of college-level writing and even the perceived need for such writing in the first place are, in my observation, unmoored in the present not-very-literate climate we find ourselves inhabiting in this first decade of the twenty-first century.

In a field as subjective as writing, perhaps we have always faced the problem of reaching concrete agreement concerning what college-level writing is and what it contributes to the postsecondary educational experience, but I believe the problem has intensified in the last ten or fifteen years as a result of several factors. Perhaps most notable among these are a general decline in reading and the mind-numbing effects of minimum-competency exams at all educational levels. Indeed, in the present environment, one often encounters difficulty defining college-level anything, according to many colleagues I speak to, both at my own institution and others. Not one to give up on my students or my vocation, I have drawn from eighteen years experience in the first-year composition trenches a few conclusions I would like to toss into our profession's conversation about this course's students, function, and future.

The starting point for me when considering first-year composition is student reading practice. For years, I have polled my classes to learn how much and how regularly students read prior to entering college. With regard to books, most report reading just one or two during their high school years, with the rest falling somewhere on the spectrum from many to none. Although they occasionally read Web sites, magazines, advertising flyers, etc., many students report that they do not read regularly at all, and when they do, they often find reading to be boring. Though hardly empirical, these responses, combined with further evidence from student essays and one-to-one conferences, suggest that reading is not an integral part of many entering students' communications experience. I find this point reinforced in conversations with colleagues around the country, who conclude similarly from their own observations of student comments and performance. Ironically, though, the electronic age is creating an environment overflowing with the written word. Indeed, most in the composition field recognize that our students must prepare to function in a vigorously text-based, electronic communications environment involving e-mails, memos, reports, online journals, etc.—some informal and some formal, but all operating best/providing the most effective results for those who are practiced, precise readers and writers. In such an accelerating climate of written communication, lack of practiced familiarity with reading is a significant problem for many first-year composition students. This lack of preparation and resulting short- and long-term vulnerability represent a great challenge for both first-year composition students and their teachers.

We can speculate why many of our students arrive at the first-year composition classroom with little to no reading experience. Television is one obvious choice. We've all read the commentaries and studies on this point, particularly regarding the passive and addictive qualities of the television/video medium, all of which often appear to contribute to a decline in the more active medium of reading. From the television phenomena emerges another factor: the absence of reading in households, as television, video games, etc., often replace the book and the magazine as media companions for families at day's end. Throwing their hands up in the air, many kindergarten through grade 12 teachers have accepted the decline of reading and so do not ask for as much reading from their students as was typically asked of the teachers themselves when they were in school. This is particularly true in so-called *basic* and *general* high school English classes, in my observation, which often operate under the assumption that these students are not college bound and so do not need rigorous exposure to reading and writing. Instead, students learn to succeed on state-mandated, minimum-competency grammar and five-paragraph writing tests. Ironically, these are additional contributors to the decline in purposeful, intelligent reading and writing in our schools. In the end, of course, many of these students actually do go to college, as in Florida, where a statewide open-enrollment policy grants community college admission to all high school graduates. (Speaking of "throwing their hands up in the air," I have spoken to many in the first-year composition field who themselves have noticed a subtle shift in the length of readings now offered in composition texts. Extended fifteen- to twenty-five-page articles—or longer—appear with decreasing frequency, while two- to five-page articles increasingly become the norm. As the sample textbooks arrive from publishers every semester, I hear many of my colleagues concluding that the wave of decline and acceptance of decline may well be rolling through higher education as well.)

An overall decline in reading, then, at home and in school, is certainly contributing to whatever difficulties we face in attempting to clarify what college-level writing means as a goal for first-year composition courses. A related concern involves a point one hears discussed from time to time: many of the students going to college in the twenty-first century are those who would not have attended college at all a few decades ago. Many of these students' approach to college work focuses primarily on the acquisition of credits leading to a degree that allows them to compete in a more technical, professional, and skilled job market than existed in earlier generations. Another aspect of this point is that many such students indicate—even in their papers—that they have no interest in the traditional values of college education, going back to the Middle Ages, involving a breadth of knowledge in a variety of fields, including the arts, philosophy, history, rhetoric, etc., and also involving a manner of thinking that cultivates practiced combinations of creative and critical thinking processes. In other words, these students take the college route because they see the acquisition of a college degree as the only possible pathway to their financial goals. From this pragmatic perspective, they often question the value of higher-level competence with the written word and seek primarily to accumulate credit hours toward the degree they believe will help them realize their financial goals.

We could call this the vocational versus traditional approach to higher education, and it is the result of the democratizing of postsecondary education. More people are attending college than ever before, in one of the great democratically inspired educational movements in the history of education. As a community college professor, I celebrate my participation in this movement and remain committed to bringing the best possible education to every student I teach, many of whom are first-generation college students. Some of these students rise to wonderful heights their parents or grandparents could not even have imagined for themselves. I believe, therefore, in this democratic endeavor, but I must acknowledge that this larger, democratic student body also takes its place alongside the decline in reading—perhaps emerges from that decline—as another source of difficulty in reaching a clear definition of college-level writing at the first-year composition level. With the pool of college students so much larger now than in the past, many in our field report a decline among entering students' overall experience and competence with the written word—indeed, even in their belief in the necessity of the written word in the first place. The landscape has changed for us all.

Despite the challenges apparent in the points I have made above, I believe that much can be done to improve the learning experience for both students and teachers in first-year composition courses. In particular, I suggest two major areas for practitioners to consider when reflecting on the definition of college-level writing for first-year composition. The first of these is assessment. The second involves the more vigorous inclusion of reading and reading process instruction in the composition classroom.

Looking first at assessment, professional associations have, over the years, proposed various approaches to assessment criteria in the field. The literature is replete with examples, and I won't spend time here reviewing the various approaches. Instead, I would like to make a simple proposal: that the profession not only take upon itself the identification of criteria and methods of evaluation, but also begin the process of establishing national range finders of passing and nonpassing college-level writing in a variety of typical first-year composition formats. As we know, whatever assessment we undertake in this field, a certain amount of rank ordering is necessarily involved. We can identify consistent criteria and even reliable assessment methods—but, given the growing numbers of college students and also their changing relationships to print, I do not believe we have clarity or agreement now concerning what it is we are rank ordering; that is, what a valid college composition is. In this shifting landscape of growing enrollments and morphing relationships to print, I hear colleagues around the country observe that whatever it is we are rank ordering now is not at the level of what we rank ordered in past years. Having taught first-year composition for eighteen years, I would have to say that my own impressions are much in accord with those comments. Of course, one could require empirical evidence, rather than the growing conviction of practitioners, but such a project would involve a great deal of time, and since it would also involve unearthing decades of student work, may well be unfeasible.

Even if one were not to accept the argument that the quality of student writing has declined over the last ten to fifteen years, many practitioners I speak to agree that we find ourselves adrift when it comes to what we call college-level writing and how we should be assessing it. Throughout my years teaching college composition, I have asked colleagues at my own institution and other schools to provide examples of writing that is A, B, C, and D quality, and the resulting spread of range finders is remarkable. Even when agreement on criteria may move toward a common set of standards, interpretation of those criteria in the assessment of actual student essays often offers little to no consistency. While I have seen interpretations among full-time composition teachers vary significantly, the gap between full-time and adjunct faculty interpretations is often even more profound—and understandable, given each group's respective involvement in and responsibility for defining and maintaining departmental standards. Whatever the sources of disparity may be, however, the results clearly cannot work to the advantage of our students, who experience great confusion attempting to navigate among teachers' varying assessment practices—nor can these results benefit composition program coherence, effective functioning of writing-across-the-curriculum programs, or workplace certainty concerning the skills of college graduates hired to participate professionally in this information age.

Rather than continue our present uncertainty, the assessment project I suggest would challenge practitioners to explore together and possibly even agree to a set of first-year composition assessment criteria. They then would begin the process of discussing and, again, possibly even agreeing to what examples of college writing best demonstrate the agreed-upon criteria, from levels of excellence through levels of unacceptability. Such a project would entail a long and at times possibly contentious process that might, in the end, produce no national consensus at all. I think, though, that engaging in such a national assessment project still would be worth the effort for the potential clarity it could bring to our field—even if not final clarity—and most importantly for the service it would provide our students. The entire debate concerning what college-level writing is in the twenty-first century could be aired openly, and all the affected constituencies—including students, faculty, administrators, professionals, etc.—could seek renewed understanding and perhaps also agreement that would enable all to move forward more reliably. The present variability, uncertainty, and general unease among writing teachers and students across the country could be replaced with a set of range finders that all could understand and reference in their classes/curricula. Adjustment of the range finders could be ongoing—on something like an annual or biannual basis—in order to make best use of new information affecting the field. Participation in the use of these range finders would, of course, be voluntary, but if a solid process informed the discussions and resulting decisions, then the range finders could make a valuable contribution, not just to first-year composition courses, but to all college courses in which writing is required—that is, the great majority of courses currently offered.

When the profession considers criteria for the assessment project described above, I would argue for more vigorous inclusion of reading in students' essays from the start. Four years ago, I conducted an exploration of approximately three hundred composition department Web sites in order to review curriculum and assessment practices in first-semester composition courses. At the conclusion of that review, I found that no more than twelve or fifteen of the three hundred departments demonstrated a commitment to teach the integration of reading with writing in first-semester first-year composition classes. Some departments provided for a research project toward the end of the term, but most of the programs reviewed opted to require essays relying primarily on personal experience for support of the students' main points.

Some traditional premises bear exploring at this point in the discussion. The first of these is whether the primary reliance on students' personal experience and observation in first-year composition essays is appropriate. I will say simply that I do not believe it is. If the purpose of first-year composition is to prepare students for later college work, then they should be reading and writing about what they read, as that is the sort of work they are asked to provide in the bulk of their college courses, as well as in later professional work. We have a responsibility, in my view, to help students practice as soon as possible the skills most in demand throughout their academic and professional careers. An equally important reason for integrating reading with writing in the first-year composition classroom is to help students become familiar with the sound, the flavor of the formal writing they themselves will be asked to produce as college students and, later, professionals in their chosen fields. The active integration of reading with writing throughout the composition course addresses this problem as well, in my view.[1]

As one example of reading/writing integration in first-year composition classes, the Tallahassee Community College English Department chose to adopt this approach to all ENC 1101 assignments as part of its recent Pew-funded course redesign. We are pleased with the results. With the integration of reading in each essay, faculty report stronger, more substantive student writing. We are still growing in our understanding of this change and are presently engaging in faculty workshops to accelerate our ability to work even more effectively with our students. The scope of this article does not provide for extensive discussion of this course redesign, but those interested in exploring it further may read Dr. Sally Search et al.'s documents at the following Web site: http://www.center.rpi.edu/PCR/R3/TCC/TCC_Overview.htm.

When discussing the implications of reading/writing integration in first-year composition, another area to explore involves the traditional preparation of composition instructors. The great strength of Western education lies in its ability to break down large processes into their component parts. The study of biology, for example, demonstrates this strength through its in-depth analysis of plant and animal life, from the most plainly visible down to the microscopic. Our traditional study of written language follows a similar track, as we have identified and often study separately both a reading process and writing process. Integration of the two processes, however, is not a common practice in the academy. Degrees are typically awarded in one area or the other, but not usually in the integration of the two. I begin to think such a divided approach to written language study is similar to the study of respiratory therapy in which one therapist might seek credentials in the area of inhalation, while another receives certification in exhalation. True respiration, however, requires both inhalation and exhalation, but in this exaggerated example, these specialists are not expert in the entire process, just one aspect of it. In the study of written language, we have reading (inhalation) and writing (exhalation), and yet these processes are often studied separately, rather than as integrated aspects of a larger process we could call written language.

In past generations, when first-year composition students arrived at college with more extensive reading experience than today, perhaps it was not altogether necessary for a composition teacher to conduct a serious study of the reading process, as well as a study of how the two processes work together as a larger written language process. Some I speak to, though, share my belief that the time has arrived for first-year composition instructors to become more knowledgeable about the reading process and its applications to the process of writing college compositions. As discussed earlier, we can no longer assume that the students we meet in our classrooms are experienced readers, and so if we are to help them learn to write at the college level—however that may be defined—we must also help them become experienced college-level readers, a skill for which many are either poorly prepared or not prepared at all. We cannot realistically ask our students to write college compositions if they have little or no experience reading such writing themselves. We cannot ask them to exhale if they do not also understand how to inhale. If as a discipline we continue to emphasize in our teacher training, class preparations, and teaching practices only one side of the written language process, we do so at the risk of not providing our students the skills we claim our first-year composition courses teach.

While I believe strongly in the importance of the assessment and reading/writing integration proposals described above, I realize that such a comprehensive refocusing of first-year composition courses might well produce more vigorous, more challenging assignments and grading criteria, which, in turn, might contribute to increased student failure rates and even diminished enrollment numbers—at least in the short run. As a result, the composition field might find itself on a collision course with those in administration and elsewhere who identify with the student retention movement, particularly since first-year composition represents, as I mentioned earlier, the anchor course at many postsecondary institutions. I am enough of an optimist, though, to believe that in the end all affected parties, including students, faculty, administrators, and members of the community, would benefit from such an intensive examination of first-year composition courses. If standards were raised, they would have to be raised in the context of increased support mechanisms for all students, starting ideally at the kindergarten through twelfth-grade level and moving up through college years. I am also realistic enough to understand that any examination of first-year composition courses would most likely result in other pedagogical, budgetary, etc. conflicts among faculty, students, administrators, and community members, both within the composition field and outside of it. Even so, I believe the effort is still worthwhile and could actually encourage a larger examination of college standards generally, to the benefit of all parties. Perhaps, though, now is not the time to walk much farther down this speculative path. Instead, I suggest again that first-year composition faculty and administrators embark on a process of examining the applicability of renewed assessment methods and reading/writing integration in first-year composition classes. If this effort is conducted thoroughly and in good faith, then whatever else might follow in its wake will hopefully travel a similarly positive path.

And so I conclude my reflections from the first-year composition trenches. I believe that in examining where we stand as composition teachers and where we should go next, we find ourselves at a moment of great opportunity. I am excited at the possibilities that an emphasis on reading/writing integration in first-year composition classes could bring to our assessment practices, our growth as a teaching discipline, and, most importantly, our students' academic and professional success. Alone in my office as I write this conclusion, the sky dark beyond the window and filling with stars, I look toward my desk and notice that my sleeves are already rolled up, and a stack of compositions awaits reading and evaluation. This first-year composition teaching is good work. I like it down here in the trenches, where I find in my students' successes my own success. I close by wishing great success to all those who teach and learn in first-year composition classes—now and in the years to come.

Note

1. Through phone calls, e-mails, and published work, several colleagues across the country shared valuable expertise to support my explorations of reading/writing integration and its applications to Tallahassee Community College's Pew-funded redesign of ENC 1101. By extension, their efforts also helped inform the reading/writing integration portion of this article. I here acknowledge these folks' generosity, insight, patience, and humor, and I also thank them: Eli Goldblatt, director of the Temple University Writing Program; Bridget Irish, director of the Fort Lewis (Colorado) College Writing Program; Clyde Moneyhun, director of the Stanford University Writing Center; Tom Ott, director of Developmental Studies at Community College of Philadelphia; Mike Rose, professor of Social Research Methodology at UCLA and author of *Lives on the Boundary: The Struggles and Achievements of America's Underprepared* (1989); Michael Smith, professor of English Education at Rutgers University; Karen Spear, former chair and dean at Fort Lewis College in Colorado, presently executive director of the Consortium for Innovative Environments in Learning, and author of "Controversy and Consensus in Freshman Writing: An Overview of the Field" (1997); Patrick Sullivan, professor of English at Manchester Community College (Connecticut) and author of "What Is 'College Level' Writing?" (2003); and Susan Wood, professor of English Education at Florida State University. Although I did not speak or correspond with David Bartholomae, his "Inventing the University" (1988) continues to be a great inspiration. I acknowledge and thank him as well.

Works Cited

Bartholomae, David. "Inventing the University." *Perspectives on Literacy.* Ed. Eugene R. Kintgen, Barry M. Kroll, and Mike Rose. Carbondale: Southern Illinois UP, 1988. 273–85.

Rose, Mike. *Lives on the Boundary: The Struggles and Achievements of America's Underprepared.* New York: Free Press, 1989.

Search, Sally, Missy James, Patrick McMahon, Alan Merickel, and John Pekins. "Program in Course Redesign." The Center for Academic Transformation. 2005. 8 June 2006 <http://www.center.rpi.edu/PCR/R3/TCC/TCC_Overview.htm>.

Spear, Karen. "Controversy and Consensus in Freshman Writing: An Overview of the Field." *Review of Higher Education* 20 (1997): 319–44.

Sullivan, Patrick. "What Is 'College-Level' Writing?" *Teaching English in the Two-Year College* 30 (2003): 374–90.

CHAPTER SIXTEEN

Defining by Assessing

EDWARD M. WHITE
California State University, San Bernardino
and
University of Arizona

Defining College-Level Writing: What Kind of Question Is This?

Not as simple as it appears to be. One's first instinct is to give a purely personal definition: *This* is what I take to be college-level writing. But merely personal answers to social and linguistic questions are really indulgences and quite useless. Take one example: I like to think of college-level expository writing (notice how I slipped in a qualifier) as writing that makes assertions and then develops an argument using evidence well, taking account of opposing arguments. I actually enforce that definition in my advanced composition courses. But note: most political and other public discourse, almost all of which is produced by college graduates, routinely fails this criterion. Actually, what I like to consider college-level writing is relatively rare, even in my classes. No, we cannot simply assert a personal preference and hope to get away with it on this matter, no matter how plausible, even self-evident our definition may seem to ourselves. A definition of what college-level writing is must embrace considerable consensus both on and off campus.

So we should put aside the personal and go with the pragmatic: college-level writing is the writing that is done in college by students receiving passing grades from their professors. This definition has a nice tautological economy and happens to reflect reality, a pleasant if rare bonus on such matters as this. But it is no better than my first attempt. If those posing the question were comfortable with the quality of writing produced by the average run of college students, the question would not be asked. Buried in the question is a dark surmise: present-day college students are writing so badly that their screeds should *not* be considered college level; not all students, surely, but a goodly number. In fact, the large number of basic writing programs in most American colleges, called *remedial writing* or even *bonehead English* by the less decorous public, argues for this surmise, as do the writing across the curriculum programs in perhaps a third of our universities. Too many of our writers in college are not producing college-level writing, and the world is filled with horrible examples. So the pragmatic response would not only fail to meet the expectations of the question but would be seen as evasive and nonresponsive.

I will be proposing a way around these definitional problems by way of certain testing procedures. But before we go to specific examples, we should further examine the root problem we are dealing with: Why is this question so hard to answer, so hard to deal with?

There are a number of terms like *college-level writing* that are commonly used *as if* they had a commonly agreed-upon meaning, when they do not. Let me take two other examples: *insanity* and *pornography*. My friend and occasional collaborator Bill Lutz of Rutgers University, English professor and attorney, tells me that *insanity* is a stipulated legal term, with definitions in law that differ widely from state to state. That is, *insanity* has no medical meaning, since medical diagnosis will use much more precise terms for such disorders as schizophrenia or bipolar disorder. But the term persists in ordinary speech, as a descriptor for people someone perceives as mentally abnormal in some way or other, and as a legal term for someone who cannot make moral judgments as set out in certain statutes. But we cannot pretend that there is some actual mental state that modern medicine (as opposed to earlier times) would call *insanity*. That is, the word has no actual referent in the world, but takes on its meaning from its context.

Again, I pick *pornography* as another such term, because I wound up as an expert witness in court in the 1960s, when the state of Massachusetts sought to declare that the Putnam Press edition of John Cleland's eighteenth-century novel *Memoirs of a Woman of Pleasure*, otherwise known as *Fanny Hill*, was obscene and hence publication of it could be criminal. In those more innocent days, a book could be declared pornographic if it met three tests set out by the Supreme Court. (Charles Rembar, the attorney for Putnam Press, wrote *The End of Obscenity* in 1968, which was about that case and several others he won, giving us the right to read *Ulysses* and *Lady Chatterly's Lover*, as well as *Fanny Hill*.) Later court decisions have altered those tests, so the definition of pornography has since changed. But once again we have a term whose meaning must be stipulated by learned judges, even though it remains in more or less common use as whatever someone takes to be overly sexual.

And so it is with *college-level writing*, a term with little intrinsic meaning, though in common enough use. About all we can say with assurance about it is that it is distinct from the writing produced by young children in most cases, although, as this book witnesses, teachers seem much more confident about the act of defining the term than I can be. If we are to infuse the term with meaning that will stand up in the court of educated users, we need to include within it properties and concepts that can gain some consensus, without falling into the fallacies of merely personal or meaninglessly pragmatic definitions. Perhaps our ancient discipline of rhetoric will offer some help here.

The Rhetorical Issues That Lie behind the Term *College-Level Writing*

When we apply some simple rhetorical concepts to the term *college-level writing*, we see clearly why the term lacks intrinsic meaning. Rhetoric requires a rhetorical situation, that is, a purpose and an audience, for speaking or writing if we are to take it seriously. It seems obvious that writing without either purpose or audience is at best an empty exercise that, by definition, defies any reasonable college-level designation. We cannot call writing only to be graded as having a rhetorical purpose, though it has a purpose as a kind of display, like bringing an apple to the teacher. James Britton mocked such school exercises in his classic study of British schools two generations ago, calling the writing a "dummy run" in which the ill-informed presumably enlighten the well-informed in order to gain a grade. The minute we ask what audience and purpose infuse college-level writing, the full complexity of all possible collegiate writing situations spring to life before us. Shades of what some call process pedagogy, and others call classical rhetoric, hover over this concept: we cannot deal with writing simply by examining its textual features, without considering the rhetorical situation that produced it. Many universities have taken to portfolio assessment as a way to measure and define college-level writing for this reason; portfolios by definition include a variety of rhetorical situations and forms of expression. But this sensible way to proceed as an institution will not help us solve our problem with definition, since it is an elaborated form of the pragmatic definition I dealt with in the second paragraph of this essay. For more generalizable definitions, we need to turn to the writing tests given by colleges that seek to embody in their scoring a succinct description of the writing traits they require for particular students under particular situations. These writing tests normally use scoring guides for those grading the writing, and these scoring guides take some account of the rhetorical situation for the test.

For instance, if we look at assessment situations that seek to assess student writing proficiency, we notice that we could do this at four different stages of a student's college career. When we say "college level," we need to be clear about what stage of college we are talking about. Do we mean writing ability at point of entry, as with a placement exam? Or do we mean after completion of a college writing course, as with the portfolio assessment program at the State University of New York Stony Brook popularized by Pat Belanoff and Peter Elbow? Or do we mean at the time of movement from lower-division, or community college completion, to upper-division work, as with the "rising junior" tests given by the states of Georgia and Arkansas? Or do we mean just before graduation with a college degree, as in fact the California State University graduation writing assessment requirement is implemented? Each one of these assessment points implies a different level of achievement, although that difference seems less clear when one examines some of the modalities of assessment in use. But we can't stop there. Many, probably most, graduate and professional programs (e.g., medicine, law, business) also assess the writing of those applying for entrance, seeking assurance that their new students can write at the college level. In every instance that demands actual writing, and I need not say (though I do, with a sigh) that some institutions put their faith in multiple-choice tests, as if identifying errors in test-maker prose represents an ability to produce college-level writing, student writing takes as audience some anonymous group of test readers and takes as its sole purpose impressing that group with the writer's college-level skills, whatever that may be taken to mean.

If we look at such writing rhetorically, an inherent contradiction becomes clear. The rhetorical situation of the test is usually not designed to produce the kind of writing that college students actually are expected to turn out: writing on a topic of interest to them, after some reading and reflection, with some time for feedback and revision, for an audience of peers and professors with some genuine interest in what the writer has to say. The best of these tests, such as the last example I give below, make an attempt to duplicate the rhetorical situation of college writing for that institution at the appropriate level, and thus give us reasonable working definitions. But we must generalize from these tests with great caution, always defining the situation under which the writing has been generated.

Using Test Scoring Guides as Definitions

Thus we do have documentation of what postsecondary institutions, as opposed to individuals, consider to be college-level writing from these exams, flawed and localized though they are: the scoring guides for their writing assessment programs at various levels. Many colleges, systems of higher education, and, now, the national testing firms publish a list of criteria by which they evaluate student test writing for different purposes. As I have said, some of these sit-down exams focus on entering students, usually seeking to distinguish those ready for college-level work from those who are not; some of the exams make a different distinction, between those ready for college work and those who are declared by the college board (with its advanced placement and college-level examination program tests) to write at the college level before they have so much as walked into a college classroom. Other assessments attempt to measure writing ability as students move into upper-division status or even as they apply for graduation. Again, the Educational Testing Service offers the Test of English as a Foreign Language nine times a year all over the world to ascertain if those from other language cultures can produce college-level writing in English. Can we use any of these tests or their scoring guides as rough and ready definitions?

Looking closely at the criteria for these examinations might be the best way to proceed, if only the tests would agree with each other, which they do not, or with those administering college writing programs, generally faculty with little confidence in any of the test scores they receive. While it would be absurd to pretend that college-level writing at Open Admissions Community College means the same thing as at Selective Ivy League University, or that first-year students in agriculture at Anywhere Tech wrote the same as graduating seniors in the history of science at the same institution, we would at least have working examples of what some institutions have decided on the matter for some of their students. But we have to be careful about exaggerating the generalizing power of these statements, even from a single campus. We might be able to say what Professor Smith at State University sees as college level for his class in Shakespeare, but Professor Jones down the hall would beg to differ. The exams, even the one no doubt painstakingly constructed at State University, offer generalized descriptions of standards that must be interpreted in every case by the Joneses and Smiths who make the decisions in their classes every term, usually by personal standards (see paragraph 1), which they fiercely defend when they join (as they sometimes do) college-wide scoring sessions of writing exams.

Despite all of these caveats, I will give in the next section two different scoring guides used in these exams. They have the virtue of being institutional documents, argued over and agreed on by committees, and hence are not merely personal. Some of the textual qualities they describe and presume to measure actually lead to important administrative decisions: They serve to hold back students from junior standing or even from college graduation, so they have a certain kind of credibility for their own institutions. But since no institution of higher education borrows such statements from any other such institution, we can only use them as definitions, or pious hopes, of college-level writing at one college. When we study such documents, to seek out what, if anything, they have in common, we find that the general terminology of these scoring guides depends on actual scored samples of student writing on a particular campus to flesh out their actual meaning. Therefore, I amplify one of the scoring guides by the published examples of student writing that exemplify the meaning of the criteria for that particular campus.

A Sample Scoring Guide for First-Year College-Level Writing

Here is a compact and useful scoring guide developed by a team of experienced writing faculty from the California State University system in 1988 for a variety of testing programs (White 298–99). It is intended to lead to reliable scoring of an essay question, which should be carefully developed for the purpose the scores are intended to serve. (There is an extensive literature on the design of writing assignments, much worth consulting, but rather off our topic here.) It uses the now-standard six-point scale for holistic scoring of writing.

Score of 6: Superior

- ◆ Addresses the question fully and explores the issues thoughtfully.
- ◆ Shows substantial depth, fullness, and complexity of thought.
- ◆ Demonstrates clear, focused, unified, and coherent organization.
- ◆ Is fully developed and detailed.
- ◆ Evidences superior control of diction, syntactic variety, and transition; may have a few minor flaws.

Score of 5: Strong

- Clearly addresses the question and explores the issues.
- Shows some depth and complexity of thought.
- Is effectively organized.
- Is well developed, with supporting detail.
- Demonstrates control of diction, syntactic variety, and transition; may have a few flaws.

Score of 4: Competent

- Adequately addresses the question and explores the issues.
- Shows clarity of thought but may lack complexity.
- Is organized.
- Is adequately developed, with some detail.
- Demonstrates competent writing; may have some flaws.

Score of 3: Weak

- May distort or neglect parts of the question.
- May be simplistic or stereotyped in thought.
- May demonstrate problems in organization.
- May have generalizations without supporting detail or detail without generalizations; may be undeveloped.
- May show patterns of flaws in language, syntax, or mechanics.

Score of 2: Inadequate

- Will demonstrate serious inadequacy in one or more of the areas specified for the 3 paper.

Score of 1: Incompetent

- Fails in its attempt to discuss the topic.
- May be deliberately off topic.

- Is so incompletely developed as to suggest or demonstrate incompetence.
- Is wholly incompetent mechanically.

When we look closely at the criteria for high grades on this test, we can notice that those scoring it put a particularly high value on responding to the question asked, in all of its parts and with attention to its complexity. These are the first two descriptors for most of the scores, with the quality of that student response to the question descending as the scores get lower, until the worst paper is deliberately or accidentally off topic. The third criterion has to do with organization; the worse the organization of the student writing, the lower the score. The fourth descriptor focuses on development of ideas, with supporting detail. Once again, the weaker the development, the worse the score; the lower scores are likely to have generalizations without detail, or detail without generalizations, or no development at all. The final criterion on the scoring guide has to do with correctness, clearly less important than an organized and well-developed response to the question asked, but increasingly important to the lower range of scores.

It is also useful to notice what is *not* listed as criteria for scoring of the essay test in the minds of the developers of the scoring guide. There is no mention of creativity, or style, or allusions to literature or literary devices. Such matters as these may enter peripherally into the scoring, which is holistic, meaning that the whole of the judgment is greater than the sum of its parts. But the definition of college-level writing in this particular scoring guide for an essay test yields a definition based on careful attention to the question, full and organized development of a response, and reasonable mechanical correctness given the nature of first-draft writing. Since so much of the debate about college-level writing does focus on writing tests, despite the problems we have noted, this scoring guide gives useful clues to the working definition embodied by experienced college writing teachers as they work together to grade these tests.

A Sample Scoring Guide, with Examples, for Graduation-Level College Writing

The following examination was administered in spring, 1996, at the California State University, San Bernardino (CSUSB). All campuses of the CSU have their own procedures for certifying the *upper-division* writing ability of their graduates, some by way of examinations and others through required courses. CSUSB requires an upper-division writing course offered in the various schools, but also offers an examination for students who think they already have met the goals of that course. Called the Writing Requirement Exemption Exam (WREE), it defines for that institution the kind and level of writing it demands of those receiving any undergraduate degree. As director of that program at the time, I put together the following brochure for students preparing to take that test. As with the previous scoring guide, it was devised as a practical working document, based on the practice of grading teams over a number of years, and so has the authority of an empirical definition.

It is important to notice the difference between the requirements of the WREE exam below and those of a lower-division or entry-level impromptu test. In the first place, only upper-division students are permitted to take the test, so its concern for college-level writing is beyond the first-year requirement that takes up so much writing program time and attention. Passing the test fulfills the university upper-division writing requirement for graduation. In the second place, the test is defined as a challenge examination for an upper-division course; that is, it looks for the same outcomes that are expected from students completing an advanced general education writing class. (In fact, most students satisfy the writing requirement by passing the course and do not attempt the test.) In the third place, the test is based on readings that are announced well in advance of the test, in an attempt to establish a rhetorical situation closer to that of most college courses. While not all test takers will read, discuss, and reflect on the essays in advance—so pervasive is the expectation that a writing test will be impromptu—they are given the opportunity to prepare and order their thinking about the readings before they sit down and see the particular questions they are asked to write on. And finally, the testing time is three hours, enough time for organizing, drafting, revision, and editing of the writing.

The question and the four responses that follow illustrate the demands of this testing program and give its definition of college-level writing.

CALIFORNIA STATE UNIVERSITY SAN BERNARDINO
WRITING REQUIREMENT EXEMPTION EXAMINATION
Spring, 1996

This examination is based on two essays that appear in Lynn Z. Bloom and Edward M. White, *Inquiry* (Englewood Cliffs: Prentice Hall, 1993): Thomas Kuhn, "The Route to Normal Science" (pp. 147–156) and Isaac Asimov, "Those Crazy Ideas" (pp. 370–380).

You will have three hours to plan, write, revise, and edit your response to the following question. Be sure to read the question carefully, for responses that do not handle carefully all parts of the question will not pass, no matter how well they may be written.

Your response will be graded according to the degree to which you demonstrate:

1. Ability to understand the essays and show that understanding through written summary, analysis and integration of ideas and passages from them into your own essay;
2. Ability to develop a single, coherent essay in which you develop and support an idea of some depth;
3. Ability to use source material properly: to use a consistent and accepted format for citation of sources and to use quotations to support, not to substitute for your own ideas;
4. Ability to respond to a specific question in clear prose that does not distract the reader by mechanical or grammatical errors.

WRITING TOPIC:

Write a unified, coherent paper comparing and contrasting the two essays. In the course of your response, address the following questions:

- What is alike and what is different in the two authors' ideas about how science progresses?
- To what degree do the two authors agree about the definition and importance of "normal science"?
- What similarities and differences do you see in the authors' respective uses of the terms "paradigm" and "crazy ideas"?
- To what degree does your own experience with the same issues in your own field of study support or not support the conclusions of the two authors?

Four Sample Student Essays in Response to the Question

High Pass

"Merging Creativity and Process:
the dual engines for scientific advancement"

In Isaac Asimov's "Those Crazy Ideas" and Thomas Kuhn's "The Route to Normal Science" the keys to scientific advancement are explained in ways that allow a lay reader to easily understand both the requirements and preconditions for scientific exploration. Asimov concentrates on the elements of creativity. Kuhn develops the rationale for and importance of paradigms. Together the characteristics and attributes of creativity which Asimov discusses and the evolution of procedures delineated in Kuhn's essay reveal the prerequisites of discovery and the orderly advancement of research.

Isacc Asimov's writing is described as "encyclopedic, witty, with a gift for colorful and illuminating examples and explanations" (p.370). He is quick to point out that he doesn't really know where ideas come from, but he has concluded that those people we generally consider creative share several important characteristics:

1. The creative person must possess as many "bits" [of information] as possible, i.e., he must be broadly educated.
2. The creative person must be able to combine "bits" with facility and recognize the combinations he has formed; i.e., he must be intelligent.
3. The creative person must be able to see, with as little delay as possible, the consequences of the new combinations of "bits" which he has formed; i.e., he must be intuitive.
4. The creative person must possess courage (and to the general population may, in consequence, seem a crack pot).
5. A creative person must be lucky (pp 374-8).

He describes, within these characteristics, the essentiel elements and tools which a creative person possesses and can lead to major breakthroughs. He uses the example of Charles Darwin and Alfred Russel Wallace and their work on developing the theory of evolution as examples. It was only when each of them had read Thomas Malthus's *An Essay on the Principle of Population* that they were able to move from an observation of evolution to a governing principle controlling the phenomenon. Both men used their accumulated knowledge "bits" in combination with new "bits" garnered from reading Malthus's work to come up with new combinations (characteristic #2, above) and consequences (#3 above).

Kuhn applies much of what Asimov postulates in his description of the development of the fields of science. He proposes that it is only when a group of scientists have reached a general, if tacit, agreement on "a common set of assumptions, theories, laws, or applications" (p.147) that real progress in a given arena can be made. Much of "The Route to Normal Science" is devoted to elaborating on this postulate. He says, "In the absence of a paradigm or some candidate for paradigm, all of the facts that could possibly pertain to the development of a given science are likely to seem equally relevant. As a result, early fact-gathering is a far more nearly random activity than the one subsequent scientific development makes familiar" (p.151). He illustrates his point by describing the various schools of exploration which led to the early theories of electricity. "What the fluid theory of electricity did for the subgroup that held it, the Franklinian paradigm later did for the entire group of electricians. It suggested which experiments would be worth performing and which . . . would not" (p.153). He demonstrates "how the emergence of a paradigm affects the structure of the group that practices the field" (p.153). Indeed, in various disciplines, we have come to be paradigm driven.

The use of a shared paradigm, which can and does graduallly mutate, not only undergirds scientific research, but also lies at the foundation of cultural development. Every culture has at its core a central model, shrouded in the mists of time, around which it coalesced. With the passage of time, this model acquired iconic status, and became the source of myth and legend. Eventually, entire thought systems emerged, men shared their parochial knowledge, and in the resulting eclectic were born mores, customs, traditions, legal systems, economies, governments, and so on.

All these developments can be related to the essential elements of Asimov's and Kuhn's arguments: that creativity is essential to the generation of ideas and that exploration and progress occur most rapidly when there is a shared paradigm to assist in structuring and focusing activities. Perhaps the best example of this in recent memory is the Manhattan project. When the United States brought together the group of astrophysicists and support personnel who ultimately developed the atomic bomb, certain established principles of thermodynamics and physics were well understood and accepted by the entire staff. Additionally, all were thoroughly familiar, indeed inculcated, with the principles and methods of scientific inquiry. Thus, from the outset there was an implied paradigm shared by the team. The exigency of time, however, demanded that provision for change—paradigm shift—be integral to the culture of the group. Therefore, when one of the scientists got one of Asimov's "crazy ideas," he had the freedom to explore it. The project team, brought together as a group of "brain busters," a collection of thinkers and scientists, was conceived in part in the hope that they would cross-fertilize one another into startling breakthroughs (p.377). When the idea of implosion emerged, the young astrophysicist was willing to expose himself to ridicule (he possessed courage) because he had synthesized sufficient information through experiments to make the leap to this new theory. As his idea was explored and expanded by the rest of the team, a significant shift occured, and ultimately the paradigms for astrophysics were changed. Indeed, new branches of science emerged.

This anecdote illustrates the threads of commonality which exist in Asimov's and Kuhn's essays. While one can say that creativity (the exploration of which is central to Asimov's essay) is an essential and preexisting component in the path to scientific breakthrough, it is equally true that without orderly processes and methods, which support most scientific paradigms, are keys to discovery as well. In a world as full of information as is the late twentieth century, organizing systems and procedures are essential. Without some agreement on paradigms, our arsenals of information would leave us wrangling incessantly.

No doubt it is easier for the non-scientist to read Asimov. He expresses himself clearly and simply, writing in a style which is easy to like. Kuhn is a bit more challenging. There is a tone of rigorous and unrelenting emphasis on method and process to his essay. Nonetheless, the two share much in common, and have implications well beyond the scientific community, to which I alluded earlier in this essay. In combination, evolving paradigms and encouragement of creativity are cornerstones of societal progress, and can be and are frequently employed in the field of education. As a teacher of history, I seek to develop themes. Students can not understand those themes without first accepting some common foundation (paradigms, if you will) and then using their creative energies to generalize and relate the impact of past events on present developments. Out of this process, they come to develop their own frameworks for understanding. "The transformation of paradigms, and the successive transition from one paradigm to another" (p.149) helps lead students to the possession of a broad education and the ablity to permutate and combine that knowledge in order to form new combinations and understand their consequences (p.374-76).

Note: Quotations and parenthetical page numbers refer to Asimov, Isaac, "Those Crazy Ideas" and Kuhn, Thomas, "The Route to Normal Science," in *Inquiry :A Cross Curricular Reader*, edited by Bloom, Lynn Z., and White, Edward M. (Englewood Cliffs: Prentice-Hall, 1993).

Reader Comments on the "High Pass" examination:

This paper answers all parts of the question and demonstrates successfully all four criteria for passing: (1) It shows full and detailed understanding of both assigned readings and integrates material from the readings into a well-structured essay; (2) It develops a focused and coherent essay which has something interesting to say beyond mere summary of the readings; (3) It uses cited source material to support the central idea the paper develops and explicitly connects the citations to that idea; and (4) It is written in clear and acceptable prose which, though not perfect, does not distract the reader from the ideas being expressed.

Marginal Pass

Thomas S. Kuhn and Isacc Asimov who were both educated in the sciences, have their own unique approach to explaining how the science field progresses. Kuhn believes that science progresses by first establishing models that lay a foundation for rules and standards. This foundation provides an equal base for others to use and build upon, thus progressing.[1] Similarly, Asimov provides an example of how the concept of evolution progressed through Charles Darwin and Alfred Russel Wallace. Both Darwin and Wallace created their own base of knowledge through observation of animals throughout the world. Darwin and Wallace could see a relation among the animals, and that the animals changed over long periods of time.[2] Neither could provide the answer of why evolution occurred until they stumbled upon Thomas Robert Malthus' research that suggested that population increased faster than the food supply and cut itself down by starvation, disease or war.[3] Darwin and Wallace needed to base their research on Malthus' work and share assumptions.

The differences that surface between Kuhn and Asimov's ideas on how science progresses lies with Kuhn believing that one that studies in the field of science must first learn all the rules and standards and add upon it theoretical and methodological belief that permits selection, evaluation and criticism.[4] You must go to outside sources if it is not in the specific field already. Asimov on the other hand believes that in addition to the knowledge of "bits" that one must attain in the science, one must also be able to combine the bits and know that new information has been created, the person must be intuitive, intelligent, and realize consequences. The person must also possess courage to announce one's findings and the person according to Asimov must also have luck, on his or her side.[5] All of these criteria are required for the person to have scientific Creativity, a factor that was left out by Kuhn.

Kuhn throughout his article refers to "normal science." Kuhn defines this as "research firmly based upon one or more past scientific achievements, achievements that some particular scientific community acknowledges for a time as supplying the foundation for its futher practice."[6] I feel that Asimov would agree with this definition. Asimov in his article refers to the amount of "bits" that one must aquire in order to work out theories. Asimov takes this further, however, to go beyond "normal," into creative. I feel that Asimov, unlike Kuhn, believes that "normal science" has little importance and now provides little advancement in science.

Kuhn's paradigms are models for other scientists to follow.[7] Similarly Asimov's crazy ideas have to originate from a base of knowledge on what could be referred to as paradigms. Asimov's "bits" could be Kuhn's "Paradigms." Crazy ideas on the other hand are entirely different from paradigms. Crazy ideas are generated after digesting the paradigms and bits of information and *creatively* going beyond what a paradigm would bring as an outcome.

In the field of Public Administration, the advancement has often been determined in a consistant manner such as "normal science." There are models and assumptions that are used as rules and standards. These paradigms are taught throughout academia as a groundwork for students to then build upon. Each student is given knowledge in accounting, government processes, and theory behind government, and also foundations for budgeting and management. Unfortunately there is demise in our bureaucracies, the foundations taught in school are enough. "Crazy Ideas" are needed to help our government systems run effectively and efficiently. Of course not all of these ideas are good ones. One idea to be innovating and enhance the quality of government was Management by Objectives, (MBO) which has failed. "Crazy ideas" in public administration will keep surfacing until solutions to problems are found. Reinventing government is the current "Crazy idea." Both authors can lend support for my field of study.

End Notes

1. Lynn Z. Bloom and Edward M. White ed., *Inquiry: A Cross Curricular Reader.* New Jersey: Prentice-Hall, Inc., 1993, *The Route to Normal Science* by Thomas S. Kuhn, 147

2. Lynn Z. Bloom and Edward M. White, ed., *Inquiry: A Cross Curricular Reader* (New Jersey: Prentice-Hall, Inc., 1993, Those Crazy Ideas, by Isaac Asimov, 371-372

3. Ibid.,372

4. Kuhn, 152

5. Asimov, 374-378

6. Kuhn, 147

7. Ibid.,147

Reader Comments on the "Marginal Pass" Examination:

This paper is much weaker than the "High Pass" and barely passed after much discussion by the faculty readers. They concluded that the examination met the demands of all the questions, if minimally, and satisfied the four criteria: (1) It shows genuine understanding of both readings and some ability to use insights from the readings as part of an argument; (2) though the central idea emerges slowly and seems scattered, the paper does analyze the readings and go beyond mere summary in developing an idea; (3) though the citation system is old-fashioned and somewhat idiosyncratic, the paper does discuss its quotations and connect many of them to developing ideas; and (4) the writing is generally clear and does not distract the reader by too many errors.

Marginal Fail

Thomas Kuhn and Isaac Asimov address the issue of science and the development of new scientific ideas. These two authors present similar, as well as, different definitions and names of many key words or ideas. The progression of science and what is necessary for new discoveries is explained by these two men with many simularities and differences.

Thomas Kuhn notes that prior to the eighteenth century scientists did not share ideas and any new creative idea had to be documented with evidence. This documentation could not be from another scientist. The documentation had to be new and not referenced to another scientist's work.

After the eighteenth century Kuhn indicates that there was more of a sharing of ideas (150). This leads to Kuhn's definition of normal science: "normal science means research firmly based upon one or more past scientific achievements, achievements that some particular scientific community acknowledges for a time as supplying the foundation for its further practice (147). Asimov does not give a similar spelled out definition of normal science, however, he does give an example of science and it's process. By using Darwin's discovery of natural selection, we can see the strands of what makes science. The creation of new principles or ideas must begin with the study of an area of interest. After studying, the scientist must make observations. These observations postulate new theories and ideas. After hypothesizing, the scientists must make observations. These observations are the gathering of facts, that will subsequently help scientists postulate new theories and ideas. After hypothesizing, the scientists may share information with others.

Both men agree that there needs to be time to study information and documents for the area of interest, research. Research is the basis for new scientific discoveries. The biggest difference between these men is that Kuhn implies that research is to be from past scientific achievements only and not from any other source. Asimov, on the other hand, goes to the trouble of defining how information or "bits" are obtained. He indicates that one can be educated by others in the same field, schools, or "self educated." "Self educated" does not mean uneducated it means one obtains information by reading and by personal observation. Both men agree that research must occur.

As this research occurs, there is a process to how science progresses. Prior to looking at the different perspectives for the progession, there needs to be a definition of "paradigm" as used by Kuhn and "crazy ideas" as used by Asimov.

A "paradigm" is a term to suggest that there is some accepted examples of science theory. Kuhn notes that the paradigm allows the next researcher to take for granted certain information as stated in the "paradigm." New facts to prove the paradigm are not necessary. The similarity of a "paradigm" and "crazy ideas" is that both are startling new principles or conceptual breaktroughs (Asimov, p.371). Both are new ideas.

The greatest difference between these two phrases is that Kuhn's "paradigms" seem to be concretely founded by research and past achievements. Asimov acknowledges the importance of past achievements and their necessity but also acknowledges that a new discovery can happen by luck and hence the term "crazy ideas". Although, Kuhn does admit that spontaneous ideas can occur, he notes it is rare.

Now that we have defined "paradigm" and "crazy ideas", we can proceed to discuss the similarites and differences of how science progresses as described by Kuhn and Asimov. Asimov sets up five criterion for scientific creativity: 1) the creative person must be broadly educated 2) intelligent 3) intuitive 4) courageous and 5) lucky (378). Kuhn's progression can be made to fit into some of these 5 criterion. There are similarties as well as differences.

The first criterion is that a creative person must be broadly educated. The scientist must have a foundation of knowledge by which he studies and observes old and new information. As noted previously, Kuhn's writings imply that research must be based on previously accepted achievements or paradigms. Asimov believes that crazy ideas can occur because of past achievements, as well as new ideas that have never been tested or tried.

Criterion two is that the creative person or scientist must be intelligent, not only must the person be book smart, he must be able to combine old ideas with new ideas and to come up with new hypotheses with no reference to old achievements. Kuhn would disagree with the last statement. Again Kuhn believes new ideas must have their bases on old achievements.

Intuition is a necessity of any scientist. This is accepted by both authors. Both authors note that once "bits" of information are combined there must be the acknowledgement of what information is necessary and what information is useless. Without this immediate knowledge of what is useful and useless the scientist will waste valuable time testing inconsequential information.

The fourth criterion is courage. The scientist must be courageous. He must be willing to share his ideas with others as well as publish his new discovery. Kuhn does not agree with this idea. He notes, "The new paradigm implies a new and more rigid definition of the field

(154)." This implies that new discovery does not need the scientist's courage, since it reinforces an old achievement. Asimov contends that if a new idea is too closely related or is happened upon quickly the idea is merely a "corollary" (376). Asimov says "the more profound the breakthrough, the more solidified the previous opinions; the more against reason the new discovery seems the the more against cherished authority (378)." The fifth criterion is luck. Asimov indicates that to some degree the scientist must be lucky to come across a new discovery by means of a certain combination. Not all combinations are educated guesses or planned. Some combinations merely happen by chance. Kuhn is not completely convinced of this area. He acknowledges that some discoveries just happen; but, it is rare. He believes firmly that research produces sound discoveries that are planned.

As can be seen, there are many similarities and differences of how science is perceived by Thomas Kuhn and Isaac Asimov. The process of how the sciences progress is nearly identical, the only difference being that Kuhn believes in sound research as the basis of new discoveries and Asimov sees the importance of luck and that not all discoveries are founded on concrete research only. These differences can be seen not only in science but also in the field of education.

Often times, teachers are taught theory and practice as two separate entities. Just as Kuhn sees theory and research as the most important; some educators only see theory and research as the only important tool to take into the classroom. Asimov realizes that you need the theory and research; however, there is the practicality of the matter. Asimov sees that sucess in the classroom can sometimes be just by luck.

New discoveries or new ideas in education are continually being presented to educators. Goals 2000 is a reform document that is attempting to change how schools operate. This new program is attempting to change traditional schools into college prep pathways or career pathway for students not interested in college. Some of the document relies on research that shows our schools are not sucessful. However there are new "crazy ideas" that educators want to try. They want to try new ideas so that all students can have sucess. These new ideas require courage on the part of the educators willing to implement a new program. As educators,we must, be intuitive to know what might work and what definitely won't work. Education is a science and it has its process. This process can be two separate ideas as presented by

Kuhn and Asimov or it can be a blend of theory, research, and luck. By having a balance of the two many new discoveries and sucesses can happen.

Kuhn, Thomas. "The Route to Normal Science." *Inquiry A Cross Curricular Reader*, (New Jersey: Prentice Hall, Inc., 1993.)

Asimov, Isaac. "Those Crazy Ideas." *Inquiry A Cross Curricular Reader*, (New Jersey: Prentice Hall, Inc., 1993.)

Reader Comments on the "Marginal Fail" examination:

This paper contains many ideas, is generally clear, and demonstrates some understanding of the two readings, along with some confusion and misreading. It does not, however, develop a single coherent essay (criterion 2), moving as it does from idea to idea, nor does it use quotations to support rather than substitute for the paper's ideas (criterion 3). It basically summarizes the two readings and makes random observations about their likenesses and differences. This writer might well pass a future WREE if he or she took time at the beginning of the test to organize a coherent and focused response. The writer would be likely to pass a minimum proficiency test (which the WREE is not—this is a course equivalency examination) and ought to work independently to improve organizational skills in preparation for a subsequent WREE.

Low Fail

The two authors share a similar view that science progresses by building upon established principles. Kuhn illustrates how scientific research builds upon established principles or paradigms. He defines paradigms as structures or patterns that allow scientists to share a common set of assumptions, theories, laws or applications as they look at their fields.[1]

The two authors differ in their opinions about how new theories are developed. Kuhn states that in order to be accepted as a paradigm, a theory must seem better than its competitors, but it need not explain all the facts with which it can be confronted.[2] A theory is accepted as long as it cannot be disproved. Asimov believes that new discoveries come about through a creative process. A creative individual must possess the following characteristics.[3]

1. He must be broadly educated
2. He must be intelligent
3. He must be intuitive
4. He must be courageous
5. He must be lucky in the sense that he must be in the right place at the right time.

The two authors agree that normal science is important because it provides a foundation to build upon. Considering the overwhelming amount of facts and figures utilized in the research process, a paradigm provides a springboard for further study. It allows the scientist time to concentrate on more specific study

Crazy ideas generally go against the norm. For crazy ideas to be accepted, they must be proven. If they don't work, they're useless. Many crazy ideas are not accepted because they are ahead of their time. A receptive atmosphere is one where people are willing to accept these crazy ideas. This usually involves the element of luck. Being lucky means being in the right place at the right time.

My own experience supports the conclusion of both authors. While pursing a baccalaureate degree, in biology, I was confronted with tremendous of data.

Reader Comments on the "Low Fail" Examination:

This paper fails three of the four criteria: (1) Understanding of the two readings is superficial and confused; (2) The essay is not focused, developed, or coherent; (3) Sources are not cited (though we seem to have footnote numbers) nor are they used to support the writer's ideas; and (4) the writing, though largely free from grammatical and mechanical errors, consists of a series of disconnected observations. This writer needs to develop a writing process that allows coherent development of a focused idea and probably should plan to take an upper-division course to learn such a process.

Conclusion

The term *college-level writing* is meaningless in itself, ignoring as it does the enormous variety of institutions, rhetorical situations, levels of education, and fields of study of college students. Personal definitions tell us about the person defining the term, not the term itself, and most institutional statements are too general to be useful. The clearest way to approach a genuine definition is by way of the actual criteria and sample writings used by colleges and universities to make distinctions that matter about student performance for specific purposes. No doubt, the term will continue in common parlance to mean a vague sort of good writing, left undefined, that suits the user's particular purpose—often a lament that standards have declined from the good old days, whenever they were. But for those seeking a serious definition of the kinds of writing that colleges actually require, the best place to look is at the scoring criteria used by the institutions that have decided to take student writing as a general responsibility. While far too many colleges and universities neglect that responsibility, those that accept it and enforce it through specific courses beyond the first-year level, essay tests, or portfolio assessments are able to define what they mean and demonstrate that most of their graduates eventually attain that ability.

Works Cited

Britton, James. *The Development of Writing Abilities (11–18).* London: Macmillan, 1979.

Rembar, Charles. *The End of Obscenity: The Trials of Lady Chatterley, Tropic of Cancer, and Fanny Hill.* New York: Random House, 1968.

White, Edward M. *Teaching and Assessing Writing: Recent Advances in Understanding, Evaluating, and Improving Student Performance.* 2nd ed. San Francisco: Jossey-Bass, 1994.

Chapter Seventeen

Coming to Terms: Vocabulary as a Means of Defining First-Year Composition

Kathleen Blake Yancey
Florida State University
with
Brian M. Morrison
Clemson University, Class of 2004

A story

In 1999, North Carolina was developing a new set of curricular frameworks for kindergarten through grade 12, and I was invited to think with several members of the community about what those frameworks for language arts and English might look like. Margaret, the person chairing our group, is a former Parent-Teacher Association president for all of Mecklenburg County, which with over ninety thousand students at the time (and over one hundred thousand today) was one of the largest school districts in the state. At the first meeting of the group, I introduced the idea of reflection as a process we might want to include in the language arts curriculum, and was delighted at how much the idea was welcomed. When it came to writing, however, I found myself frustrated. Regardless of the approach I took, my colleagues persisted in seeing writing as grammar. Finally, in a conversation with Margaret, I said, "Margaret, I am glad to include grammar in the framework since I think some attention to grammar can do a number of good things. But honestly, writing isn't grammar. So what can we do about that?" Her reply: "It's prob-

ably not. But it's what I was taught, and I can write, and it's what I know. *So I've assumed it's what kids should know, too."*

Some Terms: Composition and Discourse Communities

The terms we—both in high school and in college—use in the teaching of writing are important, and as we know, those terms have changed over the last thirty years. Today, we talk about the teaching of writing in the vocabulary of composing processes like drafting, peer reviewing, and revising; in the language of texts like reading and interpretation and genre; and in the words of writing assessment like focus, organization, evidence, and style or voice. These terms speak to concepts and to practices that together are the stuff of composition.

Although composition in high school and college is similar, it is also very different from one site to the next in some significant ways, as two recent studies suggest. One of these, the "Portraits of Composition" study, surveyed 1,861 postsecondary writing faculty—the largest group ever consulted—about their teaching of college composition (Yancey et al.). When asked to identify one or two of their most important approaches to teaching composition, the respondents to the survey identified academic writing most often (57 percent) followed next by argument (40.9 percent). Likewise, when asked what writing practices they most used, faculty identified three: writing process, revision, and peer review. This composition curriculum is fundamentally different than that of high school, however, at least as it is portrayed both in the work of researchers like Arthur Applebee and in the more recent *Research in the Teaching of English* study of high school writing practices (Applebee, "Stability"; Scherff and Piazza). This study, based on the responses of 2,000 high school students to a survey inquiring into their writing curricula, showed a composition that is less oriented to process and more oriented to literature. According to Scherff and Piazza, of all high school students reporting on their school writing activities, the *only* students who engaged in peer revision and editing were the dual enrollment students (288–89). Moreover, the primary form of high school writing is not academic writing, as it is in college, but "literary" writing (292), and the principal exigence for writing instruction, echoing Britton's study some thirty years ago, is test preparation. The high school composition curriculum thus differs from its college cousin in part because of the influence of tests—some thirty-eight states assess students' writing with an essay (Ketter and Pool)—and in part because the focus of the writing in both classroom and test is on literature.

Put differently, the discourse communities that these composition programs inhabit are quite different—for high school composition, the English classroom and the community of literature; for college composition, the college or university discourse community, where academic writing and argument are the preferred genres.

A New Vocabulary for a New Genre

Brian discusses a new genre of writing, blogs:

> Upon first consideration, my claim is that blogs (also called weblogs) would constitute a new genre within electronic communication. However, upon reconsideration of what can constitute a blog and a survey of its various rhetorical exploitations, I am not so certain what it is. A determination would also be contingent upon the definition that I use for "genre."
>
> Simply to lay the groundwork for beginning to talk about this, I think it would be helpful to define the terms. The word "genre" is a daunting and encompassing term, and its handling is important to my current meditation. To state it simply (to save myself from an attempt at an exhaustive consideration), a genre might be called a form that generally carries its own conventions, styles, syntax, content, etc. However, just as genre can often dictate boundaries for one of its manifestations, texts can expand or defy generic classification by playing with any of the aforementioned elements that animate the genre.
>
> Blogs are a new form of electronic communication that seem to have had their first emergence nearly 18 months ago, but have since spread all over the Internet and now seem to be a ubiquitous presence in cyberspace.

Defining Terms

We often think that we define terms, but terms also define us. And in the context of postsecondary composition instruction, that's a problem, according to Greg Colomb. On the Writing Program Administration (WPA) listserv, he notes,

> [T]he terms students bring to our classes are not up to the job. They are a hodgepodge of folk theory, terms invented locally by various K–12 teachers, handbook terms based on antique and false theories of language, and a little MTV and Reading Rainbow thrown in. Terms like "attention grabber" or "the clincher" are too vague and too easily misunderstood. As Jay [Gordon] points out, not only is the language students bring or teachers invent seldom helpful, it is most often detrimental to a writer's performance.

Colomb further notes that what he sees as our reluctance to make use of appropriate terms intentionally cannot be because the students are not *ready* for sophisticated terminology, especially when we think about the terms students learn in other disciplines:

> Besides, are we seriously going to say that any of the following terms are too difficult for students who are contemporaneously learning organic chemistry and calculus: claim, reason, evidence, acknowledgment and response, warrant, noun, verb, character, action, topic, stress, old information, new information, topic string, main character, point of view, problem statement, common ground, destabilizing condition, cost, response, solution, etc. What do we say about ourselves when we say that we want to work in a field with NO special terminology?

Not least, Colomb helps me understand my earlier discussion with Margaret:

> Few writers in or outside the academy have an adequate vocabulary for talking about writing because WE FAILED to teach them such a vocabulary back when they were our students. Past failures are hardly a good reason not to do what's best now.

Which leads me to ask: What are the terms of composition today—and in the early part of the twenty-first century?

New Genres, New Spaces, New Terms

Brian:

> Another interesting point about blogs is their use of space, which tends to vary. Beyond utilization of both written and visual material, the use of space varies between postings and blogs from snippets of information or language to lengthy arguments, comments, reportings, etc. The use of space that I have encountered thus far tends to fall on the lengthy side of the spectrum. Whereas instant messaging and chat rooms generally involve transmission of small, quick messages, blogs make provisions for the kind of organization, coherence, and length that *feels* like a print document.

A Term for Our Consideration: First-Year Composition as *Brokering*

Deciding on key terms is not an easy task, but it is an interesting intellectual task. When creating a syllabus, I locate the material of the course in key terms that lead to key questions; it's a way of identifying what matters, of helping to provide a language for thinking and writing (see Figure 1). The students and I use these terms throughout a semester. Sometimes I ask students to map key terms so that we can tease out relationships, especially the relationships among terms that students are creating. Over the course of a semester, we see how relationships shift, extend, amplify. Sometimes—as in a course on genre, voice, and technology—I ask students to use the key terms as the basis of their reflections, in portfolios and out.

As members of a discipline, how do we decide on key terms? One approach might be to review documents like the WPA Outcomes Statement, which is itself marked by key terms like *genre* and *process*. Another, complementary approach might be to think about how we understand the role of first-year composition in the academy. Is our purpose as it was in the time of World War II, to assure that students could communicate so that they could win battles (Good, *Writing*)? Is our purpose another one associated with the past, to introduce students to literature (Yancey et

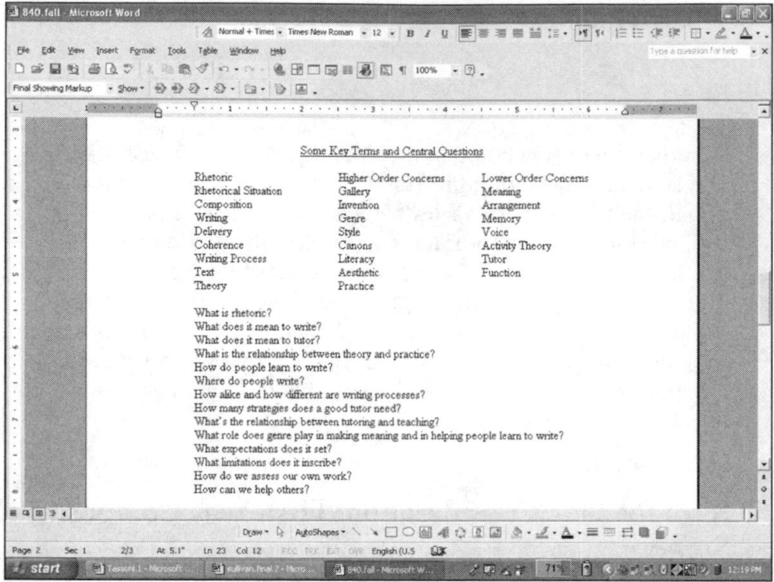

Some Key Terms and Central Questions

Rhetoric	Higher Order Concerns	Lower Order Concerns
Rhetorical Situation	Gallery	Meaning
Composition	Invention	Arrangement
Writing	Genre	Memory
Delivery	Style	Voice
Coherence	Canons	Activity Theory
Writing Process	Literacy	Tutor
Text	Aesthetic	Function
Theory	Practice	

What is rhetoric?
What does it mean to write?
What does it mean to tutor?
What is the relationship between theory and practice?
How do people learn to write?
Where do people write?
How alike and how different are writing processes?
How many strategies does a good tutor need?
What's the relationship between tutoring and teaching?
What role does genre play in making meaning and in helping people learn to write?
What expectations does it set?
What limitations does it inscribe?
How do we assess our own work?
How can we help others?

FIGURE 1. *Key terms.*

al.)? Is it to socialize students? Is it to prepare students for the classes in writing that they will encounter later? Apparently, the purpose is to help students write, but in what context?

Elizabeth Wardle, drawing on activity theory, sees our role as that of a broker. She says,

> FYC teachers . . . are faced with a very difficult task: preparing students for the varied genres used across the university and in its disciplines when the teachers themselves are usually involved in only one of those disciplines. FYC teachers faced with this goal for FYC are asked to be what Wenger (1998) calls "boundary brokers." Brokering is a connection made by a person with memberships in multiple activity systems; brokers "introduce elements of one practice into another" (p. 105). The immediately apparent problem with FYC teachers in English departments who are asked to be brokers is that they do not usually have the multiple memberships brokers need in order to translate, coordinate, and align between the perspectives (p. 109) (and genres) of the students, the English department, and the various disciplines with which students will become involved.

She seems to have a point; the report of the writing faculty in the "Portraits of Composition" study is that we teach academic writing (Yancey et al.), and yet, as Wardle claims, too often these are contexts we don't have the expertise to broker. At the same time, I still find brokering a compelling metaphor. Question: If we aren't brokering the conventions and genres of other disciplines, what are we brokering? Does this metaphorical term work?

Models of Composition

In the old model of composition, we were not sure if we could require typed copies of essays. In a less old model of composition, not that long ago, we focused exclusively on print, even as we moved to word processing. Most of us continued to teach and assess writing without *seeing* that the writing composed with a word processor that allows one to **bold** and *italicize* and

- format

is quite different from the writing that is created with pencil and paper and different still from (merely) typing a final copy. A newer model is writing for the screen, to see the screen as the vehicle for delivery and to use the parameters and the resources of the screen as another composing space. A future model is to use all these composing spaces and put them (and the processes we use in each) in dialogue with each other, using terms like *medium* and *remediation* and *genre* and *rhetorical situation* to help students think about practice, and to use reflection as a means of articulating practice and creating a theory from practice. The term *circulation*—among rhetorical situations, among various media—allows us to consider how we compose now. If we were to use circulation as a central term, how might that shape composition?

Another Story: The Things They Carried

The University of North Carolina at Greensboro offers a dual enrollment program called Fast Forward. Each summer, high school English teachers from different counties gather on the college campus to think about how they teach composition, to share assignments and response strategies, and to compare what they do with practices in the college writing program. The teachers enjoy each other, and they like focusing on a writing curriculum.

I was invited to create an assessment program to see how well this dual enrollment program worked. Put in the form of a question, we wanted to know: How do the students who complete this program fare on college campuses? To answer this question, we completed several tasks: reviewing portfolios, analyzing self-reported grades of students and retention rates, and, not least, interviewing students. The interviews were the most informative. We talked to eleven students who attended a range of institutions, including the University of North Carolina, North Carolina State University, and North Carolina A&T University. They told a story of writing located in key terms, and they explained how those key terms allowed them to create a theory allowing them to construct college writing tasks and complete them well. In other words, they pointed much more to the terms—like rhetorical situation, audience, genre, conventions, and evidence—than to the practices. In high school, the students had developed practices that they could carry with them into college, and that, they said, was good. What was even better was having a language that helped them think about how to make sense of writing assignments and how to begin working on them and how to begin to see if they were successful.

In college writing circles, we often talk about transfer, about the ability of students to take what they have learned about writing in our early classes and take it to other sites of writing, including other classrooms. These conversations are often characterized by frustration since the research (e.g., Haswell; Sternglass; Carroll) suggests that students do not in fact transfer very much or very well. What's the point, we might well ask.

What I want to ask is *what* is it that we hope will transfer? It seems to me that these Fast Forward students have articulated for us what can transfer: practices, yes, but theory—our theory of writing, which is the material of the curriculum and *their* theory of writing as they have lived it. Put together, this is a combination worth transferring. As important, being explicit about this transfer—about what this means and how it works—means that students are likely to take it seriously.

It also of course means that we would need to change our curriculum.

Whither Blogging?

Brian:

> The columnist Dave Barry uses a blog to post humor, anecdotes, and announcements. A number of bloggers in the United Kingdom recently published, in a blog, a writing discussing whether blogs are "fair" because of the influences of socioeconomic factors and gender. One blog I discovered involved the daily reportings and happenings in the life of a European prostitute. Another one is used to discuss opposition to war. This is just a mere sampling of the uses of the space in weblogs that are to be found on the Internet. I think, amongst the larger number of bloggers, there are possibilities for blogs that have not been fully explored and exploited.

Terms for Faculty

If composition in the twenty-first century—a century already well underway—is to change along the lines sketched out above, faculty too will need new terms. And another way to think about this is to consider first-year composition as a foundation for advanced writing. If we thought of first-year composition (FYC) that way, we might well build a program that shifts from process arhetorically applied to practices that are situated and a program that moves from whatever theme the faculty prefers to a content and theory that are, well, *composition*.

Robert Connors, in the Afterword to *Coming of Age*, talks about such a writing curriculum, one that rewrites literacy education. He focuses on advanced composition, which relies of course on the foundation we find in FYC. He says,

> the changing socioculture of college English departments is central here, and it must be seen as the basis for the centrifugal forces that have traditionally kept advanced composition a congeries of unrelated courses taught by staffs with no essential mutual interests, courses related only in being composition beyond freshman English. We are all living in the back wash of the creation of an English curriculum that features this unconnected and relatively primitive curricular lineup of writing courses, as juxtaposed to the God's Plenty of the literature curriculum, with its many proliferating mansions. (144)

The program, according to Connors, is "a program for an entirely new conception of undergraduate literacy education . . . based on the centrality of writing rather than literature" (150). If we thought of writing in *this* way, what foundation might we create? If faculty were to come to terms in this way, what might those terms be?

They might, I think, include:

- *Composition*: which includes how we write, where we write; how art informs writing; how the composing that is writing is like and unlike other composings, in music, in art, and so on.
- *Material*: which includes what spaces we write on and in and what tools we write with, and how some of those tools (like software) can write us. Or: composition is a material practice: what differences do different materials and tools make in what and how we write and what and how we become?
- *Visual*: which includes, as John Trimbur suggests, the typefaces we use; and as Ann Wysocki suggests, the interface of the page; and the processes of storyboarding that contribute to complex electronic documents.
- *Practice*: which refers to the processes we use to write as well as the communities in which we use these processes.
- *Theory*: which refers to how we make sense of what we know, informed by the thinking of others; and created by ourselves as we learn more. What are the theories of writing that we share with students? What theories of writing do we invite students to create?
- *Rhetoric*: which as theory and practice refers to fundamental concepts like rhetorical situation, pathos, logos, ethos, identification, knowledge, truth, and ethics that inform all writing.

- *Circulation*: which refers to how information is distributed, and in today's world, that means putting print and electronic in dialogue with each other; it means as well considering how specialized knowledge is articulated for experts as opposed to lay people; and to the patterns of information and overlaps—print papers and Web sites and blogs and text messaging and books.
- *Transfer*: which refers to the ability to take what one learns in one site and to use it in another.
- *Broker*: which refers to the role that we play in assisting students as they enter college and as they move on. This term provides a way of thinking about what we broker: writing theory and practice, negotiated through reflection.
- *Reflection*: the process of reviewing so as to understand and sometimes to self-assess and sometimes to project, which Donald Schön talks about as reflective transfer, which relies on prototypes to think about best practices and to make theory.

New Practices, New Terms

Writing is changing more quickly than we can record those changes. We went, in what seemed an instant, from hard copy print to wireless classrooms where students simultaneously text message and e-mail. Indeed, this summer, in the new Seattle Public Library, I sat next to a young woman engaged in such multitasking, and no one paid any attention to it. It's the new normal of composition—much of which takes place out of school.

In school, we tend to think of the new normal as using the Web for fairly traditional tasks:

> There was a time when researching a high school or college term paper was a far simpler thing. A student writing about, say, Count Ferdinand von Zeppelin, might have checked out a book on the history of aviation from the local library or tucked into the family's dog-eared Britannica. An ambitious college freshman might have augmented the research by looking up some old newspaper clips on microfilm or picking up a monograph in the stacks.
>
> Knowing where and how to find information, they agreed, was just the beginning. Interpreting, sorting, evaluating, manipulating and repackaging information in dozens of forms from thousands of sources—as well as having a fundamental understanding

> of the legal and ethical uses of digital materials—are also important components. (Zeller C1)

And no question, this kind of information literacy is challenging all of us. At the same time, we are all engaged in new forms of writing, which is why, as we see in Brian's writing, one assignment asks students to think about these new forms and to define them and to learn about them—for them of course, and for us all. Brian, who at the time of the writing of this essay was a senior, looked at blogs; another student, Jason, has looked at instant messaging; and still other students, like those in a first-year class, have looked at what writing looked like in the 1940s.

Writing, then, is the content for the college class in writing.

Eyes Wide Shut: College Composition and the Future

Tina Good, in mapping out a history of writing based on articles in *College English*, shows that at mid-twentieth century, college writing classes served two purposes: introducing students to literature and ensuring that student writing prepared them for the roles the country needed them to play, especially in the Second World War. Ironically, writing was both utilitarian and canonical. During the second half of the twentieth century, as we know, writing, much like a boat tacking, changed course, primarily through the language and activities of writing process. That's what we see in the "Portraits of Composition" survey (Yancey et al.), and that's what we see in the WPA Outcomes Statement—and that's what we see, to a greater or lesser extent, in the many textbooks that are intended to serve writers in the first-year course. But that *process* language and *process* activity have been used to serve many purposes, even those of the 1940s, though more often now they are intended to serve what Elizabeth Wardle calls the brokering function, what the "Portraits" survey called academic and argument writing.

But I think it's past time that we tack again: I am arguing that we have a good deal to broker, and that what we have to offer relies much less on what awaits our students in other classes and much more on what we can all learn about writing now.

Toward that end, I have identified a set of ten terms—an incomplete list, to be sure—that gives us a core to think with. In revisiting them now, that list seems very full. On the one hand, it contains what I want my first-year students to know, certainly. Yet on the other hand, I also want them to study writing, that of the past, that of the present, and that of the future, and I have suggested the barest outlines of one such assignment; we have seen that assignment embodied in Brian's work.

What I am proposing is a full agenda, a full content, and a beginning for a college composition that has a content: composition.

Works Cited

Applebee, Arthur N., and Judith A. Langer. *Contexts for Learning to Write: Studies of Secondary School Instruction.* Norwood, NJ: Ablex, 1984.

Applebee, Arthur. "Stability and Change in the High-School Canon." *English Journal* 81 (1992): 27–32.

Barry, Dave. "The Unofficial Dave Barry Blog." 12 June 2006 <http://blogs.herald.com/dave_barrys_blog/>.

Britton, James. *The Development of Writing Abilities (11–18).* London: Macmillan, 1975.

Carroll, Lee Ann. *Rehearsing New Roles: How College Students Develop as Writers.* Carbondale: Southern Illinois UP, 2002.

Colomb, Greg. "Re: Toulmin Method: Terms in Writing Education." Writing Program Administration. Arizona State University. 1 March 2005 <http://lists.asu.edu/cgi-bin/wa?A2=ind0503&L=wpa-l&D=1&O=A&P=451>.

Connors, Robert. Afterword. *Coming of Age: The Advanced Writing Curriculum.* Ed. Linda K. Shamoon, Rebecca Moore Howard, Sandra Jamieson, and Robert Schwegler. Portsmouth: Boynton/Cook, 2000.

Haswell, Richard. "Gaining Ground." *Gaining Ground in College Writing: Tales of Development and Interpretation.* Dallas: Southern Methodist UP, 1991.

Good, Tina. *Writing Assessment: An Autobiography of English Studies*. Unpublished dissertation, 2005.

Ketter, Jean, and Jonelle Pool. "Exploring the Impact of a High-Stakes Direct Writing Assessment in Two High School Classrooms." *Research in the Teaching of English* 35 (2001): 344–93.

Scherff, Lisa, and Carolyn Piazza. "The More Things Change, the More They Stay the Same: A Survey of High School Students' Writing Experiences." *Research in the Teaching of English* 39.3 (2005): 271–304.

Schön, Donald. *Educating the Reflective Practitioner*. San Francisco: Jossey Bass, 1987.

Sternglass, Marilyn S. *Time to Know Them: A Longitudinal Study of Writing and Learning at the College Level*. Mahwah, NJ: Lawrence Erlbaum, 1997.

Trimbur, John. "Delivering the Message: Typography and the Materiality of Writing." *Rhetoric and Composition as Intellectual Work*. Ed. Gary A. Olson. Carbondale: Southern Illinois UP, 2002. 188–203.

Wardle, Elizabeth. "Can Cross-Disciplinary Links Help Us Teach 'Academic Discourse' in FYC?" *Across the Disciplines*. 2004. 11 June 2006 <http://wac.colostate.edu/atd/articles/wardle2004/>.

Wenger, Etienne. *Communities of Practice: Learning, Meaning, and Identity*. New York: Cambridge UP, 1998.

"The WPA Outcomes Statement for First-Year Composition." *WPA: Writing Program Administration* 23.1/2 (1999): 59–67. 11 June 2006 <http://www.english.ilstu.edu/Hesse/outcomes.html>.

Wysocki, Ann Frances. "Monitoring Order: Visual Desire, the Organization of Web Pages, and Teaching the Rules of Design." *Kairos* 3.2 (1998): <http://English.ttu.edu/kairos>.

Yancey, Kathleen Blake, Teddi Fishman, Morgan Gresham, Michael Neal, and Summer Smith Taylor. "Portraits of Composition: How Writing Gets Taught in the Early 21st Century." Conference on College Composition and Communication. San Francisco. 2005.

Zeller, Tom. "Measuring Literacy in a World Gone Digital." *New York Times* 17 Jan. 2005: sec. C, p. 1.

III

Student Perspectives

Chapter Eighteen

The Great Conversation (of the Dining Hall): One Student's Experience of College-Level Writing

Kimberly L. Nelson
University of Iowa, Class of 2006

On Monday, September 9, 2002, as a first-year-student at the University of Iowa, and after having been on campus for less than three weeks, I walked into my second class of the morning, an honors seminar in the humanities, and sat down, completely pleased with myself and how college was going. The professor was sitting across from me, so I smiled and nodded "good morning." As I did so, I noticed a small stack of white, typed sheets sitting next to her customary cup of coffee, yellow legal pad, and blue pen. As the bells of the Old Capitol began to chime, signaling the end of the passing period, the professor handed the sheaf to the girl on her left, watched it start its way around, and began to read aloud. We were instructed to write a six- to seven-page paper on a subject of our choosing, but that related in some way to fantasy fiction. The paper could be argumentative, persuasive, a demonstration of knowledge, or simply a discussion of something we found interesting. This was our first writing assignment, definitely a significant step in the semester, but even more importantly, and certainly more terrifying for me, was the fact that it was the first essay assignment of my college career, and I was one of the only freshmen in the entire honors class. Over the next month, as I worked on the essay, struggling to realize the full potential of my resources, I learned that to write at the college level requires not only a thorough knowledge of the material to be discussed, but also a cogent, thoughtful, and passionately presented synthesis of that material.

Immediately after receiving the assignment, and in spite of the panic it aroused, I began to jot down notes; even then, I knew broadly on what topic I wanted to write. The honors seminar, entitled "Other Worlds, Other Realities" addressed fantasy and science fiction literature from Frankenstein to the slipstream and magic realism of today. However, in addition to those modern forms of the genres, our reading list also included a pair of writings by J. R. R. Tolkien, his short story entitled "Leaf by Niggle," and his essay "On Fairy-Stories." In these writings, loosely conjoined by Tolkien's examination of the artist's role in society, I found someone I could admire, an author who was an incredibly creative man committed to art as well as academics. Nevertheless, I was also baffled as to why such an apparently brilliant philologist would expend his energies creating a fantasy world like *The Lord of the Rings*, and I desperately wanted to understand the man behind the words. Yet, while I certainly did not suffer from a lack of interest in the subject, the scope of the assignment and the breadth of my inquiry quickly overwhelmed me.

Back at the dorms that afternoon, I sat down and tried to bang out an essay proposal. After an hour, I had a five-page outline and a source list that included not only the short story and essay, but also *The Hobbit*, the entire *The Lord of the Rings*, biographical information on Tolkien, and several of the reviews of him and his oeuvre we had read in class. How was I ever to cram all of my interests into a six- to seven-page paper when Tolkien said and addressed so much? I did not, in the attempt to write the essay, want to do an injustice to the man or his work. Almost everything he said seemed important and interrelated, and I did not want to leave out even one meaty or beautiful quote. Over the next few days, as I grappled with my topic and proposal, the emotional and intellectual maelstrom I passed through came to remind me of my experience a few years earlier in my high school Modern British Literature class.

Just as I was now passionately curious about J. R. R. Tolkien and *Tree and Leaf*, I had been similarly excited about writing an essay on our most recent British Literature book, *Pride and Prejudice*, but again, had possessed little clue as to where to begin. In that situation, my English instructor had helped me realize that the trick to tackling such a broad question was to reread, reanalyze, and hone the assignment and my subsidiary questions into one central question. In this way, I could construct the essay by choosing individual quotes and specific details from the text that both interested me and provided evidence for my answer.

However, my difficulty with the *Pride and Prejudice* paper stemmed not only from the format of the question, but the fact that it was the class's culminating essay. Despite the effort I had put into completing the course's previous written assignments, I had repeatedly failed to generate thoughts and language that would create the awe that I so wished to instill in my instructor, and I desperately feared failing again. As I wrote that semester, I had pictured my younger brother, a talented musician, who, in his auditions, always strives to make his adjudicators stop, take pause, and put down their pencils. I greatly respected my British Literature instructor and the topic she had assigned, and wanted to create a similar reaction between her and my essay. Using the teacher's previous lessons on refining topic questions, I had already picked my quotes, made an outline, and drafted a thesis, checking off all the individual steps on our writing rubric as we had been taught, but as the due date approached, I had still not actually begun my first draft.

The night before the essay was due, while my mom was fixing dinner, I crept downstairs, notes and outline in hand, plopped myself down on top of the kitchen island, queried, "Mom?" and out of frustration, started to cry. What was the point, I asked, of working hard that night on that essay if in the morning, when I turned it in, I would still fail to earn my teacher's respect and regard? I mumbled that it was better just not to turn it in at all, than face the humiliation of another mediocre response from my instructor. My mother, a veteran parent and teacher, stood silently over the stove for a moment before turning around and fixing me with a stern, but not unconcerned, glare. It was no skin off the teacher's nose, she said, if I did not turn in that essay, but its absence would certainly not impress my instructor in the way that I wished, or satiate my desire for validation. She turned back toward the oven and we sat in silence, but after a few moments she asked over her shoulder, "What have you got so far?"

For the next hour, she let the chili burn as I explained my theory of Mr. Darcy and *Pride and Prejudice*. When I had finally finished, and taken a gulp of air, she chuckled and said, "You have the potential to do with words what your brother does with music—add vibrato, adjust speed, and hit the note in just the right way. But, if like him sometimes, you doubt yourself or do not practice, you will never reach that level of performance. You have got to take the risks if you want the reward." Later, I would come to understand that while sitting in the kitchen, talking to my mom, I was making my first utterances in the "conversation of mankind." As Kenneth A. Bruffee notes in Capossela's *Harcourt Brace Guide to Peer Tutoring*, "Reflective thinking is something we learn to do, and we learn to do it from and with other people. We learn to think reflectively as a result of learning to talk" (128). That night was the first time I ever talked through an essay with another person, a practice that has now not only become a habitual part of my writing process, but an absolutely necessary one as well.

At eight o'clock that evening, I finally decided to take the chance, put my head on the chopping block, and start to write. As I did, I began to pay closer attention not only to individual sentences, but to discrete words and phrases as well, and in so doing, I realized that I *could* do with words what my brother did with music: vary my tone, timbre, and cadence to draw out that desired awe from my audience. A week later, when the instructor returned the essays, my efforts were richly rewarded. The second page of my paper was mark free except for "Cool!" written in electric blue ink next to a sentence that I am still proud of, nearly four years later. I had written,

> Darcy certainly belongs to a higher social rank than the Bennets, and his manners and mind are no doubt superior, but in his actions toward Bingley and Jane and his decisive inaction concerning Wickham, his pride crosses the line into a detrimental character trait. However, pride is not the only factor in the equation of his mistakes; the whims of society also play a role.

In that section of my essay, I had shown a connection between two quotes that appeared more than thirty pages apart in the text, and I had even ended with a transition to my next paragraph. I had shown both the instructor and myself that just as my brother was a young but passionate and serious student of music, I was a young but passionate and serious student of the art of writing.

Throughout Modern British Literature, and especially during the *Pride and Prejudice* essay, I had seen the importance of clear thought, crisp organization, interpersonal communication, and a host of other foundational essay-writing skills. However, by the end of my high school career, I had yet to participate in any real semblance of a literary debate. I had no experience with criticism or the comparison of academic articles. Now, barely a month into my first year of college, the professor of my honors seminar fully expected me to do all of those things while experimenting with holding a collegiate level of discourse, and once again, I found myself doubting my abilities.

The dorm I lived in as a first-year student, and still live in, is shaped like a giant eight-floor, cinderblock shoebox. While one of its narrow ends sits perpendicular to the street, the other looks back west, down the hill, toward the Memorial Union and eventually the Iowa River. On the south side of each floor there is a lounge, whose only redeeming qualities are several groupings of large, comfy chairs, and a wall of picture windows that face Old Brick, a very old Presbyterian church that is now a modern social venue on campus. At eleven o'clock on Friday, September 20, my friends found me sitting in the third floor lounge alternately looking up at swarms of bats in the steeple above and students in the pedestrian mall below, perfectly perplexed by my paper topic. Drawing both practical lessons and confidence from my reminiscences of my trials in Modern British Literature, I had taken a deep breath and limited my scope of inquiry to "On Fairy-Stories" and "Leaf by Niggle." Earlier that week, after finally turning in a workable essay proposal, I had decided to uncover the man behind the words by starting with a close rereading and reanalysis of those two tiny texts, but Tolkien was proving an elusive and wily old Englishman.

By now, my poor copy of *The Tolkien Reader* was a palimpsest of neon-colored sticky notes and highlighted passages, thoughtful annotations, and frustrated expostulations. I had walked through "Niggle's Parish" several times, and repeatedly sat in the lecture room, listening to Tolkien theorize about the values of fantasy literature, but still, I felt that I was no closer to the big picture. I knew that I needed to talk to people about the essay, but my thoughts were hopelessly jumbled, painfully plain, and completely unoriginal. Tolkien's quotes on fairy stories and anecdotes and arguments about juvenile pleasure reading were starting to solidify into vicious, repetitious, and unproductive circles of thought, and I did not want to experience this mental miasma, let alone inflict it on anyone else. Worse yet, my rough draft was due in one week. As I flicked off the light and left the lounge that evening, I decided that while it had been a good idea to start my research by limiting my field of vision, it was now time to reexpand my scope of inquiry. If I was not yet ready to speak to other people about Tolkien, then perhaps I was at least ready to listen.

The next morning, I hiked down the hill to the library, and after deciphering the building's arrangement and puzzling out the Library of Congress System, I made my way to the fourth floor and what I came to think of as The Aisle of Tolkien. I had gone to the University's main library envisioning merely a larger version of my high school library, and hoping to unearth maybe a half dozen biographies on Tolkien. Instead, I found at least five dozen books on all aspects of his life and work. Shocked but excited, I waded in. As I sat reading one huge compendium on Tolkien, I noticed that several authors repeatedly referenced a text by Colin Wilson. I was extremely impressed with the clarity of Wilson's writing, as well as his overall interpretation, and I suddenly found myself wishing I could read his book.

On the off chance that it might be sitting somewhere in the stacks, I decided to go take a look. A few minutes later, I returned to my sunny cubicle, Wilson's *Tree by Tolkien* in hand, and stumbled across a quote that seemed to clarify almost automatically the world of Tolkien. Wilson had written, "[C]ertain people are dreamers and visionaries, and although they may seem relatively useless to the community, they embody values that the community cannot afford to forget" (20). The Hawkeyes had a huge football game that Saturday afternoon, and from my chair, I could look out the window onto the library's back parking lot, and see some twenty groups of people tailgating and apparently listening to the game on their car radios. While I do not remember whom we were playing that day, or even if we won, I do remember feeling as if I had suddenly slipped into scenes portrayed in two of my favorite books, Chaim Potok's *The Chosen* and Laurie R. King's *The Beekeeper's Apprentice*.

As I flipped back and forth between one author's examination of Wilson's analysis of Tolkien, Wilson's actual words, and Tolkien's original essay, I felt just like King's young Oxford student, Mary Russell, or Potok's school-aged Talmudic scholar, Danny. Both of those adolescent academics, while sitting in their respective libraries, had experienced the wonder and challenge of academia for the first time. Now, like them, I was listening to multiple levels of textual analysis for the first time in my life, and once again participating in the conversation of mankind, though this time, is was certainly at a much deeper level. In an article I first read in Modern British Literature, Donald G. Smith, a teacher at Apollo High School in Glendale, Arizona, explains that when reading, we can

> [S]top, reread, look up explanatory and supporting materials and then pick up the conversation where it left off. We can mull over a line until we see its worth. We can add out own perceptions, questions, and applications. We can disagree, attack, defend. In short, we can take part in the Great Conversation of humanity. (21)

When I walked back across the Pentacrest and up the hill to my dorm late that afternoon, notes and library books tucked safely in my book bag, I felt like a real college-level scholar. However, by Sunday afternoon, the rosy glow of academia had started to fade.

Once back from the library, I began to organize my notes. I planned to group them by topic and argument, and then, whip out my so recently new highlighters and officiously color code my quotes to match sections I had noted in *The Tolkien Reader*. Finally, I would arrange the different colored sections, creating a vibrant visual representation of my essay's argument. Then it hit me: I had proposed a topic, but had never established those two elements key to almost every essay, an argument structure and a thesis. My thoughts were still just a jumbled mass, and now, I had three times as much information and my rough draft was due in five days, not seven. It was definitely time to recall the good old lessons of British Literature and seek out people with whom I could hold a conversation. Legal pad in one hand and lunch card in the other, I walked up and down the floor, knocking on my friends' doors, seeing if they wanted to go to dinner. Once we had all taken seats in the cafeteria, I looked around that table, and asked, "So, do you mind if I talk about Tolkien?"

At first, I just threw out random quotes and information. Then, as I started to get a sense of what I had read, and what of it I liked and did not like, I began to make connections, saying, "but Auden says this . . .," or "yes, but about Wilson's argument that. . . ." By the end of dinner, not only was I asking questions and making arguments about specific passages, my friends were too, and everyone was excited to see how the essay would turn out. I repeated this interlocutory flood several times over the next few days to myself and to anyone who would listen, and in the end, it worked. I decided to argue that Tolkien had written *The Lord of the Rings* for two reasons, because he viewed his role as "a subcreator of a fantasy secondary world" as both useful on a broad scale and pleasurable on a more personal level, and that these raisons d'être were evident in *Tree and Leaf*. Even though I did not start writing until Thursday afternoon, I was rather confident that I could create a solid first draft. I had already done several verbal and mental drafts, and by Friday morning, the day on which I was to hand in my essay and read it through with the professor, I had a rough draft with which, I must admit, I was quite smitten. However, it should come as no surprise that I was definitely less starry-eyed when I walked out of my writing conference less than half an hour later.

My professor had carefully worked through my essay, underlining awkward passages, glossing sections, and stopping to ask for clarification. By the end of our twenty minutes together, my essay was not quite a sea of blue ink, but it might as well have been. I was adrift amidst the questions she had asked: what purpose does art serve, what role should the artist play, what happens in the act of subcreation, when does subcreation occur, why is perfection so important in the creation of a secondary world? Staving off hopelessness by returning once again to what I knew,

I realized that I needed to create a workshop-like atmosphere such as the one I had participated in during my final year in high school in my Advanced Placement Language and Composition class.

Several times during AP Language and Composition, the other students and I drafted essays and submitted them to our classmates and teacher. Then, over the next week, after we had read each other's essay, we reviewed the drafts in a roundtable format. In that class, surrounded by fourteen students, all of whom were eager to improve the quality of their writing, as well as an instructor who was herself a masterful writer, my knowledge and use of written language was once again heightened. Before that class, I had never been conscious of the power of a single pronoun. Then, when I started one paragraph in a personal essay about my love of rollerblading with the phrase, "Right before you get to the bridge there is this perfect curve," one of my classmates wrote on my paper, "Deliberate? I don't want to be in the piece yet, or at all! I don't know how to skate, so seeing this pronoun makes me nervous." I grinned at the smiley face drawn next to the comment. No, I had not thought about the authorial consequences of my pronoun usage, but I silently vowed to my reader that I would from then on. In a book I would not read until much later, Toni-Lee Capossela notes that "Writers improve when they use the questions of a thoughtful reader to shape their work, then eventually begin to ask themselves the same questions" (2). Hanna Arendt adds simply, "For excellence, the presence of others is always required" (qtd in Capossela 1). During every writing cycle, the ideas and questions of my fellow AP Language and Composition students pushed me to become a better writer and gave me a completely new set of questions with which to scrutinize my writing.

Looking back on my experiences in AP Language and Composition while staring at my recently mutilated first draft, I realized that I needed to create my own personal writer's workshop here at the University of Iowa. I had already created a verbal forum based upon my experiences in Modern British Literature, but now I needed a place to test my actual, written ideas. I started hesitantly, e-mailing my first draft to my parents. Then, once they had replied and said I sounded more logical and looked to be improving, I showed it to a few close friends. Similar to AP Language and Composition, some of my peers gave great comments on ideas and structure, while others looked intensely at my sentence-level work and grammar. Both kinds of scrutiny helped me improve my essay. All of us had each been taught different things about syntax and structure by our high school English instructors, and this variety allowed an informal writing center to develop on our floor our first year.

However, even with all of this kind attention, I still felt that something was missing, so I took the plunge, and went to the campus Writing Center. There, one night at the beginning of October, I experienced a frisson moment. The consultant and I sat hunched over a round table, desperately trying to discover what was missing in my essay, because it was obvious that something was. Finally, she made as if to speak, halted, and then started afresh. "Explain to me again why Tolkien wanted to do all this?" I sat silently for a minute, and then started to think aloud:

> Well, he didn't create his fantasy world for himself alone; he didn't have to, it had already been in his head for a long time. However, to utilize what he believed to be fantasy's valuable abilities, he needed to let readers experience it, but he had to help them because it was so new. He had to make it detailed and based in reality so that it would be understandable. Then, if he wanted to be a subcreator, the ultimate level of writer for him, Tolkien had to give up his creation to an audience. Without an audience, his secondary world could not exist, could not flow into reality.

I turned back to her to see if all that made sense. A slow grin was slowly creeping up the side of her face. She pointed to my notepad, "Write that down—quick!" In that moment, I had finally connected "Leaf by Niggle" and "On Fairy-Stories," the utilitarian, allegorical story and the high, theoretical essay, ultimately paralleling the development of the short story's main character, the artist, Niggle. By the morning of the final due date, I had not only shown "Flowing into Reality" to friends and family, but had taken different sections of it to the professor several times, and actually visited the campus writing center twice.

A few days later, when the professor returned our essays, I had proof that all of my hard work, as well as the hard work of my coaches, peer readers, and listeners, had paid off. Written on the last page, in that now familiar blue ink, was the comment, "Excellent—cogently argued; your claims are well supported by quotations and relevant details. I'm impressed with the improvement from first draft to final version." My essay, which had started as a furtive monologue, had slowly but surely ballooned into a full discourse, whose interlocutors included over a dozen texts, as well as my friends, family, and professor.

While I must admit that among my original motives for working so hard on the Tolkien essay was the importance of the grade I would receive, by the end of the month-long writing process, the worth of the score had greatly declined, and upon finally receiving it, the good marks were actually a bit of a letdown. At first, I was puzzled by this, but then realized that what I had really desired was not a grade, but validation that my thoughts and efforts, though only those of a first-year student, were important to both my professor and my academic community. My instructor's willingness to repeatedly sit down with me and look at my writing, as well as her end comments had shown me that I was valued, more than any letter grade ever could. Bruffee argues that "Normal discourse is what William Perry calls the fertile 'wedding' of 'bull' and 'cow,' of facts and their relevances: discourse on the established contexts of knowledge in a field that makes effective references to facts and ideas as defined within those contexts. In a student who can consummate this wedding, Perry says, 'we recognize a colleague,'" or a college-level writer (132). More than any grade I have ever received, the attention, time, and collegiality of a teacher dedicated to my growth have sustained and pushed me through the many challenges I have encountered as a student writer.

While working on *this* essay, I chose to define college-level writing not merely through a list of skills, but rather, through a reflection on my growth as a writer, since over the last few years I have learned that college-level writing is as much about process as it is about product. Sometimes, my writing method has been a violent expenditure of energy similar to my work on the Tolkien essay. Other times, it has meant merging materials from disparate courses to gain new perspectives on a topic, and often, it has taken shape as a battle to condense ideas for time and space.

Rarely, but it has happened, I have received assignments in college that neither call for nor expect college-level writing. These papers are worksheets in essay form, whose creators are not interested in involving students in academic discourse, but merely testing them in a way in which the curricula calls for. As Lil Brannon and C. H. Knoblauch note in their essay, "On Students' Rights to Their Own Texts: A Model of Teacher Response," published in the *Harcourt Brace Guide to Peer Tutoring*, "The incentive to write derives from an assumption that people will listen respectfully and either assent to or earnestly consider the ideas expressed" (217). While the evaluations these assignments proctor are likely necessary, they do not inspire much more than an obligatory effort, as it is painfully obvious that no one cares. Thankfully, these negative experiences have been brief and short in my college career.

A few months after the completion of my Tolkien essay, my professor asked if I was interested in a becoming involved with Writing Fellows, a pilot program being developed on campus. A peer-based tutoring program, Writing Fellows seeks to improve students' writing abilities by stressing the importance of peer conversation and drafting. I leapt at the chance to become further involved in the writing community at the University of Iowa. Currently, I am starting my third semester as a peer tutor, and have seen with every assignment, student, class, and semester the importance of sharing and refining ideas both verbally and in writing. As E. M. Forester once said, "How do I know what I think until I see what I say?" (qtd. in Capossela 17). However, I have also seen that college-level writing can be amorphous, changing its specific shape, though not its general form, from student to student. One of my first peer tutees was a fifty-year-old English language learner whose passion and intelligence were being swallowed up by the devilish intricacies of the English language. Instead of the normal fifteen- to twenty-minute meeting I usually held, we worked together for three hour-long sessions that semester, trying to make her incredible ideas on women's studies visible through her disjointed syntax. While her essays, even after those long sessions, were far from error free, I would argue that her writing was certainly college level, and her efforts would have shamed her fellow teenaged, native-speaking classmates, who frequently came not only to their meetings with me, but to their classes unread and unprepared. Few of them wrote essays that engaged the material as thoroughly as hers. Experiences like that one, in addition to the lessons on theory and grammar, have made Writing Fellows one of the most challenging and exciting experiences of my college career. They have allowed me to shift my position in the conversation of mankind, and become an interested listener as well as a fervent speaker.

Nearly two years after completing the Tolkien essay and taking what I consider to be my first steps as a college-level writer, I am continuing to hone my dialogue, expand my skills, and move to the next level of college-level writing. Recently, I have begun work on my senior interdisciplinary honors thesis, an experience that I hope will serve as a good transition from college-level to post-college-level writing. It has become obvious to me, through Writing Fellows and my classes in general, that college-level writing is a dynamic term that means a number of things. Mastering materials and research methods, engaging the readings, grappling with increasingly sophisticated grammar, and synthesizing information from disparate sources are all part of becoming a college-level writer, but primarily, that degree of attainment requires giving yourself over, as a student and writer, to the desire to create meaningful and elegant connections between texts, ideas, and readers. Throughout all of my classes and writing assignments, I have held to the belief that if we, as participants in a community of writers, want to raise our discourse to that of college-level reading, writing, and thinking, and, if we want our work to be knowledgeable, cogent, thoughtful, and passionate, then we must do as Nancy Mairs urges, "nourish and strengthen one another: listen to one another very hard, ask hard questions too, send one another away to work again, and laugh in all the right places" (qtd. in Capossela n.p.).

Works Cited

Brannon, Lil, and C. H. Knoblauch. "On Students' Rights to Their Own Texts: A Model of Teacher Response." *Harcourt Brace Guide to Peer Tutoring*. Ed. Toni-Lee Capossela. Fort Worth, TX: Harcourt Brace College, 1998.

Bruffee, Kenneth A. "Peer Tutoring and the Conversation of Mankind." *Harcourt Brace Guide to Peer Tutoring*. Ed. Toni-Lee Capossela. Fort Worth, TX: Harcourt Brace College, 1998.

Capossela, Toni-Lee. *Harcourt Brace Guide to Peer Tutoring*. Fort Worth, TX: Harcourt Brace College, 1998.

King, Laurie R. *The Beekeeper's Apprentice, or, On the Segregation of the Queen*. New York: St. Martin's, 1994.

Potok, Chaim. *The Chosen*. New York: Ballantine, 1967.

Smith, Donald G. "Speaking My Mind: Why Literature Matters." *English Journal* 89.2 (1999): 19–21.

Tolkien, J. R. R. *The Tolkien Reader*. New York: Ballantine, 1966.

———. *Tree and Leaf: Including the Poem Mythopoeia*. New York: HarperCollins, 2001.

Wilson, Colin. *Tree by Tolkien*. London: Covent Garden Press, INCA Books, 1973.

Chapter Nineteen

Putting on the Sunglasses: The Argumentative Thesis as the Keystone to "Good" College Writing

Mike Quilligan
Indiana University, Class of 2004

In his essay "What Is 'College-Level' Writing?" Patrick Sullivan suggests the following standards for defining college-level work:

> A student should write in response to an article, essay, or reading selection that contains at least some abstract content[, which] should demonstrate [. . . a] willingness to evaluate ideas and issues carefully[, s]ome skill at analysis and higher-level thinking[, t]he ability to shape and organize material effectively[, t]he ability to integrate some of the material from the reading skillfully[, and t]he ability to follow the standard rules of grammar, punctuation, and spelling. (16–17)

My own experience with what is and is not "good" college writing has been based on both my experience as a peer writing tutor at Indiana University (IU) and my contemporary experience in the undergraduate classroom setting. I've seen both sides of the college writing process. The essence of the shift from high school (or other precollege) writing to college writing is the shift from indicative writing to explicative writing. What I've seen suggests that the trick to teaching good college writing is teaching the argumentative thesis statement. Sullivan's other concerns (grammar, structure) are subordinate to teaching students how to effectively articulate their thoughts—once the initial thinking process has been modeled and the student is more comfortable, *then* the other concerns can warrant greater focus.

In the high school model, the first paragraph usually has some sort of catchy introduction, often personal, that ends in the topic of the paper. These topic sentence theses are usually benign enough. A quick glance through my own high school writing is telling: "What has made [Superman] such a huge icon, one of the great American heroes? That is what this report intends to show" (from my sophomore year) and "In light of [evidence], the United States should re-assess its policy towards Cuba to reflect [a] post-Cold War ideology, of rapprochement rather than isolation" (from the end of my senior year). While these sentences do indeed introduce the topic of the essay to the reader, they *only* introduce. Since college writing is more focused on argument and couched positions, these sorts of introductions become outmoded rather quickly in the transition from high school expectations to college ones.

The way in which IU (my frame of reference) goes about breaking incoming students of this habit is by requiring a first-year composition course.[1] The curriculum is designed to use mass media criticism as a structural model for students to begin writing argumentatively. To this end, the course begins with essay summary and response assignments and works its way up to analysis and a film comparison. Students are made to integrate their readings into their writing, and (theoretically) to use the strategies from the readings as models to explicate their own ideas about the material they are discussing.

The problem with this sort of modeled approach, however, is that the students often seem unable to integrate ideas in assigned readings with their own. One common concern of many of the students I talked to or tutored throughout their semester of first-year composition was that they were unsure how to acknowledge the author's critical stance while at the same time incorporating their own observations and arguments into their essays. Students would sometimes create a reading of an advertisement or a film in advance, and then fabricate evidence within the piece itself to fit the interpretative vision they thought they were supposed to have. The students had misunderstood their instructor's criticism, and misread it as an enthusiasm for the specific sort of criticism voiced in the article: if the student had just read Deborah Tannen or Naomi Wolf, for example, they turned in essays that were ostensibly feminist even though their own language clearly indicated their ambivalence toward or even active disagreement with the very views they thought they were supposed to present.

This is much the same problem as in the 1988 John Carpenter movie *They Live*. In the film, the central character (played by Roddy Piper) discovers sunglasses that reveal certain humans to really be imposter alien monsters. These aliens have a hypnotic device that beams out sleep-inducing waves, and makes anyone who isn't wearing the sunglasses see them as normal humans. These aliens have absolute control over media as well: with the sunglasses, the real messages of billboards and magazines become evident—"Obey," "Reproduce," "Consume," "Conform," and so on. At one point in the movie, Piper's character tries to convince his friend Frank to put on the sunglasses, knowing that Frank will understand Piper's bizarre behavior once he's seen this for himself. The problem, though, is that Frank *won't* put on the sunglasses. They fight for several minutes. At the end of the fight, Frank puts on the sunglasses and realizes his error.

This conflict could, perhaps, have been averted had Piper's character presented himself differently—let the sunglasses speak for themselves, for instance—rather than merely asserting over and over that Frank "Put on the glasses!" It seems like this method of presentation might be the key to teaching the transition to college writing as well—if a student's high school-style paper is asked "So what?" and thus *forced* to become argumentative, or is compared with an academic essay on the same topic, it seems as if the student should be more able to see the differences between what he or she is doing versus what he or she is expected to do.

The easier thing, and I think the thing that happens more often resultantly, is that like Piper in the movie, students are frontloaded with impatient demands. One of the advantages that should be better exploited is that the students generally are already familiar with the popular culture they're studying. In their book *Saturday Morning Fever: Growing up with Cartoon Culture*, Timothy and Kevin Burke emphasize the connections that mass culture forms between strangers: "'People I didn't know had the same experiences as me even though they lived hundreds of miles from me!'" (83).

With this in mind, perhaps such a curriculum (at IU or anywhere) could be slightly shifted to accommodate the innate cultural knowledge that the incoming students have. Rather than watching, say, *American History X* in class, primed for viewing racism, for what may be the first time (or a time that is chronologically close to the first time), watch something that students already have some basic familiarity with—*Superman*, or a Disney movie, or *Sesame Street*—something that there is experience with from a world without critical perspective. Then, the experience of viewing isn't a new one, but a revelation equivalent to putting on the sunglasses.

The ideas that have been indicated in texts to the students about the social view of masculinity, or of advertising culture, or any of the sorts of altered perspectives that can lead to the shift to the critical—the argumentative—mindset will more readily jump out, since the experience is not a new one with a new critical lens, but a familiar one with a radically altered perspective. With these new perceptions, then, students should be better able to understand the sort of writing that is expected of them, and can proceed with that writing—argument based, evidential, and original.

Note

1. An extraordinarily common practice, to be sure. However, since assuming that approaches from school to school are the same would seem to go against the very explicit purpose of this volume, I'll deal with the specific setup of the IU approach. It also seems worth mentioning here that my experience with this first-year course has been limited to conversations with instructors and former students, as well as tutorials with students enrolled in the class. Thus, though I have an outsider's perspective, I feel it is an educated one.

Works Cited

Burke, Timothy, and Kevin Burke. *Saturday Morning Fever: Growing Up with Cartoon Culture*. New York: St. Martin's Griffin, 1998.

They Live. Dir. John Carpenter. Videocassette. Orion Pictures. 1988.

Sullivan, Patrick. "An Essential Question: What Is 'College-Level' Writing"? *What Is "College-Level" Writing?* Ed. Patrick Sullivan and Howard Tinberg. Urbana, IL: NCTE, 2006. 1–28.

Chapter Twenty

Bam

Amanda Winalski
Temple University, Class of 2004

An afternoon of placement testing, one of the more delightful events scheduled during the four-day orientation for incoming students at Temple University, promised to reveal individual academic potential, thereby ensuring that students would be assigned courses according to their abilities. These exams, the administration explained, would guarantee that those who had already mastered calculus would not be sentenced to a semester of remedial algebra, while those unfamiliar with rules of punctuation would have the opportunity to pore over a grammar book or two before plunging into Chaucer. Thus, in theory, a few hours of multiple-choice questions dictated students' academic standing relative to those of their peers. In theory. (Of course, that individuals—whether because they were greedy for high marks [easy As] or because they believed the test results overestimated their potential—could ultimately elect to take courses the university deems too easy for them seems to render these administrative suggestions obsolete.)

Many students ignored the university's pleas to take the exams seriously, handing in their packets minutes after the tests had begun, while others hunched over their desks, furiously underlining passages and scribbling notes. I was in the latter group, determined to demonstrate mastery of the fundamental skills that core classes promised to develop.

I learned I was exempt from English Composition a few hours after I had completed the three-part test. Although I had finished the exam early and handed my papers in with confidence, I was surprised that the university urged me to skip the required class. The test had been a rip-off of the verbal component of the Scholastic Aptitude Tests (SATs); we read passages, filled in blanks, corrected grammar, and defined words. (In fact, a particular section of the reading comprehension—a page from Poe's "The Cask of Amontillado," followed by five or so multiple choice questions—appeared as a review for the advanced placement tests in my 11th-grade literature class.) According to the university, the questions were representative of the subjects covered in English Composition; therefore, students with strong backgrounds in and familiarity with these topics, as demonstrated by their performances on the exams, were excused from the basic course that taught the fundamentals.

Although I was eager to dive into the more exciting classes outlined in my major, I admit that I was apprehensive regarding the idea of exemption. Yes, I could conjugate verbs and summarize main ideas, but wasn't it presumptuous to assume I could prance straight from high school English courses to a class filled with college upperclassmen? Wouldn't a transitional preparatory class be beneficial? When I approached an academic advisor with my concerns, he scoffed at my anxiety. He told me the introductory course was easy, boring, and a waste of my time. Although his suggestions were dripping with disdain and elitism, I followed the advice. My first-year roster did not include the composition course. (Fortunately for incoming students, this advisor is no longer employed at Temple.)

The apprehension I had regarding my decision to skip the introductory course faded as the academic year continued. My professors and I followed a very simple routine: they assigned paper topics, I spent hours (days) choosing the exact adjectives and sentence structures that best expressed my ideas, and I was rewarded with As and metaphorical pats on the head in the form of scribbled praises and exclamation points. I relished compliments from my instructors, nearly all of whom awed me with their seemingly endless knowledge of literature and language, and triumphantly read the comments aloud to my parents. I was convinced I had found the formula for good college writing—or, more cynically, the formula for an A paper. (In a first-year student's mind, there is hardly a difference between the two.)

During high school, I operated under the assumption that what I wrote was much less important than how I wrote. For four years, my papers screamed "Style and structure essential, content optional!" I realized that teachers concentrated so intensely on revising dangling modifiers and comma splices that they tended to ignore the actual ideas embodied in the essay. More simply: the student's ability to communicate effectively (and not *to effectively communicate*) had precedence over the raw quality of the ideas. Armed with this knowledge, I dressed up the content of my papers. Longer sentences, larger words, and creative uses of punctuation, I reasoned, compensated for merely average content. Indeed, attempting to dazzle a professor with eloquent rhetoric was a dangerous endeavor; an extra comma or a superfluous adjective was just as likely to receive a murderous red slash. It was not, however, just as likely to receive a minus. Too many semicolons resulted in a gentle reprimand. Simple sentences and one-syllable words earned lower grades.

Of course, work that impresses a ninth-grade teacher accustomed to students who cannot be bothered to use apostrophes or punctuate sentences will not necessarily electrify a college professor who reads thousands of pages of student essays each year. In high school, students often assume that a thesis sentence guarantees a passing grade. One who clings to this assumption while making the transition to a university should either amend these preconceived notions regarding writing or learn to expect poor grades. Thus, it is obvious that that which is sufficient for a high school paper is not predictably adequate for a college paper. (Furthermore, who attends college with an ambition of adequacy?) Without a doubt, then, there is something unique about college-level writing. But *what*? And why is it that some individuals learn to write at this mysterious level, while others require a course introducing its concepts?

I could not have begun to answer these complex questions had I not enrolled in a particular course concentrating on the grammar and linguistics of language. Do not mistake me: I did not coast through my years at Temple. I wrote and rewrote, revised and re-revised. I never handed in a paper until I was certain that, regardless of whether another party could improve upon the text, *I* had written as well and as passionately as I could. Still, the hours of huddling over my notebook were devoted to perfecting my rhetoric rather than the ideas it expressed. I strove to find balance in my writing. I wanted to be neither simple nor pretentious, but a brilliant writer who expertly worked between the extremes. I wanted to sound intelligent, but not such that my reader suspiciously pawed through a thesaurus or dictionary, ready to accuse me of littering my works with SAT words; I wanted to sound comprehensible, but not to the extent that the reader grew bored. Therefore, in addition to creating outlines and rough drafts, I allotted equal time to improving my papers. During revision sessions, I made sure I weaved in enough five-syllable words with bare nouns and verbs, and that my flowery, paragraph-like sentences were offset by short, declarative remarks. (This because a professor once kindly advised me, "Not every sentence needs a semicolon. Don't be afraid of the simple sentence.") So, as I struggled to find the balance between "I need to demonstrate academic prowess by using big words!" and "I can't irritate my reader by trying to set sentence-length records and using eight words when two will suffice," I welcomed the course on grammar, a class characterized by worksheets and discussions rather than term papers.

The class—and its ridiculously entertaining professor—instantly became one of my favorites. The first half of the course was dedicated to the archaic rules of grammar and punctuation (thus/therefore, further/farther, I/me). The second half concentrated on the relation between linguistics (what we do say) and grammar (what we *should* say, as dictated by *the rules* and those obsessed with following them). Although I devoured the daily worksheets, I was a bit nervous about the final assignment. The instructor asked us to write a few pages about the course. The subject was straightforward and simple; however, I knew that despite the hours I would spend editing my prose, my paper would be flooded with monumental grammatical errors, invisible to any reader save he or she who did not shriek in horror at finding a dangling modifier in a campaign letter. (That the professor was obviously joking did nothing to assuage my fear of committing similar grammatical atrocities.)

When I finally handed in my paper, I was confident that it was representative of my best ability. I wrote about the transition I experienced while in the class. I drew a character arc that showed my evolution from a bratty high school student obsessed with correcting any individual who dared to utter blasphemy such as, "I could care less." Now, I wrote, I understood that one's diction does not reveal his or her intelligence. A writer should learn the standards of grammar to facilitate communication; however, there is nothing inherently wrong with a writer who chooses to use the passive voice or to nominalize verbs. Yes, I reasoned, a writer may invent words when the dictionary just cannot capture a certain idea, and he or she may use collective pronouns to avoid sexist language. When a writer is comfortable with the rather arbitrary rules governing the conventions of English, he or she can choose to modify or even dismiss these standards. This is not to say that an eager student should reject accepted rules of possession and declare that *its* is an improved version of the *it is* contraction. One should only scoff at the grammar check if he or she knows the meanings would be better expressed by ignoring its suggestions. Thus, I presented an essay that reflected my appreciation for the course, and I impatiently waited to receive my praise and collect my A.

This time, however, the professor did not follow the formula.

I was shocked by the hideous B- that engulfed page six of my paper. Despite that semester of diligent grammar study, I made mistakes on every page. I was not penalized harshly for my awkward commas or unclear modifiers; rather, the professor accused me of a literary crime far more frightful: I had not answered the assigned question.

I choked down the well-meaning criticism, then destroyed the evidence of my failure. I was not upset about the grade because I knew I must have earned it. I was upset that I had disappointed both my instructor and myself. According to the vicious red attack, I had ignored half of the assignment. I was so obsessed with illustrating my character growth that I had not included even a sentence about the linguistics component of the course. I did not appreciate the irony that my written tirade combating the importance of obsessing over detail insufficiently fulfilled the assigned requirements because I had failed to pay attention to detail.

I had completed a course on grammar and linguistics, which emphasized and challenged the meaning of standard literary rules, and I then proceeded to break one of the most fundamental conventions of communication: I did not address the subject of discussion.

Stripped of the illusions that good writing required merely an impressive vocabulary and an enthusiasm for sentences that cannot be spoken in a single breath, I had to reevaluate my definition of a successful college writer. It was clear that multisyllabic words and superfluous punctuation could not salvage an essay devoid of content. I further noted that a writer should actually *consider* the topic before concocting phrase structures and stringing together adjectives in her head. Such constructions could dress up an inadequate answer; however, unless accompanied by equally worthy content, they could not express anything greater than poorly applied writing skills. Thus, the argument would be pretty. Nothing else.

What can this lengthy, at times painful, anecdote reveal regarding the controversy of college writing? A college writer must anticipate the reader's response. Once the writer has conquered the grammar check and can confidently justify using the passive voice or splitting an infinitive, he or she begins to demonstrate a level of comprehension and application that I would consider characteristic of the *college-level* label. Those who bow before the grammar check and heed every suggestion—whether because they doubt their abilities, overestimate the power of the computerized rulebook, or think the reader will use any grammatical error as evidence of ineptitude or justification for a grade reduction—can only improve their writing by first tending to their confidence.

There does not (yet) exist a checklist for the requirements that compose college-level writing. The transition from high school to university writing is not as simple as the memorization of a few grammar handouts; rather, it consists of a student's willingness to learn, understand, and modify the rules that govern language in order to communicate ideas. One can easily write five pages of nothing that sounds lyrical or drainingly intellectual or fill five pages with brilliant thoughts that are presented in bullet statements. To achieve a balance between the two is to be a successful college writer; it is a goal to which one must aspire every time he or she picks up a pen. Thus, writing at this level is perhaps an ongoing process that necessitates a persistent willingness to try, fail, and try. (Writers will always lament the forced revision process in which, with waves of nausea, they cross out adjectives and adverbs, leaving nude nouns and bare verbs.) After all, despite my transcendental literary experience, I still cannot help but insert those extra commas, without which my writing would *clearly* be gibberish. (No need to address further my ostensibly haphazard use of parenthesis, italics, and dashes, which I gleefully excuse by maintaining I choose to ignore certain conventions in order to communicate more colloquially.)

And thus the process continues.

IV

Administrative Perspectives

Chapter Twenty-One

College-Level Writing: A Departmental Perspective

James M. Gentile, Chair
Department of English
Manchester Community College

Most undergraduate institutions offer a course in college writing. Variously called First-Year Composition, Expository Writing, or Language and Rhetoric, this course has had a long and contentious history. As Robert J. Connors notes, debate about college writing courses can be characterized in terms of "alternating periods of . . . *reformism* and *abolitionism*" (47). This debate reflects a variety of complex and evolving professional, curricular, and political concerns within higher education.[1] Although this debate continues, the composition course remains a constant at most institutions. In fact, today it has become much more than an autonomous course within an English department. The college writing course typically functions within the context of institutional programs and outcomes—as a prerequisite for other courses and as a central component of most colleges' core curriculum requirements.

This essay attempts to situate the composition course within a larger, college-wide context. Doing so, it will identify the issues that help shape the varied definitions of writing that must be addressed by a department as it tries to teach this course. This essay will also explore the conceptual tension between *college writing*—any writing assignment completed by a student in a college course—and *college-level writing*—any such assignment that requires a significant level of cognitive engagement. As a department chair, I offer here a personal perspective on these many issues.[2]

Institutional Issues

Standard Course Syllabus

A department's understanding of college-level writing is embodied in its standard course syllabus, a syllabus that typically identifies course objectives. Those objectives might focus on higher-level critical reading, thinking, and writing skills, and they might also imagine a type of writing that both evidences those skills and demonstrates mastery of the conventions of academic prose. The objectives of the standard syllabus at my college, for example, focus on writing grounded in those critical skills—"strong analysis and higher-level thinking" about texts studied in class—as well as a writing consistent in formal terms of "essay format, voice, and organization" ("English 111"). Clearly, the emphasis on higher-level thinking makes the realization of these objectives problematic because often such thinking is only beginning to emerge in many first-year college students. Furthermore, this model does not specify outcomes that are easily measurable. (Determining the degree to which students read and write *intelligently*, *rigorously*, *abstractly*, *critically*, *resourcefully*, and *effectively* is a challenge. The only thing clearly measurable on our list of objectives is the word count required.) While this model does not necessarily represent a norm, it does present one framework in which the larger issues of college-level writing can be addressed.

A standard course syllabus represents not only a departmental but also an official institutional definition of college-level writing. Though developed by the department, such a syllabus typically goes before both a Curriculum Committee and a Faculty Senate for approval. Such might be said of any standard syllabus. And yet, while no department exists independent of its institution, perhaps no department other than English finds its work tied so extensively and integrally to the institution. Its reading and writing curriculum is designed, at least in part, to prepare students for the type of work necessary for most other college courses they will take. The importance of this role is indicated by the common presence of the composition course throughout a curriculum, whether as a general education or a degree requirement or as a prerequisite for another course. This institutional presence is expanded when the college is a public one within a large community college or state college system. Often its curriculum will be tied to that of other institutions in the state for reasons of articulation and transfer. And even if it is not a public institution, the college still must be responsive to common standards of college reading and writing.

General Education Requirements

When we situate the composition course within an institution, it is likely that the formal rather than the cognitive qualities of college writing will be emphasized. This is especially true when the course fulfills a general education or core curriculum requirement because such requirements are typically organized around distinct outcomes. At my college, where Composition fulfills the English requirement, these outcomes focus on writing characterized by its formal qualities alone: "clear focus," "logical pattern of development," "adequate support," "effective attribution," varied sentences, "standard conventions of grammar and sentence structure" ("General Education, Mode 2").

As to higher-level thinking as an outcome in a general education program, it is probably situated primarily (if not exclusively) in courses other than English. This is the case at my college. The shift in focus is evident, for example, when comparing the outcomes for English and humanities. The English outcomes ask students to "recognize," "write," "arrange," "formulate," "obey"; the humanities outcomes ask students to "engage," "discover," "communicate." The humanities outcomes value the student's ability "to discover larger patterns or relationships, discriminate among multiple views, and make connections to other times and people, their works, beliefs and cultures" ("General Education, Mode 2"; "General Education, Mode 3"). The implication is that the composition course focuses less on these abstract abilities and more on concrete and easily measurable skills. The issues involved here are at the center of a discussion now occurring at my college as well as at many others: how can general education outcomes be realized and even measured?

The Degree Requirement and the Course Prerequisite

Even if it does not expressly function as a general education requirement, the standard composition course typically functions as a degree requirement. Thus, it would seem to represent a type of reading and writing characteristic of college work. However, an English department's conception of college-level writing may not be evident in all of the college writing assignments required of students in credit-bearing courses. Common writing assignments in other departments might include personal responses, journal entries, article summaries, case studies, lab reports, researched reports, and essay exams. Such assignments are all valuable ways to learn and to demonstrate learning, and yet they are distinct from the major writing assignments in most composition courses. If this essay had been written by a chair in a department other than English, the definition of college-level writing undoubtedly would reflect such differences.

These differences might determine whether the composition course is identified as a prerequisite for entrance into specific college courses. Some departments may require the course for its larger objectives, others for its ostensible outcomes. Still others might find eligibility for an upper-level developmental course adequate preparation. For example, at my college many social science courses and even some science and humanities courses do not require the college-level writing course as a prerequisite. Among the introductory courses without Composition as a prerequisite are American Government, Anthropology, Art History, Criminal Justice, Earth Science, Economics, Ethics, Film Study, Geography, Geology, History, Music History, and Philosophy. In contrast, courses in mathematics do have such a prerequisite. After consulting with the English department, the mathematics department concluded that the mathematics textbooks they use and the problem-focused curriculum they have developed—which requires students to read through problems and to explain in prose the mathematical process—require students to have strong reading, thinking, and writing skills. This example suggests the importance of dialogue among disciplines to explore the role of reading and writing within the curriculum. Whether that dialogue occurs in fact or not, the composition course—as a degree requirement—remains an integral component of every curriculum.[3]

Articulation Agreements

Efforts at articulation call a department to view its curriculum—and hence its definition of college-level writing—in the context of other colleges. Institutional efforts at articulation can have a positive impact on curriculum, encouraging a dialogue among departments and motivating the department seeking articulation to ensure its program meets high standards. The Executive Summary of the "Access to the Baccalaureate Project Survey" conducted by the American Association of Community Colleges and the American Association of State Colleges and Universities emphasizes that the primary barrier to the acceptance of the associate's degree as the "equivalent" of the first two years of baccalaureate work has been "the perception that community college graduates are simply less well-prepared academically . . . " (2). Thus the practical and enormously important challenge is to create a curriculum whose definition of college-level writing is consistent with that of transfer institutions and to prepare students for actual success at such institutions. As an English department chair, I am reassured by the fact that part-time faculty who teach at various universities in our state confirm that in terms of objectives, pedagogical approach, and even textbook selection, our composition course is consistent with the comparable course at other universities. I am also reassured by the more anecdotal evidence of the success of our transfer students at competitive private institutions.

At public colleges, when articulation efforts are made at the system-wide level rather than the institutional level and when common course numbering initiatives subsequently arise, the local definition of college-level writing can be seriously challenged. The local development of curriculum makes common course numbering especially difficult. In our twelve-college system, for example, there are fourteen different developmental courses, including courses in reading, in writing, and in reading and writing, and focusing on writing skills ranging from the sentence, to the paragraph, to the essay. Many of these courses are offered at only one or two institutions; not one of them is offered at more than eight. Some of these courses are offered by English departments, some by basic writing or basic skills programs. Most of these courses are part of unique developmental sequences. And yet each course is deemed necessary on at least one campus to prepare its students for the common course in college-level composition. Certainly there may be a greater consistency than this complex of courses suggests; some of the objectives of individual courses may be contained in other courses. Nonetheless, by their very existence these courses suggest distinct pedagogical approaches to developing reading and writing processes as well as distinct priorities concerning those processes.

Departmental Issues

As a department chair, I continually address these multiple definitions of college-level writing. Many of these definitions are not necessarily inconsistent with but instead are only a part of our departmental understanding of such writing. However, as chair and as faculty member, I would argue that a departmental definition should be taken as a standard. And yet, experience tells me that any established standard of the college level is difficult to realize even at the departmental level. Within each department we find a complex of competing definitions—those of its students who have varied needs and expectations, those of its developmental courses that imply a precollege-level writing standard, and those of its faculty who have distinct and sometimes differing priorities and experiences.

Assessment and Placement

The reality of varied student needs and expectations affects an English department even before students matriculate at an institution. Those needs and expectations certainly shape efforts to teach college-level writing. Central to that effort are issues both of initial assessment and of placement. The former calls for a consideration of what basic abilities are necessary for *success*, how those abilities can be effectively determined, and then how those abilities can be realistically evaluated. In its "Writing Assessment: A Position Statement," the Conference on College Composition and Communication (CCCC) clearly identifies the challenge of creating effective assessment strategies. The complexity of the undertaking, the Statement emphasizes, is grounded in the "competing tendencies . . . to measure writing as a general construct" and "to measure writing as a contextualized, site- and genre-specific ability." In assessment for placement, such contextualization is a challenge, but as the Statement emphasizes, such "assessment—when conducted sensitively and purposefully—can have a positive impact on teaching, learning, curricular design, and student attitudes" (Conference).

Institutions—especially four-year institutions—have varied information with which to place entering students, ranging from secondary school course work, to statewide secondary-level competency tests, to the College Board Scholastic Assessment Test (SAT; now revised), to the American College Test (ACT) English Test, to the College Board Advanced Placement Tests in Language and Composition or Literature and Composition. Institutions can also administer their own assessment tests, choosing a nationally available standardized testing program or developing their own assessment mechanism. Three popular standardized programs—the College Board Accuplacer and WritePlacer programs, the Educational Testing Service (ETS) English Placement Test, and the ACT COMPASS/ESL or COMPASS e-Write—all offer some form of assessment in reading skills, language or sentence skills, and writing skills. (These programs can also assess ESL students, a consideration especially significant at the community college level but one too complex to address in the context of this essay.) The decisions made concerning which components of such tests to use and what cutoff scores to set all reflect a department's definition of college-level writing. However, such tests—especially those in essay writing (and especially when assessed by what the ACT refers to as "cutting-edge electronic scoring technology" and what the College Board refers to as its artificial intelligence IntelliMetric)—and such scores—which are often meaningful at a high and a low end and less useful in the middle range—can also undercut such a definition. This is the very dilemma articulated in the CCCC Position Statement.[4]

Even when a department develops its own mechanism such as an essay exam, this single writing sample likely will require an attitude toward the writing process inconsistent with the departmental definition of college-level writing. Practices valued such as writing in response to thoughtful reflection on ideas and developing an essay over time with multiple drafts cannot be easily duplicated during an exam situation. Even the physical process of producing a text might be different from that actually used by students. Being required to write by hand rather than composing on a computer (with its resources for spelling and grammar and its capability of easy revision) might affect the writing sample. The motive for writing—not primarily out of interest but for placement—and the related desire to meet the unclear standards of some unknown audience further complicate efforts to assess meaningfully. And even the audience itself—those reading the essays—are reading in a way that gives them an incomplete insight into the writer. Nonetheless, despite these limitations, the effort to attempt such assessment is an important one.

Basic Writing and the College-Level Curriculum

The assessment of student abilities is firmly grounded in the departmental definition of college-level writing. Students must enter the composition course with a foundation in the processes of critical reading, thinking, and writing. Without that foundation, the transition to the college-level curriculum will be a challenge. English departments are faced with providing such a foundation through basic writing courses. These courses offer another perspective on the issue of college-level writing. They suggest that certain types of writing are not yet college level and other types (those completed near the end of the semester) are approaching college level. These are the multiple distinctions with which the department, the instructor, and the student must struggle.

Such distinctions can be illustrated in reference to the basic writing sequence at my college. By the end of that sequence—which students might enter at one of three levels—students must demonstrate an ability to write in response to texts, to craft an analytical essay centered on a controlling idea, to develop that idea in the body of the essay, to organize their ideas so that they flow logically, and to express themselves with relative clarity. Certainly students will be asked to demonstrate these same abilities at the end of the college-level course. What will distinguish basic writing from the college level will be the writing situations established. At the college level, it is expected that the assignments will be more challenging, the standards for assessment more rigorous, and the independence of the writer greater.

Faculty and Pedagogy

Thus, beginning with a definition of college-level writing, a department must determine its students' readiness for such writing and create a curriculum that will address students' varied needs. Even after it has done both, a department still has to ensure that students encounter a curriculum consistent with its definition. This can be a special challenge for a department such as mine which typically offers between eighty to ninety sections of basic writing and college-level writing courses each semester. While each section does not have to duplicate the others—such a goal would be undesirable and probably unrealizable—each section must share common objectives and outcomes and must be grounded in common philosophical and pedagogical premises.

At a time when courses are taught increasingly by part-time faculty, issues of hiring, orienting, and mentoring all determine the extent to which a department can reach a collective understanding of college-level writing. This is not to suggest that it cannot happen; all departments have a core of part-time faculty who have chosen to teach part time, who have a long relationship with the department and its curriculum and its students, and who have a strong commitment to professional development. Most departments can attract new faculty from graduate programs from which they have in the past found faculty who have taught a curriculum and who share a pedagogy common to their own. Finally, most departments must also hire some instructors so close to the beginning of classes—because a part-time instructor unexpectedly leaves or because course sections must be added to meet enrollment demands—that it is difficult to provide the preliminary support necessary to confirm consistency with the curriculum.

The challenge of preparing new faculty often lies in the fact that they have years of experience at varied institutions. Unfortunately, that extensive experience may be at schools whose definition of the college level is different from the department's definition. During interviews, the range of curricula, materials, and pedagogy all ostensibly representative of college-level writing classes often becomes dramatically evident. Perhaps more revelatory are the responses I receive when I ask applicants to review a student essay and then "workshop" with me as if I were the student. Their identification of the essay as either a basic writing sample or a college-level sample as well as their identification of varied types of issues as significant—ranging from spelling to depth of critical thinking—gives me insight into their abilities as teachers as well as into the curricula that they have taught. The significantly varied responses I have encountered over the years reveal a significant lack of consensus among English departments as to what constitutes college-level writing.

Textbooks

For a department to sustain its own definition of college-level writing, it must identify materials and assignments as well as *best practices* in terms of instructional methods. Selecting a common textbook offers an excellent example of a departmental definition being tested. A textbook can function as a concrete representation of a curriculum and can figure prominently in a department's ability to realize its curriculum in the classroom. A quick search of the online catalog of any of the major publishers indicates the variety of texts available to support a college-level curriculum. Thus even when a department believes it has identified a standard for college-level writing, it is evident that its definition is one of many.

A visit to the "Freshman Composition" section of McGraw Hill, for example, illustrates this complexity. The section offers selections organized under such categories as Handbooks, Research Writing Guides, Dictionaries, Readers, Rhetorics, Argument, and Writing Across the Curriculum. Under "Readers," there are forty-six options (several cross-listed as both college-level and basic writing texts) ("Freshman").

The readings selected by the editors of these texts, the introductory apparatus included, and the assignments suggested offer within each text not simply another approach to what is college-level writing but another definition of it. And the popular *alternative tables of contents*—identifying modes, purpose, genre, discipline, theme (itself sometimes an alternative to an already identified thematic approach)—suggest that even within the same text, the editors are offering different and perhaps even competing definitions of the college level.

Best Practices

The definition of college-level writing is also shaped by the instructional methods a department identifies as *best practices.* Decisions concerning the teacher-student dynamic; the types of assignments, their nature and frequency; the effective use of classroom time; and the role of instructional technology will necessarily determine the ways in which students learn to write and come to value writing. For example, material presented in class can establish writing priorities: extensive emphasis on reading as a comprehensive rather than interpretive act, or extensive emphasis on writing as a formulaic rather than organic process, or extensive emphasis on "correctness" rather than expression will necessarily affect the type of writing produced.

Much of my time as chair is devoted to working with faculty to meet the challenge of realizing our curriculum. The support I offer, necessarily in conjunction with full-time faculty, will range from selecting textbooks, to identifying representative student essays, to creating professional development opportunities, to mentoring. All of this support will determine the extent to which the department is able to achieve consistently and effectively the objectives of the curriculum. Unfortunately, it is often easier to say what it is not, rather than what it is. Thus a department often must resort to negative models—textbooks that offer writing prompts inconsistent with the curriculum, student essays that do not succeed, or mentoring support meant to rectify rather than develop. Such models further complicate the effort to define what college level is.

Support Services

In addition to the faculty, the departmental definition must find consistency with the definition of college-level writing imagined by support services at the college. Again, ensuring consistency is a challenge, especially when tutors are often unfamiliar with a particular curriculum and instructors. It is possible that only their broad understanding of college-level writing is consistent with the departmental definition of such writing. If tutors do not interact with the English department, the consequences in developing student understanding of college-level writing can be serious. This is further complicated in an age when tutoring can also occur online.

My college has an advantage in meeting these particular needs—full-time English faculty members coordinate and participate in our Tutoring Center, Writing Center, and online tutoring programs. They can ensure a synergy between these areas and the department. The tutors' familiarity with the curriculum, their visits to English classrooms, even their occasional transfer from tutoring to teaching positions in the department all suggest ways in which support services can help a department function consistently as it seeks to define and develop college-level curriculum for its students.

Final Assessment

Having developed a system to assess students for placement, having created a curriculum to address varied needs, and having identified instructional materials and methods appropriate for realizing objectives, a department must consider whether those objectives can be assessed. Whether it chooses assessment by classroom instructor or by committee, whether it chooses assessment by an exit essay or by portfolio, a department must evaluate whether the work that receives a grade that meets a departmental prerequisite for registration in future courses or that merits transfer credit indeed embodies its standard of college-level writing. A department is inevitably faced with multiple writing samples and it must determine the stage at which such writing passes into the realm of the college level. Again, a department is called to an act of definition.

Conclusion

As I initially argued, an English department's commitment to reading, writing, and critical thinking must underlie its definition of college-level writing. That commitment reflects the department's own as well as its college's larger commitment to *academic literacy*. Defining such literacy is beyond the scope of this essay. Here I will refer briefly to a report prepared by the Academic Senate for California Community Colleges, *Academic Literacy: A Statement of Competencies Expected of Students Entering California's Public Colleges and Universities*. That report, grounded in a survey intended to determine the extent to which entering college students demonstrate such literacy, identifies the "elements of academic literacy [as] reading, writing, listening, speaking, critical thinking, use of technology, and habits of mind that foster academic success" and emphasizes that "the inseparable skills of critical reading, writing, listening and thinking depend upon students' ability to postpone judgment and tolerate ambiguity as they honor the dance between passionate assertion and patient inquiry." The report defines "reading [as] a process that requires time and reflection, and that stimulates imagination, analysis, and inquiry" and argues that students must be taught to be "active makers of meaning and . . . to think critically, to argue, to compare, to own an idea, and to remember." The report defines writing as a process intended to "deepen and extend discourse in the pursuit of knowledge" and explains that

> college faculty assign writing to get to know how students think, to help students engage critically and thoughtfully with course readings, to demonstrate what students understand from lectures, to structure and guide their inquiry, to encourage independent thinking, and to invite them into the on-going intellectual dialogue that characterizes higher education. (Academic)

This definition of academic literacy emphasizes that reading and writing are *processes*. Thus, as the report indicates, students entering college must have a strong foundation in these processes that then will be developed and reinforced throughout a curriculum. The thirty-year history of Writing Across the Curriculum programs is informed by this belief. The fact that such programs typically situate the teaching of reading and writing within either an English course or a discipline course raises the issue of where the teaching of academic literacy should be primarily centered. The fact that English faculty are trained (at least by practice) to teach reading and writing, that they are placed in classrooms in which the diversity of students complements teaching such skills independent of a single discipline, and that they teach a class that can clearly be identified as a requirement for all incoming students (many of whom may not yet have a particular academic interest) supports an argument for centering it in an English department.

Focusing on the English department as such a center, the distinction between college writing and college-level writing becomes salient. Writing that is focused on a controlling idea, that is well developed, that is logically organized, and that is clear does not necessarily demonstrate the level of critical thinking characteristic of academic literacy. Similarly, writing assigned in other classes such as summaries or reports undeniably offers a valuable way for students to learn and to express their learning but does not necessarily offer a way to acquire fuller academic literacy. Students need assignments characterized by a complexity grounded in three factors: the degree of cognitive engagement required by the material, especially as it reflects an interpretive act; the academic setting for the writing, especially as it is defined by the writer-reader dynamic; and the ethical dimension of that dynamic, especially as it is affected by the academic assignment.

I believe that the degree of cognitive engagement identifies within college writing that which is college-level writing. Here, Bloom's taxonomy of cognitive educational objectives, with its progression through knowledge, comprehension, application, analysis, synthesis, to evaluation, is informative of the higher-level cognitive abilities students must develop. The college-level writer, in my judgment, should demonstrate as a reader and as a writer a control of all of these. Writing that values formal proficiency over content, or writing that does not challenge in its content, cannot fully embody a college-level writing standard in the context of academic literacy.

Bloom's taxonomy can serve as a paradigm for construction of a college-level curriculum in reading and writing. While a basic writing curriculum might need to focus on the earlier objectives, a college-level curriculum needs to centralize the latter objectives. Challenging students to progress through those cognitive objectives as readers—to understand, analyze, and evaluate single texts—and as writers—to demonstrate those abilities in reference to single and multiple texts—will provide an opportunity for intellectual growth. That opportunity calls the student to move beyond the self; to think in the context of others, and of texts, and of ideas; and then through that process, to move back to the self, informed and critical. That new self continues to mature both in the particular composition class and in other classes outside the department.

While the student's cognitive development obviously underlies the entire academic experience, that development can be expressed fully in the composition classroom. Such a classroom, when its focus is on reading and writing, causes the student to identify himself or herself as a *reader* and as a *writer* and in turn to become conscious of the text as an interaction of writer and reader. The student especially acquires a consciousness of *academic audience* and is called to write for that audience. Basic assumptions about that audience and its expectations in terms of focus, development, and correctness would inform college-level writing. As the student begins to meet these expectations, he or she gains a sense of comfort in the academic community. That comfort informs his or her *voice* as a writer. Thus, writing within such a setting has implications in terms of formal and linguistic considerations as they identify college-level writing.

In the academic setting, formal standards apply both to college writing and college-level writing. However, the extent of the writer's cognitive engagement—especially the young student writer's engagement—will often be reflected in the essay's formal proficiency. Dealing with unfamiliar, complex, perhaps contradictory ideas or texts will necessarily result in a writing whose formal proficiency must be evaluated in the context of its ideas. In a class, the students who do not engage in the subject fully, who focus on the obvious, or who avoid ambiguity might actually write the more formally proficient essays. Formal proficiency should be a standard of college-level writing; however, what constitutes such proficiency, especially as demonstrated by the writer engaged in a new cognitive process, must be considered. If we were to define college-level writing simply by formal criteria, the student's struggle with a new act and a new form might suggest he or she is not actually engaged in an act of college-level writing.

Related to these formal considerations are linguistic ones. Correctness of expression must be identified as a standard of any writing, and particularly of college-level writing. Here we must grant less flexibility than we need to grant when assessing formal proficiency. However, while a student must learn to communicate clearly, the focus of a composition course should not be on *correctness*—grammar, punctuation, spelling—alone. Correctness should be a criterion for assessment, but not the primary one.

The academic setting centralizes the final component of college-level writing: the ethical one. Certainly all writing is grounded in the writer's awareness of his or her ethical responsibility. However, the nature of academic writing—its interpretive or argumentative focus, its logical appeal, and its grounding in sources—centralizes this responsibility. College-level writing—and college writing in general—requires a type of writing in which students will be asked, as my department's mission statement indicates, "to argue fairly, to use language fairly, and to use sources fairly" ("English Department Mission"). The cognitive and formal elements of college-level writing are grounded in this larger ethical issue.

Students will not develop academic literacy, or even college-level writing abilities, in a single semester. Both will be framed by the composition course, modeled and attempted in the course. Both will be developed and reinforced in subsequent courses, as well as in the workplace and in students' personal lives. This realization makes possible a composition course in college-level writing. Putting the emphasis on the development of academic literacy shifts the focus from product to process. Within this perspective of college-level writing as a process, assessment is necessarily formative rather than summative.[5] While a portfolio may be produced and a final grade may be assigned, writing is presented throughout as an ongoing process. Within this frame of reference, almost any writing assignment can be viewed as a formative one and almost any product created by a student—a student responding fully in the context of his or her formative development—is moving toward college-level writing. And as a department helps prepare a student to address college writing assignments that require college-level writing skills and to move toward fuller academic literacy, the department's larger institutional role becomes clear.

Notes

1. For an excellent brief history of the composition course in American college education, see Connors, "The Abolition Debate in Composition: A Short History."

2. I would like to acknowledge my colleagues at Manchester Community College whose collective insight into our reading and writing curriculum is reflected in many of the specific observations made in this essay. I would especially like to acknowledge Jeanine DeRusha, Michael DiRaimo, Kim Hamilton-Bobrow, Ken Klucznik, and Rae Strickland for their critical and editorial input into this essay.

3. Our department is currently conducting focus groups involving faculty within single departments or related departments in order to understand better how reading and writing figures in their curriculum. Since the original composition of this essay, our department also helped to coordinate a campus-wide Professional Day focusing on the role of reading and writing in the curriculum. This program increased understanding of the range of needs of our entering students and initiated a dialogue which continues. It led many departments to review prerequisites for many of their courses.

4. Information on various assessment mechanisms can be found at the following sites: ETS: http://www.ets.org/aboutets/index.html; SAT: http://www.collegeboard.com/student/testing/newsat/writing.html; ACT: http://www.act.org/aap; Accuplacer: http://cpts.accuplacer.com/docs/StudentGuide.html; COMPASS: http://www.act.org/compass/index.html.

5. These concepts of evaluation and assessment were first articulated by Michael Scriven in "The Methodology of Evaluation."

Works Cited

Academic Senate for California Community Colleges. *Academic Literacy: A Statement of Competencies Expected of Students Entering California's Public Colleges and Universities*. Intersegmental Committee of the Academic Senates. 2000. 9 Sept. 2004 <http://www.academicsenate.cc.ca.us/Publications/Papers/AcademicLiteracy/main.htm>.

American Association of Community Colleges and American Association of State Colleges and Universities. "Access to the Baccalaureate Project Survey." Executive Summary. 9 May 2003. 1 Oct. 2004 <http://www.pathtocollege.org/pdf/EXECSU.pdf>.

Bloom, Benjamin S., Bertram B. Mesia, and David R. Krathwohl. *Taxonomy of Educational Objectives: Cognitive Domain*. Vol.1. New York: McKay, 1956.

Conference on College Composition and Communication. "Writing Assessment: A Position Statement." 1995. National Council of Teachers of English. 28 Sept. 2004 <http://www.ncte.org/about/over/positions/category/assess/107610.htm>.

Connors, Robert J. "The Abolition Debate in Composition: A Short History." *Composition in the Twenty-First Century: Crisis and Change*. Ed. Lynn Z. Bloom, Donald A. Daiker, and Edward M. White. Carbondale: Southern Illinois UP, 1996. 47–63.

"English Department Mission." Academics, Manchester Community College. 2006. 7 June 2006 <http://www.mcc.commnet.edu/academic/divisionsLAEnglish.php>.

"English 111: College Reading and Writing (English * 101: Composition)." Standard Course Syllabus. Manchester Community College. Manchester, CT. December 1997.

"Freshman Composition." McGraw Hill Higher Education. 2005. 7 June 2006 <http://catalogs.mhhe.com/mhhe/viewNode.do?node_type=c&catid=931722>.

"General Education Component Checklist, Mode 2: English Composition Learning Outcomes." *Manchester Community College Catalog. 2006–2007*. Manchester Community College. 7 June 2006

<http://www.mcc.commnet.edu/students/resources/pdf/0607cat.pdf>.

"General Education Component Checklist, Mode 3: Humanities Learning Outcomes." *Manchester Community College Catalog. 2006–2007*. Manchester Community College. 7 June 2006 <http://www.mcc.commnet.edu/students/resources/pdf/0607cat.pdf>.

Scriven, Michael. "The Methodology of Evaluation." *Perspectives of Curriculum Evaluation*. Ed. Ralph Tyler, Robert Gagné, and Michael Scriven. Chicago: Rand McNally, 1967.

Chapter Twenty-Two

A Lot Like Us, but More So: Listening to Writing Faculty Across the Curriculum

Susan E. Schorn, Coordinator
College of Liberal Arts WAC Initiative
University of Texas at Austin

The editors of this volume asked me a very specific question: "How, if at all, do standards of 'college-level' writing change if faculty from departments outside of English weigh in on the subject?" As an administrator in a university-wide, cross-disciplinary writing program, and a teacher of composition, I have a sort of catbird's seat from which to consider this question. Accordingly, I solicited opinions from some of the hundreds of instructors teaching Substantial Writing Component (SWC) courses at the University of Texas (UT) at Austin. The SWC program at UT Austin is decentralized, and although it is built around a very basic set of course requirements, it does not bind instructors to a single set of learning outcomes. Thus our teachers, in eleven colleges and schools across campus, represent a cross-section of definitions of college-level writing outside of English.

Taking Patrick Sullivan's essay in this volume as a starting point, I asked SWC instructors in a wide range of disciplines a number of questions, including:

- What is college-level writing?
- How does it differ from, say, high school writing?
- Can we define what college-level writing looks like? Should we do so?

- Can we define the purpose of college-level writing?

The responses I received indicate that writing instructors outside English share virtually all of our many concerns about student writing. Moreover, as a group, they share our disagreements over the content, purpose, and need for standards. In short, they are a lot like us, only more so. I see this as a good thing. My sense is that, rather than trying to reconcile these many definitions into a single standard, we can do more to improve student writing by looking for the reasons behind the definitions. In fact, when we look at the range of ideas about writing across disciplines, we may become more comfortable with the level of disagreement we find within our own field. Disciplines obviously have divergent goals, but college writing must meet all of those goals. The differences among disciplines demand a more dynamic set of writing standards that are adaptable, as we assume all writing should be, to purpose, audience, and occasion.

In response to my first two questions, a professor in the School of Business provided a detailed, five-point list of skills:

College-level writing should demonstrate the following:

- High level of accuracy (grammar, punctuation, spelling)
- Discipline-relevant vocabulary (e.g., business students should be able to use economic, financial, and management vocabulary appropriately)
- Discipline-relevant style (e.g., business students should use business-related formats and structures for writing such as memos, letters, reports)
- Ability to clearly and concisely relay a message (appropriate use of topic sentences, highlighting, introductions/conclusions, etc.)
- Writing that meets the intended purpose (demonstrates an understanding of the audience and goals of the message) (Loescher)

Compare this response to the more general (and more ambitious) standard laid out by a professor of economics:

> The rough first stab I can offer is: College-level writing succeeds in communicating college-level content. A written product (es-

> say, paper, monograph, etc.) achieves the standard of college-level writing if it could reasonably be included among college-level readings, assigned to be read by a relevant class of college students with the expectation that it would contribute to the students' learning in a way and to an extent similar to what instructors expect of the readings they typically assign. (Trinque)

These instructors approach their definitions of college writing quite differently. One foregrounds correctness and the other stresses content. They are representative of the range of responses I received. And yet, the two definitions are not mutually exclusive; indeed, the professors could actually be describing the same ideal piece of writing.

Moreover, the instructors I surveyed clearly appreciated the interplay of small- and large-scale issues as they tried to define college-level writing. A professor of history, for example, narrowed the difference between college and high school writing down to three seemingly minor, but to her, telling, points:

> I get seniors who are still tightly wedded to the five-sentence paragraph, who think they will go to hell if they write "I," and who can't imagine that [the professor] might be really truly interested in what they actually think (because I'm asking them to write on historiographical matters that are unsolved). Those three problems seem most clearly to define the difference between college and [high school] writing. (Frazier)

When she goes on to discuss the purpose of college writing, this professor reveals why these high school writing habits are so troublesome to her:

> I teach a period of history (European Middle Ages and Renaissance) that attracts students with many pre-conceived ideas. I'm happy enough if I manage to help them overcome those prejudices and see the sources we read in order to write about them freshly. (Frazier)

No doubt the preconceived ideas about history she wants her students to overcome are reinforced by their preconceived ideas about writing. The ability to write "freshly," to contribute new ideas and perspectives, requires thinking that isn't bound by counterintuitive rules. Here, the instructor is concerned about how an overemphasis on such rules unfits her students for college writing—a somewhat different perspective from that of the business professor. This concern may reflect the demands of her discipline, or her personal experiences as a teacher, or some combination of the two. Whatever the source, it is a valid concern, and it arises because she is trying to accomplish a reasonable and worthwhile goal: getting students to reconceive history.

A professor in art history described the difference between high school and college writing this way:

> For me it has to do with level of research (deeper and more sophisticated—no encyclopedias, for example), quality of analysis (there has to be some at the very least and it has to demonstrate a broader knowledge of the subject than the paper can or should represent), and the presence of an actual argument. (Canning)

Surface error is not what comes first to the mind of this instructor (though, knowing her, I am sure it bothers her when she sees it). She is looking for research ability, analysis, and argument. In fact, she sounds a lot like a composition teacher to me!

None of these responses is likely to surprise a composition instructor. We know all the things mentioned by these teachers are important. We understand the professional pragmatism that motivates these instructors' goals. We might disagree with the business professor's emphasis on surface issues if we felt it impeded a student's development, but we would probably admit the importance of error-free writing in the workplace. None of these descriptions could, I think, be called unreasonable. The question is: Can they all simultaneously be "right"? Can all these definitions and expectations be made to live together in harmony?

I believe they can. The result may be inelegant—a palette of definitions for different majors and careers rather than a single, neat standard, perhaps—and the process itself will certainly be noisy, but involving faculty across disciplines in defining college writing has many benefits. Such a process broadens an institution's understanding of the purpose of writing and sharpens awareness of writing's myriad uses. Standards devised by a cross-disciplinary process are more thoroughly interrogated and better understood by all parties. Giving all instructors a voice in setting the standards gives them a stake in improving student writing.

The key, I believe, lies in looking at the goals and expectations these faculty members bring to writing instruction, and how they mesh with those of English and composition faculty. I use the term *mesh* carefully; rather than expecting faculty in various disciplines to share the exact writing goals and expectations of English faculty, we should collectively discover where our goals coincide, where they diverge, and why. This helps everyone concerned determine who bears responsibility for meeting various goals.

Responsibility, admittedly, can be a sticky problem—one that emerges quickly when faculty outside of English are asked to describe the relationship between basic composition and writing in their discipline. For example, a professor of government replied to my questions by describing a dichotomy that professors of English (at least) would probably call false:

> In political science, clarity, precision, and analytic rigor are valued very highly. Eloquence and literary flair are less prized. (Madrid)

The economics professor was more forthright:

> . . . [I]t might be worthwhile to compile a set of definitions for each discipline as an instructors' resource. One benefit I imagine is to free instructors from the possible default position that they are to function as satellite English professors, using the content of their course as an opportunity for remedial instruction. That students might improve their skills in composition is not unwelcome, but quite beside the point. (Trinque)

I am guessing most English teachers will bristle at this instructor's use of the word *remedial.* There does still persist a sense among the disciplines that students *progress* from writing English papers to writing lab reports or business presentations. Housing basic composition courses in the English department reinforces this perception. Setting composition courses adrift in programs that offer no major does not help. These kinds of curricular structures imply that one *advances* from the study of English and composition to the study of more complicated things as one matures; as if Adam Smith were a more highly evolved being than William Shakespeare, or the contemplation of the tax code required more maturity than understanding Aristotle's rhetorical triangle. Yet, curiously enough, when I distribute our institution's "Grading Criteria for First-Year Writing" to instructors across campus, many of them immediately co-opt the criteria for use in their own, junior- and senior-level, classes. When they get an opportunity to examine the standards we hold our students to, they are less inclined to dismiss them as remedial. This, then, is another benefit of involving instructors from the disciplines in discussions about college writing: they come to better understand and appreciate the work we do in English and composition.

Discussing standards and criteria with these instructors also provides an opportunity to share with them the scholarship we writing professionals wallow in on a daily basis. Some instructors in other disciplines think of grammar as someone else's problem—namely, ours. They wonder what on earth we did during those fifteen weeks of First-Year Composition when we should have been teaching basic grammar. To many teachers in other disciplines, it is news that assigning grammar exercises will not magically produce error-free writing. They may not understand the relationship between what they call composition skills and critical thinking ability. They may have completely unrealistic ideas of the sort of writing students have done in high school. Here, our background knowledge can do much to enlighten them, to the benefit of their students. (In my experience, instructors in education and educational psychology are most likely to understand the developmental aspect of writing; faculty in these disciplines often make especially good allies if you are having trouble communicating with other disciplines.)

Of course, discussing standards with many instructors does not mean accepting or validating all those standards. At some point, consolidation is necessary or the approach becomes pointlessly reductive. If each individual instructor sets his or her own standards, there is nothing standard about them. But there is good reason for writing instructors to expend at least some energy in that direction. In any act of writing, the standards, for content, correctness, purpose, and so on, ultimately reside in a tacit agreement between writer and audience. If the standard, whatever it is, is not met, the reader either fails to understand or refuses to read the writing. Thus, developing any standard for college-level writing requires spectacular generalization of what is really a quite individual relationship.

It is less than ideal, but on some level necessary. Based on my work with instructors across the curriculum, it seems eminently possible to work toward a comprehensive set of learning strands related to writing. These would admit the need for, and benefit of, different emphases among strands, and different levels of performance, in different disciplines, institutions, and situations. Such a set of standards, while perhaps not as easily explained to state legislatures as a single rubric, is far more reflective of how writing really happens.

Creating such standards is good for us as composition instructors because it makes us more aware of the needs of students in majors other than English. We serve these students better when we know the full trajectory of their writing development in college, rather than just the stages that we guide them through. The process is good for instructors outside our field because it makes them aware of what we do—and what we don't do. It helps them better understand what *they* contribute (or should contribute) to their students' writing and critical thinking skills.

Having spent so much of this essay discussing differences, I would like to close by examining a common thread among the responses I received. It became clear as I read these instructors' thoughts that they all shared one specific goal for student writing. It is a goal dear to composition teachers. For these instructors in other fields, the goal is intimately connected with both the ideal and the intensely practical facets of their disciplines. The instructor in the School of Business expressed it this way:

> If I had to pick one thing that separates adult-level writing from adolescent-level writing, it is the ability to reflect the needs of the audience in your writing. To be able to empathize with the reader and present the material in a way they can best receive and comprehend it. As part of the college journey, the adolescent needs to learn to empathize on this level and to leave behind the self-centered focus of youth. (Loescher)

Now, this is the same professor who provided the five-point list of grammatical, disciplinary, and stylistic skills quoted earlier in this essay. But she takes pains to say that the *one thing* that denotes "adult-level" writing, to her mind, is empathy with the audience. Not just *awareness* of the audience, but "the ability to reflect the needs of the audience" and "leave behind the self-centered focus" of the immature writer.

A teacher in the School of Nursing strikes a similar note in her response:

> You have to write to a wide variety of people, both inside your institution and outside. . . . Most writers don't spend nearly enough time understanding the people to whom they'll be writing. (Johnson)

Not just knowing who your readers are, but *understanding* them. This is a call for empathy much like that voiced by the business professor. Both teachers are concerned with the *practical* need for such empathy. It is, to them, simply necessary to good communication. And good communication is necessary to succeed in both their respective fields.

Along similar lines, the professor of Germanic studies worried that her students are too focused on "figuring out" the audience's point of view. This concern at first seems to contradict those voiced in the previous quotations, but the reverse is actually true:

> The difference with "high-school writing" seems to be (and this is someone talking who has grown up in another educational system) that the students tend to assume that there is one correct answer to each question and one correct way to write it down. What they want from me is the "formula" that they can use. What I am trying to teach them is to *find* their own voice: develop their own opinion as opposed to trying to figure out mine. This, however, also means that they have to *prove* their point. (Hafner)

This professor's emphasis on "finding" voice and "developing" opinion is telling. She has observed her students using her as a stand-in audience for their writing—a tactic we have all probably witnessed. Why go to the trouble of trying to visualize a hazy professional or public readership when the teacher with the grading pen makes such a convenient substitute? If the student writer can just decode the biases of the faux audience embodied in the professor, he or she need never learn to empathize with amorphous, multifaced, imagined audiences (admittedly, a difficult task for any writer). But if students follow this course, the professor notes, they lose the opportunity to interrogate their own views—the very reason many of us in composition stress audience awareness in the first place. They will never develop the ability to prove a point or defend their opinions to real-world readers. They will lack both audience awareness and self-awareness. And this, according to these instructors, is what will keep them from being college-level writers.

In the College of Communication, a professor responded to my questions with his own list of desired student writing skills. But he too specifically mentions the writer's approach to audience as central to college-level writing:

> The move from high-school-level to college-level writing is, to my mind, a move toward a much greater consciousness and self-consciousness concerning the role of writing. That is, on the one hand, college-level writing involves a greater appreciation for the located-ness of the sources used and the subjects talked about. . . . On the other hand, the student's own writing should demonstrate a sense of audience: Am I writing this for people who have seen this film or to introduce it to people who have not seen it? Am I analyzing a film's formal qualities or am I concerned with its reception by viewers? What are the preconceptions my audience is likely to hold toward this film, this genre, this country's films, and the like? How will I either work with those preconceptions or attempt to change them through my writing? (Siegenthaler)

Again we see the concern for self- and other-awareness. Note too that this professor not only wants students to ask questions about audience ("Am I writing this for people who have seen this film or to introduce it to people who have not seen it?"), but expects them to then actively adjust their writing, so that they may, as Ronald Lunsford puts it elsewhere in this collection, "talk to people who see the world differently" (190): *How will I either work with those preconceptions or attempt to change them through my writing?* Students of this professor must embrace the possibility that opinion is changeable through open discussion. If they cannot admit this possibility then they can never develop the skills to change opinion. And furthermore, they will never develop the ability to rationally modify their own opinions, or even interrogate them at all. And thus, the instructor in me feels compelled to add, they will be unable to tell when their own opinions are being changed, perhaps even grossly manipulated, by others.

My respondents were striking in their persistent concern over the quality that Ronald Lunsford, in his essay, calls "attitude." Moreover, they see this quality as integral to the work of people in their respective professions. Clearly, a writerly attitude is not merely something we demand in English or composition. The need to talk to people who see the world differently, rather than simply yelling at them, is integral to all disciplines—even the "objective" sciences, the ever-so-pragmatic world of business, and the life-and-death world of health and medicine. This fact strikes me as a vindication of our focus, in composition, on the ability to question, reflect, persuade, and listen. All too often I have been faced with students who not only did not want to seriously consider a different viewpoint, but felt it was unfair of me to require them to do so. It is heartening to know that instructors in other disciplines will continue to emphasize this important skill, and work to teach it to our students. Anyone involved in that great struggle, I think, deserves to have his or her opinions about writing heard.

Works Cited

Canning, Charlotte. "RE: Questions on 'college-level' writing." E-mail to author. 21 June 2004.

Frazier, Alison. "RE: Questions on 'college-level' writing." E-mail to author. 16 June 2004.

Hafner, Susanne. "RE: Questions on 'college-level' writing." E-mail to author. 16 June 2004.

Johnson, Regina. "College Level Writing." E-mail to author. 15 Sept. 2004.

Loescher, Kristie. "RE: Questions on 'college-level' writing." E-mail to author. 9 July 2004.

Madrid, Raul. "RE: Questions on 'college-level' writing." E-mail to author. 21 June 2004.

Siegenthaler, Peter. "Questions on 'college-level' writing." E-mail to author. 28 June 2004.

Sullivan, Patrick. "An Essential Question: What Is 'College-Level' Writing?" *What Is "College-Level" Writing?* Ed. Patrick Sullivan and Howard Tinberg. Urbana, IL: NCTE, 2006. 1–28.

Trinque, Brian. "thoughts on 'college-level' writing." E-mail to author. 24 June 2004.

CHAPTER TWENTY-THREE

The Recursive Character of College Writing

CHRIS KEARNS
Assistant Dean of Student Services
University of Minnesota

Acknowledgment of another calls for recognition of the other's specific relation to oneself, and . . . this entails the revelation of oneself as having denied or distorted that relation.

STANLEY CAVELL, *The Claim of Reason*

If our explanations or our understanding of the universe is in some sense to match that universe, or model it, and if the universe is recursive, then our explanations and our logics must also be fundamentally recursive.

GREGORY BATESON AND RODNEY DONALDSON, *A Sacred Unity*

When I took my first position as a graduate student instructor of composition and comparative literature more than twenty years ago, universities typically paid scant attention to mentoring graduate assistants in pedagogy. Although there were some discussions of the application of rhetorical and expressive models of composition to undergraduate writing—I, like many colleagues from that era, found myself developing an understanding of what is at stake in undergraduate writing in coffeehouses and library carrels as I graded papers, talked with fellow instructors, and prepared my thrice-weekly classes. At the time, I little suspected we were cultivating insights into the recursive character of college writing that would remain a mainstay of my professional academic work for the next quarter century and would ground my understanding of student development within the context of the educational process to the present day. Although we do not normally discuss college writing in such terms, the recursivity of undergraduate prose, its complex form of self-generating reflexivity, not only distinguishes university-level composition from more basic forms of writing instruction, it also provides the essential tools necessary to understand and take greater responsibility for the ways our relationship to language maps the surrounding world and orients our attention prior to any conscious decisions on our part. College writing, in other words, provides an opportunity to form the contents of our consciousness and the effectiveness of our communication and also to shape the constitution of our character.

These days I spend most of my time as an assistant dean directing student services, career support, and liberal arts academic advising at a Big Ten university. A uniquely rewarding aspect of this role is provided by the opportunity to work with undergraduates from scores of academic disciplines at all stages of their undergraduate careers. Because I focus on composition and forms of literacy when I teach, and also because I believe composition serves as a core educational competency for all majors, I frequently find myself talking with students about the role of college writing in the educations and lives of undergraduates.

One recent pivotal conversation about college writing occurred in an hour-long discussion with a young man completing a technology-related degree. He indicated considerable dissatisfaction with the writing training he had received at the university, saying that although he was well educated to work as a Web designer and computer programmer, he had a strong interest both in improving his ability to express himself personally and in developing business communication skills. Given his sparse training in writing and communication more generally, he felt the technical components of his education were insufficiently connected to his personal interests and his professional goals. His education, therefore, seemed incomplete in ways he found troubling. "I've always done creative writing," he noted, "but there's no place for it in my degree, and I don't show anyone what I write anymore." The disconnect between his education and his personal writing was problematic, in part, because it was through such creative writing that he had first discovered and articulated his interest in computers.

Even more troubling for this technology student, though, was his lack of professional writing experience. He asked how he was expected to succeed in the work world if he did not know how to put his ideas into writing in ways that made sense to nonspecialists. "Unless we learn how to write and how to talk effectively," he said, "guys like me end up in cubicles working for people who do know how to communicate." At that point, the young man made a comment that I subsequently found reverberating throughout conversations with other undergraduates over the next few months. Speaking in a semiapologetic tone, he said, "I almost feel like I have to shame guys like you into giving us a better education."

An avid reader of our campus newspaper, my young friend knew about the drive to improve graduation and retention rates, the push to incorporate business-style performance and accountability measures in higher education, and the appetite for data-driven decision making at upper levels of educational administration. These were some of the topics he wanted to discuss with me as a way of thinking about future options and whether he might like to work in university education. He was disappointed that the focus on objective outcomes measures had, as he saw it, diverted attention from students as people with a full set of interests and life goals, disposing universities and colleges instead to view undergraduates from the perspective of educational bottom lines. Although his characterizations were both incomplete and at times extreme, I found myself inwardly agreeing with a number of his criticisms. "We are left to ourselves to learn about leadership and management in the real world," he summarized. "We aren't taught to speak or write or communicate our ideas. Those of us in technology aren't usually very good at speaking with people in power to begin with, and this means many of us can't have the kind of careers we want."

Sensing that such concerns might have broader applicability to undergraduates as a whole, I wanted to talk about them with my first-year advisory board, a group of some ninety newly matriculated undergraduates interested in involvement opportunities at the university and in improving our approach to undergraduate education. Because they are new to the university, we typically focus on transition issues between high school and college and on topics related to adjusting to college-level expectations and workloads. I asked this group about their high school experiences with writing, how well prepared they felt for college, and what they hoped for from the undergraduate writing experience. As anticipated, many of the same themes stressed by the technology student reappeared in the discussion of humanities and social sciences undergraduates and also featured prominently in the conversations of arts and exploratory students.

One common frustration with high school writing education was driven by the sense that much of the work was repetitive and geared toward addressing group deficiencies rather than developing individual strengths. One young woman commented on her experience of high school composition by noting, "Sometimes it feels like we have to keep going backwards for a certain percentage of the class, as if there's no bar you can count on as a starting point for the whole class." She was eager to study writing in a setting characterized by standards and a steady progression of skills. I did not share with her that one of the most common complaints of students who have completed our writing-across-the-curriculum series is precisely that it lacks a common set of expectations and is all too frequently perceived as being calibrated to redress weaknesses rather than building on the educational foundations already in place.

Another undergraduate commented on the general lack of intellectual challenge in her previous compositional work by observing, "Writing in high school was always so obvious. It was like: 'compare and contrast these two books' that had obvious similarities or differences." Although a number of the students reported positive experiences, especially in connection with outstanding individual teachers and with honors or advanced composition courses, my impression of the general consensus was that our incoming freshmen were frustrated with their preparation for college-level composition. On the whole, they did not know what to expect regarding the type of work they would be required to do, and they consequently had little sense of how well or deficiently positioned they were to cope with the demands of college-level writing.

Through their self-descriptions, the students tended to divide into two groups, a small contingent who felt they were ready for college writing, and a much larger group of students who were uncertain of the state of their preparation and worried that they might not have the skills or background to be successful in composition. On the whole, the students who felt positioned for compositional success indicated they had taken an integrated approach to writing in high school, one that emphasized the interdependence of writing, learning, and thinking. Most students in this group had found themselves pushed to improve their skills and mentored to view writing as an open-ended process. These were attitudes they were now bringing to the college classroom. In explaining the importance of writing instruction to her educational prospects in college, one of the more confident undergraduates related: "Not being able to write is like not knowing your name. You're just completely paralyzed. I think they all go hand-in-hand—reading, writing, and communicating. I mean, you can't really develop one without all the others."

By way of contrast, the students who felt uncertain about or poorly prepared to cope with college-level writing tended to describe approaching composition as a compartmentalized, quasi-mechanical exercise unconnected with the rest of their education. "I never had any individual feedback from my English teacher," one of these students said. "It was all: here is your assignment; here are the guidelines, here is your grade." Regardless of their sense of the state of their preparedness, the majority of students agreed that what they wanted from their college writing experience was a chance to incorporate it into the rest of their education. Furthermore, a surprising number mentioned the need and desire to develop their own individual prose voices. They wanted their writing to sound like them. Finally, most of the students registered an awareness that they needed experience with many different types of writing, including analytic and expressive prose, research writing, disciplinary specific texts, and technical writing.

After meeting with my first-year advisory board, I discussed the question of college-level writing with a junior majoring in

English who also volunteers on a part-time basis to help tutor high school composition students. She had shared many of the frustrations of the first-year students at the outset of her own undergraduate education. But she had since made an important discovery concerning the connection between writing and thinking. This represented a change from her precollege attitudes toward composition. Although she had been a prolific letter writer in high school, preferring that nearly anachronistic form of communication to e-mail, she said she had never been committed to her compositional homework. "College was the first time I felt bad if my case wasn't strong," she explained, "or if I just whipped up something at the last minute and handed it in like I did a million times in high school." I asked her why she had found writing letters easier than drafting papers before coming to college. She indicated there were two crucial differences between letters and papers: In her letters she cared about what she was saying and she also cared about her reader. Neither attitude characterized her approach to high school papers.

Although I did not indicate as much at the time, investing simultaneously in one's position as a writer and in the needs of one's reader are two of the three steps necessary to take a recursive approach to composition. This student had, in other words, begun mastering the basics necessary to succeed at collegiate composition even though she had done so outside the confines of her formal high school course work. Speculating about why she changed her attitudes toward composition as an undergraduate, she said, "I felt like my writing became a lot more personal in college, because the topics I chose to write on were usually my own." She went on to describe a Shakespeare essay she had written the previous semester. "That paper was the first time I felt like I made connections that were really mine," she recalled. "And even though I finished the course, I'm still not done with the paper; I'm still working on it. I think it may become my senior thesis."

We also discussed what I regard to be the three most common approaches to writing that students bring with them from high school. (In my view, some students have no interest in writing whatsoever, and it is difficult to fathom their understanding of a university education. But even the students who bring an interest in writing to college usually have formed no clear conception of writing itself and instead see undergraduate writing primarily as a means to other ends.) These common approaches to writing tend to divide into three camps. The first group views writing as a transaction or performance designed to please the instructor in order to earn a reward. Students, they believe, submit papers in return for grades. The resulting grade point average serves as a barometer of *institutional success*. For some, this means that collegiate writing is pure theater, a game of guessing what the teacher holds behind his or her back and of saying whatever the teacher wants to hear. Others subscribe to a contractualist view of the student/teacher relationship. They judge that the instructor is gratified and grades are secured by following long-established rules. Both attitudes interfere with learning. The undergraduates who approach their papers in the spirit of politically motivated guesswork are altogether too pliant to accompany their writing by any inward change of perspective. Similarly, the contractually minded students tend to believe they have already acquired the fundamentals of composition through their work in high school English classes and they often do not open themselves willingly to instruction and advice that might help them become better writers.

Furthermore, the second group also typically views writing as an extension and declaration of the self. Members of this cohort exemplify what Charles Taylor calls "expressivist youth culture" (*Varieties* 82). As Taylor outlines, the rise of this culture is rooted in Romantic ideals regarding the primacy of the private individual, the value of authenticity, and the quasi-moral imperative of self-discovery. It is driven both by an expanding consumerism and by the kind of self-concern that was once the purview of the wealthy. As part of "the expressivist turn" in the Western world view, Taylor argues, youth has become accepted as a distinct stage of life to be distinguished both from childhood and from the responsibilities of adulthood.[1] In college composition classes, expressivist undergraduates tend to regard writing as an organic process to be evaluated on the basis of its sincerity or intrinsic beauty rather than according to *external* criteria such as coherence or cogency.

The third group regards writing as an instrumental tool rather than as a transaction or a form of personal expression. For instrumentalist students, college composition consists of a collection of techniques and protocols for communicating information in the service of presumably higher-order goals such as creating a portfolio for prospective graduate schools or job opportunities, promulgating strongly held cultural values or religious beliefs, or producing insights into science or the humanities. Although they are often interested in grades as well, instrumentalist students are primarily concerned with being right or effective with respect to the larger aims toward which they are directed.

I told the English major that I still found those three approaches to composition dominant among undergraduates, and I shared sample comments from my first-year advisory board that seemed indicative of each of the three views. "College-level writing starts with such attitudes," I said, "but we fail our students if we make it easy for them to believe the most important feature of undergraduate writing is to be found in the academic record it builds, the personal expression it affords, or the causes it enables us to advance." College-level writing cannot begin to come into its own, I maintained, until we discern that all of these attitudes are tied together by a single common thread that needs to be cut.

Despite their varying aims, the three most common approaches to undergraduate writing are all fundamentally monological. Whether students are focused on the institutional recognition represented by grades, the travails of finding one's voice, or other goals that might be furthered by effective composition, they remain unaware that writing is not and cannot be private.[2] Rather, the kind of writing required of college students always involves an awareness of at least two consciousnesses: that of the writer and that of the implied reader.[3]

I am afraid my explanation sounded ferociously theoretical or phenomenological, however, and was not the sort of pragmatic advice the English major was seeking as she thought about how best to improve her own writing and that of her high school students. Nonetheless, I believe an awareness of the characteristics and ramifications of the kind of consciousness lying at the heart of successful undergraduate prose provides the key both to understanding what distinguishes college-level writing from other forms of composition and to articulating why learning to write at the college level is vital to all areas of communication, analysis, and self-comprehension.

In order to become clear about college writing, we need to recognize that the process of acquiring the dialogic consciousness necessary to successful undergraduate prose cannot begin until *after* students have learned the rules of basic composition. Precollege writing courses focused on issues of mechanical competency do not require the same dialogic focus and, for this reason, are best regarded as epistemologically distinct from college composition classes.[4] Although their work is predicated on the prior completion of such learning, teachers of college-level writing must do something much more complex than instructing students to follow rules. In addition to concerns related to formal correctness, college-level composition teachers need to bring their students to recognize that the desire to be understood requires us to find ourselves in relation to the purposes and needs of the reader, who must serve as a partner in shaping our language. These were the first two steps of recursive writing that the English major had taken for herself when writing letters in high school.

Whatever its topic or aim, the essential feature of composition confronting all thoughtful undergraduates is that it establishes a real human relationship. In this sense, all writing is inescapably social. Consequently, how the student accepts or avoids responsibility for clarifying the shape and content of the writing relationship is simultaneously an ethical and an epistemological matter. That is to say that good writing is an issue not only of what the student knows but also of how the student chooses to live the knowledge that forms of thought always entail forms of life, and that both must be shared if they are to be meaningful. As Richard Lanham writes in *Revising Prose*, a book I continue to draw from when teaching, "this is why we worry so much about bad prose. It signifies incoherent people, failed social relationships" (64).[5]

When student writing does fail, it is most often because, unable to break free of the bewitchment of self-concern, the writer does not sufficiently respect the reader. Care for those with whom we find ourselves connected is not simply a social value, it is also an intellectual virtue necessary for undergraduate writers wanting to perform at the college level. J. Hillis Miller clarifies the tension between care for others and narcissism toward the self when, in *The Ethics of Reading*, he argues, "respect is properly the conception of a worth which thwarts my self-love" (17). Hillis Miller goes on to maintain that respect requires me to recognize and incorporate a necessity or law that originates from beyond the narrowly conceived self which, nonetheless, takes it up as its own and is thereby transformed. If students hope to learn what college writing has to teach, they must work at just such a respect-based self-transformation. More specifically, they must develop the critical capacity to read their own prose from the perspective of their audience in a way that puts the needs of the reader on an equal footing with the needs of the writer. This, I think, is an insight toward which most strong undergraduate writers are groping, but it is difficult to develop in isolation.

Such reasoning suggests that college writing proper begins whenever an undergraduate takes the first consequential step from self to other on the grounds of care for one's audience. This is best done by opening oneself to the fact that meaning does not *belong* to the writer; it *unfolds* in the shared space of acknowledgment between the reader and the writer. Effective communication depends on readers recognizing themselves in the way they were already comprehended by the writer who prepared the page before them. Naturally, the writer must first have accurately anticipated this self-recognition by the reader.

The underlying dynamic between the writer and reader indicates that the basic coherence of compositional advice such as "understand your audience," or "clarify the importance of your argument" is poorly grasped if understood exclusively in terms of *techniques* designed to secure institutional recognition, to further individual expression, or to achieve private aims. Although it requires considerable effort to do so, such counsel is better viewed as being rooted in the confounding logic of intersubjectivity. In this logic, *mastery* may prove indistinguishable from *subjection to necessity*, and freedom may best be realized through self-constraint. Such apparent paradoxes bring us before the problem that often leads to college writing being described poorly or not at all: intersubjective logic cannot be articulated without a conceptual apparatus that most students find baffling. Students and teachers working to develop a natural and convincing prose voice are therefore understandably reluctant to embrace an arcane description of what they are trying to do. But to avoid working through the interpersonal complexities of undergraduate composition is, in a significant sense, to miss both the point of college writing and one of education's most important opportunities.

The primary reason intersubjective logic so often eludes our prosaic grasp is that it is endlessly recursive. As Gregory Bateson has argued, recursive systems are found in most self-shaping processes—especially those involving communication and information dissemination (*Angels Fear* 161; *Mind and Nature* 182–84). Essentially, recursion is a form of self-governing, circular causality found in the feedback loops at the core of all self-directing systems. Examples of these might include university governance, college composition, and even—one hopes—the development of individual character. However, the circular causality of recursion cannot be adequately represented by traditional linear logic, and the paradoxes that result when the latter attempts to map the former have remained a mainstay of philosophical reflection and vexation since Epimenides grappled with the puzzle of the Cretan liar.[6] Nonetheless, if students are to write successfully at the college level, they must, at a minimum, develop an understanding of the recursive role of the writer in intersubjective terms.

This means students have to find a way to conceptualize the writer not on the basis of the private self, but, rather, as one pole of a relationship. Inasmuch as the theory of logical types teaches that no set can include (or exclude) itself as a member of that set, the process of cultivating this understanding also obliges students to negotiate a transition between logical levels of discourse.[7] The role of a writer connecting with a reader, in other words, cannot be fully represented from within the writer/reader relationship. Instead, students must adopt a third position, one capable of embracing both poles from somewhere outside the writer/reader dyad. Ideally, this third position will be modeled for the student by the teacher whenever the latter acts as a *critical reader*. In the context of composition, critical readers work to align and develop the relationship between the writer and the implied reader by cultivating a greater awareness of how the role of each shapes the other.

The moment students accept the role of critical reader of their own prose, they begin to transform the dyad of writer and implied reader in the direction of a self-overcoming dialectic, the aim of which is to return to and more effectively grapple with its point of origin.[8] This recursive role is not easy to undertake, however. It is complicated by at least two considerations. First, it has to coordinate a minimum of three consciousnesses—those of the writer, the implied reader, and the critical reader. Second, as has already been mentioned, it has to coordinate these perspectives by bridging at least two logical levels required by the process of composition. One level is that of the writer presenting a case. The other level is that of the critical reader undertaking a double description of that presentation from the perspectives of both the writer and the implied reader. Because the recursive character of this process makes it difficult to model and to discuss, most students need to be guided through the experience of self-revision by seasoned teachers. But even if our students thereby encounter the recursivity of college writing at first hand, they are not well served unless they are also given the conceptual tools to begin thinking about the meaning and potential of that experience.

I would argue that the recursive moment of critical reading ought to be more fully articulated both in our conversations with undergraduates and in our composition classrooms because it represents the pivot on which the ethical and epistemological importance of college writing turns. Through recursive revision, undergraduates can take a more conscious level of responsibility for the way they engage the surrounding environment. If taken seriously, critical reading and revision thereby helps students understand that we live in a world of relationships rather than operating on a field of things. It does this by positioning them to more reflectively construct the social world we hold in common and to recognize the extent to which college writing is ultimately an act of self-composition. Unfortunately, my discussions with undergraduates, instructors, and administrators indicate this is an insight that has not yet arrived in many of our classrooms and educational policy decisions.

Because, at its best, writing is an act of declaring ourselves and our connections with a larger scheme of things, writing is or ought to be about life and our place in it. From my perspective, there is no more important intellectual work college students can do. I am concerned, though, that many features of the university system (like the trend toward responsibility-centered management, the adoption of the instrumental languages of business at the expense of the self-reflective idioms of art and the humanities, and the sometimes reductionist field-coverage principle that shapes academic professional life) complicate any attempt to position college writing to do this important work. If becoming clear about your relationships to a larger world (which only emerges through those relationships) is a fundamental feature of college writing, it would be helpful if the university provided a model for such effort by exercising a firmer grasp of its own structure and motivations. I believe, though, that we seldom achieve clarity about ourselves. This necessarily presents obstacles for teachers and students alike, while at the same time demonstrating that even senior administrators can and should continue to learn from the college writing classroom.

Notes

1. See *Varieties of Religion Today*, especially pages 79–86. See also *Sources of the Self*, especially pages 368–90.

2. The best known and most powerful arguments against the possibility of private language are to be found in Ludwig Wittgenstein's *Philosophical Investigations*. Wittgenstein's key insight for college-level writing is that competence in communication requires one to engage the forms of life that provide the context for all collective understanding. Wittgenstein makes this point when he notes that "to imagine a language means to imagine a form of life" (8). Without entering into or, at a minimum, imagining a shared life within which communication can unfold, there can be no meaningful exchange or mutual comprehension. As Wittgenstein observes, "It is what human beings *say* that is true or false; and they agree on the *language* they use. This is not agreement in opinions but in forms of life" (88).

3. My point of departure for thinking about the implied reader is Wolfgang Iser's argument that the implied reader is encoded by the writer

through the strategic positioning of "gaps" in the text that the reader is invited to fill. The writer, in other words, offers the reader an interpretive project or set of projects to be completed in collaboration with the writer's formative design. See Iser's *The Implied Reader* and *The Act of Reading: A Theory of Aesthetic Response*. See also Umberto Eco's related construct of the *model reader* in *The Role of the Reader*. For a useful overview of thinkers critical of Iser's position, see Jonathan Culler's *On Deconstruction*, pp. 73–78.

4. My sense of the dialogic draws heavily on the work of Mikhail Bakhtin and his related concepts of polyphony, carnival, and literary architectonics. Bakhtin, in turn, drew on the writing of Dostoevsky, for whom the dialogic was roughly synonymous with consciousness. As Bakhtin comments, "Dostoevsky could hear dialogic relationships everywhere, in all manifestations of conscious and intelligent human life; where consciousness began, there dialogue began for him as well" (40). Consciousness, in short, never belongs to one person in isolation. It always exists on the border between a self and an other. This, I believe, is a foundational lesson to be learned and applied by students of college-level writing.

5. Stanley Cavell makes an excellent related point when he observes, "we are endlessly separate, for *no* reason. But then we are answerable for everything that comes between us; if not for causing it then for continuing it; if not for denying it then for affirming it; if not for it then to it" (369). From this perspective, college writing requires undergraduates to focus on their relationship to their readers and on how this relationship has been miscarried by the writer.

6. See especially pages 54–60 of *Mind and Nature: A Necessary Unity.* Bateson there argues that, because it ignores the reality of time, formal logic offers an incomplete model of how causality actually operates. As he observes, though, "we use the same words to talk about logical sequences and about sequences of cause and effect. . . . When the sequences of cause and effect become circular (or more complex than circular), then the description or mapping of those sequences onto timeless logic becomes self-contradictory" (*Mind and Nature* 54). Bateson discusses these issues in connection with Epimenides and the paradox of the Cretan liar on p. 108–9.

Bateson developed his theory of recursion near the end of his career in order to avoid the pitfalls of logical paradox and to think more effectively about ecology, systems design, and cybernetics. As Bateson made clear in his posthumously published collection of essays entitled *A Sacred Unity: Further Steps to an Ecology of Mind*, recursion is a form of reflexivity or circular causality through which things return "all the time to bite their own tails and control their own beginnings" (191). I believe college-level writing is distinguished precisely by its insistence that students undertake the endlessly iterative and paradoxical process of meeting themselves in the act of marshalling their own origins.

7. Whitehead and Russell developed the theory of logical types in the *Principia Mathematica* in order to solve and understand the source of a number of paradoxes in symbolic logic and other forms of thinking concerned with aggregates. As they write in the introduction to that work, "it is believed that the theory of types, as set forth in what follows, leads to the avoidance of contradictions and to the detection of the precise fallacy which has given rise to them" (Russell, *The Basic Writings of Bertrand Russell* 161).

Influenced by the efforts of Russell and Whitehead throughout the *Principia Mathematica* to demonstrate that we must employ a theory of logical types if we wish to avoid logical contradictions, both Ludwig Wittgenstein and Gregory Bateson developed distinctive understandings of the relationship of language and meaning to the contexts in which they were produced. Wittgenstein focused on "forms of life," and Bateson focused on "ecology." Both men disagreed, however, with the ultimate aim pursued by Whitehead and Russell, and concluded that the goal of eliminating all paradox from human communication was illusory. Drawing on the theory of logical types in light of the considerations urged by Wittgenstein and Bateson, it would appear that a key lesson of college-level writing involves *context sensitivity*. Students need to develop an understanding that what makes perfect sense in one frame of reference may prove to be complete gibberish in another.

8. Students of Hegel will here recognize the ternary scheme of the Hegelian *Aufhebung*, the dialectical process whereby a thesis is preserved, transcended, and cancelled in a synthesis which can serve in its turn as a new thesis. The clearest explanation Hegel provides of his dialectic can be found in his *Encyclopedia of the Philosophical Sciences*, the first part of which is *The Logic*. See section 11 (pp. 15–16), where Hegel writes, "to see that thought in its very nature is dialectical, and that, as understanding, it must fall into contradiction—the negative of itself—will form one of the main lessons of logic" (*Hegel's Logic* 15). Please also see section 48 (p. 76–79), where Hegel discusses what he sees as shortcomings in Kant's use of theses and antitheses to model the antinomies of reason. Finally, see section 81 (p. 115–19), where Hegel observes, "wherever there is movement, wherever there is life, wherever anything is carried into effect in the actual world, there Dialectic is at work" (116). For a description of the dialectical process that anticipates many elements of Bateson's model of recursivity, see page 10 of Hegel's preface to *The Phenomenology of Spirit*. Regarding the dialectic through which truth unfolds itself in the interplay between thought and the material world, Hegel there writes: "It is the process of its own

becoming, the circle that presupposes its end as its goal, having its end also as its beginning; and only by being worked out to its end, is it actual" (*The Phenomenology of Spirit* 10). Readers interested in the secondary literature treating Hegel's dialectical method might begin by consulting *A Hegel Dictionary*, pp. 81–83.

Works Cited

Bakhtin, Mikhail. *Problems of Dostoevsky's Poetics*. Ed. and trans. Caryl Emerson. Minneapolis: U of Minnesota P, 1984.

Bateson, Gregory. *A Sacred Unity: Further Steps to an Ecology of Mind*. New York: HarperCollins, 1991.

———. *Mind and Nature: A Necessary Unity*. Cresskill, NJ: Hampton, 2002.

Bateson, Gregory, and Mary Catherine Bateson. *Angels Fear: Towards an Epistemology of the Sacred*. New York: Bantam Books, 1988.

Cavell, Stanley. *The Claim of Reason: Wittgenstein, Skepticism, Morality, and Tragedy*. Oxford: Oxford UP, 1979.

Culler, Jonathan. *On Deconstruction: Theory and Criticism after Structuralism*. Ithaca: Cornell UP, 1982.

Eco, Umberto. *The Role of the Reader: Explorations in the Semiotics of Texts*. Bloomington: Indiana UP, 1979.

Hegel, G. W. F. *Hegel's Logic* (part 1 of *Encyclopaedia of the Philosophical Sciences*). Trans. William Wallace. Oxford: Oxford UP, 1975.

———. *Phenomenology of Spirit*. Trans. A. V. Miller. Oxford: Oxford UP, 1977.

Inwood, Michael. *A Hegel Dictionary*. Oxford: Blackwell, 1992.

Iser, Wolfgang. *The Act of Reading: A Theory of Aesthetic Response*. Baltimore: Johns Hopkins UP, 1980.

———. *The Implied Reader: Patterns of Communication in Prose from Bunyan to Beckett*. Baltimore: Johns Hopkins UP, 1974.

Lanham, Richard. *Revising Prose*. 4th ed. Boston: Allyn and Bacon, 2000.

Miller, J. Hillis. *The Ethics of Reading: Kant, de Man, Eliot, Trollope, James, and Benjamin*. The Wellek Library lectures at the University of California, Irvine. New York: Columbia UP, 1989.

Russell, Bertrand. *The Basic Writings of Bertrand Russell, 1903–1959*. Ed. Robert E. Egner and Lester E. Denonn. London: Allen & Unwin, 1961.

Taylor, Charles. *Sources of the Self: The Making of the Modern Identity*. Cambridge: Harvard UP, 1989.

———. *Varieties of Religion Today*. Cambridge: Harvard UP, 2002.

Wittgenstein, Ludwig. *Philosophical Investigations*. 2nd ed. Trans. G. E. M. Anscombe. Oxford: Blackwell, 1953.

Whitehead, Alfred North, and Bertrand Russell. *Principia Mathematica*. 2nd ed. 3 vols. Cambridge: Cambridge UP, 1925–27.

Chapter Twenty-Four

College Writing, Academic Literacy, and the Intellectual Community: California Dreams and Cultural Oppositions

Sheridan Blau, Director
South Coast Writing Project
Departments of Education and English
University of California, Santa Barbara

After forty years of teaching university writing courses, with a half-dozen years as the director of my campus writing program, several terms of office chairing or serving on college and university committees that oversee campus and university writing requirements and credit policies, and more than a quarter of a century directing a Writing Project site, working with writing teachers at every level of education (and in the meantime publishing essays and textbooks on the teaching of writing), I might reasonably be expected to have some definitive answers to the question of what is college writing. Unfortunately, my years of experience and research have mainly shown me why it is so difficult to answer that question, why the question itself may not be meaningful, and why college writing remains such a problematic domain for college and university policy makers who would like some authoritative basis for making decisions about such related questions as what counts as college writing as distinct from what constitutes precollege or remedial writing, what distinguishes college writing from high school writing, and what students engaged in or completing college writing courses should be expected to know or be able to do.

In this chapter I want to address these and some related problems that have perennially vexed college writing programs and those who oversee them, not to offer the last word on any of those questions, but to interrogate and possibly reinterpret them in ways that may illuminate our understanding of the problematic nature of college writing and its relationship to the teaching of writing at other levels of education. My discourse will be anecdotal as well as theoretical, and much of it will take as its starting point two problematic documents—a generation apart—in which the collective engine of higher education in the state of California conspired to define college writing for the guidance of those who prepare students to engage in it and to establish some rational basis for policy on questions about funding and the award of academic credit for various kinds of writing courses.

When Is It a College-Level Course and When Is It a Precollege Remedial Course?

I'll begin with the practical and economically pertinent question of what defines a college writing course or a creditable college writing course as distinct from a course that represents a remedial writing course and therefore one that either should not be counted as transferable from one college to another or that should not be counted as a baccalaureate-level course in computing student credits toward college graduation. The economic ramifications of this question are enormous for colleges and state educational systems that worry about it, because it impacts the credits granted to transfer students from community colleges to four-year colleges and it can mean that large numbers of first-year students will be enrolled in writing courses for which they will not or should not receive credit toward graduation. The persistent hope of many cost-conscious university administrators in California over the past two generations has been to distinguish what is remedial from what is college-level instruction in order eventually to outsource all remedial instruction to the community colleges, which are legislatively mandated and funded (as the university is not) to provide a number of remedial and non-baccalaureate-level courses to students who need them.

From the perspective of auditors or any politicians who might ask about the cost-effectiveness of state-funded, degree-granting university programs, any courses that use faculty resources without producing credits that advance students toward graduation are wasted courses and improperly used resources. Thus, if the problem of distinguishing between college-level and precollege- or remedial-level courses can be finessed or ignored in periods of budgetary plenty, it is certain that it will command attention in periods of budgetary famine.

Nor would it occur to any university administrator or state auditor or to most academics in most disciplines that the task of distinguishing between college-level and remedial (or precollege) instruction in writing should be a particularly problematic one. It certainly seemed self-evident a generation ago that colleges and universities should be able to define a baccalaureate-level course in terms of the course content or focus of instruction and in terms of the prerequisite skills and knowledge that the course required of students who enrolled in it. Hence, in the early 1980s, in response to academic senate debates at a number of University of California campuses about the dubious status of courses designed to enable students to meet the university-wide Subject A requirement (a writing proficiency requirement that students must satisfy before enrolling in standard university-level first-year English courses), and at a time of ballooning enrollments in remedial writing courses at campuses of the California State University, the state administrative apparatus in higher education in collaboration with the academic senates of the University of California (with 8 general campuses), the California State University (with 23 campuses), and the California Community College System (with 109 colleges) appointed an intersegmental committee of faculty and administrators to resolve the perplexing but apparently answerable question of how to define a baccalaureate-level writing course and the level of student knowledge or skill required for enrollment in such a course.

After some months of consultation and two statewide conferences to allow for articulation and discussion among educational segments, a report was published by the joint academic senates of the three branches of public higher education in California under the title, *Statement of Competencies in English and*

Mathematics Expected of Entering College Freshman (1982). Most of the pages of the report were actually devoted to appendices describing the placement tests in writing used at various campuses (this was five years before the University of California established its university-wide writing proficiency examination) of the three segments of higher education in California, and presenting sample papers from each segment representing four different levels of student performance ("clear pass, marginal pass, clear fail, marginal fail") on those tests, along with comments explaining the reason for the ranking.

Ironically, Ed White (see "Defining by Assessing" in this volume) would argue that those sample papers and explanatory comments provided the true or most valid answer to the question addressed in the report about how to define college-level competency in writing, but the report proper focused instead on the brief statement of competencies, which purported to define college-level writing in terms of eleven "Writing Skills" said to be "fundamental for successful baccalaureate-level work." These include the ability to generate ideas, to formulate a thesis, to construct a coherent paragraph, to organize an essay logically, to use varied sentence structure, to select appropriate words, to adjust word choice and sentence types for different audiences and purposes, to avoid plagiarism, to use evidence to support opinions, to use a dictionary, and to proofread and revise. Students whose prose didn't demonstrate such abilities could be said to require remediation in pre-baccalaureate-level courses; courses designed to teach these skills of academic writing were therefore said to be remedial. Likewise, courses that directed instruction toward more sophisticated rhetorical, logical, and conceptual matters were properly designated college-level courses, appropriate for students who had already mastered the fundamentals of style and structure that were said to be the marks of college-level writing.

State educational agencies heralded the new statewide document on college writing as a major intersegmental accomplishment marking the beginning of a new era of intersegmental articulation and rational vertical curriculum development in composition. Intersegmental statewide conferences of writing teachers were convened at various campuses of the University of California to introduce the new intersegmental statement of competencies in writing to teachers at every level of instruction and even across the curriculum. Teachers at every level enthusiastically attended these conferences and happily met in warmly collegial sessions where college and university writing instructors and interested professors from a variety of disciplines sat side by side with elementary, middle school, and high school language arts teachers to discuss how they could all use the new intersegmental document to guide curriculum and instruction in the teaching of writing, and where (at least at the conference I attended, and, no doubt, at others) the college composition teachers were initially shocked but then wildly amused to hear an elementary school teacher modestly and hesitantly observe that the standard for college-level competency in writing as defined in the new intersegmental document described what she required of student writers in her 6th-grade class (thus contradicting Ed White's presumably unassailable assertion in his chapter in this volume that the only thing we can say with assurance about college writing is that it is distinct from the writing of young children).

This observation was then seconded by a number of upper-elementary and middle school teachers (mostly from our local site of the National Writing Project), who claimed that they too expected students in their classes to learn and exhibit all of the same competencies apparently expected of entering college students (apt word choice, sentence control and fluency, paragraph coherence, organizational and argumentative logic, observance of conventions, ability to proofread and revise, and so on) and that their writing instruction generally focused less on basic skills of transcription than on more substantive concerns such as the development and relevance of ideas, adequacy of information, and rhetorical effectiveness. It would appear, therefore, that they too were conducting their classes at a level appropriate for a fully creditable college or university class, according to the specifications of the intersegmental document on college-level writing instruction.

Moreover, they observed, the basic skills on which remedial writing classes were apparently expected to focus seemed to them (as it did to many specialists in the teaching of writing) an inappropriate focus for writing instruction at any level, if students were ever to learn how to write effectively. Thus the definition specified for a remedial course as distinct from a college-level course seemed a recipe for ensuring the continuing remedial status of the very students who were forced to enroll in those courses to correct their need for further remediation. To add to the deconstructive findings of the discussion groups, many college teachers (from a number of disciplines) in these same intersegmental groups began to acknowledge that many of their upper-division students—students who were getting by in college with satisfactory grades—appeared not to have mastered some the competencies that were presumably prerequisites for writing in college and that elementary teachers were claiming to have taught successfully to students in grades 6 through 8.[1]

As far as I know, nothing was ever formally published (and has never been published in any form or forum until now) reporting on how elementary and middle school teachers at various regional conferences had exposed the nakedness of the imperial intersegmental statement of 1982 on remedial and college-level writing in California. But I distinctly remember that after what was touted as the first round of a year-long series of regional intersegmental conferences on remediation and college-level writing, the university and the academic senates of the other units of higher education in California suddenly and mysteriously lost interest in sponsoring follow-up conferences or in continuing to advertise or distribute the intersegmental booklet they had formerly announced and distributed as a uniquely valuable resource for teachers of writing at every level of education.

This story, which, I confess, I tell with pleasure as a story at least in part about the humble wisdom of classroom teachers and the foolish hubris of academic bureaucrats, will be misleading if it is taken merely as a story of academic ineptitude, rather than as a story about the genuine difficulty of specifying levels of competence in writing that might distinguish college-level writers from precollege writers or the curriculum and content of college writing classes from high school college preparatory writing classes. Quite aside from the fact that the celebrated document on college-level competencies may have identified the wrong competencies, every experienced teacher who has taught in a range of secondary schools and colleges knows that any attempt to define the boundary between college and high school writing instruction or student writing, without reference to the particular schools and classes to which the definitions apply, is likely to yield misleading generalizations and educationally dubious policies about student placement and academic credit. High school English teachers who moonlight as composition teachers in local colleges often report that their baccalaureate-level college classes are much less sophisticated than the tracked top-level classes they teach in the neighboring high school. Equally dramatic contrasts are frequently observed, of course, by teachers who move in the other direction or from one college to another or one high school to another or even between different college preparatory classes within the same comprehensive high school.

Thus, while it is reasonable to assume that there is as vast a difference between college and high school writing courses as there is between most colleges and most of the high schools from which they recruit their students, it is nevertheless impossible to construct a general model of high school and college instruction or competency in writing that will be sufficiently predictive of the actual performance of students and teachers and college communities to render the model educationally useful or accurate in making policy decisions about academic credit or course equivalency for any individual students or for all secondary schools and colleges. Decisions on such matters will always have to be made to serve bureaucratic efficiency rather than educational purposes, except insofar as bureaucratic policy wisely allows and encourages academic administrators to make policy decisions on a case-by-case basis, using as evidence, wherever possible, the actual writing produced by the student seeking credit for having completed a college-level writing course (see Ed White's essay in this volume).

College Writing as Academic Literacy: A Second Generation Definition

It took exactly twenty years, or one generation, before the state institutions of higher education in California—again under pressure to reduce or otherwise reallocate the responsibility for providing remedial instruction in writing for college students entering the higher education system—attempted to produce another and more authoritative document specifying what constitutes college-level competency in composition and what therefore defines the instructional responsibility of high school college preparatory writing courses, which are presumably designed to turn out students who are ready to perform at a level of competency expected of entering college freshmen. The new document, published in 2002 by an official statewide higher education body known as the Intersegmental Committee of the Academic Senates (ICAS) and authored by a joint committee of faculty (all of whom regularly taught writing in their courses) representing the Academic Senates of the University of California, the California State University, and the California Community Colleges, carries a title that reflects both the interests of the key faculty members who shaped the content of the document and the aims of the faculty organizations that sponsored it: *Academic Literacy: A Statement of Competencies Expected of Students Entering California's Public Colleges and Universities* (presently available online and from outreach offices at the University of California, California State University, and California Community Colleges).

That is to say, the intellectual aim and admirable achievement of the ICAS document and of its expert authors is to describe the academic literacy tasks and underlying intellectual competencies that are typically required of students enrolled in introductory college courses in composition and across the academic disciplines. But the political and economic assumption apparently made by the document's sponsoring institutions of higher education and evidenced in the second part of the document's title is that it is the responsibility of secondary schools to equip students with these very skills and competencies *before* those students enter California's institutions of higher education. Presumably, then, it is not the responsibility of colleges and universities to teach the same skills, except in remedial courses that cannot or should not count toward a baccalaureate degree and that in a well-ordered educational system (as university administrators and faculty senate committees, not to mention legislators, continuously remind university directors of composition) should not be the financial responsibility of a university program. The document is itself deliberately silent about the economic and political issue of remediation, but its sponsors acknowledge their agenda in this regard in a preface over the signatures of the academic senate chairs of the three sponsoring higher educational systems, where the document is introduced as "an update of the original 1982 *Statement of Competencies in English Expected of Entering College Freshman*," a document I have already described, that was explicitly conceived by university administrators and sponsoring academic Senate committees as an effort to reduce the expensive problem of remedial writing courses across California's higher education system and particularly to reduce the need for basic writing courses (courses satisfying the infamous Subject A requirement) on the campuses of the University of California.

There is no doubt that some of the skills and competencies called for in the ICAS document are presently and appropriately taught and required of students in college preparatory high school classes and even in middle school classes (or earlier) for students headed for an academic track in high school. The writing competencies identified by the ICAS document include, for example, the following (slightly rephrased for economy and felicity):

- Generate ideas for writing by using texts in addition to past experience or observation
- Duly consider audience and purpose
- Employ a recursive prewriting process
- Develop a main point or thesis
- Develop a thesis with well-chosen examples
- Give reasons and employ logic
- Vary sentence structure and word choice as appropriate for audience and purpose
- Revise to improve focus, support, or organization
- Proofread and edit to correct surface errors

But we move into a much more problematic borderland region of the academic universe when we come to the more subtle and advanced skills of writing and many of the competencies that are identified by the ICAS document with "habits of mind," "critical thinking," and the "reading writing connection." Under these various rubrics we find such competencies as:

- Structure writing so that it moves beyond formulaic patterns that discourage critical examination of the topic and issues
- Critically analyze or evaluate the ideas or arguments of others
- Synthesize ideas from several sources
- Conduct college-level research to develop and support . . . opinions and conclusions
- Critically assess the authority and value of research materials that have been located online and elsewhere
- Read texts of complexity without instruction and guidance
- Experiment with new ideas
- Generate hypotheses
- Synthesize multiple ideas into a theory
- Challenge and interrogate one's own beliefs
- Respect facts and information in situations where feelings and intuitions often prevail
- Demonstrate initiative and develop ownership of one's education

I do not believe my experience or perception eccentric when I assert that in forty years of teaching college students at three highly respected and very selective research universities, I have never taught a first-year- or sophomore-level English class (and I'm talking exclusively about nonremedial classes in literature as well as in composition) where most of my students arrived at my class experienced enough and competent enough in academic literacy not to need intensive instruction in the very academic literacy skills, competencies, or habits of mind described by the list above as prerequisites for admission to college courses.

And what are we to make of the competency that with no apparent irony is identified explicitly as "conduct college-level research to develop and support . . . opinions and conclusions"?

Can colleges and universities reasonably expect that students will acquire college-level competency while they are still in high school? Well, yes, by the logic of this document, which insists at every point that its thoughtful and well-researched catalog of the skills, competencies, and habits of mind that are required for effective academic work in college ought to be instilled in and acquired by students while they are still in high school. "All the elements of academic literacy," the ICAS document authoritatively announces in speaking of skills and competencies that are required for success in college-level courses (2), "are expected of entering freshman across all college disciplines. These competencies should be learned in the content areas in high school. It is therefore an institutional obligation to teach them." That is, it is the responsibility of the institution of the high school to teach them.

Thus the corporate voice of higher education in the state of California says precisely the same thing I remember some disgruntled faculty members saying to me during the years when I was the director of Composition on my own University of California campus. Virtually every term, one or more of the teachers—most of them recent recipients of the PhD in English, teachers we had hired specifically to teach writing courses and especially our sequence of first-year English courses—would come to my office to complain that the students in their various first-year English classes were not ready for the course, because these students had no idea how to frame a coherent argument, could not interpret the assigned texts, needed help in reading conceptually complicated material, or seemed disinclined to grapple with complex or subtle intellectual problems. My response to them was very close to what I would also like to say to the institutional sponsors of the ICAS document on academic literacy. If students could do all of these things at the time they entered your class, why would we need you to teach them?

The Discourse of a Culture and the Culture of Discourse

I do not mean to argue here that most of the skills, competencies, and habits of mind necessary for successful work in college should not be nurtured and taught in high school. The recent success of an "academic writing task force" of high school teachers, representing sites of the California Writing Project, in developing assignments, assessment tools, and instructional strategies for teaching academic writing in high school demonstrates that high school students can and actually want to engage in much more sophisticated reading, writing, and thinking tasks than are ordinarily set for them in high school. But this does not mean that the academic skills and competencies expected of students in college and university courses are likely to be taught and learned in high school in a way that will satisfy the expectations of most college and university faculty members or that such skills can be taught and acquired in high school in a way that will ever relieve college and university faculty of their own responsibility for teaching the same constellation of skills.

It may even be unrealistic, if not foolish, to expect some of the more sophisticated of these skills to be taught and learned in high school at all. In what imaginable school district, for example, will we be able to find significant numbers of college preparatory high school classes where most students are being taught (and actually learning) to structure their writing so that it moves beyond formulaic patterns that discourage critical examination of the topic and issues? And in what state anywhere are public high school students generally being taught to read texts of complexity without instruction and guidance or to challenge and interrogate their own beliefs or to demonstrate initiative and develop ownership of their own education?

Those may be habits of mind that inform the performance of highly competent students in college (and surely they appear among the most talented students in high school classes as well), but they are also habits of mind that to a very large extent distinguish the culture of the university from the culture of the high school. Public high schools and school boards throughout California and in virtually every other state (especially in an era of government-mandated assessment programs) typically favor and provide substantial funding for the purchase of formulaic programs of instruction in composition for high school students—programs that are designed to substitute obedience in the application of a formula in place of any act of independent or critical thinking. Of course, smart, experienced, professionally sophisticated high school teachers, who are themselves writers, know the advantages of helping student writers learn to be guided more by the shape of their reflective thought than by a prefabricated outline. But such teachers will be the first to admit that their instruction generally runs counter to the culture of their school and even the culture of their department and certainly to the current national culture of assessment.

In fact, the function of the first year of college for most students from most high schools—when they look at it retrospectively—turns out to have been largely to debunk much of what they learned in high school, to get them for the first time to challenge and interrogate their own beliefs, to prod them for the first time toward taking charge of their own learning, and to initiate them into an academic and intellectual community, which is to say, to an entire culture whose most distinctive features are those that render it wholly unlike the culture of the high school. Nor is there any generation in the history of public education in America for which this hasn't been true.[2]

Moreover, insofar as a culture is defined largely by it discursive practices, the features that most fundamentally define the genres of academic discourse in the university, including the ways speakers position themselves in relation to their audience and authorities in their field, precision and exactitude in expression, a critical stance toward received opinion and one's own assumptions, a sense of responsibility to contribute to an ongoing discussion or debate on a significant question, and many of the other practices identified by the ICAS authors with *academic literacy*—all of these are cultural practices that can only be learned through participation in a culture as an active member, including the practice of participation itself. Nor would it be incorrect to claim that one of the principal aims of a college education in any field is to initiate students into the discourse and discursive practices of that field, just as it is the particular function of first-year writing courses to initiate students into the discursive practices that are shared across the disciplines and define the broader culture of the university community.[3]

Having criticized placement and credit policies based on unsustainable generalizations about the academic culture of high schools, I am nevertheless now arguing—I hope not inconsistently—that it is fair and reasonable to acknowledge that high schools and colleges—most especially research universities and highly selective colleges, but virtually all colleges in their official aspirations—represent different kinds of academic and intellectual communities. One could fairly say, in fact, that most high schools (excluding highly selective independent schools and a few highly specialized public secondary schools) do not identify themselves at all as intellectual communities and may not even serve primarily as academic communities.

Public high schools are supported by local communities as institutions designed to reflect and preserve the parochial values of the community and of the parents who send their children to local schools, where they expect local community values to be confirmed and reproduced, not to be interrogated and culturally analyzed. Critical thinking in most high schools and in most state documents on curriculum standards refers to such formal operations as providing reasons to support a claim. It does not entail questioning the efficacy of the reasons or the values that constitute the warrants for the reasons. Colleges and universities—particularly research universities and highly selective colleges—are typically charged with the responsibility of advancing the frontiers of knowledge, which includes a mission to teach students to question their assumptions, to challenge commonplace wisdom, to interrogate the values and ideology of their own community and tradition as well as those of communities and cultures that are alien and even threatening to them. Such interrogations would not be tolerated in most high schools in most communities, where the thinking it characterizes would be regarded as dangerous if not seditious (see Blau, "Politics and the English Language Arts").

The Cultural Challenge of College Writing

Insofar as I have been critical of the California intersegmental document on academic literacy for attempting to pawn off on the high schools the responsibility that belongs to institutions of higher education to teach students the skills and habits of mind—the discursive practices—that colleges and universities expect their students to exhibit, I may be accused of and I am willing to plead guilty to the charge of having committed the intentional fallacy. For while the document insists that it is the responsibility of the high schools to teach these skills and continually refers to the list of skills as representing the competencies required of *entering* college students, it never asserts that colleges should therefore be relieved of their responsibility to teach the same skills and competencies to college students. It is my knowledge of the history and funding sources for such documents that leads me to be critical of what I take to be the document's bureaucratic intention. In the meantime, however, it also seems clear to me that the faculty authors of the document did not themselves share the intention I am attributing to its sponsors. And for this reason or for reasons having nothing to do with intention and everything to do with execution, I think there is good reason to celebrate what the document achieves in cataloging the skills of academic literacy and the underlying habits of mind that together define what the document calls *competencies* and which we can call *discursive practices* (both terms are apposite for their respective auditors), and in also calling upon high school teachers in every discipline to teach these same competencies and practices.

Read as an articulation document outlining for high schools the discursive practices that students should be taught and experience in college preparatory courses, the document constitutes a worthwhile effort to reform the intellectual culture of the high school and to lend the collective authority of the state's institutions of higher education to the teaching practices and intellectual goals of the best informed and most literate teachers in high schools—teachers whose practices and values may well put them in an oppositional relationship to the practices of many of their colleagues, to the official curriculum of their school, and to the newer standards promulgated by state agencies and presumably tested on state-mandated standardized assessments.

And what the oppositional posture of many outstanding writing teachers may suggest is how much the character of intellectual discourse or the discourse taught in college writing courses and valorized implicitly and explicitly in research on college writing is a discourse that positions the writer outside of the American cultural mainstream represented most notably by the culture of the American high school and by what we might characterize as the discourse of Main Street and middle America.

But, of course, there is nothing uniquely American about the opposition between what I am identifying as intellectual discourse or the discursive practices of the intellectual community and the contrasting practices of the public at large, or more distinctively, the discourse of the marketplace and the bureaucracy. The intellectual community—distinguished by discursive practices or habits of mind that entail interrogating commonplace assumptions, questioning the values of the community, moving beyond formulaic patterns of thought to examine issues and topics critically, and experimenting with new ideas (see the ICAS list above)—has always been and must always be in something of an oppositional or critical stance with respect to whatever constitutes the prevailing or conventional culture of any community.

In a politically healthy community, intellectuals are celebrated and protected precisely for the critical and challenging role they serve and teach. In corrupt and pathological societies—like totalitarian and fascist societies—intellectuals are among the first groups to be declared enemies of the state and among the first citizens to be sent to concentration camps or gulags, as they were in Hitler's Germany and in Stalin's Soviet Union, and as they continue to be in every regime built on the manipulation and contempt for citizens and for truth.

College writing, I am suggesting, is a species of intellectual discourse, and the powers of language and mind that it calls upon and develops are those that enable students and citizens to become participants in an academic community that is itself a segment of the larger intellectual community. But colleges and universities do not define the intellectual community and they do not constitute the only sites for initiating new members into that community. Many leading intellectuals—certainly in the generation ahead of my own—were never college students, yet became leading American intellectuals and eventually distinguished university professors. I'm thinking of literary critics like Phillip Rahv and R. P. Blackmur (both of whom were my own teachers), both of whom edited leading intellectual journals before and after World War II, and ultimately became powerfully influential and widely published literary critics and professors of literature, though neither of them had ever enrolled in an undergraduate college or university program of study.

Not only is it the case that colleges do not own and are not the only sites for cultivating intellectual discourse; it is also the case that most people who attend and even graduate from college do not take up all or most of the practices that define intellectual discourse and never become members of the intellectual community. Indeed many college teachers of composition can hardly be counted as intellectuals themselves and surely some colleges can hardly count themselves as intellectual communities, while some secondary schools or communities of teachers that include elementary teachers surely qualify as intellectual communities.

Among the many contributions that the National Writing Project has made to the American educational community, one of the most profoundly important, enduring, and revolutionary is the concept that a writing project site is most fundamentally a community of teachers that serves as a professional and intellectual community—a community whose members are drawn from the ranks of classroom teachers who teach at every level of education from elementary school through graduate school, but who are linked by their common commitment to improving their own professional practice by sharing their teaching practices with each other, by interrogating and reflecting on their practice through their conversation and writing, and by regularly sharing their writing with each other—including the writing they do in their roles as reflective practitioners, researchers, and creative writers. In this way communities of writing project teachers who teach in kindergarten through grade 12 along with their colleagues who teach in community colleges and four-year colleges and universities have become the kind of intellectual communities that colleges and universities themselves have always claimed to be and have frequently aspired to be, but in their modern corporate and bureaucratized incarnations have often failed to become, except in certain privileged and protected precincts of their institutional structures.

Moreover, in functioning as productive intellectual communities where knowledge is produced as well as consumed, shared as well as honored, where learning is nurtured and disseminated for its own sake and for the satisfaction and benefit of those who learn—and where all this learning and knowledge production transpires without the interference of hierarchies of power (such as administrators, teachers, students) and without bureaucratic or economic structures of reward or advancement, the writing project demonstrates—as workman's circles and various groups of workers, and artisans have demonstrated throughout the past century and more—that intellectual communities and intellectual discourse may thrive and be acquired by community members in a number of settings outside the control of universities or any academic institutions.

What this meditation on the sites of intellectual discourse seems to be suggesting, then, is that what defines college writing is less essentially about what defines college than it is about what defines the discipline of writing. For it is the discipline of writing or writing practiced as a discipline of mind that makes writing the most effective tool for discovering and clarifying thought and thereby the principal instrument for intellectual discourse. Hence writing as intellectual discourse is nurtured and valorized and serves as the most effective instrument for sustaining the community of learners in those colleges and universities that function as legitimate intellectual communities, while its intellectual power may be ignored and regarded as subversive in academic institutions—like most high schools and, no doubt, some colleges—where education is focused largely on training students to standards of behavior and academic performance that are determined less by a transcendent commitment to liberating and refining thought than by a parochially defined and politically expedient interest in transmitting a given ideology and sustaining whatever happens to be the dominant bureaucracy of power.

Hence the National Council of Teachers of English (NCTE)—an organization of English and language arts educators representing all levels of education—takes a permanently subversive role with respect to most dominant regimes of American power in making two widely publicized national awards each year on behalf of the power of writing to clarify and liberate thought: the Doublespeak Award, an award of shame given each year to call attention to a glaring example of intellectually dishonest and deliberately obfuscating prose of the kind characteristic of political discourse in George Orwell's novel *1984*, and the George Orwell Award, honoring an author or editor or published work that contributes to intellectual honesty and clarity in public discourse. With these awards, made by an organization and supervised by committees that include teachers at every level of education from elementary school through the university, NCTE demonstrates that the writing distinguished as college writing and celebrated as a discourse important to acquire and master for participation in academic and intellectual communities is not different from the writing that the discipline of composition or the broader field of the English language arts desiderates as the model for instruction and practice at every level of education, but differs instead from all the varieties of manipulative and ethically compromised writing that all students and all citizens in an intellectually healthy democratic society must learn to resist rather than produce.

Notes

1. Anyone skeptical today about the practicability of an elementary school writing program conducted at the level described by the teachers in my anecdote need only visit the classrooms of exemplary writing project teachers or Google the phrase *six traits writing* to see what has become the most widely used rubric for teaching and evaluating writing in the elementary classrooms of many teachers—the six traits rubric and instructional guide developed at the Northwest Regional Educational Laboratory specifically for use in the elementary grades. Those six traits include voice, word choice, ideas and content, organization, fluency, and conventions.

2. See Russel Durst's ethnographic study, *Collision Course* (1999), for a vivid account of the conflict between the culture of the high school or the home culture and the culture of the university.

3. In speaking of discursive practices that characterize the culture of the university, I may be accused of subscribing to what David Russell (60–65) characterizes as the myth of a universal educated discourse, which is often used as a rationale for the very institution of first-year English courses and what Russell and others regard as an equally misguided notion of what is known as "general writing skills instruction." Without refuting his argument about how discursive practices differ across

disciplines and the activity systems they entail, I think it remains fair to posit a set of intellectual values, social responsibilities, and habits of mind that are valorized widely in the intellectual community and promoted across disciplines in the university, and that are represented by the list of competencies ratified by academics from widely disparate disciplines in the 2002 California intersegmental document. Just how extensive these common practices may be can be disputed, but surely some commonalities in values and practices are indisputable if not self-evident: don't distort the truth or misrepresent evidence, check and acknowledge sources, evaluate evidence, contribute to an ongoing discourse, recognize counterarguments, and so on.

Works Cited

Academic Senates for California Community Colleges. *Academic Literacy: A Statement of Competencies Expected of Students Entering California's Public Colleges and Universities*. Sacramento: Intersegmental Committee of the Academic Senates of the California Community Colleges, the California State University, and the University of California, 2002. 7 June 2006 <http://www.universityofcalifornia.edu/senate/reports/acadlit.pdf>.

Academic Senates of the California Community Colleges, the California State University, and the University of California. *Statement of Competencies in English and Mathematics Expected of Entering College Freshman*. Sacramento: The California Roundtable on Educational Opportunity, 1982.

Blau, Sheridan. "Politics and the English Language Arts." *The Fate of Progressive Language Policies and Practices*. Ed. Curt Dudley-Marling and Carole Edelsky. Urbana, IL: NCTE, 2001. 183–208.

Durst, Russel. *Collision Course: Conflict, Negotiation, and Learning in College Composition*. Urbana, IL: NCTE, 1999.

Russell, David. "Activity Theory and its Implications for Writing Instruction." *Reconceiving Writing, Rethinking Writing Instruction*. Ed. Joseph Petraglia. Mahwah, NJ: Lawrence Erlbaum, 1995.

White, Edward. "Defining by Assessing." *What Is "College-Level" Writing?* Ed. Patrick Sullivan and Howard Tinberg. Urbana, IL: NCTE, 2006. 243–66.

Continuing the Conversation: A Dialogue with Our Contributors

One of our primary goals for this collection was to begin a thoughtful, wide-ranging discussion about college-level writing. To help promote this conversation—and to make our work on this project more interactive—we established a companion Web site where additional work and discussion about this important issue could be posted.

We asked contributors to post their finished essays there for others to read and discuss, and we invited each contributor to post at least one follow-up response. We are very pleased with the results of this online conversation. Although not every writer was able to contribute, many were, and the resulting dialogue was, we believe, substantive and important.

We are including in this section of the book a brief sampling from this conversation. We invite you to visit our Web site and read the follow-up work of our contributors in its entirety. You may also post your own comments if you wish. Our Web site is located at http://www.mcc.commnet.edu/faculty/collegewriting/. We hope that you will find the conversation here to be as interesting and as insightful as we did.

Samples from Contributors' Follow-Up Comments

Reply to: Muriel Harris's "What Does *the Instructor Want?" —Amanda Winalski*

This article recalls the struggle undergraduate students endure when painting their prose to appeal to a particular audience. The theory perfectly fits my undergraduate experience; however, I believe the idea can advance one cynical step further.

The anxiety regarding the academic standards for a particular class was often manifested within the first assignment. Who doesn't remember the panicked, urgent question, "WHAT does this teacher expect?" Generally, the apprehension was soothed by the return of that assignment: the students realized whether the professor emphasized grammar, deducted points for page-long paragraphs, or firmly enforced the citation rules. However, there was another prejudice that could not be so easily determined. True, a student understands her audience better after she has received the red-inked feedback. But the process of writing for a particular reader has another layer to it. In college, a student learns to cater her writing not only to a particular audience, but to a particular individual: she may spend the entire semester unpeeling her professor's classroom rhetoric to reveal personal prejudices that affect his role as the reader. When a student pays attention to the specific language of her professor's lecture, or his attempts at humor, she can more clearly understand her job as a writer. For example, a progressive historian might wince if he read a student paper referencing "Viet Cong," while another professor might not consider the term pejorative. Similarly, a professor who espouses traditional grammatical theory might tear apart a student's haphazard or arbitrary use of the feminine or collective pronouns.

But does this mean that successful college writers perform background checks on their professors to determine the particular ideologies that dictate how each will receive a paper? Must a student put on her libertarian hat for one professor, then adopt a socialist perspective for another? Of course not. A college writer must find the balance between knowing her audience and maintaining her integrity. Thus, she needn't pretend to adopt all the biases of her audience; rather, she must have an understanding of these biases such that she will know how her reader will interpret her essay. When a writer can more fully anticipate the reader's response, she can write more persuasively, perhaps more successfully.

Kittle Is on Target —Merrill Davies

Peter Kittle's essay first attracted my attention because of the title. I thought that if he did not consider the problem the high school teacher's fault, he couldn't be all bad! His essay brought to mind my own "pilgrimage" in teaching writing. I have come to some of the same conclusions he has, although by a different route. As a teacher at the high school level for 31 years, I have often struggled with teaching students who are unprepared for high school writing as well as how to prepare students for college writing.

I totally agree that blaming the previous teachers serves no good purpose. I decided that if I blamed middle school teachers for the students who could not write at the high school level, I would also have to give them credit for the ones who could. That idea did not particularly appeal to me, and it also made me realize that students come to us with all kinds of talents and abilities (and lack thereof) that must be taken into account. In the end it just does no good to try to figure out why they arrived at a particular level of ability when we get them; we just have to teach them. It reminds me of what my neurologist said about my migraine headaches. He said that trying to find the cause of the headaches was such a chore that it was usually better just to treat the symptoms.

I arrived at the idea that "students write best when they have something to say and someone to say it to" as I coached debate, mock trial, entered student writing in contests, and conducted various projects at school. I noticed that when I made writing assignments just to teach a particular mode of writing, such as persuasion, description, etc., I would often get groans, sighs, and complaints, and often not good quality writing. I would also find it hard to get students to help one another. They just didn't seem to care one way or another.

However, students would spend hours poring over debate or mock trial briefs, arguing over wording, placement of ideas, or effective examples of support. They would also seek my advice and listen to my suggestions. Students learned persuasive technique willingly when it offered them opportunities to earn trophies and recognition in debate and mock trial. They also had an audience other than the teacher.

In the 1980s one of my friends decided to design and implement a recycling program at our school. He asked me to work with my students in developing a brochure to inform the school and community of the program, and later asked us to design a manual explaining how the program worked which could be used by other schools to replicate similar programs in their schools. I found that my students paid attention to their writing and sought help in wording the brochure and the manual.

In the early 1990s I partnered with the American Literature and American History teachers in our school to lead students in conducting research on our community. Our plan involved interviewing many older residents to learn their individual stories and to publish them in a booklet. We decided to use the format of a magazine article, similar to a profile of a person, for each of the articles. This booklet was to be sold in the community for a nominal fee to cover printing costs. Again, students responded positively and were eager to learn, because they had something specific to say and had an audience.

I continued to seek ways to make "real" writing assignments to students and coach them in the process. In 2002 my students produced a video to promote our school's service learning program. The intent was to provide the school with something to show incoming freshmen to encourage them to participate in this voluntary program. It turned out to be an impressive statement, written and produced by the students.

During all these projects, not only did students produce better writing, but they also learned to give valuable, meaningful feedback to one another as they talked about how their potential audience would perceive their messages. These projects also helped me to become more of a mentor or coach to the students as they wrote instead of always being the authority figure.

Throughout my teaching career, I encouraged (and sometimes required) students to submit writing for specific writing contests. I also coached them in writing speeches and presenting them for various contests. Although the audience may not have been quite as clear as some of the other projects I have mentioned, there was an incentive and a wider audience than the teacher, so students usually wrote better. I had several students who won cash awards, trips, etc. for their work, and this inspired others to try. Two students (at different times) won a week in Washington, D.C., to participate in the Washington Workshops.

I realize that this does not really address the issue of "What is college level writing?" directly. However, I believe that when students have multiple opportunities to do "real" writing in high school they will be more likely to be successful in college.

Audiences and Ideologies —Peter Kittle

"Writing in college, as elsewhere, happens among people, in real places, over time, for a vast range of purposes. When people writing in college environments write, we see embodied instances of college writing."

This quote, from Jeanne Gunner's anti-essay, really resonated with the rich description of a "college writing" experience given by Kim Nelson. Nelson's piece precisely embodies a kind of college writing that is predicated not simply on an institutional demand (although a class assignment set the ball in motion), but on an explicit desire to engage in an academic, intellectual community. And while Nelson mentions that she considered making a list of skills to define "college-level" writing, her decision instead to take us through her own literacy practices provides a wonderful anecdote in support of Gunner's adamant desire to resist the reification that simple list-making fosters.

I was struck as well by the similarities between Gunner's ideological critique of the desire to delineate a somehow always-applicable definition of "college- level" writing and Sheridan Blau's discussion of the types of communities housed in various educational institutions. While reading his piece, I found myself feeling uncomfortable with the ways that Blau (despite many qualifying statements) seems to essentialize high schools as non-intellectual, even non-academic spaces—but I think that, in part, this is because I simply do not wish to believe that such is the case. The grim reality is that public schools, as institutions subject to the whims of policy makers, are enmeshed in a system which disembodies learning so that it may be quantified and branded as successful or failing. A grim sadness is elicited in me to think of our school system as being non-academic and even anti-intellectual—even though I know of many teachers who actively resist institutional inertia—but it makes Gunner's call to resist such boxing of college writing all the more imperative.

A final connection that I noticed was to Muriel Harris's discussion of the intricacies of audience and writer. I couldn't help but see that so much of the content of the essays in this collection is necessarily political, having ramifications that go far beyond our disciplinary concerns. In this era of No Child Left Behind, when our professional lives as educators are increasingly under fire, I wondered how we could think differently about an audience for this book. I suspect that, like Harris's student whose paper didn't satisfy the engineering professor, our work in this volume would likely be shrugged off by many politicians and bureaucrats who only know the "business" of education from their experiences as students. While I applaud this book, and the work we did as contributors, I think that we need to find a way as a discipline to make ourselves heard beyond the discipline. I thank Harris's essay for helping me to think about doing something about the serious threats to writing instruction raised in the works of Gunner and Blau.

What Can We Learn from These Essays? —Merrill Davies

Since writing "Whistling in the Dark" a few weeks ago, I've been reading the essays and comments by other writers attempting to answer the question "What is college-level writing?" and trying to synthesize the information into something which might be helpful from the viewpoint of the high school English teacher trying to prepare students for college. Despite the fact that it is very difficult for college professors to agree on a specific definition of "college-level" writing, I have come to the conclusion that high school teachers do need more information in order to help students be ready for college writing and that these essays do, in fact, provide some ideas about what could be done.

Let's begin with why we need more guidance in preparing students for college-level writing. It is obvious that most of the time high school teachers have focused almost exclusively on grammar, mechanics, and formulaic kinds of writing, and colleges have increasingly expected students to focus more on content. Generally there seems to be a big gap between what we have often told students they need to know and what they actually have to do in college level writing. The fact that more and more colleges are refusing to fund remedial programs means that parents are expecting high schools to get their kids ready for college. Some school systems (like the system I taught in) are now starting accelerated programs and "guaranteeing" college readiness. If the system promises that its students will be ready for college, English teachers need to know what that means in terms of writing.

But it's difficult even for college professors to define college-level writing. There are several reasons for this as mentioned in many of the essays. First of all, we have to determine whether we mean entry-level college writing, writing during college, or exit requirements. For the purpose of this discussion, I think we'd best stick with entry level expectations if it is to mean anything to the high school teacher. I say this because many of the essays talked about whether students were ready for college-level writing or not. But then we also have to deal with college-level writing in other ways. The student who has been praised for his/her flowery writing in creative writing classes may be sorely disappointed when a science professor reads a lab report. College-level writing differs greatly according to the task, and unfortunately, many students enter college with the idea that he/she only needs writing skills in the English class. They have little idea about different kinds of writing except the sense of modes of writing (i.e., descriptive, narrative, persuasive, etc.). Another difficulty in defining college-level writing has to do with different expectations at different colleges and/or universities. Some prestigious private colleges may expect much more than others and some areas of the country have differing requirements.

But even with all these difficulties, we see some common ground among the different essays regarding what college-level writing is. This common ground gives us a starting point and could lead to some helpful insights for the high school teacher who wants to get students ready for college. First of all, the high school teacher has not been totally wrong—college-level writing does assume a competency in grammar and mechanics, as well as organization of thought. Although the college professor may not be as tough on these areas as the high school teacher thought, it is still evident that college writing demands a good command of the language, including accuracy in usage, as is evident in Patrick's essay and several others. Beyond accuracy in writing, another rather common theme in many of the essays is an assumption that students will have developed some critical thinking skills. This idea was mentioned or implied in most of the essays in some way or another. Audience awareness is a definite expectation in college writing also, according to most of the essays. Unfortunately, many high school students are quite oblivious to whoever might read what they have written. Some other elements of college-level writing were mentioned, but those mentioned above were the most common.

So how can we make use of what we have learned? Assuming that one of the goals of this discussion for me would be to learn how to better prepare secondary students for college-level writing, I would suggest four things: (1) Secondary teachers should read these essays; (2)

Area college professors and high school teachers should engage in dialogue to better understand what students need to do to prepare for college; (3) Both high school and college teachers should study College Board writing expectations on the new SAT; (4) High school teachers should work with students to learn specific expectations in writing at colleges, especially those out of the area where they live.

A Response to Peter Kittle, Sheridan Blau, and Milka Mosley —Kathleen McCormick

When read together, your three essays intersect so well to help to establish a clear distinction between teaching writing in high school and teaching it in college. The bottom line is that regular high school English classes and college-prep courses are not college courses, nor should they be. I think that these three essays should be given to the kind of faculty Peter discusses at the college level who complain that freshmen students are "unprepared for college writing." As Sheridan notes in relation to those college faculty who find their students unable to synthesize, analyze, etc. to their satisfaction, "if students could do all of these things at the time they entered your class, why would we need you to teach them?"

All three of you demonstrate clearly why high school writing may well need to be largely "formulaic" and show that this is not necessarily a negative—high school students frequently lack the experience to write well without explicit guidance or formulas from their teachers. You show us that high school writing under most circumstances necessarily seeks to conform—and why wouldn't it, given the material conditions of standardized testing, pre-determined curricula under which students and teachers are working, and large class sizes. You explain how class size usually prevents the assigning of more complex writing. Most high school English teachers clearly work hard to teach literature and writing while inserting PSAT, SAT, SAT II, and AP prep into their lessons. But what they are teaching about writing must often be different from what college teachers emphasize.

At the moment, all three of you argue that Writing Projects are the best way that English teachers in the schools can find support for more creative ways of teaching writing—teaching revision, teaching ownership of one's writing, etc. But, as you point out, these methods require more work and cannot be embraced by everyone. There are times when it seems that Sheridan's essay was written to provide further evidence for Peter and Milka's essays. He astutely notes in reference to those teachers who collaborate with Writing Projects:

> Of course, smart, experienced, professionally sophisticated high school teachers, who are themselves writers, know the advan-

> tages of helping student writers learn to be guided more by the shape of their reflective thought than by a prefabricated outline. But such teachers will be the first to admit that their instruction generally runs counter to the culture of their school and even the culture of their department and certainly to the current national culture of assessment.

If the teaching of writing in most high schools will ever truly become more obviously "college preparatory," we would need a thorough overhauling of the material realities of high school English teaching—class size, testing, textbooks, and of course a change in how writing is addressed in schools of education. In the absence of all of this, we should adopt more realistic assumptions about the relationship between writing in high school and writing in college. Your three descriptions of how different students are in high school and college—something that doesn't seem to get addressed enough in the literature—should help all of us to recognize that, under the current conditions of public schooling, we cannot and should not expect students to have a seamless transition from high school to college.

What's Missing from This Conversation? —Muriel Harris

As I read the essays in this collection, enjoying the insightful ideas, the voices from various corners of the campus and types of educational institutions, and the variety of lenses through which we all think about college-level writing, I realized we're missing an adjective to qualify that term "college-level writing." As the scholarship of contrastive rhetoric and my own experience as a tutor in a writing center have convinced me, we're discussing "American college-level writing." As we know, the rhetorical ideals we teach are based on those that are valued in American academic writing. But other cultures value other ideals that some of our students bring along with them to college composition courses.

In our Writing Lab, I've seen drafts of papers that would appear to be not well written but that in the writer's mind qualifies as good writing. What I see might be the endlessly long sentences that meander through what to us would be a paragraph or two. But some Spanish-speaking students, especially (in my experience) those who grew up in Puerto Rico and had an excellent high school education were encouraged—even rewarded—for those endless sentences. At other times it's the seemingly monotonous sentence pattern that marches like a drumbeat across the page. To my ear they need variety in structure and length. But some languages stress (or are almost restricted to) parallel structure, and that limits the writer's interest in using subordinate sentence structures. When I ask such a writer to read the paper aloud (a standard tutorial practice to let the student hear her own text) and ask how it sounds, the student often looks pleased by what she heard.

Less obvious are those vague papers that just don't have a clear-cut point because, to me, they are stuffed with gauzy metaphors that don't help to move ideas forward. And here we meet up with a student from another language group where metaphor is an excellent vehicle in which to couch ideas. A straightforward declaration of the point (what we would term "the thesis sentence") might sound overly direct, even rude. When students learned to write in that culture, they also learned to move gently to the point, not to announce it overtly at the beginning of the paper.

A major issue that comes up when students from other cultures write research papers is the fact that in some cultures it is an insult to cite a source from an authority in the field or to offer a reference to a literary source. To do so implies that the reader is less than literate, not well-read, or not acquainted with what is known about the subject. American emphasis on citing all sources is a concept that is difficult to grasp for some of these students.

I could go on and on citing examples of student writing that simply don't fit in the standard mold of American academic writing. These influences are embedded in the culturally derived values that accompany the students' instruction in writing. Whereas conciseness is preached in American business and technical writing, some cultures value copiousness. Organizational patterns in American academic writing don't encourage digressions, but digression is acceptable in the rhetorical values of some cultures.

The problem with such differences in rhetorical values is that most are never verbalized to the student or to us as these students write for us. The disconnect is when we would assess the writing as inadequate while such students see their writing as incorporating standards instilled in them in previous classrooms (classrooms, that is, outside the United States). Once we recognize this divergence in students' papers, we can help these writers understand that in American classrooms, they need to learn to write prose that is acceptable by American standards. In my experience, this isn't as obvious as it sounds. I remember a series of tutorials with a charming Asian woman who simply couldn't bring herself to compose a thesis statement, much less insert it in the first paragraph of her paper. "I am not such a bad-mannered person," she would say quietly, but adamantly. I never won her over to my attempt to argue that she would not be giving up her writing preferences, just adding a new one adapted to a different audience.

So, just a final plea to us all that we keep in mind in this conversation that we are discussing *American* college-level writing, not *all* college-level writing. We know this, but just as it's problematic when some students aren't aware of the standards by which they view their writing, so too can some instructors overlook the possibility that when some writing doesn't meet their standards, they may need to take a second look in order to figure out what is causing the difference.

Index

Editors

Patrick Sullivan teaches English at Manchester Community College in Manchester, Connecticut. His work has appeared in *Teaching English in the Two-Year College*, *The Journal of Adolescent and Adult Literacy*, *English Journal*, *The Community College Journal of Research and Practice*, *The Chronicle of Higher Education*, and *The New York Times*. He enjoys spending time with his wife, Susan, and his two children, Bonnie Rose (who is a senior at the University of Connecticut as a fine arts major) and Nicholas (who is finishing up high school and is a big fan of Bob Dylan!).

Howard Tinberg is professor of English at Bristol Community College, where he directs the Writing Lab. A past editor of the journal *Teaching English in the Two-Year College*, he is committed to advancing the scholarship of teaching across all subjects and all institutions. Tinberg is the 2004 recipient of the Council for Advancement and Support of Education (CASE)/ Carnegie Community College Professor of the Year.

Contributors

Sheridan Blau is a former president of the National Council of Teachers of English and serves as a member of the National Writing Project Taskforce. He has published widely in the areas of literature, composition, pedagogy, and the politics of literacy. He is a senior faculty member in the departments of English and education at the University of California, Santa Barbara, where he directs the South Coast Writing Project and Literature Institute for Teachers, and formerly directed the campus writing program and the teacher education program in English. Now completing his fifth decade as a teacher of English and teacher of teachers, he sometimes contemplates retiring to become a full-time potter.

Lynn Z. Bloom, Board of Trustees Distinguished Professor and Aetna Chair of Writing at the University of Connecticut, is a specialist in autobiography, composition studies, creative nonfiction, and essays. Her discovery of the contemporary essay canon is the subject of her twenty-first book, *The Essay Canon* (in process). Her creative nonfiction includes "Teaching College English as a Woman," "Living to Tell the Tale: The Complicated Ethics of Creative Nonfiction," "Writing and Cooking," and "(Im)Patient." As her marriage approaches the half-century mark, she and her husband are happy to include grandchildren and daughters-in-law in frequent family parties, swimming and hiking activities, and world travels.

Merrill J. Davies is a retired high school English teacher. After thirty-one years in the classroom, she still enjoys helping people perfect their writing—usually by reading doctoral dissertations now. In addition, she enjoys reading good books (not chosen because of curriculum requirements) and doing her own writing. She also spends more time with her husband, Bill, her two daughters, Melanie and Lori, their husbands, and her six beautiful grandchildren.

Michael Dubson has an associate's degree in liberal arts from Parkland College, a bachelor's degree in English and a master's degree in composition theory from the University of Massachusetts at Boston, and a graduate certificate in publishing from Emerson College.

He has taught college writing "professionally" since September 1990, mostly in the Massachusetts community college system. He has worked at Massachusetts Bay Community College, Bunker Hill Community College, Middlesex Community College, Roxbury Community College, and Massasoit Community College. He has also taught at Suffolk University and the University of Massachusetts at Boston. In between teaching, he has written short stories, newspaper articles, and a play. A product most relevant to this project is *Ghosts in the Classroom*, a collection of essays written by adjunct faculty members about teaching as adjunct professors. He is currently working on a play inspired by his adjunct experiences and hopes to have it produced next year. He has been happily married for twenty-two years, and is seriously depressed that the Baby Boomers are starting to turn sixty—especially Cher.

James M. Gentile currently co-chairs the English department at Manchester Community College in Connecticut. He also coordinates through the Connecticut Distance Learning Consortium online tutoring in writing at MCC and serves as the college's teaching and learning consultant, organizing professional development opportunities both for the college and the community college system. Additionally, he is the co-director of the Connecticut Poetry Circuit. James has a doctorate in American literature from Columbia University.

Jeanne Gunner is associate provost for academic programs and professor of English and comparative literature at Chapman University in Southern California. She has been a writing program administrator at the University of California, Los Angeles and Santa Clara University and continues to teach writing courses in her current position. For the past four years, she has been doing fieldwork on the development of ideological literacy in impoverished communities in El Salvador.

Muriel Harris, professor emerita of English, is happily retired from Purdue University, but not from the world of writing centers. She continues to edit the *Writing Lab Newsletter*, attend conferences, and promote and write about writing center theory and pedagogy with evangelical fervor ("Clearly the most invigorating, effective setting for working with writers yet devised," she argues). She continues to work on revisions of two composition handbooks, *The Prentice Hall Reference Guide* (now available in the sixth edition) and *The Writer's FAQs* (soon to appear in a third edition). And she proudly babbles about her incredible family that, in her unbiased opinion, includes the world's most intelligent, delightful grandchildren.

Jeanette Jordan teaches English and directs the writing center at Glenbrook North High School in Northbrook, Illinois. Professionally, she is active in the International Writing Centers Association and enjoys collaborating with colleagues. Personally, she is consistently amazed by her two daughters, ages four and six, who keep everything in perspective for her. She is thankful that her Glenbrook North colleagues **Karena K. Nelson, Howard Clauser, Susan E. Albert, Karen M. Cunningham,** and **Amanda Scholz** responded to her pleas for help. Writing this chapter was "truly a collaborative effort."

Chris Kearns is assistant dean of student services for the College of Liberal Arts at the University of Minnesota. He lives with his wife and son in Minneapolis, where he enjoys kayaking, ice skating, acoustic guitar, and exploring used book stores.

A former high school teacher, **Peter Kittle** is currently associate professor of English at California State University, Chico. He teaches preservice teachers in the English education program, and collaborates with practicing teachers through the Northern California Writing Project. Ever eager to challenge stereotyped notions of the tweedy academic, Kittle regularly indulges in such nonprofessorial pursuits as vert skateboarding and mountain unicycling. He lives in Chico with his wife and three sons.

Ellen Andrews Knodt, professor of English at a four-year branch campus of Penn State University, has taught writing at middle school, high school, community college, and college and university levels. Active in the Conference on College Composition and Communication, she has written or edited three writing texts and published many articles on writing and professional issues. Her literary interests focus on modern American literature, especially the writing of Ernest Hemingway. She presents her analysis of Hemingway's work regularly at international conferences and in journals and essay anthologies. She enjoys playing tennis and cheering at Nittany Lions football games.

Cynthia Lewiecki-Wilson is professor of English and director of college composition at Miami University, where she teaches theories and practice of composition and disability rhetoric on the Oxford campus. Previously she taught at Miami's two-year Middletown campus for twelve years. She describes herself as a lover of collaborative teaching and writing, travel, and shopping trips with Ellenmarie.

Alfredo Celedon Lujan loves coaching varsity basketball so much that he retired from it after thirty-one years—no more boarding yellow buses or driving vans for him! He had his 2005 Christmas vacation without basketball practices for the first time in three decades. Does he miss coaching? Only when he misses sixteen-hour days. He now enjoys spending more time with his family: Amy, Amanda, Mabel, and Peter. He has more time to write and to recreate (he has lost thirty-five pounds). He loves walking his white lab, Brutus, every single morning at daybreak when the sun rises over the Sangre de Cristo Mountains. And he loves his summers on the shore of the Benjamin River in Maine.

Having served as director of rhetoric and writing at Clemson University, head of the department of English at Southwest Missouri State University (now Missouri State University), and chair of English at University of North Carolina at Charlotte, **Ronald F. Lunsford** now serves as professor of English and co-coordinator of the English Learning Community at UNC Charlotte. His hobbies include golf, traveling with his wife, Nancy (when she lets him), and taking constant delight in his children, Tamara (and her husband Chad) and Christopher.

Kathleen McCormick is professor of literature and pedagogy and head of the Expository Writing Board of Study at Purchase College, State University of New York. The author/editor of seven books, including *Reading Our Histories, Understanding Our Culture*, and *The Culture of Reading and the Teaching of English*, which won the Modern Language Association's Mina Shaughnessy Award, she is currently coediting *Approaches to Teaching Italian American Literature, Film, and Popular Culture* and working on a book-length memoir. She is the coeditor of the MLA volumes on *Approaches to Teaching Joyce's* Ulysses, a coauthor of *Reading-to-Write: Exploring a Cognitive and Social Process*, and the textbook *Reading Texts*. She has won a National Writing Program Administrators' Award and a number of teaching awards.

Milka Mustenikova Mosley was born and raised in the city of Kavadarci, Macedonia. Ever since she was a little girl, she adored the sound of the English language. She loved watching American movies and copying American pop songs from the radio. In the fifth grade, she was thrilled to learn that her class was selected to take English as a foreign language. From then on, English became her favorite subject throughout the rest of her schooling. When the time came to select an undergraduate major, the choice was easy. She entered the School of Philology and majored in English language and literature at the Sts. Cyril and Methodius University in Skopje, Macedonia.

She has studied English morphology, phonetics, syntax, Old English, literature and everything connected with it, and loved it all. Twenty-five years ago she moved to Georgia and is delighted that she is able to continue to nurture her love for the language by teaching both high school and college-level English to American students.

Kimberly L. Nelson is a member of the class of 2006 at the University of Iowa. She graduated with a double major in English and anthropology, and she also served as a Writing Fellow for the English department.

John Pekins worked first in reading/writing education at the School for Individualized Learning, a publicly funded alternative middle and high school in Tallahassee, Florida, from 1979 to 1988, and afterward at Tallahassee Community College, from 1988 to present. He has a BA in English and an MS in reading education/language arts from Florida State University. When not teaching, he enjoys his family (including two children—ages eleven and sixteen), practices Zen meditation, plays golf, reads, and writes. His most recent publication is a book of golf poems, *Getting a Good Read*, coauthored with thirty-five-year golfing partner and prize-winning poet P. V. Le Forge.

Mike Quilligan is a graduate of Indiana University, the class of 2004. He earned a double major in English and history. When he's not selling used books or shilling Cajun food, he enjoys science fiction books and movies (as is perhaps evidenced by the allusions in his piece in this volume), comic books, and psychedelic pop music.

Susan E. Schorn coordinates the Writing Across the Curriculum Initiative in the College of Liberal Arts at the University of Texas at Austin. She has been a writer for Star Date Radio, a professor of English, and a self-defense instructor. She holds a total of four college degrees in studio art and English, as well as a black belt in Kyokushin karate. She currently has three dogs, three cats, two parakeets, two children, and one husband of seventeen years.

Ellenmarie Cronin Wahlrab is instructor of English and curriculum coordinator at Miami University Middletown, where she teaches composition courses and studio writing workshops. She describes herself as a lover of interdisciplinary collaboration, designing (curriculum, house rehabilitation, systems, crafts), and shopping trips with Cindy.

Edward M. White has written or edited eleven books and about one hundred articles or book chapters on writing, writing instruction, and writing assessment. As we go to press, he is completing his fifth textbook for college writing students and the fourth edition of his book for teachers, *Assigning, Responding, Evaluating*. During the 1970s, he was coordinator of the Writing Improvement Program for the California State University (CSU) system, with statewide responsibility for entry-level and midcareer assessment for the 330,000 students then in that system. He has also served two terms on the Conference on College Composition and Communication Executive Committee, in the 1970s and again in the 1990s. After taking early retirement in 1997 as emeritus professor of English at the CSU San Bernardino campus, he joined the University of Arizona English department, where he continues to teach graduate courses in writing assessment, writing research, and writing program administration.

Amanda Winalski will graduate from the Boston University School of Law in 2007 and plans to go into health law litigation. Ultimately, she would like to be an advocate to protect women's reproductive health against legislative threats. She lives with her guinea pig Tommiey. They both love to run. Amanda runs fifty miles a week, every week, while Tommiey runs laps around his plastic house every morning at four or five o'clock in the morning.

Kathleen Blake Yancey is Kellogg W. Hunt Professor of English at Florida State University, where she directs the graduate program in rhetoric and composition, and vice president of the National Council of Teachers of English. Having just moved to Tallahassee, she is learning to love eating summer tomatoes in January. In her spare time (should she have any), she enjoys reading, playing bridge, and most of all, hanging out with her husband, son, and daughter. **Brian M. Morrison** graduated as an English major in 2004 from Clemson University, taught high school for one year, and is now pursuing an MA in library science and media studies.

This book was typeset in Sabon by Electronic Imaging.
Typefaces used on the cover include ITC Stone Serif Bold and Semibold.
The book was printed on 50-lb. Williamsburg Offset paper
by Versa Press, Inc.